The Milita

The Case and Ca. ... ...e Duke of Cambridge
in an Age of Reform

By Kevin W. Farrell

UNIVERSITY PRESS OF
NORTH GEORGIA

University Press of North Georgia

North Georgia College and State University
Dahlonega, GA

Copyright 2011, University Press of North Georgia

All rights reserved. No part of this book may be reproduced in whole or in part without written permission from the publisher, except by reviewers who may quote brief excerpts in connections with a review in newspaper, magazine, or electronic publications; nor may any part of this book be reproduced, stored in a retrieval system, or transmitted in any form or by any means electronic, mechanical, photocopying, recording, or other, without written permission from the publisher.

Published by:
The University Press of North Georgia
Dahlonega, Georgia

Publishing Support by:
Booklogix Publishing Services, Inc.
Alpharetta, Georgia

ISBN: 978-0-9792324-2-8

Edited By: Timothy May
Cover Design: Lee-Anne Eliot
Cover Photo: Sheila Farrell
Book Layout: April Loebick & Matt Pardue

Interior photos are all taken from the public domain

Printed in the United States of America, 2011

For more information, please visit: http://www.upnorthgeorgia.org
Or e-mail: upng@northgeorgia.edu

UNIVERSITY PRESS OF
NORTH GEORGIA

For Sheila

Table of Contents

INTRODUCTION:
The Legacy of a Royal Duke's Career

London is filled with impressive statues and monuments to the great figures–and more obscure characters–of British history. Many are easily recognized by both historians and the general public. A magnificent statue of Lord Nelson sits high atop a column over Trafalgar Square, massive Wellington Arch is situated at the end of Buckingham Palace Gardens, the Victoria Monument stands majestically outside Buckingham Palace, a statue of Cromwell is positioned rather ironically before the Houses of Parliament, and a suitably bleak and pale Cenotaph rises in the middle of Whitehall to commemorate the British dead of the First World War.

In the middle of the street having the same name as that section of London–Whitehall–stands another impressive statue: an army officer seated on a horse across from the Horse Guards building just south of Trafalgar Square. Thousands of people pass by it every day in cars, buses and on foot without giving this larger-than-life memorial much attention. The lettering on the plinth on the left side reads, "FIELD MARSHAL HIS ROYAL HIGHNESS GEORGE, DUKE OF CAMBRIDGE K.G., G.C.B., &c.," and on the right side it reads, "COMMANDER-IN-CHIEF OF THE BRITISH ARMY 1856-1895. BORN 1819. DIED 1904." While the passing of a century has not diminished the statue, the man to whom the statue is dedicated is largely forgotten.[1] This book investigates the important military and political changes that his life and career reflected, and more importantly, it reveals how the crucial relationship between the army, the Crown, and Parliament were affected at a key juncture in British history.

At first glance it might seem odd that the career of Prince George, Duke of Cambridge, royal duke and first cousin to Queen Victoria, should be so neglected. The Victorian era is one of the most heavily investigated periods of British history; scholars have devoted great effort to understanding the principal characters and minor figures of the age and readers continue to devour books of all types on the period. A particularly popular area of

---

1 I first saw this statue during a visit to London in March of 1980. Enthralled by the spectacle of the Horse Guards, I noticed a very important-looking statue dedicated to the Duke of Cambridge. Located in an area dominated by the Ministry of Defence and near other famous military monuments such as the Cenotaph and the statue of Viscount Montgomery, I assumed Cambridge had to have been a major historical figure and my curiosity was piqued. A little-known biography of Cambridge contains a similar account of the statue, Ethel M. Duff, *The Life Story of H.R.H. the Duke of Cambridge* (London: Stanley Paul & Co., 1938), 11-12.

research has been the monarchy, its transformation and political influence, and yet, despite this enduring interest, there clearly remains much more to be said. In the words of a leading scholar in the field, "The difficulty with the study of the British royal family since 1837 is that there has been too much chronicle and too little history, a surfeit of myth-making and a dearth of scholarly skepticism."[2]

This book examines the Duke of Cambridge's important relationship to the Crown while he served as Commander-in-Chief of the British army from 1856 until the Gladstone Ministry's end in 1874.[3] It places his life and actions in the context of his times. Although it is obviously quite difficult to rehabilitate the legacy of a man who resisted the use of khaki uniforms even in the desert, this book demonstrates that Cambridge was not a two dimensional figure obstinately opposed to any and all types of change. His career intersected an important period of transition for the British military and the monarchy, one that until now has not been sufficiently explored.

Historians studying this period have benefited from the tremendous amount of correspondence and government documents contained within the National Army Museum, the Public Records Office, and the British Library, to name but a few of their repositories, as well as the published diaries and correspondence detailing the attitudes and opinions of many of the important political, royal, and military figures of the era. Unfortunately, a great deal of the Duke's correspondence has remained largely unexplored or at least unreported; this material is essential to a better understanding of the changing nature of the army, the Crown, and Parliament during a crucial period of British history. Thanks to the gracious permission of Her Majesty Queen Elizabeth II and the staff of the Royal Archives, this author had extended access to the Royal Archives at Windsor Castle, wherein a very large amount of the military and private correspondence of the Duke of Cambridge remains well preserved. In the pages that follow, a more complete and accurate understanding of the role of the Duke of Cambridge will be presented and the result will be not only a new understanding of Cambridge, but more importantly, also of Queen Victoria, her ministers,

---

2 David Cannadine, "The Last Hanoverian Sovereign?: The Victorian Monarchy in Historical Perspective, 1688-1988" in A.L. Beier, David Cannadine and James N. Rosenheim (eds.), *The first Modern Society: Essays in Honour of Lawrence Stone* (Cambridge: Cambridge University Press, 1989), 129.

3 The official title of the Duke of Cambridge was "Officer Commanding-in-Chief" for the period from 1856 to 1887and then "Commander-in-Chief" from 1887 to 1895. For the sake of simplicity, the term Commander-in-Chief will be used to describe the position for both periods.

and her government, providing a significantly revised understanding of the relationship between Crown and Parliament, and the army.

The long tenure of His Royal Highness (H.R.H.) George William Frederick Charles, 2nd Duke of Cambridge, as Commander-in-Chief from 1856 to 1895 has traditionally been regarded as the major counterweight to a period that otherwise witnessed profound change in the administration of the British army. Not surprisingly, the majority of works devoted to the Victorian army deal with Cambridge only in a cursory manner; when he is addressed, in either political or military studies, he is invariably cast as little more than the main obstacle to serious reform, but little more than that.[4] While serving as the Adjutant General, Sir Garnet Wolseley expressed the view of many in favor of reform when he wrote, "All the Secretaries of State [for War] here in my time, have suffered at his [the Duke of Cambridge's] hands, and have had all needful reforms in the Army so blocked by him that one and all were determined never to have another Prince here."[5]

It is now clear the monarchy under Victoria looked quite different at the end of her reign than at the beginning. As a leading scholar on the monarchy, David Cannadine has aptly demonstrated "by the end of her [Victoria's] reign, the monarchy was less powerful, more popular, more splendid and more imperial than it had been at the beginning."[6] As true as that might be, and as well documented as the political influence of Victoria may now be, the appointment–and subsequent long tenancy–of

---

4 A telling example is Sir John W. Fortescue's dated but definitive thirteen-volume history of the British Army that mentions the Duke of Cambridge as Commander-in-Chief *only three times*. John W. Fortescue, *A History of the British Army*, 13 vols. (London: MacMillan and Co., 1910-1930); vol. 13, pp. 55, 557 and 559. Most studies of the British Army of the Victorian period that mention Cambridge focus on his role in preventing or delaying effective British army reform. See Brian Bond, *The Victorian Army and the Staff College, 1854-1914* (London: Eyre Methuen, 1972); Gwyn Harries-Jenkins, *The Army in Victorian Society* (London: Routledge & Keegan Paul, 1977; Edward M. Spiers, *The Army and Society, 1815-1914* (London: Longman, 1980); Jay Luvaas, *The Education of an Army: British Military Thought, 1815-1940* (Chicago: Chicago University Press, 1964) and *The Military Legacy of the Civil War: The European Inheritance* (Chicago: University of Chicago Press, 1988); and Hew Strachan, *European Armies and the Conduct of War* (London: Routledge, 1983).

5 Letter by Sir Garnet Wolseley to the Adjutant General, undated, reproduced in Brian Bond, "The Late-Victorian Army," *History Today*, 11 (1961): 618. Wolseley was writing to the queen's Secretary in opposition to the succession of the Duke of Connaught to his office. Brian Bond, "The Late-Victorian Army," *History Today*, 11 (1961): 618.

6 David Cannadine, "The Last Hanoverian Sovereign?: The Victorian Monarchy in Historical Perspective, 1688-1988" in A.L. Beier, David Cannadine and James N. Rosenheim (eds.), *The first Modern Society: Essays in Honour of Lawrence Stone* (Cambridge: Cambridge University Press, 1989), p. 127-128.

her cousin, the Duke of Cambridge, is an area which lends crucial insight into Victoria's political and military outlook.[7] Just as Cambridge's role has been neglected in the important works dealing with the British army as a whole, so has the interaction between the Queen and her cousin been overlooked as a source to explore the political and military influence of Queen Victoria. Although written over sixty years ago, Frank Hardie's introduction in *The Political Influence of Queen Victoria* could still well apply: "I have said very little about the relations between the Queen and her cousin, the Duke of Cambridge, as Commander-in-Chief from 1856 to 1895, and of her influence on Army questions generally, because…the obsoleteness of the subject deters me…"[8]

Yet, an essential linkage between two of the most important and investigated institutions of modern British history, the military and the monarchy, can be found in the career of the Duke of Cambridge. Apart from a biography written over four and one-half decades ago, his legacy has been almost entirely neglected since the time of his death.[9] In attempting to make the case why the former Commander-in-Chief of the British army mattered, his most recent biographer, Giles St. Aubyn, argued:

> The biographer in his choice of a victim is confronted with a dilemma. Either he writes about famous people of whom little new can be said, or he selects a lesser-known person, the subject of a mass of unpublished documents, who nevertheless is too obscure to catch the public's fancy. How well known the Duke of Cambridge is today is difficult

---

7 In addition to David Cannadine's essay, above, see, G.H.L. Le May, *The Victorian Constitution: Conventions, Usages and Contingencies* (London: Duckworth, 1979), especially chapter 3, "Queen Victoria and Her Ministers," 42-96. A major shortcoming is that it devotes only four pages (pages 77-80) to the Queen's interaction with Cambridge, and only then regarding the well-documented issue of the abolition of Purchase and other Cardwell reforms. Naturally, that is an important area that will be addressed below, but it overlooks other important, less-well-known areas of interaction.

8 Frank Hardie, *The Political Influence of Queen Victoria 1861-1901* (London: Oxford University Press, 1935), 7. Giles St. Aubyn in *The Royal George,* is the closest anyone has come to addressing this interaction and it is only tangential, "The history of the office of Commander-in-Chief and is largely the struggle between the Crown and Parliament for control of the armed forces." p. 107.

9 Giles R. St. Aubyn, *The Royal George: The Life of H.R.H. Prince George, Duke of Cambridge, 1819-1904* (London: Constable, 1963).

to tell, but of three things I am certain. First, as Commander-in-Chief of the Victorian Army for thirty-nine years he occupied the centre of the political stage at one of the greatest moments in our History. Secondly, the material for his life and times, much of it unpublished, is important, extensive and exciting. Thirdly, the Duke enjoyed a fascinating and momentous life.[10]

Unfortunately, such an explanation is less than satisfactory for a work of serious scholarship. This book will not be a biography of the Duke of Cambridge, for, try as one might, the sad truth is that in many ways, contrary to what his biographer wrote, Cambridge was a rather dull figure and at times even quite absurd. That, however, is not an excuse for ignoring Cambridge's contributions to the history of the Britain's army, monarchy and political system. What Cambridge's biographers failed to do, and what students of the British military and the monarchy have not yet done, is to place his career properly in the context of the changing relationship between the army and the Crown during the reign of Queen Victoria.

In the early spring of 1819, Princess Augusta, wife of the seventh and favorite son of King George III, Adolphus, Duke of Cambridge, gave birth to a son, George.[11] At the time, this royal birth was an important event for the monarchy, and therefore Great Britain, because it presented a male grandson as heir to the English throne. Scarcely two months later, however, young Prince George's opportunity to become king was ended by the royal birth of Princess Victoria on May 24 to infant George's aunt and uncle, Edward, Duke of Kent and Victoria, Princess of Saxe-Coburg.[12] The significance of these two births lay beyond their timing and their royal nature, for each would go on to head important institutions in Great Britain: the military and the monarchy. If by the end of the reign of Queen Victoria the monarchy had undergone a considerable transformation, it was

---

10 *Ibid.*, vi.
11 See Roger Fulford, *Royal Dukes: The Father and Uncles of Queen Victoria* (London: Gerald Duckworth & Co., 1933) for a dated, but useful and entertaining account of the sons of George III.
12 The best biography on Queen Victoria is Elizabeth Longford, *Queen Victoria: Born to Succeed* (New York: Harper & Row, 1964).

equally true that by the time George, the Duke of Cambridge, relinquished command, the office of the Commander-in-Chief had also. And while the monarchy survived the passing of both individuals, the office of the Commander-in-Chief did not last long after Cambridge left it. Why this should have been is one of the major themes of this book.

Apart from the monarchical and political aspects of the Victorian era, the general topic of the British army of that period has been an unending source of both serious and amateur investigation ever since. Much work has been done on British army administration reform and the development of a school for the professional education of senior officers, the Staff College.[13] During the past several decades, historians have also thoroughly investigated the reforms of Viscount Edward Cardwell.[14] Scholars have also addressed in depth the failure of reform after the Crimean War.[15] Interestingly, however, very little effort has been devoted to the most senior ranking uniformed army officer in Great Britain, the Duke of Cambridge, whose career spanned thirty-nine years. Only two serious biographies of Cambridge have been written since his death in 1904.[16] The extant works on Cambridge do little to improve our understanding of

---

13 Brian Bond, *The Victorian Army and the Staff College, 1854-1914* (London: Eyre Methuen, 1972) is the definitive single-volume investigation of the subject.

14 In addition to journal articles by Brian Bond, Albert Tucker and Arvel B. Erickson, to name only a few, there have been several important biographies and monographs dealing with reform in the British Army during the second half of the 19th century: Brian Bond, *The Victorian Army and the Staff College, 1854-1914* (London: Eyre Methuen, 1972); Gwyn Harries-Jenkins, *The Army in Victorian Society* (London: Routledge & Keegan Paul, 1977; Edward M. Spiers, *The Army and Society, 1815-1914* (London: Longman, 1980); Jay Luvaas, *The Education of an Army: British Military Thought, 1815-1940* (Chicago: Chicago University Press, 1964) and *The Military Legacy of the Civil War: The European Inheritance* (Chicago: University of Chicago Press, 1988); and Hew Strachan, *European Armies and the Conduct of War* (London: Routledge, 1983).

15 Entire sections of good libraries are devoted to the topic. For a solid and readable overview see David Chandler, ed. *The Oxford Illustrated History of the British Army* (Oxford: Oxford University Press, 1994). Related topics include the significance of the Volunteer Movement of 1859 as well as the various campaigns and actions of the British Army of the Victorian era.

16 The two biographies are William Willoughby Cole Verner, *The Military Life of H.R.H. George, Duke of Cambridge*. 2 vols. (London: John Murray, 1905) and the aforementioned biography by Giles St. Aubyn, *The Royal George*. In addition to Verner and St. Aubyn, there have been two other works devoted specifically to the Duke of Cambridge. The first appeared shortly after Verner's biography, an edited compilation of Cambridge's military and personal correspondence, Edgar Sheppard, ed., *George Duke of Cambridge: A Memoir of His Private Life Based Upon the Journals and Correspondence of His Royal Highness*, 2 vols. (London: Longman's, Green and Co., 1906). The other is Ethel M. Duff, *The Life Story of H.R.H. the Duke of Cambridge*, certainly not an historical account due to its unsubstantiated rumor from the perspective of the daughter Rev. A.W. Bailey, who had known Cambridge.

either the transformation of the military or the monarchy during this vital period in British history.[17] The concluding paragraph from the most recent work by St. Aubyn demonstrates this point overwhelmingly. If all that can be discovered is that the Duke's preservation of traditions and customs "was the salvation of the Queen's Army," clearly there remains much more to be done in this area.[18]

Whereas historians have neglected the life of Cambridge, the most contentious issue of his tenure–the so-called Cardwell reforms–has been thoroughly investigated. The changes implemented under the Secretary of State for War, Edward Cardwell, were intended to modernize the British army. These included abolition of flogging and the purchase of commissions, introduction of significantly shorter enlistments, reform of the War Office, and other important changes. The debate over the Cardwell reforms has been a lively one. Ever since Hampden Gordon called Cardwell the greatest war secretary since the Napoleonic Wars, the historical debate has naturally found him at the center.[19]

While Cardwell is generally regarded as the champion of reform, the Commander-in-Chief, the Duke of Cambridge, has been consistently portrayed as his nemesis. Although written over seventy years ago, Gordon's work characterized the two men in a manner that has persisted to the present day. According to Gordon, in Cardwell, "England had found a great Secretary for War in the clear-sighted and resolute person of the Rt. Hon. Edward Cardwell...this remarkable statesman achieved reforms in the space of five years the importance of which can hardly be overstated."[20] The image Gordon created of the Duke of Cambridge portrays a man whose "...ideas were extremely conservative. A man 'to whom a new idea was perdition.'"[21] However, it now seems clear that the Cardwell reforms were not nearly as sweeping as their supporters have argued, and army organization between the Crimean and Boer Wars underwent little

---

17 A century old, Verner's biography is useful for its published primary sources, but it fails to place the life of Cambridge in the context of the times and offers very little critical insight–it is on the whole, a traditional lengthy Victorian biography. Although more contemporary in style, St. Aubyn suffers from many of the same shortcomings as Verner's two-volume work.

18 St. Aubyn, *The Royal George,* 341.

19 Hampden Gordon, *The War Office* (London: Putnam, 1935), 59.

20 Ibid., 57.

21 *Ibid.*

effective change.[22] How could it be that the country which spearheaded the Industrial Revolution and became the most successful colonial power the world has ever seen by the end of the 19th century was one of the last European powers to create a modern army? Part of the explanation must lie with Cambridge. Cardwell was new to the scene, whereas Cambridge could in many ways be seen as the physical embodiment of the Crown and the army. Examining the Cardwell reforms without understanding Cambridge is to overlook half of the issue.

Although it is quite useful to examine the Duke's role in reforming the British army, Wolseley's quotation cited above is revealing; it points out not only that the Duke appeared to be opposed to reform, but also that he was a "Prince." Even though the military history of the 19th century may very well be an "obsolete" topic, to borrow Hardie's description, the changed role of the monarchy and its relationship to the military remain, with good reason, vibrant areas of investigation, still factors in British political life to the present day. While the 19th century witnessed a dramatic change in the character and role exercised by the monarchy, the one area of influence to which the Crown held on most fiercely was its relationship to the military. Queen Victoria deeply cherished what she understandably viewed as "her army." As the cousin to the Queen and former direct heir to the throne, the Duke of Cambridge exercised what authority he did have both by virtue of his position as Commander-in-Chief and the fact of his royal birth. The amount of real power of the former was, in his case, tied directly to the latter.

The struggle between Parliament and the Crown for mastery of the army could be traced back to the Glorious Revolution. It was during Cambridge's tenure that the army witnessed once and for all the final triumph of civilian control. Although Cambridge viewed his primary mission to be one of preserving the "Royal Prerogative"–the Queen's belief that in many ways the army was her own–and preventing undue civilian interference in the command, discipline, and efficiency of the army, ultimately he was far less successful than he would have liked.

---

22 Although the debate has continued unabated since he wrote them, Brian Bond's argument is the convincing position. See especially, Brian Bond, "Prelude to the Cardwell Reforms, 1856-1868," *Journal of the Royal United Services Institution* 106 (May 1961), "Edward Cardwell's Army Reforms, 1868-1874," *The Army Quarterly and Defence Journal* 84 (1962) and "The Effect of the Cardwell reforms on Army Organization, 1874-1904," *Journal of the Royal United Services Institution* 105 (May 1960).

Under Cambridge's leadership, the issues of civilian control and army reform would be tested, sometimes very publicly. Despite his best efforts and even with the Queen's assistance, Cambridge would not succeed in thwarting major changes in the army's organization and administration. By the end of the first Gladstone Ministry in 1874 it was clear not only that the matter was settled permanently, but also that the Queen and her cousin understood at long last they had lost. Although Cambridge continued in office for some two decades after the definition of his duties had been resolved at his expense, his importance as a military, political, and even as a royal figure was substantially and permanently diminished. In the end, rather ironically, it would be through the same royal connection that initially assisted his entry into office that Cambridge was finally forced to retire from it. Thus it was that the end of a struggle dating several centuries ultimately came to an end and changed forever the relationship between the military, the monarchy, and Parliament.

CHAPTER 1:
The Military and the Monarchy to 1837

The connection between the military and the monarchy is a historical one, as both institutions are rooted in antiquity and directly related to each other. It is no coincidence that in the classical era and throughout the pre-industrial period of western civilization, the greatest kings and emperors were generally very effective military commanders; by definition, they had to be. Almost without exception, a ruler's foundation was based upon the loyal support of a capable army able to conquer enemies both within and without the kingdom or empire.[1] At least until the end of the Middle Ages and arguably until the 19th century–George II of Great Britain (b. 1683; r. 1727-1760) and especially Frederick II of Prussia (b. 1712; r. 1740-1786) are two notable examples–monarchs were expected to be military leaders.

Although many kings and emperors were inept militarily, historically the measure of a monarch's position was his ability as a warrior.[2] Despite the subsequent importance of Christianity as the foundation of a king's legitimacy–eventually articulated as the notion of the divine right–the role of a monarch as chief warrior did not disappear until fairly recently, and any survey of the surviving European nobility reveals a healthy dose of dress uniforms and shiny medals. As a historian of the Middle Ages has observed, "The origins of Europe were hammered out on the anvil of war."[3] Although war may be too precise a term to describe the situation in Western Europe after the fall of Rome, the result was an intensified requirement for power to be exercised first and foremost by capable warriors as the political and bureaucratic infrastructure of the Roman Empire disintegrated. Throughout the entire medieval period, the influence of Germanic tribes affected the subsequent political systems that developed throughout all parts of Western Europe. The *comitatus,* or war band, became the basic political unit, and tribal chieftains were often elected on the basis of their martial prowess. Feudalism was as much a response to economic necessity as it was a military system to create stability. It also served as the nucleus for what eventually became the European aristocracy.[4]

1 For a broad-ranging survey on the relationship between power and its ceremonial representation in pre-industrial societies, see David Cannadine and Simon Price, eds., *Rituals of Royalty: Power and Ceremonial in Traditional Societies* (Cambridge: Cambridge University Press, 1987).

2 See J.H. Burns, ed., *The Cambridge History of Medieval Political Thought* (Cambridge: Cambridge University Press, 1987), for an excellent introduction to this rather complex topic.

3 R. Allen Brown, *The Origins of Modern Europe* (London: Boydell, 1972), 93.

4 For a brief, but effective summary of the influence of warfare on the political development of western Europe see Michael Howard, *War in European History* (Oxford: Oxford University Press, 1976), 1-19.

Charlemagne (b. 742; r. 768-814), the greatest king of the Franks, became emperor of the largest European empire between the fall of Rome in 476 and the rise of Napoleon (1769-1821). It was his unparalleled ability as a military leader that propelled him to lead France, while his capable administration and personal willpower enabled him to fashion an empire out of a desolated Western Europe.[5] The fusion of Christianity with the Germanic customs formed the basis for European culture and political organization. The feudal system varied widely in Europe, yet throughout the continent it remained primarily a political and military organization. In England, as throughout Europe, kings were first and foremost warriors, and kings of medieval England–Richard I (b. 1157; r. 1189-1199), Edward I (b. 1239; r. 1272-1307), Henry V (b. 1387; r. 1413-1422) to name a some of the more successful ones–were judged as much for their ability as warriors as they were for their effectiveness at ruling. The two characteristics were directly related. The long and effective reign of Elizabeth I (1533-1603) from 1558 to 1603, following the reign of another, less successful, woman, brought with it religious and political stability transforming England into a united state possessing a powerful navy and flourishing commerce.[6] Although Elizabeth was not a warrior, she exercised military force capably and successfully fended off the armed might of Spain. Even if the individual combatant role of the sovereign may have faded, it certainly did not disappear with the dawn of the modern era.

During the 17th century the constitutional position of the English monarch was fundamentally changed.[7] The role of the king underwent a substantive transformation, and the beginnings of a constitutional monarchy could be discerned so that, in the words of one historian, by "1714 the potential theoretical power of the monarch had been greatly diminished, its real practical power greatly enhanced."[8] Furthermore, though the nature of the army may have changed as well,

5 See Heinrich Fichtenau, *The Carolingian Empire* (Toronto: University of Toronto Press, 1978).
6 See Wallace MacCaffrey, *Elizabeth I* (London: Edward Arnold, 1993). For a survey of the changes in England during the age of the Tudors, see John Guy, *Tudor England* (Oxford: Oxford University Press, 1988).
7 See Mark Kishlansky, *A Monarchy Transformed: Britain 1603-1714*, The Penguin History of Britain, ed. David Cannadine (London: Penguin, 1996). See also, J.P. Sommerville, *Politics & Ideology in England 1603-1640* (New York: Longman, 1986), Christopher Hill, *The Century of Revolution 1603-1714* (New York: W.W. Norton, 1961), Barry Coward, *The Stuart Age* (New York: Longman, 1980) and J.G.A. Pockock, *The Ancient Constitution and the Feudal Law: A Study of English Historical Thought in the Seventeenth Century* (New York: Cambridge University Press, 1987).
8 Kishlansky, 341.

the relationship between the military and the monarchy remained a crucial aspect of both institutions. The legacy of Oliver Cromwell (1599-1658) affected the history of England in many ways, among them the relationship between Parliament and the Crown and the relationship between those two institutions and the army.

Although the year following the Glorious Revolution of 1688 is usually considered the official date for the start of a standing army in England due to its Parliamentary funding and royal control, the dual association of the king as head of state and military commander lasted throughout the 16th century. With the accession of the Hanoverians in 1714, the monarchy and newly united kingdoms forming Great Britain entered yet another phase, one which saw the formation of the British nation.[9] While George I (b. 1660; r. 1714-1727) and George II were generally not dedicated to affairs of state, their reigns had profound implications on the role and character of the monarchy. The Hanoverians' discomfort with the English language and their pronounced German mannerisms did not enhance the popularity of the monarchy, but both father and son continued the close association between the military and the monarchy. Both men were accomplished army officers with extensive combat experience. George I had commanded the imperial forces during the wars of Marlborough while George II will always be remembered as the last serving British monarch to lead his troops into battle.[10] In true Germanic tradition, the first two Hanoverian monarchs were soldier-kings. Into such a military heritage both the Duke of Cambridge and Queen Victoria were born, and it was a background the royal cousins would embrace without hesitation.

---

9 Material on the topic is exhaustive, but the definitive work on the creation of the British nation and monarchy, national identity, patriotism and war is Linda Colley, *Britons: Forging the Nation 1707-1837* (London: Yale University Press, 1992).

10 George II led his troops into battle at Dettingen during the War of the Austrian Succession on June 27, 1743. Despite their other faults, both kings were the source of most of the reforming initiatives within the British army in the first half of the 17th century.

I

Shortly after Cambridge died, his official biographer observed, "With all his devotion to the Army and his keen enthusiasm for his military duties, His Royal Highness was always something more than a soldier."[11] He was more than a soldier indeed, for he was the first cousin to Queen Victoria. From his birth, George was intimately connected with both the military and the monarchy. It is therefore not surprising that in terms of worldview, life experiences, and familial background, the Duke would share much in common with his first cousin, Victoria. Although not readily apparent in the early stages of their lives, as the two grew older, their mutual trust, fondness, and concern for one another would also result in each having influence over the other. For both, a key ancestral consideration was the essential military part of their family history beyond their royal blood.

The tradition of the German states in general, and the Hanoverian tradition in particular, held that aristocratic positions were intrinsically interwoven with military command.[12] Although the historical connection of Brandenburg-Prussia and the Hohenzollerns is a conspicuous example of a kingdom where political rule and military command were so closely connected as to be one in the same, the relationship of king or elector as the senior army officer was common throughout the Holy Roman Empire. Thus when George I acceded to the British throne, in addition to his German manners, German language, and German mistresses, he brought with him the German tradition of having been an army officer.[13] George had repeatedly served with distinction in battle on the continent, and despite the lack of majesty that accompanied his reign, his military expertise and experience stood in marked contrast to that of his doleful predecessor, Queen Anne (b. 1665; r. 1702-1714). He instituted changes that permanently altered the nature and traditions of the British army by attempting to introduce German methods of soldiering into Great Britain.

11 Edgar Sheppard, ed., *George Duke of Cambridge: A Memoir of His Private Life Based Upon the Journals and Correspondence of His Royal Highness*, Vol. 1, *1819-1871* (London: Longman's, Green and Co., 1906), vii.
12 Although primarily focused on Prussia, Gordon A. Craig, *Politics of the Prussian Army 1640-1945* (New York: Oxford University Press, 1955) presents a useful account of the importance of the army to monarchical power and political rule. See also, among others, Hajo Holborn, *A History of Modern Germany 1648-1840* (New York: Knopf, 1971).
13 Though dated, but still useful, see John H. Plumb, *The First Four Georges* (New York: Macmillan, 1957).

Although George achieved mixed results and was unable to root out the practice of purchasing commissions, he did raise the standards of training and discipline.[14] His most lasting contribution was standard individual arms drill throughout the entire army, although standardization of unit drill did not occur until the end of the century.[15] George I's reputation for martial ability was superseded only by one individual: the Duke of Marlborough (1650-1722). When George I ascended to the throne, Marlborough returned from self-imposed exile to command the army. By this time, however, the Duke suffered somewhat prematurely from the effects of old age, and he died eight years later. Notably, Marlborough's title of "Captain-General" was not bestowed upon a replacement until 1745, when a prince of the blood and grandson of George I, the Duke of Cumberland (1721-1765), received the title and took command of the army.[16]

Whereas George I had held a close association with the army, his son and successor, George II, surpassed his father's interest in military affairs. Although he may not have equaled the ardor of his Prussian cousins, King William Frederick I (b. 1688; r. 1713-1740), known as the Soldier King because of his obsession with drill, discipline, and tall soldiers, or Frederick II, one of the great battle captains of history, George II devoted even greater attention to army matters than his father. Whatever his shortcomings as a sovereign, he was a capable military commander. At Dettingen in 1743, George dismounted his horse and, with sword drawn, personally led his English and Hanoverian infantry in a counterattack that proved instrumental in winning the battle. The king had demonstrated not only great personal bravery, but good tactical sense as well. Moreover, in addition to having taken direct part in combat during the War of the Austrian Succession, George studied his army with great interest. Not only the King of Great Britain, he was also Elector of Hanover, a fact which mattered more to him than his role as the British king, but he also identified himself as an army officer. He regularly wore his red-jacketed uniform when dealing with military matters and was a major force for army reform. Like his father, George II was opposed to the practice of

---

14 Through his intervention, Purchase was regulated in 1720 and 1722 but not abolished. Purchase will be addressed in depth in chapters 7 and 8.
15 See Correlli Barnett, *Britain and Her Army 1509-1970: A Military, Political and Social Survey* (New York: William Morrow & Co., 1970), 176-177.
16 Alan J. Guy, "The Army of the Georges 1714-1783," in David Chandler, ed., *The Oxford Illustrated History of the British Army* (Oxford: Oxford University Press, 1994), 98-99.

selling commissions, but he also recognized that to eliminate the practice entirely would be extraordinarily difficult.[17]

As did his great-great granddaughter, Victoria, a century later, George II jealously guarded not only the control of his army, but also the promotion of its senior officers, and he strove to prevent outside interference into what he regarded as his prerogative. In 1751 a Royal Warrant ended the practice of regiments being named after their commanding officer, while another Royal Warrant that year prohibited the placement of personal coats of arms on regimental colors.[18] During his reign, George II issued three warrants that progressively tightened controls over the appearance and quality of uniforms.[19] Matters of pay, tactics, and weapons were also areas of great interest to the king. Perhaps one of the most significant and lasting contributions of the two Georges was the continued determination to centralize and make the officer corps of the army a more professional organization. In short, George II believed the army must be above party politics and that senior rank was not dependent upon political views.[20] This royal attitude has continued to the present day and remains a lasting contribution of the Hanoverians. It was a legacy both Queen Victoria and the Duke of Cambridge would take very seriously over a century later, and remained a key underpinning of their opposition to the subordination of the Commander-in-Chief to a civilian minister, specifically, the Secretary of State for War.[21]

As George II and his first-born son and heir, Frederick Louis (1707-1751), the Prince of Wales, detested each other in the best Hanoverian tradition[22]–Queen Caroline (1683-1737) infamously described her son as

17 Anthony Bruce, *The Purchase System in the British Army, 1600-1871* (London: The Royal Historical Society, 1980), 22-28.
18 Guy, "The Army of the Georges 1714-1783," in Chandler, 98.
19 *Ibid.* The controls were implemented in 1729, 1736 and 1751.
20 Hew Strachan, *The Politics of the British Army* (Oxford: Clarendon Press, 1997), 28-29. An exception that proved the rule occurred in 1764 when Lieutenant General Henry Conway, MP for Thetford, was deprived of the colonelcy of his regiment, the Royal Dragoons, because he voted against the government. Conway's supporters protested that an appointment could only be forfeited for an offense, not politics. Although George III did not reinstate Conway, the king never again interfered with commands on the basis of political opposition, and Conway himself went on to become Commander-in-Chief.
21 This will be addressed in chapters 7, 8 and 9.
22 Beginning with George I, the repetitive antagonism between father and son–in the case of George II and the future George III, grandfather and grandson–besides becoming a predictable familial relationship, developed a political component as well in that political opponents of the monarch would align themselves with the Prince of Wales, who in turn became the center of political opposition against the king.

"the greatest ass and the greatest liar and the greatest *canaille* and the greatest beast in the whole world"—the two men differed significantly in disposition and calling. It is not surprising therefore, that Frederick did not undertake a military career and was in many ways the opposite of his father. However, to portray Frederick as solely the opposite of his father would be a gross oversimplification—he recognized the flaws of his Hanoverian predecessors and attempted to draw allies and supporters from a broad array of political groupings.[23]

King George II's third and only other surviving son, William Augustus, the Duke of Cumberland, was an accomplished soldier and continued the German military tradition of his father and grandfather. Entering the army at age 19, he saw extensive action during the course of the War of the Austrian Succession. Significantly, he fought with his father at the Battle of Dettingen and received a wound which would never heal. Despite his growing corpulence and festering leg wound, Cumberland pursued a very active military career as Captain General of the army. He introduced the *Regulations* of 1748, an attempt to standardize all aspects of army life, and released a second work, *Standing Orders,* in May of 1753.[24] In addition to being a capable military commander, Cumberland possessed that far rarer quality of giving thought to the subject as well.

All of these accomplishments aside, Cumberland was most famous for a single military action within the British Isles. In 1745 he was recalled to England to suppress the Jacobite Rebellion from Flanders where he had been fighting the French in the War of the Austrian Succession. Prince Charles Edward Stuart (1720-1788), better known as Bonnie Prince Charlie or the Young Pretender, son of James Edward (1688-1766), the Old Pretender, initiated "the Forty-Five" Jacobite rebellion in Scotland to seize the British Crown. After months of skirmishes, Cumberland defeated the forces of the Young Pretender at the Battle of Culloden Moor on April 16, 1746. In the course of the battle, Cumberland's forces killed approximately 1,000 Highlanders and captured an additional 1,000 more, but the summary execution of prisoners earned Cumberland the infamous nickname of "the Butcher."[25] After Culloden Moor, Cumberland returned to the continent to lead the British forces against the French, but was

---

23 Colley, 206-207.
24 The book was based upon Cumberland's orders while in command of the British forces in the Low Countries from 1745 to 1748. From Guy, "The Army of the Georges 1714-1783," in Chandler, 99.
25 Barnett, 192-194.

defeated by French Marshal Maurice de Saxe (1696-1750) at the Battle of Lauffeld near Maastricht on July 2, 1747. Although Cumberland achieved additional fame in the protracted defense of Maastricht, the city fell to the French on May 7, 1748. The Treaty of Aix-la-Chapelle ended the War of the Austrian Succession on October 18, 1748. Cumberland's downfall came a decade later in the beginning of the Seven Years' War. Once again in command of an allied army, this time with 10,000 English and 40,000 Prussian troops, Cumberland was defeated by a French army under the command of Marshal Louis d'Estrées (1695-1771) at the Battle of Hastenbeck in Hanover on July 26, 1757. This defeat allowed the French to occupy Hanover. As a result, Cumberland's father, King George II, relieved him of command.

Despite the unhappy ending, the Duke of Cumberland had established a precedent for a royal duke who chose the military as a career and attained the highest position within the army, what was then termed Captain-General but would later be Commander-in-Chief. Although later in life the "Butcher of Culloden" may have appeared a "fleshy Cyclops, breathing with difficulty through his asthma, and limping from a suppurating wound in his leg," he had once proved himself a brave and capable army officer.[26] During his career Cumberland had also alienated many fellow officers and acquired, with some justification, the reputation of being a martinet through his untiring efforts to bring German-style discipline into the officer corps.[27] These attempts rankled many officers, as did the efforts of Cumberland's father, George II, whose devotion to Germanic discipline went against the English officers' tradition of aristocratic privilege and individualism.

After 1748, Cumberland became the primary target of those opposed to the German military tradition imported to Britain by George I and George II. Frederick, the decidedly unmilitary Prince of Wales, and his political allies portrayed Cumberland as being too closely attached to the army and a threat to the constitution. Cumberland's reputation remained damaged after Frederick's death, and there were even rumors to the effect

---

26 The quotation describes the appearance of the Duke of Cumberland at the marriage of George III to Charlotte of Mecklenburg-Strelitz when Cumberland presented the bride, from Roger Fulford, *Royal Dukes: the Father and Uncles of Queen Victoria* (London: Gerald Duckworth & Co., 1949), 16.

27 Prussian-style discipline on the continent was so severe that between 1713 and 1740, 30,216 men deserted the Prussian army to escape it–a fantastic number considering the army grew from 40,000 to 83,000 men during this period. From Craig, 7-9.

that Cumberland had played the same role to the adolescent Prince George as had "Crookback Richard" to the princes in the tower.[28] Yet in spite of Cumberland's incomplete efforts to improve the army and his ultimate disgrace in defeat, this royal duke had set a high standard for military service, perhaps one which became clearer after his death.[29]

In barely half a century, the Hanoverians had established a close association with the British army, despite their primary loyalty to Hanover. In addition to the many other family characteristics which the two Georges brought to their new country, including the tradition in which each sovereign became bitterly estranged from his heir, they added the Germanic approach to the army. Although George I, George II, and the Duke of Cumberland attempted to fashion the British army along the lines of various German armies, they were not successful. However, they reinforced the practice of the monarch taking a close interest in all things military and royal princes being accepted as active officers at the highest levels. Even though the Hanoverians obviously did not create the close association between the military and the monarchy, they added a new vitality to the traditional association between the army and the king. Many of the issues affecting the morale and discipline of the army occupied the attention of the Duke of Cumberland and remained over a century later when the Duke of Cambridge assumed the position of Commander-in-Chief, although Cambridge would see things from a combined German and English outlook. Significantly, the early Hanoverians viewed the army as their private domain rather than that of Parliament.

II

The connection between the military and the monarchy would be continued, modified, and in some ways strengthened during the long reign of George III (b. 1738; r. 1760-1820). Although George himself did not undertake a military career–that distinction was left to most of his brothers and sons–his reign witnessed a defining period of British and world history, most importantly the Industrial Revolution and the long struggle against France following the French Revolution. In the course of the several wars

---

28 Guy, "The Army of the Georges 1714-1783," 108-109.
29 It is telling that the first outdoor statue of a soldier to be erected in London was of the Duke of Cumberland in 1770.

against France and the loss of the American colonies, a national identity was shaped while the monarchy and governing classes became genuinely British, and Britain became a world power.[30] Upon his accession, George III made it clear that he considered himself to be English and cared very little for Hanover; his reign clearly represented a new phase in British history.[31]

Famously, George's children were a scandalous lot who, in contrast to their father, did little to further the dignity of the monarchy. More troubling than their behavior was the very real possibility that not one of them would produce a legitimate heir.[32] The greatest chance for succession evaporated when Princess Charlotte (1796-1817), the only child of the Prince Regent, died along with her stillborn son on November 6, 1817.[33] Accordingly, the possibilities for succession shifted dramatically as George's six other surviving sons and five surviving daughters were now the potential source for an heir to the throne. The possibility of the Prince Regent divorcing his wife and remarrying a younger bride was not great.[34] As for the other children of George III, they were all quite advanced in years with the youngest being well past middle age, and, in the words of an eminent royal biographer, they "inspired the nation about as much as the

---

30 See Colley, 147-236.

31 For a useful account of the legacy of the Hanoverian kings and their connection to the reign of Queen Victoria, see David Cannadine, "The last Hanoverian sovereign?: the Victorian monarchy in historical perspective, 1688-1988" in A.L. Beier, David Cannadine and James M. Rosenheim, eds., *The First Modern Society: Essays in Honour of Lawrence Stone* (Cambridge: Cambridge University Press, 1989).

32 Although quite dated, Fulford, *Royal Dukes: the Father and Uncles of Queen Victoria*, remains a solid introduction. For a more critical analysis of his reign and its impact on the political powers of the monarchy, see Christopher Hibbert, *George IV* (Harmondsworth: Harmondsworth, 1976).

33 Charlotte, Princess of Wales, led a short and rather unhappy life. Separated at an early age from her unfit mother, Caroline of Brunswick, whose own conduct was equally as scandalous and disreputable as that of her husband, Charlotte was placed into the care of her cold and unfit father, the Prince Regent. The Prince Regent sought to marry her off at the first opportunity. He did just that in May 1816 to Prince Leopold of Saxe-Coburg, who would later become Leopold I, King of the Belgians.

34 The Prince Regent, subsequently George IV, was a shocking example of excess and degeneracy. As Prince Regent from 1811-1820, he was the acting king as his father, George III, had become quite delirious and incapable of ruling. An apt and compact assessment of George IV finds that "...in the character of his brilliant son [George IV] there was little that was healthy; nothing that was simple." Roger Fulford, *George the Fourth* (New York: Capricorn, 1963), 16. To borrow the assessment of a contentious biographer of Queen Victoria, it was doubtful that the Prince, who "presented a preposterous figure of debauched obesity, could ever again, even on the supposition that he divorced his wife and re-married, become the father of a family." Lytton Strachey, *Queen Victoria* (New York: Harcourt, Brace and Co., 1921), 7-8.

procession of Banquo's descendants inspired Macbeth." [35] Regardless of the character of their moral behavior, what the surviving sons of George III had in common–except for the Prince Regent and the Duke of Sussex–was a military career. Apart from the Duke of Clarence, who chose the navy, the Hanoverian sons cemented the already close connection between the military and the monarchy. While they may have diminished the popular view of the royal family–they certainly did not enhance it–the sons of George III made an army career commonplace.

After the Prince Regent, the other surviving children of George III at the time of the death of Princess Charlotte in 1817 were Frederick (1763-1827), Duke of York and Albany,[36] William Henry (1765-1837), Duke of Clarence, later William IV (b. 1765; r. 1830-1837), Charlotte (1766-1828), Princess Royal and later queen of Würtemberg, Edward Augustus (1767-1820), Duke of Kent, Augusta (1768-1840), Elizabeth (1770-1840), Ernest Augustus (1771-1851), Duke of Cumberland, subsequently King of Hanover, Augustus Frederick (1773-1843), Duke of Sussex, Adolphus Frederick (1774-1850), Duke of Cambridge, and Mary (1776-1857), subsequently Duchess of Gloucester and Sophia (1777-1848).[37] Out of this impressive but rather dizzying array of offspring, there were certain children who were obviously incapable of producing an heir. The three unmarried princesses, Augusta, Elizabeth, and Sophia were all over the age of 40 by 1817, so that short of a quick marriage followed by a miraculous conception, there was no hope of any of them producing an heir. As for the two married daughters of George III, Charlotte, queen of Würtemberg, and Mary, the Duchess of Gloucester, they had thus far been unsuccessful; considering their advanced ages, an heir was unlikely. As for George's other sons, none had conceived any legitimate children by the time of the Charlotte's death. Clearly the future for succession was less than promising.

Although the lives of the Royal Dukes were uneven, if not scandalous (and therefore quite interesting), their lives are of only passing interest for

---

35 Longford, 17.

36 Young Prince Frederick had the rather unique privilege of becoming a bishop at the age of seven months; in the words of Roger Fulford, "The infantile, but Right Reverend, Father in God was admittedly an unusual character to meet in English family life." Fulford, 21.

37 This lengthy list includes only those children who were still alive at the time of the death of Princess Charlotte. In addition to the eleven children alive at her death, three more had preceded her: Octavius, Alfred and Amelia.

the purposes of this book and therefore shall be addressed only briefly. Of greater importance, however, was the impact of their lives and careers in modifying, strengthening, or weakening the relationship between the military and the monarchy. Neither George III nor the Prince Regent undertook a military career, in itself an important break from the tradition of Georges I and II. William IV, who succeeded George IV (b. 1762; r. 1820-1830), resumed a direct link between the Crown and military service, as he had seen service as a naval officer. Despite the break in direct connection to the military during the reign of two monarchs, the connection between military service and the Crown was strengthened through the younger sons of George III; it was now expected of Royal Dukes to serve in the military.

The Duke of York, next in the line of succession after the Prince Regent, Frederick, had a troubled marriage which was quite unlikely to produce a child. Even though Frederick had been married since 1791 to the niece of Frederick the Great, Princess Frederica, the two did not spend much of their married life under the same roof. Even the death of Charlotte in 1817 and the increasingly urgent need to ensure the line of succession were insufficient to bring the two of them together long enough to produce an heir.[38] Regarding the Duke of York specifically, however, two aspects of his life would foreshadow those of his nephew, George, the second Duke of Cambridge: York considered the army to be his primary profession and he went on to attain the highest possible rank as Commander-in-Chief of the British army. His army career began when he was gazetted to the rank of colonel at the age of seventeen and sent to Hanover by his father, where he would receive his military education in the German tradition.[39] While on the continent, York reviewed Prussian garrisons in Westphalia and observed Prussian maneuvers in 1782.[40] Within a year of his return, he was promoted to the rank of major general shortly before his twentieth birthday, followed by a subsequent promotion to lieutenant general less than a year afterwards.

---

38 Fulford, *Royal Dukes*, 35-39.
39 During his year in Germany York met Frederick the Great, King of Prussia, and was greatly impressed by his methods. It was only natural for a royal prince to learn about the army in Hanover, since prior to the French Revolution the German states in general were considered the best location in Europe to receive a military education. The successes of Frederick the Great influenced the armies of not only the other German states, but the rest of Europe as well. The familial ties to Hanover made it only natural to start there.
40 Jeremy Black, *European Warfare 1660-1815* (New Haven: Yale University Press, 1994), 149.

After France declared war on Britain in early 1793, King George III selected the Duke of York to command the British army in Flanders. Despite some initial success, including the capture of the Valenciennes on July 26, 1793, overall York did not prove to be a gifted commander. He was hindered in his efforts by the difficulty of leading a poorly trained British force which was part of a coalition that included the Dutch, the Hanoverians, and the Austrians. By the summer of 1794, the British force under York had been forced back into Holland where it prepared for its winter quarters. While York's army suffered greatly from lack of adequate winter supplies, the Duke left his men and returned to England in December where he was promoted to the rank of field marshal, despite his failure in Belgium, and assumed the position of Commander-in-Chief of the British army. Clearly his royal blood helped him overcome the reversals encountered on the battlefield, foreshadowing a similar career progression for a future Commander-in-Chief, the Duke of Cambridge.[41] Shortly thereafter, York returned to the field to command an Anglo-Russian army in Holland, where the following summer he was defeated by the French and returned with his troops to Britain, leaving behind his French prisoners according to the terms of the Convention of Alkmaar.[42]

After his return to London, the Duke of York demonstrated his greatest military ability, that of a reformer. As the highest-ranking officer in the British army, he proved to be genuinely progressive during his long term as Commander-in-Chief from 1795-1809. Rather than fade quietly into obscurity following field service, he carried on in the tradition of his Hanoverian grandfather and great-grandfather, George I and George II. Influenced by the military education he had received on the continent and having experienced firsthand the inefficiencies of the British army against Napoleon, York strived to correct the army's shortcomings, many of which were the same ones his father and grandfather had sought to eliminate and would later continue to plague his nephew, the Duke of

---

41 See Chapters 3 and 4, below.

42 Space does not allow a full account of the Duke's lifetime accomplishments. A genuine professional, he faced the very difficult task of fielding the first British army (supported by a confused and inefficient alliance) against a French army infused with the new military factor of nationalism. When assisted by a capable staff, he could be an effective commander, but his greatest attribute was his willingness to listen to subordinates advocating reform, such as Sir John Moore. See A.H. Burne, *The Noble Duke of York: The Military Life of Frederick, Duke of York and Albany* (London: Oxford, 1949) and Ramsay W. Phipps, *The Armies of the First French Republic and the Rise of the Marshals of Napoleon I.* 5 vols. (London: Oxford University Press, 1926-1939).

Cambridge. Although York was unable to effect much change overall, he did make great strides in improving the training of light infantry and officer education. Furthermore, one of his developments in 1799, the creation of a separate engineer corps, the Royal Staff Corps, was used by Wellington with great effect.[43] Scandal forced him to retire, however, when his mistress, Mrs. Mary Anne Clarke, was revealed to have accepted money from officers to advance their rank.[44] Though a capable reformer, his disgraced departure from office put an abrupt end to further reforms, and it remains an unanswered question what would have become of reform had York remained in office longer.

Regardless, when the career of his nephew George, the second Duke of Cambridge, followed certain aspects of York's career, he was not much influenced by the lessons learned or even the personal example of the Duke of York. The two men were quite different in ability, outlook, and temperament, and they serve as interesting examples by which to contrast very different approaches to the office of the Commander-in-Chief when filled by a royal prince. Though not the first example, York's case represents an important precedent involving the connection between the military and the monarchy. More importantly, it occurred within living memory of the Victorian era, and York's example both contrasts and illustrates the changed positions of the army and the Crown during the era of Napoleon versus the Victorian era. York used his office and his royal birth as a vehicle to bring about much needed reform to the army, when the service–indeed, the entire kingdom–was challenged by a new and dangerous phenomenon.

Napoleon and the nationalism he both inspired and used with great effectiveness ushered in a new type of warfare. York had fought against the French and lost. Accordingly, York used his office and his status to try to bring about needed reforms in order to meet more effectively the hazards of modern continental warfare.[45] Since the British army operated

43 Gunther E. Rothenberg, *The Art of Warfare in the Age of Napoleon* (Bloomington, IN: Indiana University Press, 1978), 225.

44 An investigation in the House of Commons into charges of corruption forced the resignation of the Duke of York. Humiliation for the Duke was great as his love letters to Mrs. Clarke were read before the House and published in newspapers throughout England. Despite surviving the vote in the House (278 voted for his innocence while 196 found him guilty of "personal corruption and connivance at the infamous practices disclosed by Mrs. Clarke"), the Duke retired immediately after the vote, shocked that such a large number of MPs thought him guilty. Fulford, *Royal Dukes*, 60-61.

45 The definitive work on the topic is Gunther E. Rothenberg, *The Art of Warfare in the Age of Napoleon* (Bloomington, IN: Indiana University Press, 1978). In addition to many others, see David

on vastly different principles than the French, it was a remarkable example of reforming in an opposite direction. Whereas the French harnessed the forces of nationalism and commissioned many officers from the ranks, the British response was to ensure the maintenance of great discipline while officers were commissioned through the system of purchase. York did not try to copy the French example. Instead, he attempted to borrow the Germanic tradition of strict discipline while enhancing the administrative, logistical, and organizational aspects of the British army. Despite the personal animus of his brother, the Prince Regent, York was effective in bringing about change to a system in which inertia was substantial. His premature departure leaves the question unresolved of how much further reform could have been accomplished had he remained in office.

The Duke of York's royal nephew, the Duke of Cambridge (1819-1904), presents a dramatically different case of a royal duke in the office of the Commander-in-Chief threatened by external challenges. Whereas York sought to bring about change, Cambridge, after a brief period where he also tried to implement some new ideas, spent the majority of his lengthy tenure–which by no means ended prematurely–doing his utmost to prevent it. Like his uncle before him, Cambridge brought both his office and his royal connection to bear. Curiously, both men came to high office after failing to achieve glory and great success in battle–York, as commander of the allied army had been defeated by the French, while Cambridge, after a case of lost nerve and ostensible battle fatigue, abandoned his division command in the Crimea. The lack of great success in combat did not hinder either man in fulfilling his duties as Commander-in-Chief, but York continued to command troops operationally in the field against the French while Cambridge never returned to the field. Cambridge's struggle will be addressed in depth, but what is important here is the significance of the case of the Duke of York for Cambridge: the precedent of a royal duke holding the highest military position in the kingdom with a determined agenda had been established. Furthermore, despite the unsatisfactory end

G. Chandler, *The Campaigns of Napoleon: The Mind and Method of History's Greatest Soldier* (New York: Scribner, 1966), "Chapter 5: The Wars of the Revolution," in Michael Howard, *War in European History*, 75-93, "Chapter 4: Napoleonic Warfare" in Hew Strachan, *European Armies and the Conduct of War* (London: Routledge, 1983), "Chapter 4: The French Revolution and Napoleon" in Theodore Ropp, *War in the Modern World* (London: Collier MacMillan Publishers, 1959), 98-142, "Chapter 1: The Legacy of Napoleon" in William McElwee, *The Art of War: Waterloo to Mons* (Bloomington, IN: Indiana University Press, 1974), 1-33, and Harold T. Parker, *Three Napoleonic Battles* (Durham, NC: Duke University Press, 1983).

to York's career, overall his tenure had by no means been a misfortune for Great Britain. All of this notwithstanding, here remain substantial differences between the two cases. For York, the monarch was the father and not the cousin of the Commander-in-Chief. The comparison is further complicated by an incapacitated George III. York really had to deal with the Prince Regent, who strongly disliked his royal brother, while Cambridge for the majority of his tenure had not only the support of his cousin, Queen Victoria, but perhaps even her genuine affection.

The Duke of York as Commander-in-Chief represents the first time a royal relative had occupied the position. The Duke of Cumberland had served as Captain-General several decades earlier, but the position of Commander-in-Chief had only been revived by George III as recently as 1793–it had last been seen after the Restoration when Charles II (b. 1630; r. 1660-1685) appointed the Duke of Albermarle (1608-1670), serving from 1660 until his death. From then until 1793, the king personally assumed the role of Commander-in-Chief and appointed a Captain-General or Commander-in-Chief in a temporary position in response to a specific emergency.[46] It was therefore an important development in the relationship between the military and the monarchy when George III resurrected the permanent position of Commander-in-Chief in 1793 with Lord Amherst, Field Marshal Jeffery Amherst, 1st Baron Amherst (1717-1797), hero of the French and Indian Wars, as a result of the outbreak of another war with France. The duties were undefined and Amherst's main responsibility was to safeguard England against a French invasion.[47] Due to Amherst's advanced age and York's lack of success on the continent, King George III placed the royal duke into the office in 1795.[48] Although there was no clear definition of duties, the Commander-in-Chief was to be directly responsible to the king for control of military administration while the Secretary at War was responsible to Parliament for army finance.[49] Once again imitating future disputes, George's action did not clarify the exact relationship between the military officer responsible to the Crown and the civilian minister responsible to Parliament, a situation which would remain the subject of dispute over half a century later when the Duke

---

46 St. Aubyn, *The Royal George*, 107.
47 Charles M. Clode, *The Military Forces of the Crown*, vol. 2 (London: John Murray, 1869), 339.
48 When York assumed the office, he located himself at the Horse Guards, the same location where the office would be when the Duke of Cambridge assumed it six decades later.
49 Hampden Gordon, *The War Office* (London: Putnam, 1935), 40-41.

of Cambridge became Commander-in-Chief.[50] George III's decision was momentous; it was the first time since the Restoration that the sovereign had purposely relinquished direct control of the army.

III

All but two sons of George III strengthened the bond between the royal family and service in the armed forces, although not to the same degree as York. Prince William, the Duke of Clarence, would become King William IV after the death of his brother, George IV, in 1830 (his older brother, the Duke of York died in 1827), but in 1817 he seemed quite incapable of producing a legitimate heir. Before he attracted national attention over the issue of succession, he had demonstrated a rather mixed career as a naval officer. Clarence had spent his formative years at sea, but was not an accomplished sea captain. He was denied a squadron during the Napoleonic Wars and saw limited service. Unfortunately, during his time at sea, Clarence acquired rather rough habits and manners from his extended association with sailors, yet one positive consequence of his service in the navy was his close friendship with Lord Nelson, Horatio Nelson, 1st Viscount Nelson (1758-1805).[51] It was this association and his royal blood that advanced his rank, despite his incompetence as a sailor. Promoted to captain in 1786, he was created Duke of Clarence in 1789, and promoted again to admiral in 1799, but saw little service after 1790. Technically Clarence had been a career naval officer, but he did not enhance his own reputation or that of his family's during his time in uniform.

Clarence's inability to provide an heir was not due to difficulty fathering children, for he produced ten with his former mistress, the stout and coarse actress, Mrs. Dorothea Jordan (1761-1816).[52] After breaking

---

50 The lack of a definition of duties for both positions will be addressed in depth throughout the second half of this book.

51 A sign of that closeness is that Nelson entrusted the Duke with giving away his bride at Nelson's wedding.

52 See Claire Tomalin, *Mrs. Jordan's Profession: The Actress and the Prince* (New York: Alfred Knopf, 1995). Early in his adult life Clarence earned a reputation for indiscretion by walking throughout the fashionable parts of London with his actress "friend," Mrs. Jordan, even though by then she had several children by different fathers. In 1811, once his brother became Prince Regent, he severed his relationship with Mrs. Jordan, apparently over lack of money. She died in squalor in France in 1816 and Clarence's treatment of her made him a target of the London papers, scandal being the only time he was a national figure. See also Fulford, *Royal Dukes,* 89-108.

free from Mrs. Jordan, William eventually found a suitable wife, Princess Adelaide of Saxe-Coburg-Meiningen (1792-1849). The two married in the summer of 1818, but Parliament barely increased Clarence's income, so the two went to live in Hanover out of economic necessity. In March 1819 and within several days of the birth of the second Duke of Cambridge, the Duchess of Clarence bore a daughter, but she died within a few hours. In December that year the Duchess gave birth to Princess Elizabeth Georgiana Adelaide, but she also died in March 1821.[53] With the death of the Duke of York in 1827, Clarence became heir presumptive to the throne and was appointed lord high admiral of the navy, but was forced to resign. He would prove unable to produce an heir to the throne. With the death of George IV in 1830, Clarence became William IV, another Hanoverian monarch who had seen active service in the armed forces, but his association with the navy only weakened the relationship between that institution and the Crown.

As Edward, Duke of Kent, the fourth son of George III, was by then fifty years old, he did not seem likely to produce a legitimate heir either. Hopelessly in debt, he had once been a promising army officer, serving most of his career in Gibraltar, Canada, and the West Indies. His attitude toward discipline, however, gained him the deserved reputation of being a martinet—not a surprising characterization considering the reputation of his grandfather, George II, his uncle the Duke of Cumberland, and his great-grandfather, George I. It was Kent's obsession for excessive discipline that brought his career to a premature end in 1803 when he was recalled from Gibraltar because of his treatment of the garrison there.[54] His reputation

---

53 *Ibid.,* 114-115.

54 The Duke of Kent's recall from Gibraltar in 1803 was not the first time he had gotten into trouble over his poor treatment of his soldiers. Deep in debt from the very beginning of his military career, he left his military schooling in Geneva without leave to ask his father for monetary assistance. Furious, George III in effect banished him to Gibraltar in 1790, where he lasted less than a year because of his extreme behavior. From Gibraltar he was sent even farther away, to Canada. Even though he rose to the position of Commander-in-Chief of all the forces in Canada, he arranged for his own transfer to the West Indies to serve under Sir Charles (later Lord) Grey. In the late 18th century, Canada was a remote and unattractive posting for a British army officer; it certainly was not the mark of a successful career. He performed well in the reduction of rebellions in Martinique and St. Lucia and was mentioned in dispatches and ultimately received the thanks of Parliament. After Kent received additional promotions and an increase in income, his brother, the Duke of York, in his capacity as Commander-in-Chief of the army, sent Kent once again to Gibraltar for the express purpose of restoring discipline to the garrison there. Barely six months after his arrival, his closure of half the wine-shops on the island caused a mutiny on Christmas Eve 1802. He quickly subdued the rebellion and had the ringleaders shot, but he was recalled to England in March of 1803 and his career was effectively over. He demanded an

for harshness was such that he would not flinch in sentencing a man to one hundred lashes for leaving a button undone.[55]

In fairness, he was also reported to possess humanity, piety, and an ample amount of bravery with some enlightened ideas as well, yet his obsession with trivial minor details did not enhance his reputation.[56] By 1817, however, his lifelong habit of spending well beyond his means left him hopelessly indebted. All of these impediments could have been either rectified or overlooked in the pursuit of an heir except for one inconvenient fact: he had been living for twenty-seven years with Madame St. Laurent, who did not appear ready to move aside for any reason.[57] After the death of Charlotte, if Clarence did not marry, Kent would be next in succession, and he would need to secure a wife. On November 16, 1817, it did not seem likely the Duke of Kent would one day sire an heir, yet he would be the father of the future Queen Victoria (b. 1819; r. 1837-1901). And despite the unhappy end to the army career of yet another royal duke, the most important self-identification for Kent was that of being a soldier. His excessive insistence upon discipline was the consequence of a high sense of duty as an officer and the importance of his chosen profession. The influence of Kent's desire to be a successful army officer can scarcely be overestimated, and this was to be of great importance in the development of his daughter's worldview. Victoria would always consider herself a soldier's daughter and followed her father's example in relishing the minute details of army uniforms, insignia, and accoutrements, while the influence of her father and his passion for soldiering would have a profound effect on the continuance of the Hanoverian linkage between the military and the monarchy.

---

inquiry, which was denied, and then asked to be sent once again to Gibraltar, which was also denied. His army career was over (although he was gazetted to Field Marshal in 1805) and he retired to Brussels in 1815 to live more economically. Giles St. Aubyn, *Queen Victoria: A Portrait* (New York: Atheneum, 1992), 2-3.

55 *Ibid.*, 2.

56 Arthur C. Benson and Viscount Esher, eds., *The Letters of Queen Victoria*, 1ˢᵗ ser., *A Selection From Her Majesty's Correspondence Between the Years 1837-1861*, vol. 1 (New York: Longmans, Green and Co., 1907), 9-12. Unlike many of his siblings, he detested drunkenness and gambling. In addition, he was an intelligent and eloquent speaker possessed with a high sense of duty. St. Aubyn, *Queen Victoria*, 2.

57 Little is actually known about Madame Alphonsine Thérèse Bernadine Julie de Montgenet de St. Laurent, often referred to by the Royal Dukes as "Edward's French lady." She was a French Canadian whom he met when he was posted to Quebec in the summer of 1791. Her light-hearted character contrasted sharply with Edward's serious countenance. From Fulford, *Royal Dukes*, 157-159.

The fifth son of George III, Ernest Augustus, Duke of Cumberland, was perhaps the most unpopular man in England around the time of the death of Charlotte. Complex, ugly, and unscrupulous, he was rumored to have murdered his valet and married an immoral woman, the Princess of Solms-Braunfels, herself rumored to have murdered her two previous husbands.[58] Yet what Cumberland possessed that his brothers lacked was intelligence. It was not that the other Royal Dukes were popular, for they were not. What made Cumberland so unpopular was that he was feared while his brothers were simply regarded as irresponsible. Against the wishes of his brother, the Prince Regent, his mother the queen, and even his sisters, the Duke of Cumberland married the Princess of Solms anyway. The queen never received the duchess and the Duke of Cumberland, and his bride lived abroad for the next fourteen years. In 1817, the princess bore a daughter who died at birth, and in 1819 she bore a son, later the King of Hanover.[59] The birth of Prince George of Cumberland occurred three days after the birth of his cousin, Victoria, and the need for an heir was no longer as urgent as there were now two royal heirs born before the young Cumberland. None of that, however, could have been foreseen in 1817.[60] In addition to being an interesting, if disagreeable, historical figure, Cumberland also had seen rather extensive service as an officer in both the Hanoverian and British armies, and he remained on the continent fighting the French in Flanders, Holland, and Germany from 1793 to 1799.[61] After returning to England and being created the Duke of Cumberland, he served as the colonel-in-chief of the Fifteenth Dragoons. Despite his being a target for gossip and caricature, he was another royal duke who maintained the tradition of service in the army as an officer.

The sixth son of George III, Augustus Frederick, the Duke of Sussex, held virtually no promise of producing a legitimate heir, for he had violated the Royal Marriages Act and had wedded Augusta Murray without the king's consent. Lady Augusta, older than Sussex and with children from a previous marriage, bore Augustus two children, but the

---

58 The Princess of Solms had been married to a Prince of Prussia, and soon after his death, she was engaged to Cumberland's younger brother, Adolphus, the Duke of Cambridge, who in turn ended their engagement, and she then was married the Prince of Solms. She bore both husbands children. From Fulford, *Royal Dukes*, 210-214.

59 The Blind King of Hanover, he ascended to the throne of Hanover in 1851 and served as its last king until expelled by the Prussians in 1866.

60 *Ibid.*, 218-222.

61 *Ibid.*, 200.

marriage was declared null in the summer of 1794, and the children were therefore not legitimate heirs to the throne. Even though Sussex eventually gained custody of them, they were not considered royalty. Overall, he never figured prominently in the family, although in politics, like all of his brothers except for Cumberland, he was a vocal Whig, and by far the most consistently liberal Whig of all of the royal dukes.[62] He also never served in the army nor had much interest in its affairs.

This brief overview of several children of the fifteen that came from the marriage of George III and Charlotte of Mecklenburg-Strelitz highlights the difficulty in securing succession despite the large number of offspring as well as the close relationship between the Crown and the armed forces; the following chapter will bring to light additional individual aspects of the military and monarchical connection. The reign of George III proved to be a crucial stage in the evolution of the relationship between the army and the Crown in a number of ways. The two institutions had survived great challenges posed by the era of Napoleon and a changed position for Great Britain in the world.

Though greatly affected by the upheavals, both the military and the monarchy would carry on into the 19th century Janus-faced, retaining or attempting to recreate the glory of the past while adapting to the realities of the nineteenth century. George III continued his father's recent tradition of not undertaking a military career and severed another tradition of direct army command in creating a permanent office of Commander-in-Chief. Although immediate royal control of the army was thus ended during the reign of George III, the close association between the Crown and the army was undoubtedly strengthened because of the extended royal family. Even if the king no longer led troops into battle, his sons often did and were certainly expected to do so. Having a royal duke as Commander-in-Chief had already worked out well for the defense of the kingdom and reform of the army; it was private scandal and not professional incompetence that ended the tenure of a prince as Commander-in-Chief. Scandalous behavior of the sons of George III may not have helped the majesty of the monarchy, but it had no mitigating effect on increased expectations for a royal duke to undertake an army career.

---

62 *Ibid.*, 253-283.

CHAPTER 2:
The Royal Connection 1819-1854

The youngest and seventh surviving son of George III, Adolphus Frederick, the Duke of Cambridge, was the least known of all of George's sons, but he was the first to produce a legitimate heir after the death of Princess Charlotte in 1817. When Prince George William Frederick Charles of Cambridge was born on the continent in his father's palace in Hanover on March 26, 1819, succession for the Hanoverian line was secured and for the first two months of his life, young Prince George was heir to the British throne.[1] The birth of Princess Victoria on May 24, 1819 ended his brief claim to the throne since Victoria's father, the Duke of Kent, was closer in the line of succession, even though Kent would not live to see his daughter's first birthday.[2] The birth of Prince George of Cumberland, future George V of Hanover and son of the Duke of Cumberland, on May 27, 1819, further distanced Prince George of Cambridge from the throne because Cumberland was also closer in the line of succession.

Although George, the second Duke of Cambridge, is remembered for his exploits–and lack thereof–as the highest ranking soldier in Great Britain for the second half of the 19h century, his father, Adolphus, was himself a decorated and distinguished soldier who served in the Hanoverian army. In striking contrast to the future conduct of his son in a similar situation, Adolphus was wounded and returned to battle in Flanders as soon as possible during the wars against France during the spring and summer of 1794.[3] The experience of having been wounded in combat, as well as suffering through a trying winter campaign, had a lasting impact on the young prince and would add greatly to his reputation as a brave soldier and officer, as well as influencing his future behavior as a senior army officer. The lasting impact of the experience comes through in a letter of his to Lady Harcourt: "Thank God I have borne the campaign very well. The cold was shocking, and the marches we had to make horrid, but I luckily have escaped having any limb frozen."[4] In a subsequent letter to his father,

---

1 Longford, 17. Technically, Prince George was not the only heir to the throne, but he was the first of his generation.
2 For the sake of succession, Kent had done what he had previously thought to be impossible and left his morganatic wife, Madame St. Laurent, who retired to a convent, and married Princess Victoria of Leiningen on May 29, 1818, at Coburg and July 11, 1818, at Kew Palace. At the time of her birth, Victoria became 8th in line of succession and this pushed Prince George to 9th place.
3 Fulford, 289.
4 *Ibid.*

George III, Adolphus went on to say he would not have missed what he had gone through for anything in the world.[5] Sixty years later, Adolphus's son, George, would also correspond with the monarch regarding his combat experience, but in a markedly different tone.

Adolphus remained with the Hanoverians for the next eight years, devoting his efforts in a non-soldierly direction focusing on scientific studies and improving his ability as a violinist. In 1801, he was created Duke of Cambridge, Earl of Tipperary, and Baron Culloden. That same year, Prussia invaded Hanover at the insistence of Napoleon, angered at the disruption of trade due to British control of the seas. The French occupation, which the Treaty of Amiens ended within a year, did not affect the duke. By 1803, however, tensions with France had risen once again, although not to the point of war between England and France. A French force under General Edouard Mortier threatened Hanover once again, and Mortier insisted that Hanoverians in the service of the King of England were enemies of France. The Duke of Cambridge was now in command of the Hanoverian Army with the rank of lieutenant general and did his best to motivate the Hanoverians to offer a stiff resistance to the French threat, but overall the Hanoverians had little interest in fighting. In fact, many cities in Hanover displayed placards in French declaring them "Neutral Territory."[6] Obviously such a position did not slow the forces of Napoleon, and the Hanoverians agreed to the French occupation terms while Cambridge entered a self-imposed exile to England lasting ten years. On June 18, 1803, Cambridge transferred to the British Army as a Lieutenant General and spent his years of exile in England and away from Hanover in comfort and tranquility focused on continued self education.[7]

By 1813 the fortunes of France and Napoleon had changed, most notably as a result of the disastrous invasion of Russia. Along with the weakened strategic position of France, the attitudes of the Hanoverians toward their former prince, Adolphus, now the Duke of Cambridge, consequently improved. During the period of the Napoleonic Wars known as the War of the Sixth Coalition (1812-1814), the combined forces of Austria, Prussia, Russia, Sweden, Great Britain, and several German states finally defeated Napoleonic France, bringing an end to a quarter century of

---

5 *Ibid.*

6 *Ibid.*, 290.

7 Sir Sidney Lee, ed., *The Dictionary of National Biography*, Vol. I. (Oxford: Oxford University Press, 1917), 139.

virtually continuous warfare. The decisive event was the almost complete destruction of Napoleon's *Grande Armée* that had invaded Russia in the summer of 1812; by November of that year less than five percent of the invading army of 650,000 men returned intact to France.

Emboldened by Napoleon's dramatic defeat, Prussia sought to drive the French from all German-speaking soil. Despite Napoleon's uncanny ability to raise fresh armies in the wake of his Russian disaster and his impressive tactical victories against the allied coalition at Lützen on May 13, 1813 and Bautzen on May 20-21, 1813, the brief armistice that followed did not ultimately prevent the allied coalition from driving the French forces from all of the German states with the Battle of Nations at Leipzig from May 16-19, 1813, decisively defeating the French. Except for a lingering French force that withstood a lengthy siege in Hamburg until May 27, 1814, French forces withdrew back to France by the end of October 1813. With the French now driven from Hanover by the British and Prussians, Cambridge returned to take command of the Hanoverian army. The Congress of Vienna elevated the Electorate of Hanover to a kingdom and the Duke of Cambridge was named its governor-general. In November 1816 he was appointed to the viceroyalty–a king in all but name–in which capacity he continued until the death of William IV opened the throne of Hanover to the Duke of Cumberland.

Prior to his accession to the throne of Great Britain as William IV, the Duke of Clarence had commissioned his brother Adolphus, the Duke of Cambridge, to find him a suitable bride whom Clarence could have as queen. During his travels on the continent, Adolphus was quite taken by the daughter of the Landgrave of Hesse-Cassel. In response to the glowing description of Princess Augusta, Clarence suggested that Adolphus marry her himself, which he promptly did.[8] Adolphus, Duke of Cambridge, married Princess Augusta Wilhelmina Louisa, the third daughter of Frederick, the Landgrave of Hesse-Cassel on May 7, 1818 in Cassel and then again in London on June 1, 1818, and the desired outcome of producing an heir was quickly achieved. Less than one year later, *The London Gazette* announced the successful birth of an heir.[9] Two daughters followed the birth of George: Mary Adelaide, who would later marry Francis of Teck, and Augusta who would go on to marry the Grand

---

8 Sheppard, vol. 1, 3-4.
9 *London Gazette*, April 6, 1819.

Duke of Mecklenburg-Strelitz.[10] Adolphus remained in Hanover until the accession of the Duke of Cumberland to the throne of that country forced his return to England in 1837, where he would live a long and contented retirement until his death in 1850.

Young George was christened on May 11, 1819, in keeping with the rites of the Church of England, and was officially named George, William, Frederick, Charles.[11] Although George's father was quite eccentric–the Duke of Wellington would describe him to a friend "as being mad as Bedlam"–he was a kind and considerate father.[12] George's mother would have a pronounced influence, and like Adolphus, she was a great-grandchild of George II, sharing the Hanoverian heritage. Well read and gifted musically, she lived to be ninety-two and was able to congratulate her son on his fiftieth year of military service. She also had a keen interest in politics and attended many sessions of the House of Lords.[13] Throughout her long life, the Duchess of Cambridge maintained a close relationship with her son and her niece, Queen Victoria. As will subsequently become clear, her interests and attitudes strongly attributed to her son's development, and especially in the early years of his army career, she was able to exercise some influence with the Queen on behalf of her son.[14]

Prince George's early years were spent in Hanover with his parents, the Duke and Duchess of Cambridge. He narrowly survived a childhood bout with scarlet fever, as well as a bizarre murder attempt by a crazed assistant to his first tutor, Rev. Henry Harvey.[15] The Rev. John Wyle Wood,

10 Francis and Mary Adelaide's daughter Mary married the grandson of Victoria and son of Edward VII, George, who in turn became George V. They were therefore the great grandparents of the current Queen of the United Kingdom, Queen Elizabeth II.

11 St. Aubyn, T*he Royal George*, 4. Actually, by traditional standards he had relatively few names.

12 *Ibid.*; Fulford, *The Royal Dukes*, 304-306. As he became older, his hearing worsened to the point of his becoming deaf while his eccentricities became legendary. In church he always sat in the front pew and was known to loudly answer the clergyman's sermons. One tale attributed to him that is likely apocryphal is when the reverend came to the commandment, "Thou shall not commit murder," the Duke replied, "I don't, I leave that to my brother Ernest." He was also known to respond to the clergyman's request, "Let us pray," with "By all means," in a booming voice.

13 St. Aubyn, *The Royal George*, 8.

14 At the lowest point of his career–after leaving his division command in the Crimea–Cambridge repeatedly asked his mother to intervene to Queen Victoria so that he would be able to return home to England. This will be addressed in Chapter 3.

15 St. Aubyn, *The Royal George*, 8. Rev. Henry Harvey employed an assistant who was one night found kneeling next to the sleeping prince while holding a knife and shouting that it was duty to send the child straight to heaven.

later canon of Worcester, was George's next tutor for eight years beginning in 1828. He exerted a strong influence on the development of the young prince, maintaining a regimen of intensive study and strict discipline. With the accession of his uncle, the Duke of Clarence, as William IV in 1830, King William and Queen Adelaide (1792-1749) desired their nephew be raised in England at Windsor with the Rev. Wood remaining as his tutor.[16]

Because of this move, young Prince George formed a very close personal connection with the monarchy. Not only was George a prince of the blood, but he was virtually an adopted son of the King and Queen. Having lived at Windsor under the direct supervision of the King and Queen undoubtedly enhanced the ease with which George interacted with the monarchy later in life. Spending eight formative years as a *de facto* member of the royal family reinforced his own identification with the Crown. His worldview understandably juxtaposed his personal destiny with that of the sovereign. Later in life, when George became the Commander-in-Chief of the British army, he viewed one of his primary responsibilities as the defense of the Royal Prerogative, which to him meant control of the military forces by the Crown.[17] The link between the military and the monarchy was therefore far more to him than the working relationship between two institutions of government. It was instead a fundamental conjunction between the two most important aspects of Cambridge's life from an early and formative period, being both lofty and tangible. For Cambridge, the close linkage to royalty came at birth and was reinforced from an early age. Undertaking a military career and a life-long devotion to the army would follow soon afterwards.

I

In July 1836, Prince George left Windsor and England for Hanover. Queen Adelaide had previously sought the advice of Arthur Wellesley, 1st Duke of Wellington (1769-1852), on how best to continue the education of her young charge. To come to the attention of the premier military authority in Great Britain at such a young age could only serve to enhance the career prospects for the young prince. A letter from him to the Queen demonstrates the close and overlapping requirements for a prince of the royal blood who

16 Fortunately, Rev. Wood insisted that the young prince maintain a daily journal which he did quite scrupulously until the final weeks of his life.
17 Gordon, 20. This subject will be addressed in depth below.

would have great responsibility thrust upon him "at a very early period in his life." [18] Wellington's position was clear: a military education was not only important, but vital for a royal prince. To Wellington, the prestige and authority of the Crown were inextricably linked to the army. It was only natural, therefore, that a prince receive a military education to prepare him for "any duty to which he may be called." Another telling aspect of this letter is that Wellington lists service in Germany prior to service in England. Wellington, like the Hanoverians under whom he had served, believed the German method of warfare superior to the French. George I, George II, and the Dukes of Cumberland and York had all sought to introduce German methods of discipline, training, and administration to improve the British army. Wellington continued that tradition and physically embodied its triumph over the alternative Napoleonic approach to warfare. It was only natural, therefore, that Wellington would recommend Prince George receive his military education in the British-ruled territory of Hanover.

It would be difficult to overstate the influence Wellington, "the Iron Duke," wielded over military affairs in Great Britain. [19] Although his political career was far more contentious, his reputation as a military genius and the savior of Europe survived relatively unscathed until well after his death. When the Queen wrote to him for advice in the spring of 1836, Wellington was not yet Commander-in-Chief–he would be from 1842 until his death in 1852–but his wisdom as a military expert was unquestioned. With his triumph over Napoleon, a long, almost continuous struggle against France lasting more than a generation came to an end. It also represented the end of an even longer struggle with France dating to 1689. Britain had not only survived, it had prevailed. Following Waterloo, Britain enjoyed nearly four decades of peace and staggering prosperity. Wellington was the personification of that triumph, and the British army that defeated Napoleon was accordingly seen as a vindication of British methods over French nationalism.

Based upon the advice of Wellington, Cambridge joined the Jäger Battalion of the King of Hanover's Guard Regiment. Although George

---

18 Letter from the Duke of Wellington to Queen Adelaide, dated April 20, 1836, reproduced in Sheppard, vol. 1, 30-31.
19 The volume of works dealing with Wellington is large, but a good place to begin is Elizabeth Longford, *Wellington*. 2 vols. (London: Weidenfeld & Nicolson, 1972). The second volume, *Pillar of the State*, is especially useful in understanding Wellington's influence over the army and the country after Waterloo.

had been a colonel in the Hanoverian Guards since the age of nine, it was an honorary position that entailed no real responsibilities.[20] Now, however, he had real responsibilities, first beginning as a private soldier in the line for a month and then as a regimental officer. His duties consisted mainly of mounting guard and commanding formations of soldiers at drill. Nonetheless, he found that he loved his profession, recording in his journal, "On May 9th of this year, I mounted my first guard at the Palace of Hanover. Lieutenant Basing was on guard with me, and I must confess it was one of the happiest days of my life, for I, for the first time, felt as if I was really a soldier."[21]

Shortly thereafter, George received word from his former tutor that the King had died peacefully at twelve minutes after two o'clock in the morning of June 20, 1837. Prince George returned to England to attend the state funeral, not simply for official reasons, but also because he had spent so much time with William IV and especially Queen Adelaide. Clearly the death of William IV and the accession of Queen Victoria had serious consequences for Prince George and his entire family. Most immediately, it meant the Cambridges no longer had any function in Hanover, as the Salic Law mandated succession to a male heir, thus separating Hanover from Great Britain permanently.[22] The Duke of Cumberland became King of Hanover and the Cambridges returned to England permanently, living at Cambridge House in Piccadilly and at Cambridge Cottage, Kew.[23]

The significance of the new Queen was not lost on Prince George, and he quickly realized that everything was now quite different, "My Uncle the Duke of Cumberland has now become king of that country, and my cousin Princess Victoria is Queen of England. I am thus nearly allied in blood to two great and happy families that are governing two happy and prosperous nations [*sic*]."[24] If the death of William IV meant a great deal to Prince George, it had the greatest possible impact on Princess Victoria, who was now the Queen.[25] In contrast to the loving relationship young

20 Sheppard, vol. 1, 38; Verner, vol. 1, 11; and St. Aubyn, *The Royal George*, 19-20.

21 Diary entry of Prince George, dated May 9, 1837, reproduced in Verner, vol. 1, 11.

22 Since George I, all Hanoverian kings had not only been kings of Great Britain, but they were also electors of Hanover. The accession of Victoria ended the relationship.

23 The "cottage" at Kew had forty rooms; the Cambridge family regarded it as a country retreat. St. Aubyn, *The Royal George*, 22.

24 Journal entry, July 12, 1837, reproduced in Sheppard, vol. 1, 42.

25 The best biography on Queen Victoria is certainly the previously cited one by Elizabeth Longford, *Victoria: Born to Succeed* (New York: Harper &Rowe, 1964). The eight volume, three serial set, *The Letters of Queen Victoria*, (A.C. Benson and Lord Esher, eds., *The Letters of Queen Victoria*, 1st series,

Cambridge had shared with his parents, young Victoria had experienced a rather deprived childhood. Her mother was a widow before her daughter's first birthday; George IV had been on bad terms with the Duke of Kent prior to his death, and in the words of Victoria herself, he "took hardly any notice of the poor widow and little fatherless girl, who were so poor at the time of his (the Duke of Kent's) death."[26] A crucial consideration for the future Duke of Cambridge was that Victoria considered herself first and foremost a "soldier's daughter." Although she obviously had no personal recollection of her father, his legacy was very important to her. She once remarked that she "was proud of his profession, and I was always taught to consider myself a soldier's child."[27] This was a sentiment the Queen carried with her throughout her reign. Victoria always cherished the memory of her father as a dutiful soldier and considered it her responsibility to continue the Hanoverian tradition of close connection with the military. The close interest she showed in military issues for the remainder of her life was a combination of genuine love and a strong sense of duty. These were attitudes she would share fully with her cousin, George.

Victoria's ascension to the throne came after serious changes in the role of the sovereign had taken place. Just nineteen when she was crowned in Westminster Abbey on June 28, 1838, Victoria followed uncles who had done considerable damage to the prestige and power of the Crown, not to mention the extended precariousness of having her grandfather's ten-year bout with insanity.[28] Or, to put it differently, she was following three men best described as "an imbecile, a profligate, and a buffoon."[29] Whether her reign broke with the Hanoverian tradition that preceded it and represented a new modernity is open to interpretation, but in breaking with her predecessors, she was following the family tradition.[30] In the

3 vols., *1837-61* (New York: Longmans, Green & Co., 1907); G.E. Buckle, ed., *The Letters of Queen Victoria*, 2nd series, 3 vols., *1862-85* (New York: Longmans, Green & Co, 1926); G.E. Buckle, ed., *The Letters of Queen Victoria*, 3rd series, 3 vols., *1886-1901* (New York: Longmans, Green & Co., 1928-1931)) is the most complete published source for the correspondence and journal entries of the Queen.

26 The quotation comes from a manuscript Queen Victoria wrote in her own hand in 1872 for the purpose of preserving the earliest memories of her childhood. Reproduced in Benson and Esher, eds., *The Letters of Queen Victoria*, 1st ser., vol. 1, 15-16. It is significant that she described her early youth as "rather melancholy." The Duke of Cambridge would later remember his own childhood as quite pleasant.

27 Undated quotation, reproduced in *ibid.*, 11.

28 George IV had made the throne unpopular while William IV had restored popularity to the throne but not dignity.

29 Cannadine, "The Last Hanoverian Sovereign?," 130.

30 *Ibid.*, 151-157. A pithy description is, "the history of the modern royal family remains the history of

early years of her reign, there was truly no way of knowing how it would turn out, but the great English historian, Thomas Carlyle (1795-1881), remarked after the coronation, "Poor little Queen, she is at an age at which a girl can hardly be trusted to choose a bonnet for herself; yet a task is laid upon her from which an archangel might shrink."[31]

II

With the Cambridge family now residing in London, it was indeed a different life for Prince George. Although he had, as of yet, no official military duties in England, he began his lifelong practice of watching military reviews and being favorably impressed.[32] One occurred on March 21, 1838 that must have been genuinely remarkable. The 2nd Battalion of the Grenadiers were being inspected and drilled by the Duke of Wellington.[33] This review occurred almost twenty-three years after the Duke's great triumph at Waterloo, and the Iron Duke was then sixty-nine years old. Although it is not known whether Prince George had the goal of following in Wellington's footsteps, the sight of Wellington inspecting soldiers was indeed a memorable one for the young prince. He dined with Wellington the following day, and the event made a lasting impression. Afterward he noted in his diary that Wellington "gave a great dinner in uniform to the Officers of the Battalion."[34] Several days later on March 26, George celebrated his twentieth birthday; among the many fine gifts he received, one in particular stands out as a symbol of royal approval and the promise of success it represented. Two daughters of George III, Mary, Duchess of Gloucester, and Princess Sophia, presented George with "the whole set of the Duke of Wellington's and Lord Wellesley's despatches

---

successive waves of parvenu German invaders." See also Richard Williams, *The Contentious Crown: Public Discussion of the British Monarchy in the Reign of Queen Victoria* (Aldershot, UK: Ashgate Publishing Co., 1997). Williams argues that controversy surrounding the monarchy is not new and that the secure position achieved in the late 19th Century was the product of circumstances that no longer exist, especially reverence and sentimentality, and the relationship between the monarchy and patriotism.

31 Longford, 83.

32 Prince George, as was the custom, continued to receive numerous promotions and honorary titles. On November 3, 1837 he was gazetted to the rank of Brevet-Colonel in the British army. Verner, vol. 1, 13. RA VIC/Add. E1/1 (M), promotion document dated January 6, 1838, the promotion of Prince George from "Major-General" to "General-Lieutenant" in the army of the King of Hanover.

33 Verner, vol. 1, 13.

34 Diary entry of Prince George, dated March 22, 1838, reproduced in Verner, vol. 1, 14.

[*sic*]."[35] Although not exactly prophesy, such a gift would have been quite meaningful to a man about to undertake a military career, and it was also a great vote of confidence, especially from fellow royals.

Prince George enjoyed an active social life that maintained his personal exposure to the sovereign. For her part, Queen Victoria noticed the behavior of her cousin with some alarm, and she recorded her concerns over his conduct in her journal, mentioning to her Prime Minister, Lord Melbourne, that her cousin, George Cambridge, was "being somewhat in the hands of the fashionable ladies; Lord Melbourne said his (George's) age was a very awkward one, and that he remembered it well himself; that living for amusement was very tiresome, if you had no pursuits besides."[36] Whether or not he was becoming bored with living the life of a young socialite is a moot point because in a few months he would begin in earnest his lifelong vocation. Although the initial military education of Prince George had been undertaken by the command of his parents upon consultation with Queen Adelaide, after George's entrance into the army as a colonel by brevet in November 1837, it was his decision to make the army his career. As a member of the royal family, he was exempt from having to purchase his commission, a rather ironic quirk in the system which he would later work so hard to preserve. With the assistance of his military tutor, Colonel Cornwall, the Commander-in-Chief of the army, Lord Roland Hill (1772-1842), arranged to post Prince George in Gibraltar in September to broaden his military experience.[37] George's duty position was broadly defined as that of a staff officer.[38]

Prior to his departure from England, George attended two significant events that highlighted the intersection of his chosen career and his royal birth: the Duke of Wellington's annual dinner on the anniversary of Waterloo, June 18, 1838, and the coronation of Queen Victoria on June 28, 1838. After Wellington's dinner in honor of the officers who served at Waterloo, George expressed the impact made by Wellington.[39] Noting

35 Diary entry of Prince George, dated March 26, 1838, reproduced in Sheppard, vol. 1., 48.

36 Royal Archives Queen Victoria's Journal (hereafter referred to as "RA QVJ"): 28 May 1838.

37 The exact sequence of events is unknown. The least reliable biography on Cambridge, that by Duff, posits the possibility that the posting of Cambridge abroad was the direct result of Queen Victoria who was upset that Cambridge did not wish to marry her, although she wished to marry him. Duff, 121-123. Such a suggestion borders on gossip–the infrequent mention of Prince George her diary makes this explanation quite unlikely.

38 Sheppard, vol. 1, 52-53; Verner, vol. 1, 15; St. Aubyn, *The Royal George*, 24-25.

39 Diary entry of Prince George, dated June 18, 1838, reproduced in Verner, vol. 1, 14. George notes that Wellington "gave his great annual dinner to the officers who served on that glorious day."

with perhaps a small degree of envy, he commented, "What a glorious victory that was to be sure and how that one event has immortalized the name of Wellington."[40] As for the coronation, George recorded the events in great detail, noting with a trace of wit that "The Queen, I think, looked less well than usual, but on the whole was very graceful and dignified..."[41] After the lengthy day of ceremony, George attended a ball hosted by the Duke of Wellington where he was very much at ease and obviously quite welcome in the highest circles of military and royal society. Although such associations would not guarantee promotion to the highest military rank, there would be little opposition to his having a successful career unless he proved to be hopelessly incompetent. All in all, it is hard to imagine a young officer better positioned for success in the British army of the early Victorian era, and all he seemed to lack was experience.

It quickly became apparent that duty adjacent to the Rock of Gibraltar would be far different from the relatively carefree life George had known in London or on the continent. The next months were spent drilling soldiers and learning the basics of garrison living. The regimen included taking duty on the field officer's roster and placing each of the light companies of the five regiments under the command of the prince at various intervals; ultimately he would be acquainted with all arms of the services. Though the commanding general had written previously to the Duke of Cambridge informing him his son would not receive any special treatment on account of his royal birth, the fact that he wrote to the Commander-in-Chief of the army about a new arrival belies the truth of the matter. The young duke held the rank of colonel and was not yet twenty years old.

While at Gibraltar, Prince George's father sent him some advice regarding the interaction between politics and the army. Writing just before Christmas of 1838, the Duke of Cambridge admonished his son about the dangers of officers interfering in politics. Regardless of which party was in power, Whig or Tory, it was the duty of the officer to be above it all and merely serve the existing government.[42] Whether the future Commander-in-Chief would remain true to his father's advice will become clear in the following pages, but George left the rocky fortress with a sterling reputation. After several months on Gibraltar, he had accomplished his

---

40 Diary entry of Prince George, dated June 18, 1838, reproduced in Sheppard, vol. 1, 50.
41 Diary entry of Prince George, dated June 18, 1838, reproduced in *ibid.*, 50-53.
42 Letter from the Duke of Cambridge to his son, George, dated December 22, 1838. Reproduced in Sheppard, vol. 1, 57-58.

military duties satisfactorily, and it was now time to further his military education by experiencing other military outposts in the Mediterranean. The young prince had faced his first real military "deployment" and performed well. His career seemed to be off to a good beginning.

III

Prince George left Gibraltar on April 29, 1839 and spent the next few months sailing about the Mediterranean Sea, where he visited Malta, Corfu, and Athens, along with others. During his travels, he continued his academic studies and reviewed the units on the garrisons he visited, finally returning to England in November of 1839. While George was abroad a number of rumors circulated about being a potential match for Queen Victoria, but there is little concrete evidence to support them. His satisfaction in Victoria's selection of another came through in his diary ten days before Christmas 1839, "After dinner Papa got a letter from the young Queen, in which she announces her marriage with Prince Albert of Coburg. Nothing could have given me greater pleasure than this intelligence. I hope it may prove a happy union both to herself and to the Country in general."[43] Several days later he visited the Queen at Windsor to congratulate her and later attended her wedding on February 11, 1840.

As for Victoria's true feelings, the issue is somewhat less clear. Based upon entries in her journal, she and Lord Melbourne, the Prime Minister, at least discussed the possibility of George being her husband. On October 17, 1839, she discussed the matter with Lord Melbourne and recorded her recollections of their discussion that evening in her journal, "Lord M. talks of their [the Duke and Duchess of Cambridge] wishing George for me; 'It was clear <u>he</u> did not wish it', said Lord M., 'by his distant manner'; and I said I never could have thought of taking him–ugly and disagreeable as he was."[44] It was strange that Victoria would describe her cousin as ugly since he was viewed as handsome and charming in his youth–contemporary portraits and personal accounts affirm that he was. Most likely it was defensive posturing, and she may have secretly wished to have George as a potential mate. As the two grew older they certainly grew closer, but it is impossible to determine the truth. Based upon the entries in the diaries of

---

43 Diary entry from Prince George, dated December 15, 1839, reproduced in Sheppard, vol. 1, 79.
44 RA QVJ: 17 October 1839.

young George, it would seem he did not want to marry her since he never mentions it. Most likely, George was simply one of several who met the required pedigree for marriage to the Queen.

As for the young prince, his views on marriage were quite personal. He had no intention of adhering to the Royal Marriages Act of 1772 which mandated that the Sovereign and Parliament had to consent to the marriage of a prince if he was under the age of twenty-five. George had entered the army and so far seemed happy with his selection, despite the lack of excitement his career had thus far brought him. Marriage was another matter. With an attitude that strikes the contemporary reader as very modern, he believed arranged marriages were doomed affairs, and he had no intention of allowing the state to interfere with his.[45] Close to the time of Victoria's marriage to Albert, Cambridge met his future wife, an actress, Louisa Fairbrother (1816-1890). She was the ninth child and the fifth daughter of John Fairbrother, a printer. Quite beautiful and an excellent dancer, Louisa was clearly unsuitable to be a bride of a prince of royal blood due to her familial background and profession. Although the actual beginning of their life together is unclear, they entered into a morganatic marriage (Louisa would have no claim to title or royal property) and by all accounts their union was a very happy one.[46] Louisa would bear George three sons, George FitzGeorge, born on August 27, 1843, Adolphus, born on January 30, 1846, and Augustus, who was born June 12, 1847. There were also two older children who lived in the George Cambridge home, most likely from an earlier relationship of Louisa's.[47]

Unlike his uncles, George avoided scandal. The only public incident that called into question his reputation occurred soon after his cousin, Victoria, was embroiled in the so-called Bedchamber Plot.[48] A controversy arose suggesting he had had an affair with Lady Augusta Somerset

---

45 St. Aubyn, *The Royal George,* 31.

46 Records at St. John's Church, Clerkenwell, date the marriage as January 8, 1847, although King Edward VII later claimed that the date in the register was false. George's official biographer, Sheppard, placed the marriage shortly before George left for the Crimea. *Ibid.*

47 The most complete published account of the personal and family life of Prince George and subsequently George the second Duke of Cambridge is St. Aubyn's biography. See especially, *Ibid.*, 30-37.

48 Victoria refused to accept Ladies in Waiting representing the Tory government of Sir Robert Peel, and wished to keep an entourage composed of entirely of ladies acceptable to her, who also all happened to be Whigs. It was a genuine struggle for power that artificially preserved Lord Melbourne's influence. Longford, 111-116. The incident also hurt Victoria's public image.

(1800-1865), daughter of the Duke of Beaufort (1766-1835), and she was rumored to be expecting his child. Although unfounded, hearsay circulated throughout the newspapers, and even the Queen believed it to be true. Ultimately it took the intervention of the Duke of Wellington to smooth things over and restore good will between the Queen and the Duke and Duchess of Cambridge, as well as George.[49] Fortuitously for the Cambridge family, Wellington had personal interest in the career of Prince George. It is unlikely that a man of lesser standing could have swayed the Queen's opinion. Apart from a very tense exchange during the Crimean War to be addressed in the following chapter, from this point on, Victoria and George remained on good terms until the ends of their lives.

During the decade of the 1840s, Prince George matured into a career army officer. It is important to remember, however, that his career path was not at all typical, even when compared to a well-connected and wealthy officer of the 1830s or 1840s. Prince George *began* his career as a colonel, while the Purchase system allowed purchase of commissions only to the rank of lieutenant colonel. George therefore skipped all ranks even the most promising, wealthy, and pedigreed had experienced: ensign or coronet, lieutenant, captain, major, and lieutenant colonel. A consequence of George's royal birth and the very high rank with which he began his military career was the lack of an affiliation with a specific regiment or even a specific branch of service. For a man of gentle birth there were only two from which to choose: infantry or cavalry. Branches such as artillery or engineers were considered technical branches and promotion was by merit rather than Purchase, and therefore these branches were scrupulously avoided by gentlemen.

Thus Prince George presented the rare spectacle of being a very senior officer who had neither a regimental home nor a military specialty. His time spent in the Mediterranean in the late 1830s and the subsequent assignments in the 1840s were a trial period to experience the activities of a number of types of units and locations. Since he started his career with high rank, sending him to a variety of locations with relatively little time spent at each was an effective way to introduce George to the practices of the regular army as quickly as possible and a reasonable way to prepare him to become a general officer very quickly. A letter from his former commander at Gibraltar reveals the true nature of George's time spent

---

49 St. Aubyn, *The Royal George*, 39-41.

there–a period of basic familiarization with the regular army and perhaps the hope he would choose the branch of cavalry. [50]

Rather surprisingly, considering the reputation Prince George later acquired, it was at this stage he became known as a progressive and forward-thinking officer. On April 25, 1842, Prince George was gazetted a colonel of the 17th Lancers and commanded the regiment suppressing riots related to Chartism later that year.[51] Apparently this test of leadership went well because the official *Record Book* of the 17th Lancers recorded for the year 1842, "... H.R.H. was actively engaged in suppressing the disturbances that took place that year in the manufacturing districts, receiving the thanks of the magistrates of Leeds for the effectual efforts of the military there stationed in assisting the civil powers in preserving the peace of the town."[52] Since he was attached to a cavalry regiment, it was during this period Prince George acquired his excellent knowledge of horses and cavalry, something he retained throughout his service.

More important than his actual performance was his continued association with Wellington. The Iron Duke was once again serving as Commander-in-Chief, a position he would maintain until his death, and he wrote to Prince George on August 29, 1842, as a result of correspondence from the Queen directing Cambridge "to attend the Reviews and Field Operations of the Prussian Army on the Rhine..."[53] This letter reveals that both Wellington, as Commander-in-Chief, and George's cousin, the Queen, were both aware of and interested in the actions and career of Prince George. Of equal significance is the postscript which Wellington added to the same letter: "I repeat my proposition that Your Royal Highness should do me the honour of dining and sleeping here if you should embark at Dover. I have means of taking in any gentlemen who may attend your Royal Highness on this occasion."[54] Clearly the earlier personal relationship Wellington had with George was maintained, and the multiple invitations reveal that Wellington generally enjoyed the Queen's

---

50 Letter from General Sir Alexander Woodford to Prince George, dated December 9, 1839, Reproduced in Verner, vol. 1, 25. Woodford's garrison at Gibraltar was an infantry command.

51 George's association with the 17th Lancers would be a lasting one. In 1876 they became the 17th (Duke of Cambridge's Own) Lancer, a designation the unit currently retains. From Ian S. Hollows, *Regiments and Corps of the British Army* (London: New Orchard, 1991), 73-74.

52 Verner, vol. 1, 25.

53 Letter from the Duke of Wellington to Prince George, dated August 29, 1842, reproduced in Sheppard, vol. 1, 81.

54 *Ibid.*

cousin's company. Such attitudes would have been extraordinarily helpful in advancing the reputation and career of Prince George. Throughout most of the 19th century, it was ultimately the social reputation of an officer more than any genuine ability that determined advancement. Regimental affiliations and high command were more the result of personal connection than actual ability. For Cambridge, because of his royal birth and prominent backers, his military future could not have had brighter prospects.

The thoughts and daily activities of Prince George during the 1840s are not known because his personal diaries from this period did not survive, but records indicate he was promoted to the rank of major general on May 7, 1845, when he was twenty-seven years old. The Duke of Wellington wrote to him personally to inform him the Queen was "graciously pleased to approve" his promotion.[55] In October of the following year, Major General Cambridge was sent first to Limerick, Ireland, and in April 1847 he was given command of the Dublin District, a position he maintained until 1852.[56] The Revolutions of 1848 broke out in Europe during his command there, and Cambridge himself experienced the so-called "Smith-O'Brien Rebellion" in Dublin. Actively involved in suppressing the rebellion, which was not a serious uprising, Cambridge's command was successful and relatively quiet–especially quiet since he spent many months on "leave of absence" in London–and he left Ireland with his reputation substantially enhanced.

A letter to Cambridge dated May 27, 1848, shortly after the Smith-O'Brien Rebellion, illustrates the high regard his soldiers had for him. The author was concerned over the policy of restricting men to the barracks, and it reveals that the men believed their commander was compassionate:

> Most Noble Prince and General – We,
> the well-conducted and loyal servants
> and soldiers of Her Most Gracious
> Majesty serving under Her Royal
> Cousin in Dublin, pray of Y.R.H. to give
> Commanding Officers permission to
> grant night-passes to a few of the best-

---

55 RA VIC/Add. E1/32 (M), Letter from the Duke of Wellington to Prince George, dated May 8, 1845.
56 RA VIC/Add. E1/36 (M), Letter from Sidney Herbert to Prince George dated July 5, 1846 informing him that he had received the appointment to the staff of the Army in Ireland pending final approval from Wellington and the Queen, which came the following day, RA E1/37 (M).

> conducted men of each company: we
> the well-disposed soldiers who have
> the honour to serve under Y.R.H. would
> feel for ever indebted for such a mark of
> favor to their beloved General and noble
> Prince.[57]

Obviously such a letter must be viewed with some skepticism because its author was hoping to gain something, which he did. George was on leave in London, but he relaxed the restrictions upon receiving the letter. The incident reveals Cambridge's men had an expectation that he would listen to his soldiers. The episode is remarkable and stands in marked contrast to the leadership style of Wellington and Cambridge's Hanoverian forebears. At this time, army officers widely supported flogging, even though the practice had come under attack by some reformists outside the army. Wellington was one of its most ardent defenders, and throughout the Peninsular Wars the Iron Duke had relied upon the lash a number of times. In his opinion, as long as the army was to be manned by villains, only the "terror" of corporal punishment could maintain discipline.[58] In light of such general conditions in the army, the letter quoted above is astonishing.

Contemporary accounts of martinets active in the British army at the time stand in marked contrast to Cambridge's behavior. Individuals such as Lord Cardigan, who later achieved great fame by leading the charge of the Light Brigade at the Battle of Balaclava during the Crimean War– wearing a style of jacket which has borne his name and remained popular ever since–had attracted some notoriety for his resort to the lash for even minor offenses. One of the more publicized incidents involving Cardigan occurred on Easter Sunday, April 11, 1841. After Cardigan's regiment, the 11th Hussars based in Hounslow, attended morning services, they were marched to their barracks where a short inspection took place, and a soldier who had not fared well was flogged before the entire regiment. The Easter flogging incident added support to the abolition movement and was widely reported, to include a series of articles in the *Times*. The Secretary for War, Thomas Macaulay, faced harsh criticism in the Commons, and the influence of Wellington, coupled with the support of the Queen, retained

---

57 Reproduced in Verner, vol. 1, 28.
58 Edward M. Spiers, *The Army and Society 1815-1914* (London: Longman, 1980), 88.

Cardigan in command. Wellington was disgusted by Cardigan's conduct in this instance and many others, but he saw the interference of Parliament in army affairs as a far greater danger and wished to preserve the Royal Prerogative and limit Parliamentary influence at almost any cost. Clearly Wellington wielded tremendous influence within Parliament and Britain when it came to matters affecting the army.[59]

The issue of flogging and mistreatment of soldiers continued to be an intermittent national concern throughout this period. A soldier's death from flogging in July of 1846 gave momentum to the movement to abolish the lash, and the radical press raised the issue to one of national prominence. As a result, the House of Commons debated the issue, and it looked as if Lord Russell's Whig ministry might support abolition, but Wellington negotiated a compromise: the maximum number of lashes to be awarded by any court martial would be 50 (as recently as 1837 a general court martial could award 200 lashes). The House voted down the abolition motion, and flogging remained a part of the British army for the next thirty-five years.[60]

Besides the fear of punishment for speaking out, the social gulf that separated officers from enlisted men was large and unbridgeable, due partly to the purchase system, the method by which officers in the cavalry and infantry branches "purchased" their promotion to the next rank.[61] Furthermore, Prince George was not merely an officer, a general officer, and member of the royal family. The soldiers under his command must have had a strong indication their commander was indeed approachable; otherwise, a letter such as theirs would not have been sent. George represented a rare phenomenon for his day, considering the overall state of life in the army for the common soldier. Typical living conditions were atrocious, and the mortality rate was actually higher among soldiers in peacetime than among the general population. Although occasional attempts to improve the lot of the common soldier existed, the British army of the period remained quite unreformed and was composed of long-service "volunteers," those initially duped into joining or forced in out of economic necessity.[62] Thus, for a senior army officer, especially a member

59 Cecil Woodham-Smith, *The Reason Why* (New York: Barnes & Noble, 1998), 89-94.
60 Spiers, 88-91.
61 Generally only men of property with the right social pedigree could afford to buy their initial commission and subsequent promotions up to the rank of lieutenant colonel.
62 For a solid introduction to the topic, see Peter Burroughs, "An Unreformed Army? 1815-1868" in David Chandler, ed., *The Oxford Illustrated History of the British Army* (Oxford: Oxford University

of the royal family, to be seen as approachable by the common soldier was something rather extraordinary for the British army in the 1840s.

When Prince George's father died on July 8, 1850, he succeeded to his father's titles and dignities, becoming George, 2nd Duke of Cambridge. Shortly afterward he had an audience with Queen Victoria and Prince Albert, during which they discussed his position. On July 20, 1850 the House of Commons voted Cambridge an income of £12,000 and each of his sisters £3,000.[63] In addition to the income, the Duke was now entitled to a seat in the House of Lords, which would allow him to speak on matters debated within the upper chamber. The Queen wrote to Cambridge on August 1 expressing her devotion: "Let me repeat again, dear George, how anxious we ever shall be to be of use to you, and to show you that you have true friends in both of us who entertain truly *Geschwisterliche Gefühle* towards you."[64] The good relations between the royal cousins were clearly strong as Victoria thought of Cambridge from a sisterly perspective.

With his new title, the Duke remained in command of the Dublin District until Wellington, the Commander-in-Chief, with the approval of Queen Victoria, appointed Cambridge as Inspector-General of Cavalry on April 1, 1852. He left Dublin after five years of service with the 17th Lancers.[65] In giving up his colonelcy with the 17th Lancers, he accepted command of the Scots Fusilier Guards and moved to London where his new posting made him aware of how unprepared the army was for a modern continental conflict.[66] As Inspector-General of Cavalry, Cambridge was now very near the political center of the army. By 1852, Cambridge had served a dozen years in various capacities throughout the army. Although he had not distinguished himself in combat or even held a command outside the United Kingdom of Great Britain and Ireland, he had risen in rank quite quickly. With his posting to London he would assume *de facto* command of the entire branch of cavalry. The interest of the Duke of Wellington

---

Press, 1994), 160-188 and "Wellington's Army" in Spiers, *op. cit.*, 72-96. Other notable works on the topic are Gwyn Harries-Jenkins, *The Army in Victorian Society* (London: Routledge & Keegan Paul, 1977) and Alan Ramsay Skelley, *The Victorian Army at Home: The Recruitment and Terms and Conditions of the British Regular, 1859-1899* (London: Croom Helm, 1977).

63 Diary entry of the Duke of Cambridge, July 20, 1850, reproduced in Sheppard, vol. 1, 102-103.

64 Letter from Queen Victoria to the Duke of Cambridge, dated August 1, 1850, reproduced in Sheppard, vol. 1, 103-104. Although Victoria frequently used the "royal we," in this case she meant herself and Prince Albert.

65 Undated memorandum, "Observations on the Dublin District and Garrison," by the Duke of Cambridge, reproduced in Verner, vol. 1, 31.

66 St. Aubyn, *The Royal George*, 50-59.

and the Queen, coupled with his royal birth, made the advancement of his career relatively simple. Within months of his arrival in London, an era would end with Wellingtons' death on September 14, 1852.

Overall, Cambridge's formative years of both his childhood and military career appear to have been pleasant and without trauma. Apart from the death of his father, the greatest personal difficulty Cambridge faced was separation from considerate and loving parents to be raised by a kind but determined tutor and the genuinely loving Queen Adelaide as a surrogate mother. Cambridge came through his formative years fairly unscathed emotionally, personally, and professionally. Although Prince George did well in his military assignments, the fact that he was first cousin to the Queen certainly helped to a great degree and meriting a royal reception at each new duty station could not have been especially damaging to official evaluations of Cambridge's performance.

IV

When the Duke of Cambridge assumed the position of the Inspector of Cavalry on April 1, 1852, it was at a time when the British army had undergone almost four decades of continual neglect and ever greater reductions, regardless of which ministry ran the government. To his credit, the Duke recognized the great weaknesses then apparent in the army, including officer promotions, equipment, and training.[67] However, the Duke lacked the test of combat; despite over a decade of military service, he had not served at any hostile outposts other than Ireland, and it remained to be seen whether he could command troops in battle. Thus far his royal cousin had limited impact on his military career, although the future remained open as the decade of the 1840s had been a formative one for both of them. If he had not particularly distinguished himself as a soldier, neither had Cambridge brought discredit or scandal upon his name. As Inspector-General of Cavalry, the military career of the Duke of

---

67 As for the latter, the Duke certainly knew a great deal and had demonstrated a genuine talent for training his men while in Dublin, Verner, vol. 1, 31-60. The many detailed memoranda he wrote during this period reveal an excellent grasp of the difficulties involved in training soldiers and cavalrymen. As Inspector General, he also understood that Britain's strategic position vis-à-vis the continental powers was truly a house of cards, but he also understood the importance of the Royal Navy as serving as the main bulwark of home defense.

Cambridge was about to begin in earnest–whether he would be up to the challenge of war remained an unanswered question.

His office was located in the building of the Horse Guards, the same edifice occupied by Wellington, by now a very aged Commander-in-Chief, and the same that Cambridge would occupy again several years later in that same capacity. He was now in the locus of social, political, and administrative power of the army. There was no better avenue for furthering one's career, except perhaps returning from a combat command with a spectacular victory. Ironically, the potential for that very event served as the main reason Cambridge left his position as Inspector-General two years later, but the spectacular victory would prove elusive for him as a division commander in the Crimean War.

The Crimean War proved to be the most serious test of the British army since Waterloo and the only direct British involvement in European warfare between the defeat of Napoleon Bonaparte and the start of the First World War. Emerging victorious from the Napoleonic Wars in 1815, the legacy of victory over France would deeply affect the subsequent development of the British army for the next four decades, and the legacy of that victory continued to influence the development of the army literally until the end of the century.[68] When Cambridge moved into the Horse Guards in the spring of 1852, continental involvement remained unlikely while decades of neglect weighed heavily on the military.

The Royal Navy, according to tradition and reality, was truly the first service, and the main defense of the island kingdom was firmly based upon it. The British army was the second service for the defense of Britain, and its stated focus was orthodox warfare, or rather, European warfare. As an institution, however, the army was engaged in virtually continuous conflict in the periphery of the Empire, although its senior leadership devoted little attention to the art and science of colonial warfare. The professional focus–and here, as any time the army is discussed throughout the 19th century, the term professional is used very loosely–was on the continent, and that meant study of the Prussian and French armies. The

---

68 The number of works addressing this topic is quite large. Some of the better and more accessible ones are: Peter Burroughs, "An Unreformed Army? 1815-1868," in *The Oxford Illustrated History of the British Army*, eds. David Chandler and Ian Beckett (Oxford: Oxford University Press, 1994), 160-188; Edward M. Spiers, "Wellington's Army," chap. 3 in *The Army and Society 1815-1914* (Longman: New York, 1980); and Correlli Barnett, "Decay and Reform 1815-1870," chap. 12 in *Britain and Her Army 1509-1970* (New York: William Morrow & Co., 1970).

constant warfare experienced by the army throughout the entire 19th century had little influence on the development of staffs and strategy.[69] Discipline, tactics, and determined leadership coupled with technological superiority determined success in the colonies, while the opportunity to deploy and command large forces suited for conflict on the continent failed to materialize, prior to the Crimean War.[70]

Despite its focus on European warfare, military engagement in Europe was not contemplated seriously until the second half of the century. The central concern of foreign policy and grand strategy shifted from Flanders to India.[71] Even though the peacetime strength of the post-Napoleonic army rose past an unprecedented number of 100,000 men, the majority were stationed abroad throughout the Empire, and at its heart stood India.[72] The British victory in the Seven Years War and the favorable terms of the Treaty of Paris of 1763 had given Britain tremendous territorial gains, including control of most of North America and a very strong presence in India.[73] The defeat of Napoleon ensured the survival of the British Empire and added a few more colonies as well.

Anxiety over India and protection of its trade routes led to the only post-Napoleonic military involvement in Europe of the 19th century: the Crimean War of 1854. The immediate cause of the war grew out of a dispute involving the custody of "Holy Places" within the Turkish possession of Palestine: the churches and shrines at the supposed sites of the birth, crucifixion, and burial of Christ. Greek Orthodox monks had

---

69 The definitive work on the development of the army staff and the Staff College is Brian Bond, *The Victorian Army and the Staff College 1854-1914* (London: Eyre Methuen, 1972). See also, Jay Luvaas, *The Education of an Army: British Military Thought, 1815-1940* (Chicago: University of Chicago Press, 1964).

70 For a brief but insightful discussion of the influence of colonial warfare on the European art of war, see Hew Strachan, "Colonial Warfare, and its Contribution to the Art of War in Europe," chap. 6 in *European Armies and the Conduct of War* (London: Routledge, 1983).

71 Barnett, 274.

72 The topic of British imperialism is large and complex. See C.A. Bayly, *Imperial Meridian: The British Empire and the World 1780-1830* (London: Longman, 1989), P.J. Cain and A.G. Hopkins, *British Imperialism*, vol. 1, *Innovation and Expansion, 1688-1914* (London: Longman, 1993), Ronald Robinson, John Gallagher and Alice Denny, *Africa and the Victorians: The Climax of Imperialism in the Dark Continent* (New York: St. Martin's Press, 1961), John Gallagher, *The Decline, Revival and Fall of the British Empire: The Ford Lectures and Other Essays* (Cambridge: Cambridge University Press, 1982) and David Fieldhouse, "Can Humpty-Dumpty be put together again? Imperial History in the 1980's," *The Journal of Imperial and Commonwealth History*, XII (JAN 1984).

73 Ronald Hyam and Ged Martin, *Reappraisals In British Imperial History* (London: MacMillan, 1975), 21.

tended to them for several years prior to 1854, but prior to that the shrines had been under the care of Roman Catholics who sought the resumption of their previous privilege. Napoleon III (1808-1873) backed the Catholic claim, while Tsar Nicholas I (1796-1855) backed the Greek Orthodox causes and naturally both men saw additional gains for themselves and their countries. Nicholas's attempts to strong-arm the Turks and divide the French and British failed miserably and the French and British declared war in March 1854. It is doubtful that these international affairs concerned Cambridge when he assumed his new duties in London in the years immediately preceding the war, as he was focused on the improvement of one branch of service within the army, albeit the most prestigious one.

During Queen Victoria's long reign, there was not a year in which British soldiers were not actively engaged somewhere in the world, but the Duke of Cambridge, despite being a career officer of some six decades, saw but two engagements in one war: the Crimean War. It was his greatest opportunity and his greatest failure. In the spring of 1852, such an outcome would have been hard to predict. Cambridge arrived at the Horse Guards and immersed himself in his duties, quickly acquiring the reputation as a committed reformer. Indeed, he may have already possessed the reputation of a reformer prior to his arrival. In addition to the reforms implemented while serving as a commander in Dublin, the reform-minded journals of the time, such as the *United Service Gazette,* identified Cambridge as a kindred spirit.[74] While his standing was good with peers and well-read officers when he assumed his new position, Wellington's death on September 14, 1852, further elevated Cambridge's standing. Evidence of this new standing was clearly evident when Queen Victoria placed him in command of all troops in London who came from all over Britain to conduct the funeral procession for the Iron Duke.[75]

The duties of the Inspector-General of Cavalry required that Cambridge be the subject-matter expert on the branch, responsible for its efficiency, training, discipline, and doctrine. This made him well positioned to correspond with every regimental commander and senior

---

74 The best work on the subject of reform of the British army prior to the Crimean War is Hew Strachan, *Wellington's Legacy: The Reform of the British Army 1830-1854* (Manchester: Manchester University Press, 1984). Significantly, in the first chapter, "The Identity of the Reformers," Strachan identifies Cambridge as one of them, although he observes that his accomplishments "are not so well documented." *Ibid.*, 27.
75 Verner, vol. 1, 61-62.

commander throughout the army. In turn, he was responsible directly to the Commander-in-Chief to provide advice and report on the condition of the cavalry branch as a whole. In the two years he was in the office, Cambridge wrote several important memoranda highlighting the deficiencies of the British army. Although the Crimean War made the army's weaknesses readily apparent, the Duke was well aware of many of its extant problems before the war started. He used his office as Inspector-General as a vehicle to effect change and not simply for personal connection. Naturally, the prominence of the position would further enhance Cambridge's renown throughout the army. The ability of the office to enact reform was another matter.

Although Cambridge's lengthy memoranda were a genuine attempt to improve the cavalry branch and the army, in the end his lengthy papers stood as good recommendations without immediate effect. Although Wellington's death in September 1852 may have been a blow to army morale, it also allowed supporters of army reform a much greater voice. In the words of one such officer, the death of Wellington represented "A happy release for the Army."[76] Wellington had exercised a positive influence on Cambridge's advancement, and the Queen's decision to have Cambridge command the troops at Wellington's funeral made it quite clear Cambridge had the full support of his cousin. In fact, Cambridge's reputation was such that the Queen and the Prime Minister briefly considered Cambridge as Wellington's replacement as Commander-in-Chief.[77] Wellington himself had always favored a Commander-in-Chief of royal blood since he viewed it as a guaranteed method to protect the Royal Prerogative, the Crown's control of the army. In addition to such a pedigree, Cambridge benefited from his good reputation within the army and even among reformers. Ultimately, however, the Prime Minister, Lord Derby (1799-1869), in consultation with the Queen, decided Cambridge was still too junior for such an important position, and they instead settled on Lord Hardinge (1785-1856).[78]

---

76 Napier Papers, British Museum, Add. Mss. 49,117, fo. 65, Letter from [unidentified officer] Maugham to General Sir Charles Napier, dated October 30, 1852. Napier would die less than a year after this, but even in his retirement he was active in promoting ideas in the realm of military reform. Napier had had a long and distinguished career beginning with the Peninsular Campaign and had served extensively throughout the Empire including India.
77 Strachan, *The Reform of the British Army 1830-1854*, 35-36.
78 *Ibid.*, 36.

Surviving correspondence and memoranda indicate that Cambridge viewed his position seriously and intended to make the most of it. The most important result of his two years in office was four memoranda intended to improve the efficiency of the army: "Observations on the Organization of the British Army at Home" published in December 1852, "Observations on the Regimental Organization of British Infantry, with Suggestions for its Improvement" published in January 1853, "The Organization of Cavalry" published in October 1853, and "The Age of General Officers" published in December 1853.[79] Ostensibly written for the Commander-in-Chief, Lord Hardinge, and the Secretary of State for War and the Colonies, the Duke of Newcastle (1811-1864), Cambridge intended dissemination of his ideas throughout the army and the government. Despite his solid recommendations, he was powerless to carry out the changes and instead could only put forth the recommendations to the myriad of organizations and departments–seventeen within the army, as well as departments of state–and hope that they be acted upon.[80] In the short run, they were not. In the long run, however, his ideas were disseminated widely throughout the officer corps, and it is likely they influenced the thinking of some of the officers who read them.

Presciently, the Duke of Cambridge predicted in "Organization of the British Army at Home" that the lack of divisional organizations was a major shortcoming of the army, especially when compared to those on the Continent.[81] He observed that, "the nation not being a military one," there should still be a better coordination of the regiments and batteries within the British Isles to prepare for home defense more efficiently and recommended locations and organizations to bring it about.[82] He also urged division-level maneuvers to prepare the army for modern warfare.[83] Ironically, Cambridge predicted what would happen in the Crimea: "the confusion and uncertainty on the first outbreak of a war or an attack from without would be most lamentably and seriously felt."[84] As the next chapter

79 Verner, vol. 1, 34-60.

80 Army organization will be addressed in the Chapter 4. The best single work on army administration of the period is John Sweetman, *War and Administration: The Significance of the Crimean War for the British Army* (Edinburgh: Scottish Academic Press, 1984).

81 RA VIC/E2/52, Memorandum by the Duke of Cambridge dated December 1852, "Observations on the Organisation of the British Army at Home."

82 *Ibid.*

83 Later, as Commander-in-Chief, Cambridge would implement division maneuvers, but with mixed results. See below.

84 RA VIC/E2/52, Memorandum by the Duke of Cambridge dated December 1852, "Observations on

will reveal, chaos was indeed the result of the British army's deployment to the Crimea.

Cambridge's three other memoranda were also critical of the army's organization, administration, and equipment. His memorandum on the organization of British infantry recommended standardization of infantry regiments throughout the world, since it was otherwise "left to chance."[85] Facing a dilemma similar to the challenge facing the armies of Great Britain and the United States today in Afghanistan and Iraq, Cambridge argued that if organizations could be standardized, the rotation of regiments between home service and duty abroad could more easily be regulated. Furthermore, recruiting needs would be better anticipated and the overall efficiency of the army would be enhanced. Although sound, it would be decades before aspects of his recommendations were put in place. Cambridge showed his proposal to the Prince Consort who wrote to him on February 7, 1853, expressing his approval of Cambridge's plans, which came "recommended by every principle of common sense."[86] Even though the Prince Consort was known to be in favor of military reform, nothing came of it. Similarly, his memorandum on cavalry organization argued for a rational structuring of cavalry regiments for the same reasons.

Of the four memoranda, "The Age of General Officers" proved to be the most ironic, for the very thing which Cambridge railed against in his youth he himself would violate later in life. By examining the Army List, the list of officers on active duty, Cambridge had discovered there were thirteen general officers with over seventy years' service, thirty-seven officers with between sixty and seventy years, and one hundred sixty-three with between fifty and sixty years of service.[87] The high number of aged senior officers discouraged innovation and stagnated promotion, so he recommended mandatory retirement after fifty years of service. By contemporary standards, such a recommendation hardly sounds revolutionary, but it was then considered a remarkable proposal for a young officer to make. Cambridge himself would resist retirement after

---

the Organisation of the British Army at Home."

85 Undated memorandum by the Duke of Cambridge, "Observations on the Regimental Organization of British Infantry, with Suggestions for its Improvement," reproduced in Verner, vol. 1, 44.

86 Letter from Colonel Charles Grey, Private Secretary to the Prince Consort, to the Duke of Cambridge, dated February 7, 1853, reproduced in *ibid.*, 51.

87 Undated memorandum by the Duke of Cambridge ,"The Age of General Officers," reproduced in *ibid.*, 55-56.

he had reached fifty years of service; only at the age of seventy-six, with fifty-eight years in uniform by 1895 did he retire against his will.

The four major recommendations to come out of Cambridge's tour of duty as the Inspector-General of Cavalry–division organization, standardization of combat units, linkage of battalions to territory within Britain, and the establishment of mandatory retirement ages–were eventually carried out, but not until much later. Division organization and standardization of combat units in the British army occurred in 1901, although the linkage of battalions to territory within Britain and the establishment of mandatory retirement ages were carried through in 1871 under the tenure of Cambridge's nemesis at the War Department, Edward Cardwell, Secretary of State for War from 1868 to 1874. One innovation he partly implemented as Inspector-General of Cavalry was large-scale maneuvers. From June 14 to August 17, 1853, the Duke spent his time at Chobham observing several infantry and cavalry regiments on maneuver.[88] This was his major endeavor of 1853, and one upon which he would build when he became Commander-in-Chief several years later.

Overall, however, Cambridge accomplished little of substance while he served as the Inspector-General of Cavalry. The four memoranda he produced would later be acted upon, or more accurately, similar changes to the ones he recommended were carried out by others, ironically mainly Edward Cardwell.[89] His efforts were fruitful, however, in making it clear that he was a thoughtful officer favorably disposed to reform, making him acceptable to like-minded individuals. Although the later years of his career and their conservatism have overshadowed this aspect of Cambridge's outlook, it is clear he was capable of progressive and original thought. His royal birth made him a natural ally of those interested in protecting the Royal Prerogative. As a prince of royal blood so closely connected with the monarchy and the royal family, he hardly posed a threat to the status quo. Despite his critical comments about army organization, he was unlikely to recommend anything too radical or something that threatened the traditional organization of the army. The Duke of Cambridge had accomplished the difficult task of appearing progressive to those who

---

88 Verner, vol. 1, 59-60. As Commander-in-Chief, Cambridge built upon the experiment at Chobham. See Chapter 5.

89 As will become clear in later chapters, Edward Cardwell proved to be Cambridge's nemesis. It is therefore an ironic twist that his reform-minded proposals would be carried out at a point when he himself had become quite conservative and his progressive civilian master would fulfill them.

advocated change while not making enemies within the conservative officer corps.

V

By early 1854 while still serving as Inspector-General of Cavalry at St. James' Palace, Cambridge had become intensely interested in developments regarding Turkey and Russia despite his earlier obliviousness. Although Britain had not yet declared war, it was coming–the Russian ambassador to Britain left London on February 7, 1854, and the British ambassador, Sir Hamilton Seymour (1797-1880), was recalled from St. Petersburg the same day.[90] Cambridge heard "the rumble of a distant drum" and learned on February 9th that a force of 10,000 men was to embark immediately for the east.[91] Over the next several days he ached to learn whether he would be part of the expeditionary force, and he longed, quite understandably, to be part of the action. His hopes were fulfilled when the Secretary of State for War and the Colonies, the Duke of Newcastle, visited Cambridge at the Horse Guards in the afternoon of February 16, 1854 and informed him he would command a division headed to Malta.[92] The Queen had apparently intervened directly on his behalf to enable him to join the expeditionary force. The decision by the Duke of Newcastle to give Cambridge a command came shortly after Cambridge had visited Victoria for the express purpose of obtaining one, and on February 13 he met with Victoria and Albert to explain that he must accompany the troops. Victoria's journal recorded that "[Cambridge] would feel himself disgraced, were he not allowed to go. We agreed with him and promised to do all we could."[93]

Although Victoria makes no direct mention of pressuring the Duke of Newcastle or Lord Hardinge to give Cambridge a command, and Cambridge himself does not mention exactly how the decision was made, it was clearly a result of both his own advocacy and the Queen's. Victoria personally approved all senior promotions and command appointments, a privilege she maintained fiercely–something Cambridge would experience firsthand as Commander-in-Chief. Hardinge or Newcastle would have presented the Queen their combined recommendation for senior commanders, and if

---

90 Benson and Esher, eds., *The Letters of Queen Victoria*, 1st ser., vol. 3, 10.

91 Sheppard, vol.1, 114.

92 St. Aubyn, 60.

93 RA QVJ: 13 February 1854.

Cambridge had not been on their original list, she would have asked him to be placed on it. It is also likely they would have wanted him because of his experience as Inspector-General of Cavalry and the excellent knowledge of army organization he had acquired.

Months passed, however, before Cambridge actually accompanied the expeditionary force, resulting in fierce criticism in the London press. Before he left London and joined his division, there was much to be done. Immediately after learning his good fortune, Cambridge, "Communicated it to all my friends," and spent the next several *weeks* bidding farewell to friends and relatives. His journal entries reveal a steady sequence of dinners and social events until his departure on April 10, 1854. [94] Cambridge's appointment went largely unnoticed in the press and controversy would not have arisen had he joined his troops when they departed England. At a pre-inspection of the Scots Fusilier Guards at Buckingham Palace on February 27, 1854, it was Cambridge who received the loudest cheers (short of the royal family).[95] But when he left England on April 10, he did not follow his troops, but instead headed to Paris as the personal guest of Napoleon III. It was to be his first stop on a circuitous journey that would ultimately link him up with the men of his division some four weeks later. The Duke left England and accompanied Lord Raglan, who had that same day received his official appointment as Commander-in-Chief of the British Army in the East.[96] Prior to his appointment as commander of the expeditionary force, Raglan had never held a field command despite his advanced age of sixty-five years and fifty years of military service.[97]

Their first day in Paris was remarkably similar to those that would come after it in Paris–most of the time was spent attending either reviews or social functions and very little time was spent discussing military issues. Clearly the ceremonial obligations required of a member of the royal family infringed upon the accomplishment of actual diplomatic and military functions. Nonetheless, the major reason for Cambridge's selection as a member of the military delegation was his royal birth and great familiarity with the royalty of Europe. His presence demonstrated the British

---

94 Diary of the Duke of Cambridge, recounted in Sheppard, vol.1, 114.
95 The full account of the send off of the Royal Scots Fusiliers was reported in *Bell's Weekly Messenger*, dated March 4ᵗʰ, 1854, reprinted in Kellow Chesney, *Crimean War Reader* (London: Frederick Muller, Ltd., 1960), 26-27.
96 Fortescue, *History of the British Army*, vol. 13, 33.
97 For a scathing, but informative and amusing account of Lord Raglan's role in the Crimean War, see Cecil-Woodham Smith, *The Reason Why* (London: Constable, 1956).

commitment to the Anglo-French alliance. The first actual discussion of military issues did not occur until April 13 and lasted a mere two hours. In the Duke's own words, "The affairs of the East were discussed, but no very definite conclusion was arrived at."[98] For the rest of Cambridge's stay in Paris, it was a steady alternation between social functions and time with his wife, Louisa–more of the same that had preceded the military meeting– reviews, inspections, formal dinners, and presumably, time with Louisa and Augustus, but little actual discussion of military affairs. At last on April 17, the Emperor Napoleon III summoned Cambridge and informed him that he should proceed on to Constantinople with a stop in Vienna on the way. Accordingly, Cambridge cabled London to receive permission from the Foreign Office to go on to Vienna, and he reached there on April 22 to undertake his "secret mission" to determine the inclinations of Austria in the current crisis.[99] Lord Raglan, leaving several hours prior to Cambridge's departure, proceeded directly to Constantinople and reached the city by the end of the month.

Cambridge's time in Paris generated a fair amount of criticism in the London press. Of all the London periodicals, *Punch*, the leading satirical London journal, not surprisingly, was the most scathing. A cartoon at the end of April implied in blatant terms that the Duke was avoiding going to war and instead was whiling away his time pursuing the good life.[100] The lead cartoon portrayed Punch (representing Hector) criticizing Cambridge (portrayed as Paris) for delaying in getting to the war. Biographers of Cambridge have since argued this criticism was unfair because Cambridge was on official business, and he did link up with his division in Constantinople a month before it departed for Varna and four months before it actually reached the Crimea.[101] Perhaps Cambridge's mission to Paris demonstrated British resolve, but there were no concrete negotiations or planning and Cambridge did not acquaint himself with his subordinate units. The question of whether he made the best use of his time, even by the standards of a mid-19th-century royal still remains.

---

98 Sheppard, vol. 1., 118.
99 Verner, vol. 1, 65.
100 "Hector Chiding Paris," *Punch* 26 (April 1854): 175.
101 See Sheppard, vol. 1, 120; Verner, vol. 1, 65; and especially, St. Aubyn, 64 for a defense of the Duke against such "unjust and inept attacks."

HECTOR CHIDING PARIS.
A HINT TO H.R.H FIELD MARSHAL THE DUKE OF CAMBRIDGE
'Him Thus Inactive, With An Ardent Look
The Prince Beheld, And High Resenting, Spoke.' – Pope's Homer

Regardless of its portrayal in the London press, Lord Aberdeen's government and Cambridge himself believed the mission to Paris to have been a triumph. Lord Clarendon (1800-1870), the Secretary of State for Foreign Affairs, told him the mission to Paris had "been a great political success as it has given the French people an opportunity of publicly ratifying the policy of the Emperor."[102] The mission to Vienna was far more important than the one to Paris due to strategic considerations. Certainly the Queen and her Foreign Secretary saw it as a crucial endeavor because France was already an ally whereas Austria was uncommitted, as

102 Sheppard, vol.1, 121.

Victoria noted, "Lord Clarendon agreed with us in the great importance of George...going on to Vienna, which is desired by the Emperor of Austria [Francis Joseph I (1830-1916)], and which both from a military and political point of view is most important."[103] The Queen and Lord Clarendon both believed there was no one more suitable than Cambridge because of his military experience and knowledge as well as his royal birth.

Cambridge remained in Vienna and was a frequent guest of the emperor over the next nine days. Attending numerous state functions, his diary reveals his favorable attitude towards Vienna with phrases such as "magnificent sight," "pleasing impression," "which gave me every satisfaction," "satisfactory," and "pleased me very much indeed." Clearly he thoroughly enjoyed his time there, but his itinerary also calls into question the seriousness or effectiveness of his diplomatic endeavor.[104] There is no evidence of any substantive discussions. By the Duke's own account, he ended up with nothing more than a vague expression of good will by his Austrian hosts. It was hardly an overwhelmingly successful diplomatic mission. Regardless of how the mission was evaluated after the fact or Cambridge's perceptions while he was there, he failed. The Austrians would not commit to the alliance even though the Foreign Secretary, Lord Clarendon, curiously viewed Cambridge's mission as a success, writing to his ambassador in Austria, Lord Westmoreland on May 5: "I have only time to say how intensely we are gratified by the reception given to the Duke of Cambridge, and how admirably we think he has performed his mission."[105] On May 8, Clarendon wrote similarly to Cambridge.[106] Clearly, Lord Clarendon put the best light on an unsuccessful, or at least an incomplete, mission. Whatever the "much needed" information was that Cambridge obtained will forever remain a mystery because he learned nothing not already known–Austria would remain on the side of peace and would not actively join an alliance with Britain.

In a characteristically frank (and characteristically lengthy) letter to the Queen on April 28, 1854, Cambridge presented a more accurate assessment of his recent visit: he had not accomplished anything of

---

103 RA QVJ: 6 March 1854.
104 Diary entries of the Duke of Cambridge, dated April 28, 29 and 30, 1854, recounted in Sheppard, vol.1, 124.
105 *Ibid.*
106 *Ibid.*

substance.[107] Cambridge made it clear that Austria would not intervene directly on the side of the British and the French. Furthermore, considering the "extreme delicacy" of Austria's vulnerable borders, war was out of the question. Cambridge closed his letter with an assessment that proved to be quite inaccurate: "Rely upon it, this Country will never go with Russia… "[108] He was right in predicting that Austria would "never go with Russia" but neither would they go with Britain and France. Austria had just signed an offensive and defensive treaty with Prussia–that is where her true interests were. As recently as April 20, Austria had massed 50,000 troops in Galicia and Transylvania as a deterrent to Russian action, but there was little reason to expect an active Austrian alliance against Russia. It would never happen, and by the end of the decade Austria's true weakness would be revealed with the loss of Lombardy in the Italian War of 1859.

In many ways, the Duke of Cambridge had been well suited for the diplomatic missions to France and Austria. As a member of the British royal family, his credibility with foreign heads of state was immediate. When Cambridge arrived in Paris and Vienna, there was no doubt Britain was making a statement about the sincerity of its intentions, for Cambridge combined the roles of royal representative and military commander–a combination of ceremony and military might. Furthermore, the experience and travels of his youth made him uniquely suited for dealing with the heads of state of other powers, even on matters of great sensitivity. The substance and consequences of his diplomatic efforts are questionable, although appearance and ceremony were important. Regardless of his skills as a diplomat, it would soon be time to begin the other task for which Cambridge had been sent to the east, one which he had actively sought once it became clear war was imminent. It would affect not only his reputation and career, but also reflect and inform once again the all-important relationship between the military and the monarchy to a degree no one could have imagined.

---

107 Letter from the Duke of Cambridge to Queen Victoria, dated April 28, 1854, reproduced in Benson and Esher, eds., *The Letters of Queen Victoria*, 1st ser., vol. 3, 30-32.
108 *Ibid.*

CHAPTER 3:
The Crimea and Its Consequences 1854-1855

The level of diplomatic incompetence which brought Britain into the Crimean War was perhaps exceeded only by how the British government and its army actually conducted it. This major European conflict of the mid 19th century is remembered more for ineptitude and needless suffering than any demonstration of military proficiency. Though often regarded as the first modern war–aerial observation, tactical use of railways, telegraph, photography, and exploding ordinance all made their first wartime appearance–it is Tennyson's famous poem, "The Charge of the Light Brigade," that has immortalized the conflict in literary and historical consciousness.[1] As the military historian Correlli Barnett observed, "The Crimean War is one of the compulsive subjects of British historical writing."[2] While the war and its improbable origins and conduct have been addressed extensively, what matters here is how the experience of leading men in combat affected the subsequent career of the Duke of Cambridge and his relationship with Queen Victoria.[3]

For the military, the monarchy, and the career of the Duke of Cambridge, the Crimean War proved to be pivotal. For the army, it revealed the damaging effects of decades of neglect, budgetary reductions, and the shortcomings–or more accurately, the absence–of the army staff. The British army entered the war in the same condition as it had finished fighting Napoleon, and the resulting incompetence would create renewed demand for reform even before the fighting was over. For Queen Victoria, the war was an important development as well. It reinforced her view that the army was her own institution. The Queen followed the military campaigns and especially the heroism and plight of soldiers with avid interest and the creation of the Victoria Cross is perhaps the most visible result of her devotion to the soldiers and their accomplishments. Unquestionably the war had a lasting impact on the monarchy as numerous ceremonies, parades, and award presentations served to strengthen the association between the military and the monarchy in both the national consciousness and actual practice.

---

1 Alfred, Lord Tennyson, "The Charge of the Light Brigade," in Alfred, Lord Tennyson, *Selected Poems*, (Toronto: Dover Publications, 1992), 52.
2 Barnett, 283.
3 The recent release by Orlando Figes, *The Crimean War: A History* (New York: Metropolitan Books, 2010), is the definitive work on the war's origins and its conduct.

For the Duke of Cambridge, the war also proved to be a seminal event. Most conspicuously, it provided his first and only operational command. For the remainder of his life, Cambridge was known for having commanded the 1st Division during the Crimean War, but his actual performance was less than spectacular. The Duke failed to remain with his men when they were in action against the enemy for more than a few weeks. Understanding the sequence of events that led him to division command and subsequently led him from it reveal a great deal about the man who would go on to command the British army for thirty-nine years. More importantly, the fact that the career of a senior army officer could not only survive after he abandoned his division in combat, but also that that same officer would shortly thereafter attain the highest military rank in the British army, reveals a great deal about the fundamental relationship between the military and the monarchy as it existed in mid-19th-century Britain.

I

His diplomatic duties finished for the time being, the Duke of Cambridge reached Constantinople on May 10, 1854, after ten days at sea. Wasting little time now that he was in the major staging area for the allied war effort, he quickly assessed the situation and sought to make his division ready for combat. Upon coming ashore, he asked Field Marshal Lord Raglan (FitzRoy Somerset, 1st Baron Raglan, 1788-1855) at the British Embassy the status of preparations, and he received the happy news that he was to command the 1st Division, consisting of the Brigade of Guards under Brigadier General H.J. Bentinck and the Highland Brigade under Sir Colin Campbell (afterwards, 1st Baron Clyde, 1792-1863). This news and other first-hand impressions caused his spirits to soar and overall he believed himself to be in a good situation. He recorded in his diary that he was "most enthusiastically received by the troops" and they "appeared to be in the best health and spirits and seem as comfortable and happy as possible."[4]

The Sultan of the Ottoman Empire, Abdul Medjid (b. 1883; r 1839-1861), billeted Cambridge in the Sultan's Palace of Ferez–accommodations obviously far more lavish than those of his troops–and impressions began

---

4 Diary entry of the Duke of Cambridge, dated May 10, 1854, reproduced in Sheppard, vol. 1, 125.

to change. By his third day in Constantinople, his attitude toward his host and his host's empire had worsened considerably. In a letter to the Queen dated May 13, 1854, Cambridge revealed his opinion of the Sultan: "I confess I was not much impressed with either his appearance or general ability. He is, to say the truth, a wretched creature, prematurely aged, and having nothing whatever to say for himself."[5] In his characteristic wry humor, he went on to comment on the health of the Ottoman Empire and its people, observing, "they are all a most wretched and miserable set of people, and far, far worse than anything I could possibly have imagined or supposed. In fact, the 'sick man' is *excessively sick indeed*, dying as fast as possible; and the sooner diplomacy disposes of him the better, for no earthly power can save him, that is very evident."[6]

Despite his comfortable quarters, Cambridge was genuinely distressed at the palace's distance from his troops. Social functions were no longer his focus and the inconvenience of not being near his men was an annoyance until the division left Constantinople the following month. Since his arrival in Constantinople on May 10, Cambridge had worked hard to prepare his division for action, demonstrating great energy and enthusiasm, quickly acquiring the reputation of a demanding taskmaster. One of his officers wrote to a friend that, "The Duke of Cambridge is full of zeal…nothing escapes him, and some of the mounted gentlemen have brushed up very much."[7] Another soldier in the 1st Division observed that, "Our life is not an idle one…Our royal chief is far too fond of field days, and keeps us out five hours under arms so that we return pretty well knocked up while the day is yet young."[8]

Cambridge remained with his division from May 10 until it disembarked from Constantinople for the Black Sea port of Varna, Bulgaria, on June 13. In addition to his apparent dedication to his soldiers and the constant drilling of them, Cambridge used this time to contemplate the larger strategic and political aspects of the conflict.[9] He hoped the Austrians would reinforce the allies and he mentioned them specifically

---

5 Letter from the Duke of Cambridge to Queen Victoria, dated May 13, 1854 reproduced in Benson and Esher, eds., *The Letters of Queen Victoria*, 1st ser., vol. 3, 34.
6 *Ibid.*
7 RA VIC/F1/11. Letter from Colonel Seymour to Colonel Phipps, dated 27 May 1854.
8 Sir George Higginson, *Seventy-one Years of a Guardsman's Life* (London: Smith, Elder and Co., 1916), 129.
9 Letter from the Duke of Cambridge to the Duchess of Gloucester, dated June 5, 1854, reproduced in Sheppard, vol. 1, 129.

in letters dated June 5, June 18, and June 29, 1854, expressing, "I still hope confidently in Austria."[10] His earlier confidence from when he first arrived faded quickly as sickness took a heavy toll, writing to his aunt, the Duchess of Gloucester, "our men have been rather more sickly of late and we have had some cases of cholera," and also "we have had our people attacked by cholera and suffered greatly from this dreadful epidemic, as well as from fever. The fleet are as bad as the Armies, and the French have suffered infinitely more than ourselves."[11] Already the expedition which Cambridge had wanted so badly to join was becoming very unpleasant.

Cambridge wrote often to Queen Victoria and the Foreign Secretary, Lord Clarendon. Victoria was interested in how her cousin was faring and his connection to her is demonstrated in their substantial correspondence. A telling example is a letter Cambridge wrote to Lord Clarendon assessing the outcome of the Vienna mission: "I lost no time in transmitting your Royal Highness's letters to the Queen, who, as well as Prince Albert, was greatly pleased with them, and I can assure Your Royal Highness that Her Majesty's opinions are those also of the Government."[12] Such correspondence was common and Cambridge maintained a steady flow of detailed letters. Not only was Victoria eager to learn of Cambridge's opinions, but she used his on-the-scene assessments to attempt to influence the policies of her government. In response to the above letter of May 13, in which the Duke presented a less-than-flattering picture of the Sultan and his empire, the Queen wrote to Henry Pelham-Clinton (1811-1864), the 5th Duke of Newcastle, Secretary of State for War and Colonies, attempting– unsuccessfully–to alter the government's policy toward Britain's ally, Turkey. As she observed, Cambridge's "letter does *not* give a flourishing account of the state of Turkey."[13] Despite the Queen's feelings, there was no change in policy, but by this point the situation in the military theater was so confused that the operation bordered on chaos. The British were eager to obtain allies since they were short of troops deployable to the Crimea, but the Queen's input had no discernable impact on the conduct

10 Letters from the Duke of Cambridge to the Duchess of Gloucester, dated June 5, 18 and 29, 1854, reproduced in *ibid.*, 129-131.
11 Letters from the Duke of Cambridge to the Duchess of Gloucester, dated July 29 and August 19, 1854, reproduced in *ibid.*, 129-131.
12 Letter from Lord Clarendon to the Duke of Cambridge, dated May 8, 1854, reproduced in *ibid.*, 128.
13 Letter from Queen Victoria to the Duke of Newcastle, dated May 13, 1854, reproduced in Benson and Esher, eds., *The Letters of Queen Victoria*, 1st ser., vol. 3, 38-9.

of the war or negotiations. As for the confused military situation in the region, it was only to get worse.

II

Queen Victoria's interest in all things military–it could almost be described as an obsession–has been well documented.[14] Once fighting broke out in the Crimea, she "*never* regretted more" that she was "a *poor woman* and not a man."[15] She viewed the soldiers as her own, as they in turn viewed themselves as soldiers of the Queen, and she followed all aspects of the war in great detail. Similarly, she advocated to her ministers the great importance of minimizing the suffering of the troops and the need to overcome the bureaucratic bumbling of her ministers prosecuting the war. A letter to Princess Augusta of Prussia–a close confidant of Victoria's since their first meeting at the Crystal Palace exhibition on October 15, 1851–demonstrates further Victoria's perspective: "You will understand it when I assure you that I regret exceedingly not to be a man and able to fight in the war. My heart bleeds for the many fallen, but I consider that there is no finer death for a man than on the battlefield!"[16] In a letter to Lord Raglan written shortly after the start of the New Year of 1855, she wrote, "the Queen feels it to be one of her highest prerogatives and dearest duties to care for the welfare and success of *her* Army."[17]

Nothing better illustrates the Queen's attitudes about her troops and demonstrates the deliberate association Victoria encouraged between her reign and the army than the ceremony held on May 22, 1855, where she recognized British soldiers recently returned from the Crimea. It was a public ceremony and, significantly, the Queen presented awards to officers and enlisted men alike, making it the first such ceremony of its kind to occur in Great Britain. The medal bestowed upon the men was, and still is, the highest military award for heroism in the British army. The award was commissioned by the Queen herself and given in her name: the Victoria

---

14 Giles St. Aubyn, *Queen Victoria: A Portrait* (New York: Athenaeum, 1992), 294-296, addresses Victoria's attitude towards her soldiers rather well. See also, Longford, *Queen Victoria*.
15 St. Aubyn, *Queen Victoria*, 294.
16 Letter from Queen Victoria to Princess Augusta of Prussia, dated October 23, 1854, reproduced in Christopher Hibbert, *Queen Victoria in her Letters and Journals* (London: John Murray, 1984), 126.
17 Letter from Queen Victoria to Lord Raglan, dated January 12, 1855, reproduced in Benson and Esher, eds., *The Letters of Queen Victoria*, 1st ser., vol. 3, 86.

Cross. In 1855 it was manufactured from captured Russian cannons during the Crimean War. It serves as a lasting testament to her close personal attachment to soldiers, heroism, and the army. Her recollections in a letter to her uncle, King Leopold of the Belgians, capture perfectly her outlook:

> Noble fellows! I own I feel as if these were *my own children;* my heart beats for *them* as for my *nearest and dearest.* Many, I hear, cried–and they won't hear of giving up their Medals, to have their names engraved upon them, for fear they should *not* receive the *identical one* put into *their hands by me*, which is quite touching....*One must* revere and love soldiers such as those![18]

These were strong words indeed. Language like this, written not for public consumption, but rather to be held in close confidence by her uncle–with whom she shared many private thoughts–helps explain why Victoria resisted with great vehemence any encroachment upon her Royal Prerogative. Obviously, the army and its soldiers were a matter of great personal interest to her.

In early June 1854 the political situation changed, and with it so did Cambridge's fortunes. Cambridge's diplomatic mission might have accomplished a tangible result after all: Austria, with the support of Prussia, pressed for the evacuation of the Turkish Danube principalities. In support of France and Britain, Austria deployed 50,000 soldiers along the Danube River. In response, the Tsar withdrew his forces from the Turkish Danube principalities and with their removal away went the original reasons for the dispute with Russia.

Nonetheless, national passions remained high. French and British public opinion strongly backed the war, and the Ottoman humiliation at Sinope–on November 30, 1853, the Russian navy had sunk eleven Ottoman ships without suffering any losses–added impetus for the allies to press the war. Although the allies had not yet engaged the Russians, the

---

18 Letter from Queen Victoria to Leopold, King of the Belgians, dated May 22, 1855, reproduced in *ibid.*, 161-162.

strategic situation was now drastically turned in their favor. The Turks under Omar Pasha's leadership had been unexpectedly successful and defeated the Russians soundly at Giurgevo. While the Russian siege at Silistria had previously appeared to be a guaranteed victory, the Russians were now thwarted all along the Danube by the Ottoman army. By June 22, 1854, the Russians retreated fully and withdrew back across the Danube River. The French and British forces, poorly equipped and slow, failed to assist the Turks, although two British officers, Captain Butler of the Ceylon Rifles and Lieutenant Nasmyth of the Indian artillery, helped raise the siege at Silistria, receiving wide coverage in the London press.[19] Accordingly, the Duke of Newcastle sent a letter to Lord Raglan on June 29, 1854 in which he stated the reduction of Sebastopol and the capture of the Russian fleet were "the only means of securing an honourable and safe peace."[20] National prestige was now as important as any genuine strategic considerations.

Prime Minister Lord Aberdeen informed Queen Victoria of essentially the same thing. The Cabinet had met the previous day in a long session and determined, "the necessity of a prompt attack upon Sebastopol and the Russian Fleet was strongly urged…with the assistance of the English and French Fleets."[21] Aberdeen also pointed out that although an expedition to the Crimea should be undertaken as soon as possible, "the final decision was left to the judgment and discretion of Lord Raglan and Marshal St. Arnaud, after they should have communicated with Omar Pacha [Pasha]."[22] Regardless of the increased passions, the true condition of Britain's ability to go to war was starkly revealed through the decision "to send the reserve force, now in England, of 5,000 men, to join Lord Raglan without delay. This will exhaust the whole disposable force of the country at this time, and renders it impossible to supply British troops for any undertaking in the Baltic."[23] The unhappy consequence of the lack of available troops was a request to the French to see if they could send approximately 6,000 more troops on British transports.

---

19 See Fortescue, vol. 13, 37-40.

20 Letter from the Duke of Newcastle to Lord Raglan, dated June 29, 1854, reproduced in Verner, vol. 1, 67.

21 Letter from Lord Aberdeen to Queen Victoria, dated June 29, 1854, reproduced in Benson and Esher, eds., *The Letters of Queen Victoria*, 1st ser., vol. 3, 45-6.

22 *Ibid.*, 46.

23 *Ibid.*

This letter from Aberdeen to the Queen is revealing for several reasons. First, it demonstrated that Britain's ability to respond to a military crisis was weaker than the government had planned. Although continental commitment had been scrupulously avoided since the defeat of Napoleon, now that the situation apparently demanded action, there was little Britain could do on its own. Secondly, it revealed the true role of the Queen in affecting foreign policy–the Cabinet had reached a decision and the Queen was informed after the fact. Although she took great interest in military affairs, she could not really affect the use of the army. In turn this probably increased her desire to remain in control of those areas she could influence, such as awards, promotion of key personnel–at least through placing her signature on promotion documents–and ultimately the selection and retention of her cousin as Commander-in-Chief.

The Queen responded to the Duke of Newcastle with her characteristic thoroughness, questioning the military aspects of the deployment, noting how she was "very uneasy at the very defenceless state in which the country will be left."[24] Overall, she considered the deployment vital for Britain's interests and prestige. It was at about this time, however, that the first of many disasters would strike the allied armies. A serious outbreak of cholera hit the expeditionary force, with an epidemic affecting the French first on July 19, killing over 10,000 French soldiers; a second attack struck the British encampments on July 22, taking some 500 British soldiers' lives. The disease spread to both nations' fleets as well.[25] The buildup of allied troops continued independently of changing strategic and political situations, and despite the poor conditions on the ground, Cambridge, in command of the 1st Division, arrived with his men at Varna, Bulgaria, on the west coast of the Black Sea on the eighteenth finding it to be "a most dreadful place, the picture of filth and misery."[26] Despite the physical unpleasantness of his surroundings and the confusion created by the continuing arrival of thousands of French and British soldiers, initially the Duke's spirits were high, although he was frustrated the Austrians still had not committed themselves to direct combat which would have made "the campaign…an easy one."[27]

24 Letter from Queen Victoria to Lord Aberdeen, dated June 29, 1854 reproduced in *ibid.*, 47.
25 Verner, vol. 1, 67-68; Denis Judd, *The Crimean War* (London: Hart-Davis, MacGibbon, 1975), 37-40.
26 Letter from the Duke of Cambridge to the Duchess of Gloucester, dated June 18, 1854, reproduced in Sheppard, vol. 1, 130.
27 *Ibid.*

As weeks in the bleak port of Varna continued and conditions for soldiers worsened, Cambridge's spirits correspondingly declined. Temperatures rose well above ninety degrees Fahrenheit, and tents, barracks, and hospitals became infested with lice, leeches, gnats, fleas, and large, gray rats. [28] For the first time, the reading public in England had an unvarnished account of conditions its forces faced while at war due to the first military correspondent for the *Times*, W.H. Russell, generally considered the first modern war correspondent. Russell detailed not only the hardships facing the common soldier, but also the incompetence of many senior officers and the inefficiency of supply and administration. Lord Raglan and some British officers saw Russell's reporting as treasonous since it portrayed to the Russians the true state of the British army. Regardless, Russell's reporting led to widespread outrage in England and served as a major impetus for military reform.

Through it all, Cambridge tried to maintain his high spirits despite the international developments. When the Russians unexpectedly lifted siege at Silistria on June 9, 1854, the ostensible reason for an allied presence in Bulgaria in general, and the British presence in particular, disappeared; there was no longer a military justification for being there. When the Russians withdrew completely from the region on August 2, 1854, it was only their rejection of the allies' peace plan, the Vienna Four Points proposed on August 8, that kept the war going. The plan had the following stipulations. First, Russia was to relinquish its protectorate of the Danubian Principalities. Second, Russia would not interfere with Ottoman internal affairs, including religious matters related to Orthodox Christians. Third, the convention governing access to the Bosporus and the Dardanelles, the Straits Convention of 1841, would be revised. The final point was that the Danube River would be accessible to all nations.

As it turned out, the conditions for peace resting on a Russian pledge to remain out of the affairs of the Ottoman Empire was too large a concession for the Russians to accept. By the time negotiations were underway, the prospect of continued war no longer excited the Duke of Cambridge. He noted hopefully after first learning the Russian siege had been lifted that, "Should, however, a Peace and a good one really result it would be a very great event, for certainly these people are hardly worth fighting for! Though undoubtedly the Turks have behaved most nobly in

---

28 Judd, 38, 41.

defense of Silistria, which is a bright page in their history."[29] Although Cambridge had been thrilled to get to the fight, he seemed already to have had enough before the fighting actually began.

The primitive conditions of the battlefield and campaigning affected Cambridge personally; at the end of June he had a serious fever worsened by stomach cramps and a crippling case of gout, an ailment that would strike him recurrently for the rest of his life.[30] His troops suffered as well. Beyond the physical misery, they were overwhelmed by boredom. The Duke's weakened condition prevented him from drilling his soldiers and his health did not improve until early September, by which time his division had already left Varna aboard transports anchored in Varna Bay. Despite his flagging health, he wrote prodigiously. After several days of additional rest, Cambridge gained sufficient strength to join his soldiers afloat. A letter to Louisa, dated September 4, 1854, highlights his ordeal and that of his men, and it is clear the circumstances cause him to have different thoughts about a military career, "If God in his mercy spare me, I shall have had enough and more than enough of soldiering, and the rest of my days shall be devoted to making my dearest wife happy and to looking after our children."[31] Cambridge's morale was low and his experience in the Crimea quite unlike anything he had experienced in life thus far. Fifteen years of active service as an army officer and a lifetime as a royal prince had not prepared him for genuine hardship, and he regretted his choice of a military career. Cambridge had not yet faced the enemy or witnessed hostile action anywhere, but his resolve had already weakened considerably after only four months.

III

By the late summer of 1854 the Duke of Cambridge, his operational commander, Lord Raglan, and the senior officers in the theater doubted the wisdom of a winter campaign in the Crimea. The Russian withdrawal had eliminated the need to take the pressure off the Turkish Danube principalities, and it was clear folly to launch a winter attack on one of

---

29 Letter from the Duke of Cambridge to the Duchess of Gloucester, dated June 29, 1854 Sheppard, vol. 1, 130-131.
30 St. Aubyn, *The Royal George,* 67.
31 Letter from the Duke of Cambridge to his wife, Louisa, dated September 4, 1854, reproduced in *Ibid.*

the most fortified positions in the world, the remote fortress at Sebastopol. Furthermore, serious shortcomings in the ability to supply–let alone reinforce–the British army were, by now, painfully apparent. The British, along with their French and Turkish allies, lacked a suitable logistics base in the Crimea, and the British in particular had a woefully inadequate system of resupply. The British army possessed virtually no land transport or ambulances, grossly insufficient medical supplies and physicians, and no suitable winter clothing for its soldiers. Of all accounts of misery and neglect from the Crimea, perhaps most damning is a simple statistic: 18,058 British soldiers died during the Crimean War, but only 1,761 of them were killed directly by the enemy; the remaining 16,297 died of wounds, neglect, or disease.[32] French losses were significantly higher, although the ratios of the causes of death were dreadfully similar.

Logistical woes hampered simple tactical maneuver. The British lacked maps of the region even for commanders.[33] The inadequate nature of supply and administrative organization is demonstrated by the Commissariat having responsibility for providing water for the troops, unless through "wells, tanks, pipes or other works" in which case the Ordnance Department had responsibility. Completely unresponsive, it prevented initiative to the point that it discouraged the issue of lime juice, fresh vegetables, and even bread because regulations did not specifically allow it. Bureaucratic inefficiency was so extreme that a Commissariat official objected to Lord Raglan that the form of requisition for a new greatcoat (a document with *two schedules* and *twenty-four blanks* to be filled up in *duplicate*) should not be altered to prevent abuse: regulations "did not authorise the issue of regimental overcoats more frequently than once in three years."[34] Based upon his experience at Varna, Cambridge observed, "…the Commissariat Departments are not suited to operations in the field."[35]

Ineptitude was the norm. The transports laden with Cambridge and his division, as well as those containing the other four British divisions and a significant portion of the French and Turkish forces had difficulty moving to the Crimea. All troops were aboard by September 5, but due to

32 Judd, 192.
33 British shortcomings of administration, supply and equipment are well documented. See John Sweetman, *War and Administration: The Significance of the Crimean War for the British Army* (Edinburgh: Scottish Academic Press, 1984).
34 *Ibid.*, 47.
35 *Ibid.*

several delays, the invasion fleet did not set sail until September 7, arriving offshore at Sebastopol five days later. An astonishing revelation of the extent of the expeditionary force's incompetence is evident by noting that when the fleet set out from Varna on the September 7, neither the French nor British had any idea where they were going to land. The invasion force ultimately disembarked on September 14 at the undefended port of Eupatoria in Calamita Bay, some fifty miles to the north of Sebastopol; the operation was complete by September 18, 1854.

British officers were not the only ones opposed to beginning the assault against Sebastopol so late in the year. The commander of the French army, Marshal St. Arnaud, formerly Napoleon III's aide-de-camp during the 1851 coup and a veteran of much service in North Africa, acknowledged to Cambridge that a majority of French soldiers were against the expedition. It certainly could not have inspired confidence in Cambridge to know the commanding general of the French army did not believe in the campaign. Overall, French involvement in the war made little sense; France had no national interests in the area apart from Napoleon's vanity and his desire to appease the British. For diplomatic posterity, it did result in the first use of the term, "*entente cordiale.*"[36]

Regardless of the officers' opinion on the ground, as the Duke observed in his diary on August 8, "public opinion in England is to be satisfied at any hazard, and so the attempt is to be made."[37] Despite his initial misgivings, the Duke managed to maintain fairly high spirits. He wrote to his old friend from the Scots Fusilier Guards, General George Moncrieff, "…we are landed all safe and without opposition, and have as yet seen no Russians…"[38] Of the five division commanders under Lord Raglan, Cambridge was by far the youngest at thirty-four; the closest to Cambdrige in age was fifty-nine-year-old Sir George Cathcart.[39] Even though he was the youngest and relatively inexperienced, the royal presence of the Duke of Cambridge counted a great deal. Queen Victoria believed Cambridge

---

36 Gordon Wright, *France in Modern Times: From the Enlightenment to the Present.* 4th ed. (New York: W.W. Norton and Co., 1987), 196.

37 Diary entry of the Duke of Cambridge, dated August 8, 1854, reproduced in St. Aubyn, *The Royal George,* 68.

38 Letter from the Duke of Cambridge to General George Moncrieff, dated September 18, 1854, reproduced in Verner, vol. 1, 68.

39 Cambridge commanded the 1st Division; Sir George de Lacy Evans, age 66, fairly radical and the most competent, commanded the 2nd Division; Sir Richard England commanded the 3rd Division; Sir George Cathcart led the 4th Division; and Sir George Brown age 66 commanded the 5th Division.

should behave as a member of the royal family, finding it very important that "George sets the example" even if something unpopular should occur, such as Sir George Cathcart (1794-1854) being named as Lord Raglan's successor.[40]

Despite his youth, previous reform-oriented memoranda, and a reputation for having a solid grasp of the soldiers' needs, the Duke was by no means a progressive officer or a man ahead of his times. Although he was sensitive to the suffering of his men as evidenced by his correspondence, he was also a typical officer of the very highest social standing. To the French officers in the Crimea, who did not promote their officers by the purchase system and whose social backgrounds were more varied, the British appeared to be amateurs, which indeed they were quite deliberately. Some British officers brought their wives, while others even brought their private yachts and docked them in Calamita Bay. Virtually all British officers brought some luxury clothing to the theater. Yet even by those contemporary standards, Cambridge drew attention to himself by bringing so much personal baggage to the Crimea that it filled *seventeen* wagon carts.[41] Despite sad letters home about the privations he was suffering, it is clear it was far worse for others.

Apart from a brief artillery duel on September 17, the first hostile action occurred on September 20, 1854 and with it, Cambridge's first exposure to enemy fire. History would record the event as the Battle of the Alma. Although the Duke retained his courage, he seems to have been overwhelmed by the demands of command in battle, and his leadership suffered. The 1st Division had a supporting role in the assault across the Alma River and Cambridge did not distinguish himself–inexperience and excessive caution diminished his performance. Raglan had assigned Cambridge to support the advance of General Sir George Brown's 5th (Light) Division on the far left flank of the British frontal assault. Cambridge failed to move forward in support until Major General Airey, Raglan's controversial quartermaster general, urged him to press on the attack.[42] At one point, Cambridge even considered retreating, but was

---

40 RA QVJ: 21 August 1854; diary entry of Queen Victoria, dated August 21, 1854. Several months after this entry, Cathcart was killed at the Battle of Inkerman on November 5, 1854, making the possibility of his succession to command moot. Cathcart possessed a solid reputation as an officer, but Victoria did not support his possible replacement of Raglan because she believed that persons of high social rank should command: Cathcart simply did not have the sufficient social pedigree.

41 Judd, 29.

42 St. Aubyn, *The Royal George*, 69; Judd, 62-64.

prevented from doing so by one of his subordinates, Brigadier General Sir Colin Campbell, commander of the Highland Brigade.[43] Campbell was a highly experienced officer with an established reputation for bravery. His Highland Brigade consisted of three regiments with proud histories: the 79th Queen's Own Cameron Highlanders, the 93rd Argyll & Sutherland Highlanders, and the 42nd Royal Highland Regiment (The Black Watch).

During his initial foray into combat, Cambridge's mettle was tested, causing one of his subordinates to rebuke him calmly: "No Sir, British troops never do that, nor ever shall while I can prevent it."[44] First-hand accounts such as this are rare, but it is clear from ones such as these, Cambridge's own personal correspondence addressed below, and the glaring lack of specific accounts of the Duke in action that Cambridge was not decisive in combat. More accurately it can easily be inferred he was overwhelmed by confusion and fear to the point of inaction or worse. Without question, his first exposure to enemy fire saw him firmly fixed in place, unable to influence his command, and prevented from retreating from the battlefield only through the intervention of those he was charged with leading.

Overall, the two brigades of Cambridge's 1st Division–the Highland Brigade and the Guards Brigade[45]–demonstrated great bravery. They proved crucial to the successful assault across the Alma River and the seizure of the western high ground on its far bank. In the same manner as General Sir Colin Campbell, the commander of the Guards Brigade, Brigadier General Lord Bentinck, led his troops from the front and urged them forward against the Russians. Contemporary accounts and secondary reports of the Battle of the Alma are conspicuous in their lack of reporting on the Duke, apart from his indecision and reluctance to press forward.[46] It

43 Ian S. Hallows, *Regiments and Corps of the British Army* (London: New Orchard, 1991), 202.

44 Thomas Coleridge, *This for Remembrance* (London: Fisher Unwin, 1925), 89.

45 Like the Highland Brigade, the Guards Brigade contained three superb regiments: the Coldstream Guards, the Scottish Fusilier Guards and the Grenadier Guards. From Hallows, 162.

46 In the numerous works on the Crimean War, Cambridge is mentioned in passing as the commander of the 1st Division, if he is mentioned at all. A case in point is volume 13 of Fortescue's *History of the British Army*, arguably the most detailed history of the British army by a single author. This volume covers eighteen years of British military history, 1852-1870, and in 600 pages gives very detailed coverage of the Crimean War, yet it only mentions Cambridge in his capacity as a division commander seven times, and then only in passing. The reason is obvious: he did not play a significant role or distinguish himself. Other important works give him less coverage. Olive Anderson, *A Liberal State at War* (New York: St. Martin's Press, 1967), 36, mentions Cambridge only once, while Edward Hamley, *The War in the Crimea* (New York: Charles Scribner's Sons, 1891; reprinted, Westport, CT: Greenwood Press, 1971), 31, mentions him only once as well, as a division commander.

should not be inferred that Cambridge exhibited outright cowardice during his first exposure to hostile fire, but rather that the confusion and excitement clearly overwhelmed him to the point of inaction. Furthermore, it is telling that he, a royal duke, was mentioned in a less-than-complimentary manner in memoirs and official histories. Based upon what was to come, direct combat would not be what the Duke had expected. Even though he did not flee in the face of the enemy–he had his horse shot out from under him–he was not eager to get into the fight.

In a letter addressed to his aunt and mother, he gave an extensive account of the battle, but did not mention his own actions. His 1st Brigade fought heavily, but Cambridge was not directly involved. From his perspective, his division was on the left and in support of Sir George Browne's division. Browne's division assaulted against heavy opposition and Cambridge "went forward in the line to support," but was then exposed with his men to "a murderous fire of grape [shot]."[47] By Cambridge's own account, the fighting was heavy and his division "experienced a great loss!," suffering 400 men killed and wounded, "But by God's blessing both myself and my whole Staff have been miraculously spared," while Raglan's army as a whole lost 2,090 men and 112 officers killed and wounded.[48] It was fortunate indeed that neither Cambridge nor those in his immediate vicinity were wounded considering the casualties suffered in surrounding units. Either he and his staff were very lucky or they were out of harm's way.

Despite its relatively high cost, Britain's first battle against a European army since the Wars of Napoleon resulted in a clear victory: the Russians had been driven from strongly defended and well-sited positions. Even though the Duke's battlefield leadership was indecisive, he remained in place under fire and stayed near the front.[49] Although he had been outwardly calm, Cambridge confided in his diary, "The battlefield afterwards was an awful sight, and I shall never forget it to the last days of my life. Our escape was marvellous [*sic*], and I thank God for His gracious and merciful protection. When all was over, I could not help crying like

---

47 Letter from the Duke of Cambridge to the Duchess of Gloucester, dated September 22, 1854, reproduced in Sheppard, vol. 1, 133.

48 *Ibid.* The numbers of casualties cited at the time vary somewhat with later historical accounts of the battle. Unfortunately, as is the case with most battles, determining exact casualties is nearly impossible. The numbers cited here refer specifically to the Battle of the Alma and not the Crimean War as a whole.

49 Verner, vol. 1, 71.

a child...."[50] This striking revelation is interesting because it shows how deeply his exposure to enemy fire affected him. In a letter to Louisa dated September 22, Cambridge expressed similar sentiments: "Yesterday we spent in riding over the ground, collecting both Russian and English killed and wounded, and burying the dead. This was an awful sight and I shall never forget the horror of it as long as I live."[51] Real combat was far different from life at the garrison at Gibraltar, the Dublin district, or maneuvers at Chobham. Being a soldier no longer meant inspections, reviews, and handsome uniforms; instead it was experiencing sickness, disease, discomfort, suffering, and death.

Over the next several days Cambridge would witness many of his men wounded and dying, but his entry on the twentieth and letter of the twenty-second foretold his avoidance of combat–he could not bear to see his own men die. The Alma had been a severe fight and was the Duke's first exposure to such suffering at close hand. In one memorable incident, the Duke met a vanquished Russian general on the far bank of the Alma; the dying Russian officer requested to meet the commanding general who had defeated him and the Duke's soldiers summoned Cambridge, who came right away. Upon seeing the Duke, the Russian exclaimed, "*Mais je veux voir le Général, pas ce jeune homme-ci.*" Cambridge replied, "*Mais c'est moi, Monsieur,*" and the two men embraced and shook hands. The Russian general, who had had both legs shot off, died in his arms.[52] Such a scene would have undoubtedly made a strong impression on anyone, and there can be little doubt that it affected Cambridge very deeply.

IV

After his first taste of combat, the Duke of Cambridge had lost all desire to see any more of it. Barely three weeks into the fight, he was already looking for a way to get back to England. In a letter to Louisa dated October 12, 1854, he intimated he planned to get home virtually any way possible. Under the assumption that Sebastopol would soon fall, he wrote, "My darling, I cannot tell you how miserable I feel and how I long for the end of this dreadful campaign, for I am thoroughly worn

---

50 Diary of the Duke of Cambridge, reproduced in Verner, vol. 1, 73.

51 St. Aubyn, *The Royal George,* 72.

52 Sheppard, vol. 1, 134. The translation is, "But I do not see the general, only this young man." Cambridge replies, "It is I, sir."

out with fatigue and so are we all, and the misfortune is that we see little or no progress made...."[53] He also railed against the idea of the British maintaining a presence there much longer, explaining in rather shockingly selfish language that, "...I for one shall do *my utmost to get home* and think it cannot well be refused me...either with the army if we are all to go, or by myself, if the rest must remain...."[54] Although intended only for his wife, the letter is an indictment against the Duke of Cambridge. Such sentiments from a division commander are nothing short of shocking. Expectations of an 1850s British commander to care for subordinates were obviously less extensive than a modern equivalent, but Cambridge still had a profound duty to lead by example, especially when it came to bravery. It is therefore astonishing that after his division had been in action for only one month, he was prepared to abandon his men regardless of future operations, including the very real possibility of a bloody assault at Sebastopol. While compassion was not expected of him, a great willingness to face the enemy certainly was. Furthermore, Cambridge was directly tied by blood and rank to the monarchy and kingdom. No matter how angry he may have been with the government, he was more than just a division commander and senior army officer–he was a royal duke and therefore a very real representative of his country and its reputation. Limited action against the enemy had quickly undermined his commitment to very serious obligations. Regardless of his intentions, however, Cambridge would see battle once more.

As noted above, Queen Victoria followed the actions in the Crimea with great interest and continued to be horrified at the great loss of life. With substantial enthusiasm, she passed the details of the Alma to her uncle, King Leopold: "We have received all the most interesting and gratifying details of the splendid and decisive victory of the Alma; alas! it was a bloody one. Our loss was a heavy one–many have fallen and many are wounded, but my noble Troops behaved with a courage which was beautiful to behold."[55] Interested as always in the welfare of Cambridge, she commented, "George did enormously well and was not touched."[56] It is

53 Letter from the Duke of Cambridge to Louisa, dated October 12, 1854, reproduced in St. Aubyn, *The Royal George,* 76.
54 *Ibid.*
55 Letter from Queen Victoria to Leopold, King of Belgium, dated October 13, 1854, reproduced in Benson and Esher, eds., *The Letters of Queen Victoria,* 1st ser., vol. 3, 63-4.
56 Letter from Queen Victoria to Leopold, King of Belgium, dated October 13, 1854, reproduced in Hibbert, 126. The Queen was not the only one to exaggerate the effectiveness and the performance of

significant that aside from the Commander-in-Chief, Lord Raglan, whom she compared favorably with the Duke of Wellington, the only individual whom the Queen mentioned by name was Cambridge despite his marked lack of action in actual battle.

The next major action was at Balaclava on October 25, 1854, a scene of great stupidity and courage forever immortalized in Alfred (Lord) Tennyson's poem describing the charge of the Light Brigade under the command of Lord Cardigan.[57] In early October, Cambridge and his two brigades had relocated to the south and were positioned on the heights overlooking the great fortress of Sebastopol, the main objective of the expedition. Cambridge had argued to Raglan that the attack should have pressed forward immediately after the victory at the Alma, and Raglan felt similarly. The French, however, under St. Arnaud, were reluctant to move quickly, and Lord Raglan's penchant for politeness made the French believe he was in agreement with their position. In consequence, what could have been a quick and relatively painless victory instead turned into a costly quagmire for the allies. Cambridge was well aware of the misery his troops and observed in his diary on October 3, "I regret to say that cholera is again visiting us very severely, and is thinning our ranks sadly....Winter quarters at this advanced season are most desirable, and, therefore, the sooner we complete our work, the better for us all."[58]

A lengthy siege of the fortress at Sebastopol set in and the battles at Balaclava and Inkerman took place against the backdrop of the besieged fortress. The charge of the Light Brigade produced a stunning display of bravery at the expense of intelligence, but Cambridge did not take part in the battle at Balaclava–on October 25 the 1st Division was in a supporting role. His last experience in battle would be at Inkerman Ridge during the first week of November 1854, when the Russians, aware of the weakened condition of the British, launched a counterattack to dislodge them from their positions. Early on Sunday, November 5, in a fine drizzle and dense fog, the Russians attacked, and the battle quickly devolved into a number of small unit actions in which the British were caught off guard. Close to defeat, Lord Raglan asked the French for assistance at the last minute. Their help proved essential, and of the 40,000 Russian troops that

---

the Duke in battle–his wife, mother and son all did as well. Cambridge's son, George, attributed the entire victory to the efforts of his father.

57 Cecil Woodham-Smith's *The Reason Why*, *op. cit.* remains a very readable and entertaining account.
58 Diary entry of the Duke of Cambridge, dated October 3, 1854, reproduced in Sheppard, vol. 1, 135.

launched the attack, over one-fourth were killed, wounded, or captured against British losses of 597 men killed with 1,860 wounded.[59] The French losses were significantly less.[60] Despite not being a defeat, Inkerman was hardly the victory that the London press portrayed it to be. British losses were high–including the loss of thirty-nine battle-hardened officers–and more importantly, Sebastopol was still firmly in Russian hands. At most the battle was a Pyrrhic victory, leading the British Foreign Secretary, Lord Clarendon, to wonder whether the army could sustain another such "triumph."[61]

For the Duke of Cambridge, the events on Inkerman Ridge broke him and he would never again return to the field of battle. The fighting was fearful and it took what little enthusiasm he still had left for combat. That evening, Cambridge remembered it as "a most dreadful and fearful day, and one that I shall never forget as long as I live."[62] He recounted how the enemy had somehow positioned guns in front of the 2nd Division where the pickets should have been. Enemy fire was intense and at the request of the commander of the 2nd Division, General Sir John Pennefather, the Duke positioned his men to the right of Pennefather's 2nd Brigade.[63] Cambridge recorded "murderous fire" and how his, "poor dear old horse 'Wide Awake' [was] shot in the leg and [I] had to get on the horse of my orderly. Soon after a ball passed through the sleeves of my two coats and shirt, but most providentially merely grazed my hand, inflicting a severe blow without breaking the skin." [64]

Thus far the Duke had done well. In the face of serious enemy resistance he pushed forward, despite losing his horse and also being grazed himself. In the confusion of battle, he issued commands and directed his subordinate units in a capable manner. Soon afterward, though, Cambridge lost control and the situation devolved into chaos. In a lengthy passage in his journal partly reproduced below, he presents a less-than-flattering account of his performance as a division commander:

---

59 Judd, 108.

60 Ibid.

61 Letter from Lord Clarendon to the British Ambassador in Paris, date not listed, reproduced in Ibid., 111.

62 Diary entry of the Duke of Cambridge, dated November 5, 1854, reproduced in Verner, vol. 1, 78.

63 Pennefather replaced General Sir De Lacy Evans in command of the 2nd Division due to illness that day. Ordinarily he commanded the 2nd Brigade.

64 Diary entry of the Duke of Cambridge, dated November 5, 1854, reproduced in Verner, vol. 1, 78.

I then rode back to see whether I could not bring up some more troops, and found Sir George Cathcart just come up with his Division. I rode up to him and begged him to support me on the left, but, poor man, he would not listen to me, but persisted in sending his men down to the right into the Inkermann [*sic*] Valley. This was a most fatal error and cost us most dearly. Hurrying forward, the 4th Division rushed down the hill right into the valley below, carrying along with them many of my fine Guardsmen, who could not be restrained in their ardour. I saw the danger of our position and rode about to look for other troops when I met the 20th and 95th, and my picquets coming off duty, all of which I pushed forward to the left of our battery, as I heard that large masses of Russians were coming up. Seeing Lord Raglan at a short distance, I hurried to inform him that unless he supported us we must be cut to pieces. He desired me to try and get the men back. I rode back to the battery and found this was out of the question, as the men had gone so far down the valley, owing to poor Cathcart's fatal error. On trying to get back myself I found the Russians crowning the hill between us and the 2nd Division and regularly taking us in the flank. I had no troops in hand, and Macdonald and myself being quite alone and having got between the fire of the enemy and our own people, had regularly to ride for it in order to get back. Providentially we were unhurt, though Jem's horse was shot. On getting to the rear I found no men, but Assistant-Surgeon Wilson of the 7th Hussars collected a few stragglers, and these kept the Russians off till General Adams was enabled to come up with some of his men and drive them off the plateau. Four successive charges were made by the enemy, but they were all driven back

> when the French most providentially came up to
> our assistance.[65]

What is remarkable is the extent to which, by his own admission, he lost control of his men and was unable to rally peers or superiors to his assistance. Attempts for assistance from fellow officers or his superiors were ignored and, worse still, his own troops "in their ardour" also ignored him. Either he did not try hard enough or others simply discounted him. Neither is complimentary for a division commander in combat. Disarray had befallen his division, to the point that Cambridge was caught in the middle of fire between his own soldiers and the enemy. When it was all over, he had found no one to command but the assistant-surgeon and "a few stragglers." Strength of personality is an essential indicator of a commander's effectiveness and in this instance he failed. Faced with a very difficult situation, he did not master it.

Fortunately for Cambridge's sake, the men of his division had held their own. The soldiers of the 1ˢᵗ Division had performed very well, despite the absence of an effective division commander, and he acknowledged this. He expressed further bewilderment at his good fortune to be but one of three of the eleven general officers who went into battle and emerged unscathed. After recording the names of the fallen, he commented on the misery of the situation: "The troops returned to quarters about three, and we went over the field of battle to behold a field of blood and destruction and misery, which nothing in this world can surpass."[66] His final line that evening was a harbinger of what was to come: "After dinner I had to ride to Lord Raglan to consult with him, and on my return I was so overpowered by all I had gone through, that I felt perfectly broken down."[67] He could take no more.

In a letter to his mother and his aunt, the Duchess of Gloucester, dated November 8, written while aboard the HMS *Caradoc*, Cambridge described the battle and his actions during it. Although his division was still very much ashore, Cambridge wrote from the comfort and safety of the ship. Without elaborating, he strongly intimates he has had enough. "I myself am so completely worn out that I have been advised to go on board ship for a few days for change of air, and they even want me to

---

65 *Ibid.*, 78-79.
66 *Ibid.*, 80.
67 I*bid.*

go to Constantinople."[68] The Duke's personal physician, Dr. Gibson, recommended rest although the actual medical prognosis was unclear. In his diary entry for November 7, Cambridge stated he was "unwell," whereas in a letter to the Countess of Westmoreland he reported having been "very ill with dysentery and typhoid fever"; in yet another letter, to Queen Victoria, he referred to his illness as "fever."[69] Later accounts in the *London Illustrated News* would simply refer to his illness as "a case of the nerves" and report occasionally on the recovery of the Duke of Cambridge's "shattered health."[70] A conservative and expensive publication supportive of the monarchy, the paper apparently did not intend to disparage the reputation of the Duke and presented his illness as delicately as possible. Other contemporary correspondence used similar language. In a letter to Cambridge dated January 19, 1855, Victoria informed him that many had returned from the Crimea with "sadly shaken nerves."[71] In a letter to Louisa dated January 7, 1855, Cambridge explained that his "whole nervous system has had a great shake from continued anxiety."[72]

Regardless of the nature of his illness, Lord Raglan granted permission for the Duke to seek refuge on board HMS *Caradoc* after dinner on November 7. The following day he moved to a larger vessel, the HMS *Retribution*, where he wrote a short note to the ranking officer left in his division, Brigadier General Reynardson, who had succeeded Bentinck in command of the Guards Regiment after Bentinck had been wounded. The tone of Cambridge's letter made it clear he did not expect to return any time soon, although he did not give General Reynardson much guidance. He explained, "Lord Raglan has given me leave to go to Constantinople…for the recovery of my health…I must request you in my name to assemble the Three Battalions and to assure…I am personally most grateful."[73] No record exists as to whether General Reynardson passed along the Duke's message to the men of his brigade, although it is

---

68 Letter from the Duke of Cambridge to the Duchess of Cambridge, dated November 8, 1854, reproduced in Sheppard, vol. 1, 139.

69 Diary of the Duke of Cambridge, reproduce in Verner, vol. 1, 80; St. Aubyn, *The Royal George*, 81; RA QVJ 30 December 1854.

70 The *London Illustrated News*, January 13, 1855 and January 20, 1855, respectively.

71 RA VIC/G22/59, Letter from Queen Victoria to the Duke of Cambridge, dated January 19, 1855.

72 Letter from the Duke of Cambridge to Louisa, dated January 7, 1855, reproduced in St. Aubyn, *The Royal George*, 86.

73 Letter from the Duke of Cambridge to General Reynardson, dated November 8, 1854, reproduced in Verner, vol. 1, 81.

interesting to contemplate how they would have received it in light of their situation outside Sebastopol.

That aside, there is some evidence that the genuine concern Cambridge felt for his troops was known throughout the ranks. A noncommissioned officer in the 1st Division and a veteran of the Battle of Inkerman, Sergeant Morris of the 63rd Regiment, said of Cambridge, "No officer was more truly beloved...than was the Duke, from his constant attention to their welfare, his identity with them in their dangers and sufferings, and his ready acquiesce in anything likely to add to their comforts, or... welfare."[74] One of the most famous veterans of the Crimean War, Florence Nightingale, later recounted an experience she had shared with Cambridge on December 29, 1854, that demonstrated his compassion for his men. She remembered an incident where together they toured Scutari Hospital and Cambridge recognized a sergeant who, according to Nightingale, had had at least one-third of his body blown off. Cambridge addressed the man by his Christian name and surname and lightheartedly asked, "Aren't you dead yet?"[75] The incident brought tears to the eyes of the wounded soldier. To modern readers such an incident might not appear compassionate, but with the dry understatement common to British soldiers of the era, Cambridge's humor and compassion were exceptional.

Later in his career, the Duke would acquire the moniker of the "soldier's friend," and incidents such as these earned it. He cared for his men in a manner atypical for the standards of the day. On the other hand, his subsequent avoidance of further combat was also not expected behavior. In fairness to Cambridge, other senior officers behaved in less-than-exemplary manners. It is worth remembering that Lord Cardigan had brought his private yacht to the Black Sea and Lord George Paget, a dashing cavalry officer, left his regiment to retire for the winter of 1854-5 with his bride.[76] But for all of his faults and eccentricities, there was no doubt as to Cardigan's bravery, proved repeatedly in battle, most famously at Balaclava. Furthermore, Paget left with Lord Raglan's permission and returned to the campaign once he learned of the displeasure of the Queen. No record exists of a high ranking officer in the British army leaving the Crimean War quite the way Cambridge did.

---

74 Passage from Sergeant Morris, *The Three Sergeants*, 1858, reproduced in *ibid.*, 83.
75 Edward T. Cook, *The Life of Florence Nightingale*, vol. 1 (London: Macmillan and Co., Ltd., 1914), 384-385.
76 Judd, 120; St. Aubyn, *The Royal George,* 80.

Perhaps more troubling than Cambridge's actual departure from his command was the possibility that Cambridge had been planning to get to Constantinople and ultimately home to England for some time. His letter to Louisa dated October 12 was quite explicit: he aimed to get home as soon as possible, even if it meant coming home before his men.[77] In a letter to General Reynardson, dated November 8, Cambridge makes it clear that Lord Raglan has already granted him "leave to go to Constantinople," although Raglan did not actually grant him leave until he had been aboard the HMS *Retribution* for several days.[78] It is also significant he withheld news of his "illness" from the Queen as long as he did. When the Queen was writing congratulatory letters to Cambridge, he had already left the campaign. Even though the action at Inkerman on November 5, 1854, was an evening he would never forget, one that left him broken, he was ready to leave before that battle even occurred based upon his correspondence with Louisa. Cambridge had neither the stamina to endure a sustained deployment to a desolate area nor the capacity to withstand seeing his own men get killed. These were hardly promising traits for a division commander, a general officer, and a prince of the royal blood.

Previously, Cambridge had not been hesitant to be frank with his cousin. In a letter dated November 2, he bluntly informed the Queen of the desperateness of the situation and his own misgivings about certain aspects of the campaign against Sebastopol. He wrote, "this operation has, alas! proved itself so far more protracted and difficult than we first anticipated."[79] He thanked the Queen for the letters of congratulation he had received from her and Albert regarding the Battle of the Alma, and observed that although he was indeed grateful for his personal safety and that victory was "heart-stirring." He realized that "War, however, is a fearful scene, and I assure you the scenes we had afterwards and which we have seen since witnessed have given me the greatest horror of it."[80] In this detailed letter, he pointed out the disturbing scenes he had witnessed, but gave no indication he was ready to quit. Only several weeks later did the Queen learn the Duke had succumbed to an illness. In the meantime, the

---

77 See note 67 above.

78 Sheppard, vol. 1, 147.

79 Letter from the Duke of Cambridge to Queen Victoria, dated November 2, 1854, reproduced in *ibid.*, 143-145.

80 Letter from the Duke of Cambridge to Queen Victoria, dated November 2, 1854, reproduced in *ibid.*, 143.

letters of congratulation and approval for the conduct of the 1st Division at Inkerman continued to arrive for Cambridge as he sought relief from his bout of "ague" aboard the HMS *Retribution* in the harbor at Balaclava.[81]

The Duke of Newcastle, Secretary of State for War and Colonies, wrote a letter of congratulation to the Duchess of Cambridge, the Duke's mother, on November 22, 1854, in which he informed her of her son's "honourable mention…in Lord Raglan's Despatch," but he also mentioned that Raglan had "advised the Duke of Cambridge to go down to Constantinople for a few days to recruit his strength, which has somewhat suffered from the anxieties of the Siege, the exposure to a tent life, and the want of rest."[82] In her journal entry for November 28, 1854, Queen Victoria recorded receiving a note that was passed to her, "a very interesting letter from George, written on board the 'Caradoc' in very low spirits. He was immensely exposed…This shows how much George was personally exposed, & how great his anxiety must have been for the Guards, who were so constantly cut off & divided."[83]

Regardless of the expectations of others, Cambridge ultimately received permission from Lord Raglan to head for Constantinople, and he set sail on November 25. His condition did not improve, however, and he wrote Raglan after three weeks in Constantinople for home leave. The basis was, "as I could not in my present state of health face a winter Campaign in the Crimea."[84] Fearing the public reception of such a request, Raglan asked that Cambridge seek the recommendation of a medical board. Naturally he did and recorded the result with obvious satisfaction in his diary, "I had my medical board to-day who agreed with Gibson [the Duke's personal physician] in thinking that I ought to go home for the present, so I shall now be off as soon as I can. I am glad it is at length settled, for the doubt and uncertainty were most distressing to me."[85] Official biographers and

---

81 Whatever the extent of his illness, the Duke genuinely feared for his life on November 14, 1854 when a great gale struck the Black Sea with such force that the ships rudder was torn off and the vessel came very close to being smashed against the rocks lining the harbor. In all, 21 allied vessels were completely destroyed and eight others were seriously damaged. The impact on the already seriously flawed logistical situation was severe.

82 Letter from the Duke of Newcastle to the Duchess of Cambridge, dated November 22, 1854, reproduced in Sheppard, vol. 1, 145-146.

83 RA QVJ: 28 November 1854, journal entry of Queen Victoria, dated November 28, 1854.

84 Letter from the Duke of Cambridge to Lord Raglan, dated November 25, 1854, reproduced in Sheppard, vol. 1, 147.

85 Diary entry of the Duke of Cambridge, dated December 27, 1854, reproduced in *Ibid.*, 147-148.

published accounts of his diary do not cite the exact nature of his illness.[86]

As had been the case from the beginning, Queen Victoria followed the war and Cambridge's actions very closely. She corresponded frequently with those in the theater and received many letters which described the horrors of the campaign, as well as eyewitness accounts of Cambridge's behavior. One letter, from Prince Edward of Saxe-Weimar, presented a picture of her cousin which disappointed her. Writing from the camp before Sebastopol, Prince Edward wrote a lengthy and detailed letter–ten pages–describing the battle of Inkerman, his displeasure with the Turks, and the great storm of November 14. He also described how the Duke was in much better health, despite the storm, and that he was now on his way to Constantinople. Especially troubling for Edward, but quite telling in terms of the Duke's actual fitness as a military officer, was the fact that "plenty of ill natured people who make remarks about his going, altho' I firmly believe it was necessary for his health, but he was indiscret [*sic*] in not disguising his joy at going away...has certainly not shown the talents of a general, which had been expected of him."[87] Prince Edward's sentiments make it clear that to some of his contemporaries Cambridge's actions in combat were questionable. He showed poor ability as a general, and, more damning, he did not live up to the expectation of brave conduct under fire. If Prince Edward wrote these sentiments so frankly to the Queen, it is a fair presumption that there were others who would have held similar attitudes. It would be difficult indeed to recover one's reputation if such charges were left unanswered.

The Duke's sudden illness and departure from the area obviously did not please the Queen. Fully aware of the public relations aspect of his conduct, Victoria wrote to her cousin from Windsor Castle on December 15, 1854:

> My Dear George,
> I hope you will be back in the Crimea by this time.
> Forgive my telling you frankly that I hope you will
> not let your low spirits and despondent feelings be

---

86 Terms used are "unwell," or "physical weakness." Verner, vol. 1, 85 simply states "On 27 December, as he was still unfit to return to duty, a Medical Board examined him, and he was ordered to go home on sick leave."

87 RA VIC/G20/29, Letter from Prince Edward of Saxe-Weimar to Queen Victoria, dated November 28, 1854. Prince Edward goes on to say that he regrets having to say such unkind things about the Duke because he was "always a kind friend" to him.

known to others; you cannot think how ill natured people are here and I can assure you that the clubs have not been slow in circulating the most shameful lies about you. It is for this reason that I as your true friend and affectionate cousin, wish to caution you for the future—not to let your (very natural) feelings be known and observed by others. To your own relations of course this is another thing.[88]

Here was Victoria, as Queen, cousin, and even "true friend" telling Cambridge, for the sake of his reputation—and ostensibly for the good of the royal family and the country—to return to action before it was too late. This was pressure of the first order.

Although Cambridge received the Queen's letter on January 1, 1855, it did not deter him from following the advice of the medical board. That evening he observed, "Letters from England to the 15th all strongly urging me to go back and not to come home...At last decided...to go to Malta and wait there, at all events for a time, to let matters pass on a little and see what might turn up."[89] The same day, Queen Victoria wrote to Lord Raglan, Commander-in-Chief in the Crimea, expressing her concern over the constant sickness and poor quality of the provisions being provided to her soldiers. She was also, "much grieved to hear that the Duke of Cambridge has asked for <u>sick leave</u> and means to come home; she fears the effect of his leaving his division at the moment, when the siege seems really to be drawing to a close...."[90] The previous night Victoria had recorded a similar sentiment, "A letter from George, saying that as he could not shake off the fever, & the Dr. said he was not fit for a winter campaign, he had asked Ld Raglan to come home on sick leave! We were horrified as I am sure this will have the very worst effect!"[91]

It is in no way insignificant that Cambridge failed the test, the one test that mattered above all others for a British officer. More important— and more damning—than reservations about his ability to command was his awkward departure from the field of battle well before the war was over, when he was physically unharmed. British officers were not

---

88 RA VIC/G20/128, letter from Queen Victoria to the Duke of Cambridge, dated December 15, 1854.
89 Diary entry of the Duke of Cambridge, dated January 1, 1855, reproduced in Sheppard, vol. 1, 152.
90 RA VIC/G21/65, letter from Queen Victoria to Lord Raglan, dated January 1, 1855.
91 RA QVJ: 30 December 1854, journal entry of Queen Victoria, dated December 30, 1854.

required or even expected to possess tactical or operational competence or great intelligence. Neither were they expected to possess enlightened leadership, as countless officers who went on to achieve glory and fame often possessed none.[92] The one nonnegotiable factor was bravery in battle. British soldiers and noncommissioned officers did not expect their officers to be expert tacticians or even to share their hardships with them. The British public did not expect them to be educated or even above average in intelligence. The very system of selection and promotion by Purchase and the absence of an officer education system demonstrated the army was not a professional organization. The one unacceptable shortcoming, however, was cowardice. What Wellington and the great military heroes from Britain's past possessed above all else was calmness under fire. In fact, it was the norm for British army officers to be brave, often to the point of foolhardiness.

Although it is perhaps an overstatement to accuse the Duke of Cambridge of cowardice in the face of the enemy, he definitely did not display sustained bravery. All accounts of his life report that he commanded a division in the Crimea and fought with his soldiers at the battles of the Alma and Inkerman. Documentation is noticeably lacking, however, as to what illness pulled him from the battlefield, never to return. With that in mind, it is not just merely the continued professional success of the Duke, which by itself would be rather astonishing, but the fact that within two years of his failure in the face of the enemy he went on to serve for the next *thirty-nine* years as the highest ranking officer in the British army. Against the advice of the Queen and the almost certain derision of his fellow officers, Cambridge left the battlefield while his own men were fighting and dying. It would be hard for any officer to recover from such a situation. Clearly, the Duke's royal birth and relationship with his first cousin, the Queen, were crucial to his future fortune. The Duke's first and only combat experience could, with great charity, be described as unremarkable–his conduct in the wake of it was nothing short of failure. Obviously, Queen Victoria recognized this as well. It would take a serious turn of events for her to accept the return of the Duke, let alone his restoration to a position of prominence in the army–yet that is precisely what happened in a remarkably short period of time.

92 James Thomas Brudenell, 7th Earl of Cardigan, commander of the famed Light Brigade at Balaclava, comes to mind as an example of one who lacked both, and the Duke of Wellington, who viewed his troops as "scum" might fit into the latter category.

CHAPTER 4:
Royal Seclusion and Renewal 1855-1856

While crisis rocked the Aberdeen Ministry in London early in the new year of 1855, the Duke of Cambridge penned frequent letters to his mother entreating her to pave the way for him to return to England. He was prepared to do almost anything to avoid combat and deprivation once again. His typical refrain was that a return to England would allow him the rest he needed and deserved, but his name and honorable reputation prevented him from coming home. Despite the many expressions of good will he had received, he could only find fault with others. A frank letter to his mother dated January 7, 1855 reflected his general attitude during this time. Cambridge wrote that Lord Raglan was "an upright and honourable man," but that "as a general he is a <u>nonentity</u>..."[1] This was strong criticism coming from a man whose own actions as a general officer in combat were rather dreadful.

Although Cambridge complained he had suffered "Sleepless nights, hard, continuous work, [which] all so exhausted my nerves that if I had stayed any longer I should have had a nervous fever," the Queen would not grant him what hundreds of other officers and soldiers were receiving."[2] In a petulant tone he wrote, "They have all gone home, but I mustn't go because I am the Duke of Cambridge and as such I must personally make good the mistakes of Albert and the Government."[3] It was rather curious that the Duke of Cambridge lashed out at Prince Albert; throughout the campaign Albert's correspondence to Cambridge had always been flattering. On November 29, 1854, Albert had written to express his "rejoicing that you have come through the awful day of the 5th [Inkerman] so happily and with so great reputation and honour, and to add from my heart I envy you."[4] This was a compliment indeed for the Prince Consort to admit he envied the reputation of Cambridge. In the days that followed, Cambridge continued to criticize others, but not himself.

Diary entries and correspondence from late December and early January reveal the Duke was deeply despondent and almost frantic to get home no matter the cost to his reputation or the weight of the opinions

---

1 RA VIC/G18/119, Letter from the Duke of Cambridge to the Duchess of Cambridge, dated January 7, 1855.
2 *Ibid.*
3 *Ibid.*
4 Letter from Prince Albert to the Duke of Cambridge, dated November 29th [1854], reproduced in Sheppard, vol. 1 152.

of others. His diary entry from the start of the new year states, "Thus commences another year. Alas! its commencement is anything but cheerful!... [I resolve] to go to Malta and wait there, at all events for a time, to let matters pass on a little and see what might turn up."[5] Although ambiguous to an outside reader, it soon became clear what he meant by "might turn up." In letters to his wife and mother, the Duke admitted that he was torn between his duty as an officer on the one hand and his physical and mental exhaustion on the other, although the latter force ultimately prevailed. A letter to Louisa from New Year's Day 1855 revealed, "Now love, I have received a host of letters praying me on no account to think of coming home, that I confess I have been staggered..."[6]

Cambridge also made it clear he was aware of "the shameful lies that have been circulated about me," yet, in the end, he told her "in the strictest confidence what I have decided to do....I will go to Malta."[7] The Queen and the Duke's mother continued to write him, urging him to return to action but unaware he had already made up his mind. Cambridge clearly got the message and felt the pressure, yet despite "Letters from England to the 15th all strongly urging me to go back and not to come home,"[8] Cambridge opted for rest and recovery. On January 2, Prince Napoleon escorted him as he boarded the *Tamar*.[9] He set sail for Malta on January 3, 1855 and arrived there early three days later, where he remained for several weeks, ostensibly with the purpose of preparing to return to the Crimea.[10]

Well aware that his peers expected him to return to action, and fully conscious that "shameful lies" were being circulated, Cambridge remained determined to get as far away from the Crimea as possible. He was willing to sacrifice his reputation and his career, and for a time he did just that. Whether he could somehow rise above his recent failure and once again have "great responsibility thrust upon him," as Wellington had anticipated, did not appear at all likely in early 1855.

5 Diary entry of the Duke of Cambridge, dated January 1, 1855, reproduced in Sheppard, vol. 1, 152.
6 Letter from the Duke of Cambridge to Louisa, dated January 1, 1855, reproduced in St. Aubyn, *The Royal George*, 86.
7 *Ibid.*
8 Diary entry of the Duke of Cambridge, dated January 1, 1855, reproduced in Sheppard, vol. 1, 152.
9 *Ibid.*, 153.
10 In fairness to the Duke, there were other senior officers who had "completely broken down." Most notably, Sir de Lacy Evans, commander of the 2nd Division had already returned to England by this point, but he was almost 70 and this was his fourth war–he had a distinguished record in combat dating to the War of 1812.

I

Despite her initial reservations concerning the return of her royal cousin, Victoria did change her mind by the end of January–an astonishing change. Whereas previously she saw the need to set the example and prevent cruel talk in the clubs, she eventually relented and permitted his return. It was probably a combination of Victoria's concern over the crisis with the Aberdeen ministry as well as the quiet urging of the Duchess of Cambridge on behalf of her son.[11] Like Queen Victoria, the Duchess had initially held strong objections to her son's return. The letter cited above from the Duke dated January 7, 1855 may have done a great deal to change his mother's mind.[12] In it he complained of his suffering and closed by writing, "I must ask you, dearest Mama, to stand by me with the Queen."[13]

Although the press in London reported the condition of the Duke–the royal family was a regular feature–there was no intimation that his departure from the Crimean theater and absence from command were anything other than a physical ailment. An article from *The London Illustrated News* from January 6, 1855 is typical, describing "a favorable account of the health" and noting he was "most anxious to rejoin his division, but his medical attendants insist on his not quitting for the Crimea until his health shall be completely restored. It was thought his Royal Highness would leave towards the close of December."[14]

While the influence of the Duchess of Cambridge on Queen Victoria is difficult to know with certainty, it is a fact that the Queen was interested in the ongoing crisis of the Aberdeen ministry. Queen Victoria's diary entries and her personal correspondence reveal great concern over Lord Aberdeen's ministry and the conduct of operations in the Crimea, especially regarding the suffering of the British soldier. Previous reservations regarding her cousin were pushed to the background, and apart from those diary entries and correspondence cited previously, no additional evidence

---

11 The specifics of the fall of the Aberdeen ministry will be addressed in detail below in Part II. Lord Aberdeen's coalition oversaw the entry of Great Britain into the Crimean War in October 1853. Harsh inquiries by the House of Commons over the government's mismanagement of the war brought ended to Aberdeen's ministry on January 29, 1855.

12 St. Aubyn, *The Royal George*, 88, states that this was "The letter which finally overcame the Duchess' resistance…." He offers no evidence to support his assertion.

13 St. Aubyn, *The Royal George*, 88-89.

14 *The Illustrated London News*, January 6, 1855. The placement of the notice near the end of the paper was probably intentional.

of her thoughts regarding the Duke exists for the month of January.[15] In a matter of weeks, if not days, her feelings changed from outright opposition to resignation that there was no way to prevent the Duke's return.

Lord Palmerston (Henry John Temple, 3rd Viscount Palmerston [1784-1865]), formerly the Foreign Secretary and the Home Secretary and very shortly to be the Prime Minister, informed Victoria of Cambridge's return to Dover on January 30 in a letter that same day. Whether it was the Duchess of Cambridge coupled with the far more pressing distraction of the ongoing political crisis or the Duke's repeated requests to come home, in the end Victoria did give in. It was likely a combination of the above genuine sympathy that brought about a change of heart from the Queen regarding the return of the Duke. Writing from Windsor Castle on January 19, 1855, she reassured him on account of his "broken health" to set his mind at ease about the return home.[16] This was quite a reversal from the Queen's previous position regarding duty and appearances when she was more concerned with the indignity of a royal duke returning home while his division was still fighting. Perhaps another reason for the change was that other prominent officers, such as Cardigan, had fared poorly in the Crimea, but their reputations remained unscathed. Despite his shortcomings as a commander and a leader, Cardigan had returned to England a popular hero.[17] All in all, she might have reasoned that Cambridge's condition might be similar to that of the others who had experienced the great hardships of the Crimea. Besides, it might be better to treat him as a returning hero, regardless of the degree of heroism he actually displayed, and thus all of the rumors and cruel talk would disappear. No matter how his return was to be portrayed, however, the Queen advised caution.[18] Nonetheless, this was still a remarkable reversal and in striking contrast to a letter to Lord Raglan, Cambridge's commanding officer and the commander of the British expedition, scarcely two weeks before her softened outlook. On New Year's Day, Victoria expressed shock and concern over the Duke's action, "much grieved to hear that the Duke of Cambridge has asked for

---

15 For a detailed account of the correspondence to and from the Queen regarding the fall of the Aberdeen ministry see Benson and Esher, eds., *The Letters of Queen Victoria*, 1st ser., vol. 3, 82-105.
16 RA VIC/G22/59, Letter from Queen Victoria to the Duke of Cambridge, dated January 19, 1855.
17 Ironically, Lord Cardigan would assume Cambridge's former position as Inspector-General of Cavalry.
18 RA VIC/G22/59, Letter from Queen Victoria to the Duke of Cambridge, dated January 19, 1855.

sick leave…she still much hopes that he may remain at Malta, whence he could return quickly to his post."[19]

Despite severe criticism he would later receive as Commander-in-Chief, Cambridge's reputation seemed to have survived his abysmal performance in the Crimea. There was no public questioning of his reputation until three decades later by a ruthless critic and eventual successor, Viscount Garnet Wolseley (1833-1913). He would savage Cambridge's character and ability in a private letter to his wife: "I am heavily handicapped in having to contend not only against ordinary prejudice and obstruction, but to overcome those difficulties presented to me in the form a fat, clever, royalty….a man of the most <u>timid</u> nature…."[20] In the same letter, Wolseley further impugned his reputation, quoting Lord Airey as having said that Cambridge was "quite as great a coward morally as he is physically."[21] Several weeks previously, Wolseley had implicitly questioned the courage of the Duke when he wondered whether the Duke's son, Augustus FitzGeorge, could face enemy fire as "the father could not."[22] Such opinions, though damning, are not necessarily an accurate reflection of general attitudes because Wolseley had a very sharp tongue, strongly disliked Cambridge, and was writing to his wife in confidence. However, these letters demonstrate that Cambridge's reputation over the long term might not have survived completely untarnished in private circles, despite appearing solid in public.

Whatever fellow officers may have thought of Cambridge, negative attitudes did not make it to the newspapers and the press did not hint at anything other than sympathy, concern, and respect. A half-page etching in the January 13, 1855 edition of *The Illustrated London News* depicted the visit of the Turkish Sultan to the residence of the Duke of Cambridge in Constantinople on December 24, 1854.[23] The accompanying article portrayed the visit as an extremely favorable event, almost as if he was

---

19 RA VIC/G21/65, Letter from Queen Victoria to Lord Raglan, dated January 1, 1855.

20 Letter from Viscount Wolseley to his wife, dated November 10, 1884, reproduced in St. Aubyn, *The Royal George*, 91-92.

21 *Ibid.*, 92.

22 Letter from Viscount Wolseley to his wife, dated September 26, 1884, reproduced in St. Aubyn, *The Royal George*, 91-92

23 At a shilling per copy *The Illustrated London News* was not exactly the popular press due to its price, but inexpensive illustrated weeklies did not exist. Accordingly, most detailed coverage of royal ceremony was enjoyed by a rather select group rather than the nation as a whole. See, D. Cannadine, "The British Monarchy," 108-115.

having fun–there was no mention why Cambridge was in Constantinople rather than the Crimea commanding the 1ˢᵗ Division.[24] All that mattered, apparently, was the view of Cambridge maintained by his fellow officers and the Queen. Since many senior officers performed inadequately during the Crimean War, most were quite happy to let the matter go away while the Duke's royal birth certainly did not work against him.

Having committed to returning to England–his diary entry for January 21, 1855 read, "At length my long wished for letters (from England) have arrived, and are so satisfactory that I have determined upon starting for England at once with the first boat that goes"[25]–Cambridge set sail from Malta on January 22 and reached Dover on the thirtieth.[26] His plans were far more concrete than reported in London. A small article in The *Illustrated London News* reported that the Duke had left Constantinople and was now in Malta to recover his health as Constantinople did not improve his condition. Once it improved, the article stated the Duke had every intention of returning to the British army in the Crimea as soon as possible.[27] Regardless of the reporting, he proceeded on his course, and by his own account when he landed at Dover he was "met with a most hearty reception from the inhabitants which was most gratifying."[28] Leaving Dover at two o'clock, he reached London by six o'clock and was received by his mother, who was as relieved as the Duke that he had returned home.[29]

The following day, the Queen was in London on account of the defeat of the Aberdeen ministry. Between audiences, Cambridge responded to the Queen's summons and ate lunch with her and Prince Albert. Although he remembered the reception as being gracious, but little more, the meeting made a strong impression on the Queen. In her opinion, the Duke appeared "ill and much broken."[30] Cambridge had returned, and although it was certainly not the triumphal return for which he might have hoped,

---

24 *The Illustrated London News,* 13 January 1855.

25 Diary entry of the Duke of Cambridge, dated January 21, 1855, reproduced in Sheppard, vol. 1, 153.

26 Verner, vol. 1, 86. On his way back to England he paid a visit to the Emperor and Empress of France for several hours on the 28.

27 *The Illustrated London News,* 20 January 1855.

28 Sheppard, vol. 1, 153 and *The Illustrated London News,* 3 February 1855. The *Illustrated London News* account reflected the Duke's own impression of his reception, which the paper reported was filled with "vociferous cheers."

29 Sheppard, vol. 1, 153

30 RA QVJ: 31 January 1855, journal entry of Queen Victoria, dated January 31, 1855.

his reputation was somehow intact. The political crisis certainly helped to overshadow his return. He would spend the next several months out of the public eye as he strove to overcome his experience in the Crimea. The early months of 1855 brought momentous political change for the Crown, and this worked to the Duke's advantage since it allowed him to fade temporarily into obscurity. For just as Cambridge had returned in a "broken" condition, the Aberdeen ministry was brought down.

II

The pressure mounting against the government over the war had come to a head. Prosecution of the war and a ministry that could run it effectively preoccupied the Queen and the public. On the January 24, 1855, Victoria invited the Foreign Secretary, Lord John Russell, to lunch and was shocked to receive in reply a letter from him of his intention to resign.[31] A radical Member of Parliament (MP), John A. Roebuck (1802-1879),[32] intended to introduce a motion before the House which would censure the government's handling of the war and demand an inquiry–it is not surprising that Roebuck had acquired the nickname of "Tear 'em."[33]

Victoria was quite reluctant to change the government in the middle of a war, especially upon such short notice, so she prevailed upon Lord Aberdeen to "make one appeal to the Cabinet to stand by her."[34] It was moot, however, as neither Aberdeen nor any of the Cabinet ministers had the stomach to resist the Motion, and it was merely a matter of finding the right Prime Minister to conduct the war properly. The Cabinet and the

---

31 Letter from Lord John Russell to Queen Victoria, dated January 24, 1855, reproduced in Benson and Esher, eds., *The Letters of Queen Victoria*, 1st ser., vol. 3, 90-91. Russell's resignation letter explained, "Mr Roebuck has given notice of a Motion enquire into the conduct of the war. I do not see how this Motion is to be resisted. But as it involves a censure of the War Departments with which some of my colleagues are connected, my only course it to tender my resignation. I therefore have to request you will lay my humble resignation of office, which I have the honour to hold, before the Queen, with the expression of my gratitude for Her Majesty's kindness for many years." *Ibid.*, 91.

32 John A. Roebuck had attained national prominence in 1843 during his failed attempt to introduce a national system of secular education. He was also well known because of outspoken position against coercion in Ireland. See John Hurt, *Education in Evolution: Church, State, Society, and popular Education, 1800-1870* (London: Hart-Davis, 1971) for an in-depth discussion of the movement for educational reform in 19th century Britain.

33 Roebuck acquired the nickname because his stated policy was that he was an "independent member" of the House–he attacked those who disagreed with him on any position with great vehemence.

34 Memorandum by Prince Albert, dated 25th January 1855, reproduced in Benson and Esher, eds., *The Letters of Queen Victoria*, 1st ser., vol. 3, 93.

Queen were against the resignation of Lord John Russell (1792-1878)–
a stinging letter of January 25 made clear her "approbation"[35] and the
Duke of Newcastle offered his position as Secretary for War to save the
government, but Roebuck's Motion passed by a healthy majority on January
30.[36] Lord Palmerston wrote to the Queen late that evening informing her
of a great defeat: 305 to 148, a majority of 157 against the government.[37]
Not surprisingly, all Liberals had voted against the government.

The debate over the Motion involved a number of eyewitnesses to
the dreadful conditions at the Army hospitals at Scutari and Sebastopol
and the inadequate condition of the Commissariat. Gladstone presented
a speech which Palmerston said "exhausted the subject, and would have
convinced hearers who had not made up their minds beforehand."[38]
Palmerston related how the testimony was so eloquent and powerful that it
would have been virtually impossible for the government to survive. Lord
Aberdeen and his Cabinet tendered their resignations the next day and the
Queen had no choice but to accept. Despite Victoria's initial attempt to
have Derby form a government, only Palmerston would satisfy the public,
the House, and even the French.

Not everyone saw the wisdom of choosing Palmertson, however.
After meeting with Lord Derby to discuss the possibility of his forming a
government on January 31, Victoria recorded his frank comments in her
journal later that evening, "Whatever the ignorant public might think, L^{d}
Palmerston was totally unfit for the task, having become very deaf, as well
as very blind, being 71, & [*sic*] people having begun to find him out as a
bad man of business...."[39] As it turned out, Derby was slightly off in his
assessment: Palmerston lasted another decade, dying at his desk while still
at work on October 18, 1865. As quickly as February 6, 1855 Palmerston
had formed his Cabinet and informed Victoria of its composition.[40]

As the new government worked itself out and the winter turned to
spring, Cambridge passed his time with his morganatic wife, Louisa,

35 Letter from Queen Victoria to Lord John Russell, dated January 25, 1855, reproduced in *ibid.*, 94.
36 Interestingly, Roebuck himself was able to say only a few sentences when the Motion came up for
debate because of ill health.
37 Memorandum by Prince Albert, dated 25th January 1855, reproduced in Benson and Esher, eds., *The
Letters of Queen Victoria*, 1st ser., vol. 3, 99.
38 *Ibid.*
39 RA QVJ: 31 January 1855, journal entry of Queen Victoria, dated January 31, 1855.
40 Victoria was clearly displeased with the choice of Palmerston as Prime Minister, but she recognized
he was the best man for leading the war effort. The Earl of Clarendon would head Foreign Affairs and
Lord Panmure would take over the War Department.

who was clearly delighted over his return.[41] Apart from the occasional parade and intermittent visits with Victoria and Albert, he had no official military duties.[42] On March 11 he met with the new Secretary for War, Lord Panmure (1801-1874), who informed Cambridge there was no need to return to the Army any time soon.[43] The following day he testified for two and one-half hours before the Roebuck Committee investigating the situation in the Crimea.[44] Although Cambridge did not record his exact testimony, he was questioned in advance by Roebuck and believed his evidence "was satisfactory...and was well thought of."[45] Most likely, Cambridge focused his comments on the shipment and re-supply of cavalry units to the Crimea.

As the former Inspector-General of Cavalry, he was an authority on that branch of service. In a speech in the House of Lords on March 16, 1855, Cambridge addressed issues affecting cavalry in the Crimea, primarily deployment and supply.[46] He argued for the use of steam transports, "by each of which you would be able to send out 300 horses in the most simple and easy manner."[47] That Cambridge made a speech before the Lords–his first ever–was a significant step in his return to public life. In

---

41 St. Aubyn, *The Royal George*, 93-94.

42 Victoria rarely thought of Cambridge and no longer expressed concern over his early departure from the Crimea. Between the January 31 and October 30 she mentioned him only five times in her journal. Although it is impossible to know whether there might have been more references to him because all that survives of the journal is Princess Beatrice's abridged version of the original, it is a reasonable assumption that he was not a major figure for the Queen during this period. Surviving references are from March 7, June 6, July 4, August 11 and October 30, and these were only in passing to describe their meals together. RA QVJ: 7 March 1855, 6 June 1855, 4 July 1855, 11 August 1855 and 30 October 1855.

43 Diary entry of the Duke of Cambridge, dated March 11, 1855, reprinted in Sheppard, vol. 1, 154. The Duke appeared relieved over the outcome: "with Panmure as regards my return to the Army, which he does not consider necessary at all at present."

44 Viscount Palmerston described the purpose of the Roebuck committee to Queen Victoria to "ascertain the causes of the sufferings of your Majesty's troops in the Crimea." Letter from Viscount Palmerston to Queen Victoria, dated February 16, 1855, reproduced in Benson and Esher, eds., *The Letters of Queen Victoria*, 1st ser., vol. 3, 134-135.

45 Diary entries of the Duke of Cambridge, dated March 11, and March 12, 1855, reprinted in Sheppard, vol. 1, 154-155.

46 Cambridge had been introduced in the House of Lords by the Duke of Wellington in late July 1850 after assuming the title of his father, but other than this introduction, he had not yet appeared before the House of Lords.

47 Speech of the Duke of Cambridge before the House of Lords, March 16, 1855, reproduced in *ibid.* In his diary that evening, Cambridge recorded, "I made my first short speech on the subject of the transport of Cavalry Horses. It went off well and was well received." Diary entry of the Duke of Cambridge, dated March 16, 1855, reproduced in *ibid.*

assuming an active role in Parliament's upper house he was renewing his reputation and, rather ironically, he profited due to his status as a veteran of the Crimean War. Furthermore, he was able to speak with authority on a subject he knew well without drawing attention to his own difficulties in the ongoing war. Whether the speech was deliberately orchestrated or simply serendipitous, it was an excellent way for Cambridge to return to public life.

With the arrival of spring, in a remarkable reversal from his previous "broken" condition, Cambridge began appearing openly and proudly as an accomplished veteran of the Crimean War. The Lord Mayor of London, Sir David Salomans (1797-1893), the first Jewish Lord Mayor of London, held a reception with over 300 guests in honor of the Duke on April 9, 1855. It occurred the same day as the allies' second great bombardment of the fortress at Sebastopol. Large crowds formed outside the reception and "the cheering with which he was welcomed...was continued long after he had disappeared from their view."[48] Without intended irony, he recounted how he had witnessed some scenes characterized by great excitement and glory while others were more painful, but that it was an ample reward to have taken part in such events and to receive a hearty welcome home. In an astonishing display of feigned ignorance, the Duke wondered aloud how he could have attained such a proud and honorable position–it is unlikely that he forgot his royal birth. He went on without a hint of embarrassment to explain that he had done *nothing more than his duty* in the Crimea and appreciated the honor and satisfaction of being placed in command of troops who had nobly and gallantly served their country.[49]

That Cambridge spoke these words and his audience accepted them enthusiastically is revealing. He apparently believed what he said– the deployment and combat had come as a shock, as evidenced by his diary entries throughout the year. As an example, on February 1, 1855, Cambridge recorded, "I can think of nothing but the Crimea, and the sufferings of our dear comrades there."[50] As striking as his speech may sound in comparison to his efforts to flee the Crimea, his language is

---

48 *The Illustrated London News,* 14 April 1855. The account in the paper was highly favorable and included two large illustrations along with an article of some 1,500 words.

49 Sheppard, vol. 1, 155-156; *The Illustrated London News,* 14 April 1855.

50 Diary entry of the Duke of Cambridge, dated February 1, 1855, reproduced in Sheppard, vol. 1, 153-154. Similar thoughts followed, but eventually his thoughts turned to operational matters rather than emotional remembrances. For example, July 11, "Had letters from the Crimea, with detailed accounts of poor Raglan's death and last moments." *Ibid.,* 160.

consistent with his correspondence to his mother and his wife when he was in his most dejected state. The problems he encountered in the Crimea were beyond his control–Raglan, for example, was incompetent, while the weather and terrain, were inhospitable. Those who were not there– Victoria or Albert–could never understand *his* suffering. In correspondence explaining why he wanted to leave, Cambridge discussed his feelings and illness, not his inherent responsibility as a commander.

The celebration of the Duke's service in the Crimea continued, and he attended a parade in London on May 18, 1855 to distribute the newly minted Crimea Service Medal. That evening, Cambridge noted with pride in his diary, "I commanded the parade, and was the first to receive the medal. Everything went off to perfection; the weather was lovely…to me it was indeed a proud moment, when I stepped forward to receive the medal at the Queen's hand. I shall never forget it as long as I live."[51] These two celebrations illustrate that the Duke's return to public life occurred without complication; his evident pride reveals he remembered his service in the manner it was being publicly portrayed: he was indeed a celebrated veteran, if not a hero, of the war. Cambridge's public and private rehabilitation were complete.

The remainder of the summer was spent in relative tranquility. Cambridge made frequent visits to Aldershot to inspect troops and later that year he would complain to the Queen and Lord Hardinge about his lack of success in trying to obtain a command. He also claimed in correspondence that he was "very unhappy that they do not send me back…I would so gladly go and feel of only I would be of some use!...Altogether it annoys me more and more every day to have nothing to do…"[52] Cambridge closed this letter by stating that, "Above all what I should like best would be to return to the Army in the field, for that after all is my profession or vocation, and my whole heart clings so entirely to it."[53] This was quite a reversal from his attitude while he had actually been in the Crimea– several months of princely living had clearly rekindled his enthusiasm for soldiering.

Unfortunately, little evidence remains of Cambridge's actual efforts to get back to the Crimea other than frustration over boredom rather than

---

51 Diary entry of the Duke of Cambridge, dated May 18, 1855, reproduced in Verner, vol. 1, 86.
52 Letter from the Duke of Cambridge, addressee unknown, date unknown other than June or July 1855, reproduced in *ibid.,* 160.
53 *Ibid.*

sadness at missing the military action.[54] Although idle, he was not so desperate to return to the field that he would accept a desolate posting. On June 8, 1855, Lord Panmure offered him command at Gibraltar and Cambridge declined.[55] Afterwards, he explained that he was hoping to return to the Crimea, but outside substantiation does not exist. As for not accepting command in Gibraltar, he explained frankly to Lord Panmure, "I should wish for some employment at home."[56] When offered active command in the field, he turned it down in favor of doing the more important work of supervising levies. He probably also knew there was little chance of being sent to the Crimea. In March, Lord Panmure, the Duke of Newcastle's successor as Secretary of State for War in Palmerston's ministry, had written to Lord Raglan and informed him Cambridge would not be returning to the Crimea, "I may tell you in confidence that you will not see the Duke in the Crimea again, as I have advised him not to return."[57] Although Cambridge continued to think of the Crimea and was clearly aware of developments there, his desire to return was questionable and his efforts–regardless of their strength–were never fruitful.

As Cambridge accomplished little of substance, the Queen dedicated most of her time and energy towards following the war and influencing the Palmerston ministry. Her proven method of affecting Cabinet selections was not to object to individuals but rather their placement into specific positions to delay indefinitely their ultimate placement. In early February 1855 Victoria used this technique, highlighting Cambridge's influence on her, despite his recent conduct in the Crimea. The Queen disagreed with Palmerston's selection of Austen H. Layard (1817-1894, later Sir Austen H. Layard) as the Under-Secretary for War because of his harsh, but accurate, criticism of Lord Raglan and Admiral Sir James Dundas (1785-1862) over their incompetence in the Crimea.[58] She was "<u>not</u> against his employment,"

---

54 Although both official biographies, Verner and Sheppard, refer in passing that he endeavored "to find employment," (Verner, vol. 1, 87) neither provides any evidence.

55 *Ibid.*, 87. Verner states that Cambridge was offered a command at Gibraltar which Cambridge rejected "as he still hoped to return to the Crimea."

56 Letter from the Duke of Cambridge to Lord Panmure, dated June 8, 1855, reproduced St. Aubyn, *The Royal George*, 96-97.

57 Sir George Douglas and Sir George Dalhousie Ramsay, eds., *The Panmure Papers*, vol. 1 (London: Hodder and Stoughton, 1908), 112.

58 Sir Austen Henry Layard was most famous for excavating the ancient city of Nineveh throughout the 1840's and subsequently as a liberal politician from 1851 through to the 1869. He had been near the Crimea when the war started and witnessed the battle of the Alma. He testified before the Committee of Inquiry regarding the condition of the British Army at Sebastopol.

she was against it in the War Office.[59] A more important consideration for her, and especially Cambridge, was Layard's common birth. To have someone of modest heritage assisting the royal family, like the chemist, Lyon Playfair (1818-1898), serving on the Great Exhibition committee for Prince Albert, was acceptable, but it was not at all for someone of common birth to be involved with the direction of the army. Cambridge made it quite clear to the Queen that such a posting would have a very bad effect on the army, an aristocratic preserve.[60] Accordingly, Layard did not receive the position and he was not put forth for a government position until 1861 as Under Secretary of State for the Foreign Department, to which the Queen still objected.[61] This time, however, Palmerston was determined and he assured Victoria he would ensure that Layard would act within the policies of his ministry. It helped that this newest position did not involve the army, whereas the former one did. When it affected the army and royal control over decisions affecting it, Cambridge and Victoria were united, and in the former case, effective. It would not be the last time that the two reinforced each other's conviction regarding the importance of maintaining the Royal Prerogative, a factor which would soon figure powerfully in the career of the Duke.

Regardless of Cambridge's earlier supposed agitation over the lack of a command and military action, his anxiety increased as an end to the war in the Crimea approached. Expressing concern over the difficulty to seize the Redan, a Russian fortress within the complex of Sebastopol, shortly after he had refused command at Gibraltar, Cambridge was especially distraught over the death of Lord Raglan June 28, 1855.[62] He saw it as "a fearful catastrophe, a sad and most painful blow. It has filled all hearts with mourning and sorrow, and has afflicted me personally most deeply. His death at such a moment is an irreparable loss to the country."[63] His previous opinion of Raglan had obviously changed since serving under

---

59 RA QVJ: 5 February 1855, journal entry of Queen Victoria, dated February 5, 1855.
60 Longford, 247.
61 Letter from Viscount Palmerston to Queen Victoria, dated February 7, 1855, reproduced in Benson and Esher, eds., *The Letters of Queen Victoria*, 1st ser., vol. 3, 129-132, in which Palmerston listed the proposed Cabinet and discussed key postings–Layard was not among them. Letters to and from Viscount Palmerston to and from Queen Victoria, July 8 to July 26, 1861, reproduced in *ibid.*, 566-571. The Queen still had reservations about Layard while Palmerston regretted he had been unable to change her mind.
62 Verner, vol. 1, 87-88; Sheppard, vol. 1, 159-161.
63 Diary of the Duke of Cambridge, June 30, 1855, reproduced in Verner, vol. 1, 87.

him in the Crimea. When Cambridge learned on September 11 that all of Sebastopol had finally been captured, he accelerated his efforts to get back to "the field army," and met unsuccessfully with Lord Panmure regarding his "anxiety to command the Army in the field."[64]

The Commander-in-Chief in the Crimea, General Sir James Simpson (1792-1868), was not well, and more importantly, not an effective commander.[65] Although Lord Panmure briefly considered Cambridge, he viewed him unfit for the command. Lord Hardinge and Lord Palmerston, in conference with Lord Panmure, presented a harsh assessment, "admitting all His Royal Highness's hereditary courage, he might fail in self-control in situations where the safety of the Army might depend on coolness and self-possession."[66] Cambridge's public reputation had survived the war, but his private standing within the Cabinet as a capable combat commander had not.

After the major objective of the war, Sebastopol, had been taken and peace approached, the Duke increased his efforts to gain command in the Crimea and visited the Queen on Halloween to complain about his predicament, but even Victoria was unconvinced. He had not distinguished himself and there were others of decent birth likely to perform well–Sir William Codrington (1804-1884), for instance–before the war would be over.[67] As far as Victoria was concerned, the Duke had no one to blame but himself. The Queen expressed her dissatisfaction: "I am very sorry for poor George & feel for him, but much is his own fault (which he now sees) at not having gone back to the Crimea, as he ought to six weeks after being home."[68] This private view was quite different from the one in her letter to him on January 15, 1855, in which she referred to Cambridge as being one of the nation's heroes. With ten months' hindsight, the Duke's actual conduct now appeared to Victoria the way she first viewed it, as opposed to when the Aberdeen ministry was collapsing and Cambridge was mailing letters to his mother and the Queen in the hopes of returning home. By this point, however, the public image of the Duke of Cambridge had survived. While the Queen might have held doubts privately, publicly

---

64 Diary entry of the Duke of Cambridge, dated October 5, 1855, reproduced in Sheppard, vol. 1, 155.
65 General Simpson did not rise to task of being an expeditionary force commander and sent Lord Panmure pessimistic letters. Lord Panmure wrote back after one of them and chastised him, "But my good friend, you must *lead.*" Judd, 157-158.
66 St. Aubyn, *The Royal George*, 96.
67 Codrington did in fact succeed Simpson as commander in January 1856.
68 RA QVJ: 31 October 1855, journal entry of Queen Victoria, October 31, 1855.

no good would be done for the army or the Crown. In the meantime, the war continued on into another year.

The allies were tiring of the war and after Sebastopol was taken, the question became literally, "what next?" The French grew weary (although Emperor Napoleon III remained true) and the Austrians and Prussians continued to vacillate, while the Russians failed to launch an effective counter offensive. Against this anticlimactic backdrop, a delegation of French and British senior officers met at the Tuileries on January 10, 1856, to conduct a Council of War, but before anything came of it the Russians sought terms for a truce on January 16.

The Duke of Cambridge was the senior military member of the British delegation because of his royal blood, diplomatic abilities, and previous diplomatic meetings in Paris and Vienna. In the course of the Conference, Cambridge presented his views to Emperor Napoleon III, but his analysis of the situation, though competent, had no subsequent impact due to the cessation of hostilities.[69] Altogether, there were six meetings of the Council of War and Cambridge dutifully reported the details of each to Lord Clarendon. His analysis revealed a solid grasp of the magnitude of the logistical difficulties facing the allies, as well as the inherent difficulties of fighting as part of a combined effort. The Duke returned to England on January 20, the Russians entered into an armistice on February 25, and the Treaty of Paris March 30, 1856 formally ended the Crimean War.

Upon his return to London on January 20, there was little for Cambridge to do: he held no command and the war was effectively over. Naturally, he attended more ceremonies in light of the pending victory and he met occasionally with the Queen as well. It was also at this point, however, that the War Department was undergoing a significant transformation. This process began shortly before Cambridge was to assume, quite suddenly, the highest military rank in Britain. While the war had had a profound impact on Cambridge, his beloved institution was about to experience significant change, the effectiveness of which was not fully understood at the time.

---

69 Verner, vol. 1, 88-93.

III

Prior to the Crimean War, the army had been administered by a number of separate, distinct, and independent authorities, only one of which was the office of the Commander-in-Chief. Eight departments or offices held overlapping–and often contradictory–areas of responsibility and influence: the Secretary of State for War and the Colonies, the Home Department, the Secretary at War, the Commander-in-Chief, the Ordnance Department, the Treasury, the Board of General Officers, and the Medical Department.

The Secretary of State for War and the Colonies, a Cabinet member, had overall responsibility for the size of the army, allocation of garrisons to colonial possessions, conveyance of orders overseas, and in time of war only, the authority to select officers for command and control of operations bearing on the conduct of the war.[70] The Home Secretary was also a Cabinet member who had full responsibility for the militia and, in conjunction with the Commander-in-Chief, the geographical distribution of the army within Great Britain, as well as general military issues regarding the defense of the homeland.[71]

The Secretary at War was a junior member of the government who was a Member of Parliament and not a Cabinet member, at least in theory.[72] His office was responsible for all aspects of army finance and any issues regarding the army and the general population. The Secretary at War was closely tied to other departments because without them he could not execute any of his duties. The most important and prominent of his duties, the

---

70 Great Britain, Parliament, *Report of the Commissioners Appointed to Inquire Into the Practicability of Consolidating the Different Departments Connected with the Civil Administration of the Army.* Military and Naval Parliamentary Paper, Vol. 4 (1837; reprint, Shannon, Ireland: Irish University Press, 1971), 13, hereafter referred to as 1837 *Report of the Commissioners on the Civil Administration of the Army.*

71 Sir Robert Biddulph, *Lord Cardwell at the War Office* (London: John Murray, 1904), 7. The militia was abolished shortly after the defeat of Napoleon but it was recreated in 1852. Within the House of Commons the budget for the militia, known as the Militia Estimates, was handled by a separate committee, while the budget of the active regiments was prepared by the Secretary at War.

72 Constitutional practice dictated that the Secretary of State for War and the Colonies and the Secretary at War could not be Cabinet members simultaneously, but even prior to the Crimean War disputes frequently arose. Crimea brought the issue to a head and two separate secretary positions were replaced by the Secretary for War. For an in-depth discussion, see Sweetman, 97-127. Although the office of Secretary at War was not formally abolished until 1863, the position was never filled after Aberdeen's government. *Ibid.,* 106. Palmerston had a lengthy and influential term as Secretary at War from 1809-1820, and in many ways defined the position.

preparation and submission of the annual Army Estimates to Parliament, was inextricably linked to the size of the force to be maintained, but he had no authority over the size of the army. Other factors limited his authority. Although he could *prevent* units from moving because he controlled the budget and movement involved expense, he had no authority to move units. He also lacked control over the artillery and engineer branches and had no influence over arms and supplies. Conversely, his responsibility regarding army interaction with the civilian population and protection of civilian subjects from oppression and misconduct by the army gave him great authority regarding quartering, billeting, and the marching of troops since these activities brought soldiers into contact with civilians.[73] Despite its limitations, immediately prior to and during the Crimean War, the Secretary at War was perhaps the most powerful position connected with the army. First and foremost, the individual who occupied the position answered to Parliament not only on financial issues, but administration and discipline as well. Furthermore, routine and special actions by the army almost always involved, or at least concerned, the Secretary.[74]

Another important position–of central importance to this book– was the Commander-in-Chief. In theory, the officer who occupied this position was subordinate only to the Crown. The Commander-in-Chief's responsibilities included discipline, efficiency, soldier enlistment, and commissioning and promotion of officers within cavalry and infantry, as well as recommendations to the Sovereign for command selections overseas and in the British Isles.[75] No recommendation, however, could go forward without the previous approval of the Home Secretary for commands within the United Kingdom, while those recommended for command abroad first had to be approved by the Secretary of State for War and the Colonies. A comfortable relationship between the Commander-in-Chief and the Crown was thus clearly an advantage to the smooth administration of the army. The Commander-in-Chief commanded those forces stationed in Great Britain and Ireland but none overseas. Additional limitations on

---

73 Biddulph, 4-5; 1837 *Report of the Commissioners on the Civil Administration of the Army*, 14, 16-17.

74 *Ibid.*, 14; testimony of Lord Panmure, former Secretary at War, published in Great Britain, Parliament, *Report from the Select Committee on Army and Ordnance Expenditure*. Military and Naval Parliamentary Paper, Vol. 5 (1860; reprint, Shannon, Ireland: Irish University Press, 1971), 74.

75 All promotions were officially the prerogative of the Crown and Victoria fiercely protected this right throughout her reign. Her interest in "her army" never waned–she addressed military matters in some way, or at least considered them, virtually every day of her reign.

the office included the lack of control over troops abroad, supply of arms and stores, fortifications, and the branches of artillery and engineers.[76] To assist him, the Commander-in-Chief had three primary assistants: the Military Secretary, responsible primarily for correspondence, the Adjutant General, responsible for the personnel issues, and the Quartermaster-General, responsible for logistics and movement.[77]

The Board of Ordnance had full responsibility for the so-called "civil duties." The head of the Ordnance Board's official title was the Master General of Ordnance, and he was a high-ranking army officer. The other members were the Surveyor General, the Clerk of Ordnance, and the Principal Storekeeper. The civil duties were: provision of all arms and military stores, preparation and submission of the Ordnance Estimates to Parliament, clothing for the artillery and engineers, construction and repair of all fortifications, military works and barracks, as well as the supply of fuel, light, miscellaneous articles, provisions, and forage for troops in Britain and Ireland.[78]

The Master General of Ordnance directed the artillery and engineers in all matters of discipline, pay and allowances, appointments, promotions, and orders regarding their employment. Unlike the infantry and cavalry, the purchase of commissions was not practiced in the artillery and engineers, as Master General of Ordnance controlled all appointments within these branches of service.[79] This responsibility constituted the military function of the Ordnance Department and lay entirely in the hands of the Master General of Ordnance, assisted by the Inspector General of Fortifications, a high-ranking officer and the Deputy Adjutant General, Royal Engineers. The Inspector General of Fortifications advised on matters of works and buildings under the jurisdiction of the Royal Engineers as well as supervising the employment of engineers. The Deputy Adjutant General, Royal Engineers, administered the discipline of the Royal Engineers. Regarding artillery, the Master General was assisted by the Deputy Adjutant General of Artillery who administered the discipline of the Royal Artillery,

76 Gordon, 50; Biddulph, 3.

77 Barnett, 240; Brian Bond, *The Victorian Army and the Staff College 1854-1914* (London: Eyre Methuen, 1972), 12.

78 1837 *Report of the Commissioners on the Civil Administration of the Army*, 14, 16-17; Gordon, 14-15; Biddulph, 6.

79 Great Britain, Parliament, *Report from the Select Committee on Military Organization*. Military and Naval Parliamentary Papers, Vol. 5 (1860; reprint, Shannon, Ireland: Irish University Press, 1971), 264.

and by the Director General of Artillery who held the responsibility for armaments and ammunition, as well as providing advice on scientific questions, experimentation, and new types of weapons. Even though the Board of Ordnance as a whole had the responsibility for the management of the civil duties of the Ordnance Department, it was the Master General of Ordnance who wielded the overriding authority in all matters.[80]

The Treasury managed the Commissariat Department, which had the responsibility for provisions, fuel and light, forage, transport, and money to the troops abroad.[81] The Treasury also had responsibility for preparing the annual Estimates for the Commissariat, distinct from the Army Estimates and the Ordnance Estimates.[82] Respective regimental colonels provided clothing for the cavalry and infantry regiments, but the inspection of this clothing was the primary duty of the Board of General Officers.[83] The final administrative authority, the Medical Department, had the responsibility of providing medical stores and medical personnel.[84]

From this overview it is painfully clear that army administration prior to and during the Crimean War was unwieldy and inefficient. The army served several independent masters simultaneously without a coordinating authority; in short there was neither unity of command nor unity of purpose. The branches of artillery and the engineers were the only ones in the army that had complete unity within their organization since they operated under the direction of the Master General of Ordnance. The cavalry and infantry, however, reported to the Commander-in-Chief for discipline and efficiency, the Secretary at War for financial matters, the Board of Ordnance for supplies, and the Secretary of State for War and the Colonies for operations overseas. The Medical Department had an even more complicated administrative arrangement in that it had to report to five superior agencies: the Secretary of State for War and the Colonies,

---

80 Biddulph, 6-7; 1837 *Report of the Commissioners on the Civil Administration of the Army*, 15; as well as the testimony of Colonel W.F.D. Jervois, Royal Engineers, reproduced in Great Britain, Parliament, *Reports of a Committee Appointed to Inquire Into the Arrangements in Force for the Conduct of Business in the Army Departments*. Military and Naval Parliamentary Papers, Vol. 4 (1870; reprint, Shannon, Ireland: Irish University Press, 1971), 430.

81 1860 *Report on Military Organization*, 268; Biddulph, 6.

82 Great Britain, Parliament, *Report from the Select Committee on Army and Ordnance Expenditure*. Military and Naval Parliamentary Papers, Vol. 4 (1851; reprint, Shannon, Ireland: Irish University Press, 1971), 254.

83 Biddulph, 7; Gordon, 50.

84 *Ibid.*

the Secretary at War, the Commander-in-Chief (for discipline), the Master General of Ordnance, and the Board of Ordnance.[85]

Such an unwieldy organization was ill equipped to handle war on a large scale, as the Crimea readily demonstrated. Redundant examples are not necessary to demonstrate the inefficiency of the organization, but it is worth examining the procedure for promotions to illustrate further the inefficiency of administration. Within the infantry and cavalry the Commander-in-Chief received final approval for appointments from the Crown. To do so, he prepared a memorandum with the names of those recommended for promotion for the Queen's approval. Before it reached her, however, the Commander-in-Chief forwarded the list to the Secretary at War, who divided the names on the memorandum into two lists, one of officers serving abroad and the other for those at home. The Secretary of State for War and the Colonies prepared the commissions for those abroad and the Home Secretary did the same for those within the British Isles. Both ministers then sent the commissions forward for the Queen's signature, after which the commissions were then returned to the respective minister for countersignature.[86]

The Crimean War brought national awareness to the army and its organization, so that even if "war remained a noise far away," the British army was revealed to be far less glorious and effective than thought, thanks to the work of war correspondent W. H. Russell and the pioneering nursing efforts of Florence Nightingale (1820-1910).[87] Throughout the long 19th century, in the eyes of its officers, the army continually suffered from inadequate funding, but the Crimean War did provide impetus for limited reform.[88] Coming after almost four decades of peace, the home army became a focal point of public concern, bringing the competence of military administration, the capabilities of the high command and staff,

---

85 This was the testimony of Andrew Smith, Director General of the Medical Department since 1854 testifying in 1856 reported in Great Britain, Parliament, *Report from the Select Committee on Medical Department (Army)*. Military and Naval Parliamentary Papers, Vol. 13. 1856, 359.

86 1837 *Report of the Commissioners on the Civil Administration of the Army*, 13.

87 Barnett, 273.

88 For some brief but helpful assessments of the reforms and their effectiveness, see Peter Burroughs, "An Unreformed Army? 1815-1868," in *The Oxford Illustrated History of the British Army*, eds. David Chandler and Ian Beckett (Oxford: Oxford University Press, 1994), 160-188; Edward M. Spiers, "The Post-Crimean Period," chap. 6 in *The Army and Society 1815-1914* (Longman: New York, 1980); and Barnett, "Decay and Reform 1815-1870," chap. 12 in *Britain and Her Army 1509-1970* (New York: William Morrow & Co., 1970).

and the living conditions of the soldier before the critical examination of the press and Parliament.

After the end of the Aberdeen ministry in late January 1855, Lord Palmerston's government intended to demonstrate quickly an improved ability to prosecute the war. Accordingly, it implemented a number of changes before its end. Within eighteen months, the Duke of Cambridge was Commander-in-Chief against the backdrop of "a Cabinet of terrified men, anxious to still popular clamour and eager to show that they were doing something."[89] These and subsequent reforms will be addressed below, but it is significant that Cambridge assumed senior military leadership of an army that was restructuring without a clear plan.

IV

Once again without a mission after his return from the Council of War in Paris, the Duke attended sessions in the House of Lords to follow discussions regarding army administration reforms, visited the Queen, and attended various parades and ceremonies.[90] Throughout April he frequently attended the Court of Inquiry on matters regarding the Crimean War, and the following month he took part in yet more ceremonies celebrating British victory in the Crimea.[91] However, the Duke did more than attend military ceremonies, public celebrations, and parades. His correspondence in the months prior to assumption of Commander-in-Chief was voluminous and increasing. He wrote frequently to Victoria and Albert regarding military issues, as well as Lord Hardinge, the Commander-in-Chief, and Lord Panmure, Secretary of State for War. Prince Albert regarded himself as a genuine military authority and sought increased influence on military

---

89 J.W. Fortescue, *A History of the British Army.* Vol. 13, *1852-1870* (London: Macmillan and Co., 1930), 171.

90 Selected diary entries from February, March and April 1856: "21st February – To House of Lords to hear Lord Derby put a question to Lord Panmure with reference to the duties of the H.G. [Home Guard] and Secretary for War. The reply was highly satisfactory, and the Government are pledged to maintain the Commander-in-Chief as he at present exists. This is a great point gained."; "27th March – Started...by seven o'clock train for Aldershot. Breakfasted with General Knollys, and then accompanied him to a drill of the troops. Twenty-one Battalions were out in five Brigades and really did wonderfully well...."; "19th April – Started for Aldershot...by seven o'clock train.... Breakfasted with the Antrim Rifles, and went up to the Queen's Pavilion. It is really very nice, and nicely furnished and fitted up. The Queen started on horseback at 10.45. I rode on her right, the Prince [Albert] on her left." Reproduced in Verner, vol. 1, 94-95.

91 *Ibid.,* 95; Sheppard, vol. 1, 173.

affairs; the impact of his early death in December 1861 on genuine military reform remains an unanswerable question.[92] Albert's rank within the government and the royal family was always a difficult issue for Victoria as well. A memorandum written by the Queen dated May 1856 revealed her frustration over the ambiguity of having a husband subordinate in rank.[93]

Albert's only official influence was that of a high-ranking officer in the royal family. He held no command and did not serve on a staff. It is inaccurate to suggest his correspondence was ignored–it certainly was not–but it was addressed strictly from the perspective of courtesy rather than a chain-of-command requirement. A characteristic example occurred in late May 1856 when the Duke of Cambridge wrote to Lord Hardinge concerning the position of the rank of the commander of the Medical Department, as well as other administrative reforms concerning the army. Lord Hardinge passed along the Duke's recommendations (contained on a detailed nine-page memorandum) to Prince Albert, and he commented favorably upon the Duke's recommendations.[94] As was the case with Prince Albert's, on occasion Cambridge's recommendations were acted upon, but usually when members of the War Department viewed things similarly. Other than the power of persuasion, Cambridge himself wielded little influence over the army. That would soon change.

On June 7 Lord Panmure visited the Duke to discuss Cambridge's future. Although no record exists, it appears Panmure intended to place him into "Headquarters." Panmure was considering creating a new position, "Inspector-General of Infantry in the United Kingdom,"[95] making him responsible for the training and efficiency of infantry regiments based within the home islands. Cambridge was certainly pleased with this proposed appointment.[96] On the July 5, Hardinge sent him a more detailed proposal which would give Cambridge "under his orders about 30,000 men, besides Regiments not in camps or Garrisons."[97] It was never to be, however, because Hardinge suffered a debilitating stroke. During

---

92 See Robert Rhodes James, *Albert Prince Consort* (London: Hamish Hamilton, 1983).

93 Reproduced in Benson and Esher, eds., *The Letters of Queen Victoria*, 1st ser., vol. 3, 244-245. The issue remains to the present day.

94 RA VIC/E7/39, Letter from Lord Hardinge to Prince Albert, dated May 23, 1855; RA VIC/E7/40 H.R.H. the Duke of Cambridge's Memorandum on Promotions dated May 23, 1856.

95 Verner, vol. 1, 95.

96 Diary entry of the Duke of Cambridge, dated June 7, 1855, reproduced in *Ibid.*

97 Letter from Lord Panmure to the Duke of Cambridge, dated July 5, 1856, reproduced in *Ibid.*, 96.

an audience with Queen Victoria while both were attending a series of reviews of regiments recently returned from the Crimea at Aldershot, Lord Hardinge was stricken. Cambridge saw him before he was sent to London for a recovery that never came, noting that his right side was "helpless."[98] Hardinge realized he could not remain in position and sent his letter of resignation to Queen Victoria on July 10, 1856.[99]

Even before Hardinge wrote the letter, however, Cambridge hoped to become Commander-in-Chief. Although how he learned he was under consideration is unknown, his diary for July 9 noted, "I am likely to succeed."[100] The absence of obvious successors to Lord Hardinge highlighted the nature of the perceived–and very real–failure of the army in the Crimea. The defeat of Napoleon had elevated the careers of a number of army officers, but out of the Crimean "victory" few careers were enhanced. As one authority on the topic has noted, "Despite public hopes and indeed confident expectations, the Crimean War failed to throw up either a soldier or a politician of outstanding force."[101] When Hardinge died, there was no Wellington to compete against a prince of the blood. Even though he had not distinguished himself in the Crimea, at least he had been there and–despite actual events–was publicly portrayed as having done well. Certainly, he could be counted upon to preserve the Royal Prerogative.

With Lord Hardinge's resignation, Victoria was determined to have her cousin protect and occupy the position of Commander-in-Chief, for her sake and for the sake of the army. She asked for Palmerston's advice on July 10, 1856, but wrote him that "Cambridge stands almost without a competitor," and repeated her sentiments in her journal.[102] In a discussion with Palmerston and Prince Albert on July 9, 1856, the three concurred that Sir William Codrington would be the best officer for the position, except he was too junior and lacked a spectacular victory in the field in

---

98 Diary entry of the Duke of Cambridge, dated July 8, 1856, reproduced in Sheppard, vol. 1, 176. Hardinge would finally expire that September.
99 Benson and Esher, eds., 1st ser., vol. 3, 251.
100 Diary entry of the Duke of Cambridge, dated July 9, 1856, reproduced in Verner, vol. 1, 97.
101 Olive Anderson, *A Liberal State at War: English Politics and Economics During the Crimean War* (New York: St. Martin's Press, 1967), 37.
102 Letter from Queen Victoria to Lord Palmerston dated July 10, 1856, reproduced in Benson and Esher, eds., 1st ser., vol. 3, 251; RA QVJ: 11 July 1856, "Received yesterday evening poor Ld Hardinge's resignation, & sent it to Ld Palmerston expressing my opinion that George was almost without a competitor."

the manner of Wellington.[103] All agreed that Cambridge would be the most suitable due to "his great regimental knowledge, his experience of different armies, his devotion to the army & popularity..."[104] Significantly, the absence of victory in the field was not mentioned, nor was his conduct in the Crimea. Albert added, "for the army it would be an advantage to have a Prince of the Blood," but it might be a disadvantage for the Crown "as any attacks against him would reflect, to a certain extent on the Crown."[105] Cambridge's protection of the Royal Prerogative, coupled with his knowledge and popularity, outweighed any concerns that Victoria, Albert, or Palmerston may have had regarding his performance as a division commander. There were other suitable officers senior to Cambridge, but they were too old. Lord Palmerston had no objection to the appointment and agreed there was "no general officer senior to His Royal Highness the Duke of Cambridge to whom it would be in all respects be desirable to intrust [sic] the duties of the command of the army, and there is no general officer below him in seniority...to justify his being preferred."[106] The Cabinet met and concurred with the opinion of Queen Victoria.[107] The Queen was understandably pleased.[108]

The following day she made it clear that not only was it her prerogative to select the Commander-in-Chief, but also that she viewed the position as not being subordinate to a Cabinet Member, the Secretary of State for War, but to the Prime Minister and the Queen directly. Writing to Lord Palmerston from Buckingham Palace, she reiterated, "the mode of his appointment...does not rest with the Secretary of State...The office is not a subordinate one..."[109] Lord Palmerston agreed to the Queen's modification, and therefore the relationship between the Crown, her Prime Minister, and royal control of the army.[110] Accordingly, the Prime Minister

103 Codrington had succeeded Simpson as Commander-in-Chief of the forces in the Crimea. See above.

104 RA QVJ: 9 July 1856, journal entry of Queen Victoria, dated July 9, 1856. Queen Victoria recorded a detailed account of her meeting with Palmerston regarding the successor to Lord Hardinge.

105 *Ibid.*

106 RA VIC/E7/89, Letter from Lord Palmerston to Queen Victoria, dated July 12, 1856.

107 *Ibid.*

108 RA QVJ: 12 July 1856, journal entry of Queen Victoria, dated July 12, 1856.

109 RA VIC/E7/90, Letter from Queen Victoria to Lord Palmerston, dated July 13, 1856.

110 RA VIC/E7/91, Letter from Lord Palmerston to Queen Victoria dated July 13, 1856. "Viscount Palmerston...will adopt the course which your Majesty points out." The previous day, Palmerston had said that he and the Cabinet were in agreement with her that the Duke of Cambridge was the best choice for a successor and that Lord Panmure would take the Queen's pleasure on the matter "officially." Reproduced in Benson and Esher, eds., 1st ser., vol. 3, 252-253. This is what prompted the

wrote to Cambridge personally on July 13th informing him that "the Queen has been graciously pleased upon my recommendation to approve Your Royal Highness' being appointed to succeed Viscount Hardinge in that important post."[111] The Duke accepted immediately and, well aware he was occupying a position once held by Wellington, he understood the responsibility to be a great one.[112] Reflecting upon his selection, he wrote, "Thus I am placed in the proudest military position any subject could be placed in. It is an onerous one, but I will do my best to do myself credit."[113] A general order issued by the outgoing Lord Hardinge on July 15, 1856, made it quite clear that Hardinge had filled and Cambridge was to occupy a position held by "the greatest commander which this country has produced."[114]

In a letter to her uncle, King Leopold of Belgium, Victoria confided her mixed feelings about the selection. After her impressions of some troops recently returned from the Crimea, she reported, "George has been appointed Commander-in-Chief. There was really no one who could have been put over him; though in some respects it may be a weakness for the Crown, it is a great strength to the Army."[115] She did not make it clear whether she was concerned over how criticism of him as "a Prince of the Blood" would reflect on the Crown, or whether she still had doubts related to his fitness because of his performance in the Crimea. Regardless, for thirty-nine years she would stand by her royal cousin and maintain him in position as a shield against any encroachment of further erosion of royal control of the army.

Although the term Commander-in-Chief has been used and will be used out of convenience, Cambridge's official position was General Commanding-in-Chief as he was chief, but not the first officer in the British army. The distinction lies in that he was not at the top of the army list based upon seniority, even though he was the highest ranking officer,

clarification from Victoria as to how she saw the proper command relationship regarding her position vis-à-vis the Prime Minister, the Secretary for War and the Commander-in-Chief.
111 RA VIC/E7/93, Letter from Lord Palmerston to the Duke of Cambridge dated July 13, 1856.
112 RA VIC/E7/94, Acceptance letter from the Duke of Cambridge to Lord Palmerston dated July 13, 1856.
113 Diary of the Duke of Cambridge, Sheppard, vol. 1, 178.
114 RA VIC/E7/96, General order published by the Adjutant-General, G.A. Wetherall, issued from the Horse Guards, July 15, 1856. One issued by the new Commander-in-Chief, the Duke of Cambridge, July 16, 1856, expressed the magnitude of his responsibility, but that his personal experience "as a general officer in command of a division" acquainted him with the "heroic deeds of the army."
115 RA VIC/Y101/27, Letter from Victoria to Leopold, King of the Belgians, dated July 21, 1856.

therefore his position was a gazetted one, meaning he served in the rank temporarily but did not possess it outright. He would officially become Commander-in-Chief in 1887, the jubilee of his fiftieth year of military service.[116] He received his appointment by letters patent to the command "during our Pleasure of all and singular our Land Forces employed or to be employed in Our Service within Our United Kingdom of Great Britain and Ireland."[117]

In addition, his duties went further, including the responsibility for the "general distribution of Her Majesty's troops throughout the Empire… all questions regarding the supply to troops of government stores, camp equipage etc…all reports upon vessels intended for the conveyance of troops."[118] Specific aspects covered the command of the all regular infantry and cavalry with the United Kingdom, and when constituted, the reserve forces.[119] Thus he was responsible for the deployment of all regular forces within Great Britain and Ireland. Additionally, he held responsibility for inspection of the reserves and Chelsea pensioners, as well as the permanent staff of the militia.[120] Furthermore, since he was responsible for readiness and discipline, he controlled all military training facilities within the United Kingdom. It was Cambridge's predecessor, Viscount Hardinge, who established the permanent training site at Aldershot and instituted regular musket practice at Hythe.[121] Paramount to all of these duties was the Commander-in-Chief's responsibility to coordinate national defenses against invasion, a responsibility which the Queen assigned to him directly.[122]

---

116 RA VIC/E7/95, Letter from Lord Panmure to Queen Victoria, dated July 15, 1856; St. Aubyn, *Royal George*, 108.

117 PRO WO 43/95/15244, Memorandum on the duties of the Commander-in-Chief, counter signed by the Secretary at War and Quartermaster-General, dated September, 16 1852.

118 *Ibid.*

119 *Ibid.*; PRO WO 3/114/424, letter from Viscount Hardinge as Commander-in-Chief dated April 12, 1853, acknowledging that a field officer would inspect the Lincolnshire Militia at their annual camp.

120 PRO WO 3/114/411, Memorandum dated April 1, 1853 concerning the inspection of Yeoman cavalry; PRO WO 3/115/231, order dated October 10, 1853 for the inspection of the Chelsea pensioners in the Ayr district.

121 PRO WO 46/43/106, memorandum dated August 6, 1853 documenting Lord Hardinge's personal inspection of Aldershot Heath; Memorandum by Lord Hardinge dated February 9, 1853 instituting musket practice at Hythe.

122 Letter from Prince Albert to Viscount Hardinge, dated November 8, 1852, reproduced in Benson and Esher, eds., *The Letters of Queen Victoria*, 1st ser., vol. 2, 482-483. Albert reiterates "the Queen's request to Lord Derby that he should call upon the different departments of the Admiralty, Army, Ordnance, and Home Office to furnish a report as to how far the measures begun last spring to out our defences in a state of efficiency have been carried out, and what remains to be done in that direction–I

An area that would be of special importance to the Duke of Cambridge and would mark the most turbulent change during his time as Commander-in-Chief would be the promotion of officers and transactions involving the purchase of commissions. Since they fell under the general area of discipline, these responsibilities were also his. Thus, Cambridge had overall responsibility for the entire readiness of the army, apart from the East India Company and the Ordnance forces. With such vast duties, the three primary assistants to the Commander-in-Chief discussed above were essential: the Military Secretary, the Adjutant General, and the Quartermaster-General.

When Cambridge assumed his post in the summer of 1856, he assumed command–or more accurately, partial command–of an organization that was in flux. In contrast to how the Duke would subsequently be viewed and portrayed, when he accepted command he was young, apparently competent, and open to reform as demonstrated by his earlier memoranda as Inspector-General of Cavalry. Most importantly, perhaps, because he was a member of the royal family, he was also a Commander-in-Chief who would protect the Royal Prerogative at all costs. As made clear above, when he took office his position was subordinate only to Crown and Parliament through the Prime Minister, *not* the Secretary of State for War. He occupied his position at the pleasure of the Sovereign and would serve as a bulwark against further civilian interference and as a force for greater efficiency.[123] The history of the office has been termed "the struggle between the Crown and Parliament for control of the armed forces."[124] The thirty-nine years Cambridge served as Commander-in-Chief would affirm this.

With Cambridge in command the future of the office, the military authority of the Crown, and the future efficiency of the army were all open questions. Whether the Duke would be able to handle his new position adequately and muster the endurance he had previously lacked was

---

beg now to address you in writing. The object the Queen wishes to obtain is, to receive an account which will show what means we have *really* at our disposal for purposes of defence, *ready for action* at the shortest possible notice, and what remains to be done to put us into a state of security, what the supply of the wants may cost (approximately), and what time it would require..."

123 Hew Strachan has addressed this issue tangentially in his *Politics of the British Army* (Oxford: Clarendon Press, 1997), 44-73. However, Cambridge's personal role as a buffer for the Crown, while working for or against reform, as a military–and royal–expert opposed to increased Parliamentary control of the army or interference in its affairs has remained unexplored until now.

124 St. Aubyn, *The Royal George*, 107.

unknown. When he took over there was no way to anticipate whether he would serve merely as a mouthpiece for his cousin, the Queen, push for further and deeper reforms than the halting and uneven ones already under way, or whether he might simply occupy the office and do little more than resist change in all its guises. In time all of these developments took place, but far more importantly, neither the position of the Commander-in-Chief nor the relationship of the Crown to the army looked the same once Cambridge had occupied the position for a few years. The relationship between the military and the monarchy would be forever changed as a result of his role as Commander-in-Chief.

CHAPTER 5:
The Horse Guards 1856-1857

As with most armies throughout history and most certainly the British army of the modern era, success in war–even if costly and accompanied by numerous promises for reform during the course of it–was followed by a typical pattern. The usual course was to celebrate the victory and then quietly fall back into a period of retrenchment. While the army desired to preserve the status quo, the government sought relief from the heightened expenditures required during the war. The Crimean War at first promised to break this pattern. The staggering inefficiencies and incompetence reported in great detail to the reading public in England revealed the backwardness of the army. The efforts of Florence Nightingale especially revealed the inadequacies of the army's medical services. In the press and in Parliament the demand for reform was pronounced and widespread. Although not caused directly by army shortcomings, the war brought down the Aberdeen government and ushered in the Palmerston government. Concurrent with the mandate to win the war, the government took it upon itself to reorganize the army. While the issue of whether the initiatives produced results is a subject of historical interest, the reforms themselves changed little of significance.[1]

When the Duke of Cambridge assumed the office of the Commander-in-Chief, the army was in the middle of these post-Crimean changes. Many of the reforms implemented were hastily enacted without any serious thought given to their long-term consequences. Although he demonstrated a genuine openness to the reform of army organization as Inspector-General of Cavalry, the overriding reason for Cambridge's selection as Commander-in-Chief was that he was first cousin to the Queen. He had had sufficient time and experience in the army to justify–or at least counteract any opposition to–his placement. Whether he was inclined toward serious reform or was committed to resisting change in any fashion were not the key criteria. Based upon their lengthy correspondence and frequent social contacts, Queen Victoria understood that on many issues she and her cousin would be in close agreement. The two cared deeply for the army and were in agreement that the service belonged under royal control. Had

---

1 Despite its age, an article by Brian Bond remains a solid and concise argument against the notion that serious reform in the post-Crimean British army took place before 1868. See Brian Bond, "Prelude to the Cardwell Reforms, 1856-68," *Royal United Services Institution Journal* 106 (1961): 229-236.

it been otherwise, the fact of Cambridge's royal birth would have been overridden by other considerations.

As it turned out, Cambridge was more reform-minded than has been usually portrayed by historians. His appointment drew nothing but positive expectations from reform-minded supporters of the army, and despite the reputation he would later acquire as Commander-in-Chief, he was correctly regarded by contemporaries as being young, vigorous, and inclined to make changes.[2] An article appearing in the *Times* in July of 1856 described Cambridge's "comparative youth and comparative inexperience" as "something like a positive recommendation."[3] Significantly, the article asserted the obvious–the need for reform–and blamed the generation of officers from the French wars for the problems with the army. Cambridge was seen as a good thing, not because of his experience or qualifications, which were less than those of many other officers, but precisely because he was inexperienced and young, and therefore offered the potential for adapting the military "to the wants of the age and the exigencies of modern operations."[4]

Whether such expectations would be met remained to be seen. Shortly after announcement was made of his appointment, a journal devoted to military issues, the *United Service Magazine,* also commented favorably upon the Duke's selection.[5] As the oldest publication in England dedicated to military issues, it is not surprising that it focused on military education, the general staff, and the purchase system, all areas which Cambridge would have to address to professionalize the army. The journal merely pointed out matters which the Duke might consider rather than actual changes which he would implement, since there was of course no way of knowing. Regarding military education and the purchase system, the editors of the monthly were quite prescient, but not as they might have thought. Although Cambridge would prove to be instrumental in the

---

2 Strachan, *Politics of the British Army*, 62.

3 *Times* (London), July 15, 1856.

4 *Ibid.*

5 Article with accompanying portrait announcing "The New Commander-in-Chief" in from the August 1856 edition of the *United Service Magazine.* The article praised Cambridge as uniquely qualified for the position. Curiously, it observed he was "no carped knight, whose knowledge of the art of war has been acquired on parades and reviews: but has nobly won his spurs in the fiercest throes of battle." More remarkable still, is that the article goes on to say, "The chivalrous Prince who has now become our chief proceeded to the Crimea in a subordinate rank, and in command of his division, exhibited those qualities which, quite apart from his exalted birth, marked him for future preferment."

creation of the Staff College and improvements in military education, it was his stubborn defense of the purchase system that has forever painted him as an obstacle to all reform. Overall, however, in the summer of 1856 the question of how much Cambridge would do–and *could* do–as Commander-in-Chief with the support of the Queen was far from certain.

I

Cambridge wasted little time in attempting to influence the size and shape of the army. Both he and the Queen were disturbed at the constant reductions in the size and funding for the army, but whether their combined efforts would be able to affect its fate was yet to be determined. Regardless of what lay ahead, the Queen responded with great satisfaction to the General Order published July 16, 1856, announcing, "In obedience to the gracious order of her Majesty, General his Royal Highness the Duke of Cambridge assumes the command of the Army, which has been confided to him by her Majesty's favour, on the resignation of Field-Marshal Viscount Hardinge."[6] Writing to the Duke from Osborne House on July 19, the Queen found the General Order to be "a very appropriate one," and then with her characteristic attention to detail regarding all things military, admonished the Duke that the beards of the grenadiers of the 18th Royal Irish Regiment had been cut too short, an "important subject."[7] Naturally Cambridge reacted quickly and dictated a memorandum governing beards and moustaches.[8] He then passed it to the Queen on July 22, 1856, so she would know the army regulation.[9] Somewhat comically, the Queen's consternation over the lack of facial hair would be a recurring theme between her and the Duke in the years to come. It is open to question why she was so concerned with the matter of beards–perhaps she viewed them as proof of her soldier's hardiness–but unfortunately the Queen forgot that not all men can grow a substantial beard, and her desire that soldiers should have full beards would be impracticable to carry out.

---

6 RA VIC/E7/96, General Order, dated July 16, 1856, announcing the Duke of Cambridge as the Commander-in-Chief.

7 Letter from Queen Victoria to the Duke of Cambridge, dated July 19, 1856, reproduced in Verner, vol. 1, 116-117.

8 RA VIC/E7/110, Memorandum from the Adjutant General to the Duke of Cambridge, undated, regarding beards and moustaches.

9 RA VIC/E7/109, Letter from the Duke of Cambridge to Queen Victoria, dated July 22, 1856.

As ludicrous as this minor matter regarding beards might appear, it is important for more than just its revelation of the Queen's keen interest in the army and her interaction with her cousin. It also provides an example of an area where the Commander-in-Chief had definite control: matters of discipline and appearance. When Cambridge assumed his duties, the actual powers of his office were not written, nor were they very expansive. In theory, he was responsible directly to the Crown for the cavalry and the infantry regiments. The army was a parliamentary army–Parliament determined its budget–while the Secretary of State for War, running the War Department, was responsible to Parliament for executing the government's policies abroad.

The Commander-in-Chief commanded only the forces stationed in the home islands and his ability to command was limited by a number of factors. With no power to affect operations overseas other than to recommend officers for command, the Commander-in-Chief could only request information and read dispatches and accounts in the papers. Even his command of units at home was limited by the lack of any higher organization than division–regiments were their own, virtually independent, entities. The Commander-in-Chief issued regulations, but it was up to regimental commanders to execute them as they saw fit. Even the types of equipment and weapons used by the army were beyond his control since the Ordnance department had responsibility for them. Despite these many constraints, the Commander-in-Chief was indeed the highest ranking officer in the army, and the force of personality of the individual occupying the office could wield a great amount of influence, as had definitely been the case with Wellington. Much of what the office would become would therefore be up to the individual personal character and leadership of the Duke of Cambridge.

As would be expected with anyone assuming a new position, the Duke concentrated his first months in office on immersing himself with the responsibilities of his position, something he continued for the remainder of his life. Much of his time was engaged by correspondence with general officers and regimental commanders scattered throughout the vast British Empire. Related to this was the constant requirement for the suitability of various officers for command, promotion, and awards. In terms of administrative zeal, Cambridge was the equal of Victorian-era correspondents–his personal correspondence to the Queen, members of the government, and senior officers throughout the British army fills many dozens of volumes, each of hundreds of pages. And although he may not have exceeded the quantity of his royal cousin the Queen, he came close.[10] It was not unusual for him to write several detailed letters a day numbering eight or more tightly-scripted pages. The pace and sheer number of the Duke's letters, as well as the surety of his opinions, remained consistently high from the first weeks to the last years of his command. Just weeks into his new role, it would not be a gross exaggeration to describe the correspondence to the Queen as a flood of communication.[11]

Almost immediately Cambridge made his presence felt as he pressed the Queen and the War Office for change. Barely a week after becoming Commander-in-Chief, the Duke, with surprising confidence and perhaps a small break with tradition, urged the abolition of a policy advocated by his predecessor, Lord Hardinge. On July 24, Cambridge asked the Queen to reverse a previous change she had approved for Lord Hardinge. Rather than have brigades commanded by brigadier generals, the Duke believed that "Colonels to be appointed to command Brigades in the United Kingdom, Malta, Gibraltar, and North America should be commissioned as Major Generals with temporary Rank,"[12] to cover the additional expenses incurred by brigade commanders.[13] Although Cambridge had discussed the proposal with Prince Albert prior to approaching the Queen, it was a substantial decision to make after only a few days in office.

The Duke's confidence in interacting with the Queen was not surprising considering their lifelong association, and on occasion he was also willing to challenge her, especially concerning selection for key commands. A vacant brigade command at Malta during late summer 1856 is a case in

---

10 Whereas the handwriting of Queen Victoria is well known for its unique style, the Duke of Cambridge had his own telltale style that omitted the crossing of the letter "t" among other special characteristics.

11 RA VIC/E8/2, RA VIC/E8/3, RA VIC/E8/5, Letters from the Duke of Cambridge to Queen Victoria, dated August 2, August 2 and August 5, 1856 respectively. Together, these detailed memoranda written for the benefit of the Queen regarding proposed organization and distribution of the army as well as the suitability of select officers for regimental and battalion command highlight Cambridge's regular interaction with the Queen regarding the state of the army.

12 RA VIC/E7/111, Letter from the Duke of Cambridge to Queen Victoria, dated July 24, 1856. The Duke, with the concurrence of the Secretary of State for War, Lord Panmure, believed that brigade commanders should hold the temporary rank of Major General to enable them to meet better the expenses required of them. The Queen concurred with the recommendation.

13 Cambridge believed that "…for these officers the rate of pay of a major general…is essential to enable them to meet the expenses to which they will be exposed." *Ibid.*

point. In August he asked that Colonel Horn be given command there, despite his advanced age.[14] Although Horn was well into his *seventies*, the Duke argued he deserved command as a reward for faithful service, even if there were younger officers more capable available to fill the position. Without a hint of self-consciousness, Cambridge noted that "Colonel Horn served with the army from the time of its landing in the Crimea 'till its return to England," adding that he was "also enabled to speak to the gallantry of Colonel Horn at the Battle of Inkermann where he was wounded but did not leave the field…"[15] Although Victoria reluctantly consented, she reminded Cambridge of his previous position on age and retirement[16] and observed, again without any apparent irony, "that these appointments by selection ought to be given to as young and active colonels as possible as the only mode of obtaining a few major generals fit for general service and is therefore very sorry that Colonel Horn's name should be submitted…"[17] Although just one incident, it indicates that personal relationships and reputation were more important to the Duke than abstract principles. The placement of Colonel Horn was exactly the type of situation Cambridge had protested as Inspector-General of Cavalry. Now that the Duke was in the one position that would have perhaps the greatest influence on the selection of officers for command, he qualified his previous stance on old age.[18]

Cambridge also maintained great interest for the welfare of the common soldier and used his influence with the Queen to promote it. An example of two sergeants denied the Legion of Honor demonstrates this interest. The time limit for the medals had expired, and although their commanding officers had recommended them, an administrative oversight prevented proper recognition. Since the Queen reserved the right to approve all military decorations, on August 12, 1856, Cambridge

---

14 RA VIC/E8/12, Letter from the Duke of Cambridge to Queen Victoria, dated August 12, 1856.

15 *Ibid.*

16 See Chapter 2 for a discussion of the Duke's memorandum, "The Age of General Officers," published in December 1853.

17 RA VIC/E8/13, Letter from Queen Victoria to the Duke of Cambridge, dated August 14, 1856. Victoria stated that in the future the Duke would follow "the principle above set forth…in future recommendations, so that the Queen is not placed in the invidious position of having to refuse the appointment of officers who have otherwise well served their country."

18 Another factor might be that Cambridge believed that to reject Colonel Horn for command, despite his heroic and lengthy service in the Crimea, would make Cambridge vulnerable to painful questions about his own more limited time there.

intervened successfully to correct the injustice.[19] He would continue to do so in similar cases.[20] Actions such as these helped earn Cambridge the devotion of many of the enlisted soldiers throughout the army. More importantly, it demonstrated that to Cambridge individuals mattered, even enlisted men, but that systemically he gave little thought to the larger problems their cases represented. Both in the cases of Colonel Horn and the two noncommissioned officers, Cambridge used his position as Commander-in-Chief to remedy a situation for specific men, but did not use the examples before him to correct systemic problems throughout the army. With Colonel Horn he took the position opposite to one on which he was on record supporting. Similarly, regarding the two sergeants, he did not issue an army-wide directive looking for similar cases preventing future similar oversights. Instead, Cambridge continued to deal with problems on a case-by-case basis and not adopt a systematic approach. In his view and the Queen's view, the army remained a system of personal relationships rather than a larger rational organization.

II

The issue to which the Duke's response was the most predictable, and one where he never gave in without a fight throughout his tenure as Commander-in-Chief, was reduction in the size and strength of the army. Cutbacks to the army after Waterloo obviously contributed to its poor performance during the Crimean War. Once Napoleon had been defeated, the British army's main role was to garrison the British Empire, and the Royal Navy was charged with keeping the lines of communication open to the colonies and protecting the home islands. Whether reductions affected tactical performance is debatable, but as an institution it was clear the army was not prepared for the demands of widescale mobilization and deployment requirements for modern war. Cambridge was committed to preventing a recurrence in the wake of the Crimean War. Interaction between Victoria and Cambridge frequently dealt with preventing reductions, but since neither of them had authority over army funding, their efforts were largely unsuccessful.

---

19 RA VIC/E8/11, Letter from the Duke of Cambridge to Queen Victoria, dated August 12, 1856.
20 RA VIC/E8/14, Letter from Queen Victoria to the Duke of Cambridge, dated August 14, 1856. The Queen agreed to the Duke's request for the soldiers to receive the Legion of Honour.

Britain had had a parliamentary army for over a century and a half. Since Parliament's vote for "establishment" during the reign of William and Mary in 1692, the Crown's discipline over the army was contingent upon funding from Parliament.[21]   The defeat of Napoleon incurred tremendous cost–far greater than anything Britain ever experienced until the First World War–and afterward the government undertook strict fiscal expenditure, especially regarding the military. Between 1815 and 1880, Britain's funding for its army, in total amount, per capita and per soldier was significantly lower than military spending than that of continental powers.[22] Then as now, defense budgets are one of the most expensive and therefore tempting areas of the government expenditure to reduce. Once in office, Cambridge had the daunting task of transitioning the British army from waging war to being prepared to fight one. Begun under Palmerston in 1855, army reorganization brought real change, although not necessarily genuine efficiency.

The Duke's first year was characterized by dedication to reform and his intimate knowledge of the true condition of the post-Crimean British army proved useful. Although not immediately enacted, his ideas were sound and eventually carried out. He recommended the Medical Staff Corps become an army-wide organization rather than a regimental-level one.[23] He sought to improve the army reserve and prepare the army for rapid mobilization by linking militia regiments with active regiments. He hoped to strengthen what would today be termed officer professional education by trying to create an oversight department for military education and the addition of a fortification and surveying course at Chatham.[24] However, despite his focus on reform, the Queen's major concern continued to be martial appearance. Not facial hair this time, she was concerned that the uniform of the Director General of the Army Medical Department should be distinguishable from that of other officers of the rank of major general.[25] Her cousin's arguments in favor of army reform did not move her.

---

21 Gordon, 25-26.
22 Philip Harling, *The Waning of 'Old Corruption': The Politics of Economical Reform in Britain, 1779-1846* (Oxford: Clarendon Press, 1996), 12-13. Harling demonstrates that the quest for "cheap government" after the Napoleonic War reversed the pre-war trend towards higher levels of government expenditure. This attitude lasted until the final two decades of the century.
23 Verner, vol. 1, 117.
24 Verner, vol. 2, 446-447.
25 RA VIC/E8/19, Letter from Queen Victoria to the Duke of Cambridge, dated August 27, 1856.

Although Cambridge was a strong proponent of tradition, he was not against change, especially at the start of his tenure, and in succeeding years continued to press for the reforms mentioned above and additional ones (with mixed results). Although the relationship between the Duke and his first Secretary of State for War, Lord Panmure, was far more cordial than it would be a decade later with Edward Cardwell, even Panmure and Cambridge were often working toward different ends and clashed frequently. As a Cabinet member, Lord Panmure was responsible to the Prime Minister and the government to curtail expenditures while at the same time reassuring the country that the army was well prepared to defend the nation. The Commander-in-Chief, on the other hand, was motivated strictly by his loyalty to the army and the Queen and therefore sought to maintain the army at the highest level of effectiveness.

In his capacity as Secretary of State for War, Lord Panmure would send Cambridge the proposed budget for the coming year's annual estimates prior to sending it to the Queen for her approval. On August 11, 1856, Panmure intimated he tried to be generous towards the army yet produce a budget, "likely to pass thro' Parliament and to stand the attacks of the economists..."[26] Well aware of the great shortcomings in army administration and efficiency demonstrated during the Crimean War, Cambridge was concerned the "peace establishment" would negate lessons learned at the cost of British soldiers' lives.[27] Dissatisfied with the proposed reductions, he reminded Panmure on August 15 that Europe remained unsettled, while "At present the Army is in a most efficient state, and much has been spent arriving at that point. It would be a pity to throw this efficiency away hastily..."[28] Voluminous correspondence between Queen Victoria, Lord Panmure, and the Duke of Cambridge followed regarding the peace establishment, but in the end Parliament's desire for economy prevailed. Consistent with her intense interest in the army, Victoria besieged Panmure for information regarding the peace establishment. During the last week of August and the first two weeks of September 1856, he responded no less than three times with each answer

---

26 Letter from Lord Panmure to the Duke of Cambridge, dated August 11, 1856, reproduced in Verner, vol. 1, 118-119.

27 The term peace establishment was used to describe the post war size, organization and disposition of the British army.

28 Letter from the Duke of Cambridge to Lord Panmure, dated August 11, 1856, reproduced in *Ibid.*, 119.

prompting further questions.[29] For decades to come the Queen, the Duke of Cambridge, and the Secretary of State for War would interact in a similar manner with similar results.

Despite his deep involvement with the reorganization of the army, there was little Cambridge could do to affect the budget other than argue with the Secretary for War or the Prime Minister for more money. Seeking to maximize efficiency and balance overseas requirements while still providing necessary forces for home defense and training, he benefitted from his understanding of the true state of the army. Memoranda he had written while Inspector General of Cavalry now proved to be of greater value. He resurrected the twenty-page memorandum, "Observations on the Organisation of the British Army at Home," from December 1852.[30] It explained the army was not ready for modern war: no organization existed above regimental level, no large scale maneuvers had been conducted since the Napoleonic Wars, and the militia was ill-equipped and not trained to provide serious defense of Great Britain. Similarly, "Observations on the Organsation of the British Army at Home" and "Observations on the Regimental Organisation of the British Infantry, with Suggestions for its Improvement" identified significant problems.[31] Within the British army there was, "no uniform system adopted."[32]

Needless to say, the Duke had been unable to bring about the changes he proposed in 1852 and 1853, but his suggestions generated a great deal of interest and discussion which later saw partial implementation.[33] With responsibility for only the branch of cavalry, he had had no authority over the army as a whole. To enact widespread change would have required the full commitment of the Commander-in-Chief, the Secretary of State for War, and other departments of the army affected, not to mention Parliament, which would have had to have funded any required changes. Although the memoranda generated discussion, the Crimean War soon overshadowed Cambridge's proposals. Despite great interest on the part of Prince Albert

---

29 RA VIC/E8/27-32, Letters from Lord Panmure to Queen Victoria regarding army organization and the peace establishment, dated August and September 1856.

30 Verner, vol. 1, 34-60.

31 RA VIC/E2/54, Memorandum by the Duke of Cambridge, dated January 1853, "Observations on the RegimentalOrganisation of the British Army."

32 *Ibid.*

33 For a detailed discussion of the Duke's proposals while Inspector-General of Cavalry, see Verner, vol. 1, 36-60.

and his military secretary, Colonel Grey,[34] the Duke was unsuccessful in implementing any of his proposals prior to the Crimean War.

As Commander-in-Chief, Cambridge attempted once again to reorganize and standardize the regiments. He tried to convince the Secretary of State for War, Lord Panmure, that the army needed fundamental reorganization and improvement in training. During the last two months of 1856 alone, Cambridge wrote fifteen 15 detailed memoranda and letters to Lord Panmure and Queen Victoria to enact his desired reforms.[35] He continued his efforts well into 1857 but was unable to change much. Unfortunately for his efforts, the impetus for reform had been generated prior to his assumption of office so that, ironically, as Commander-in-Chief, he had little power to influence existing appropriations and reforms already approved. Palmerston's government had begun change almost immediately and most programs were in place prior to the time Cambridge came to office. Subsequent developments in foreign affairs, most notably the Indian Mutiny (to be discussed later), reduced demand for further reform, so that many of Cambridge's ideas had already been acted upon prior to his entrance into the Horse Guards or were neglected for a decade or more after he got there.

Despite Cambridge's inability to bring about significant change, Queen Victoria was not at all troubled for she had wanted her cousin to act as a bulwark against civilian interference with "her army" and to prevent any radical change to the status quo. Within several months of his assumption of office, it was clear the Queen was pleased by the Duke's performance and any doubts regarding his suitability had evaporated. Victoria frequently recorded her satisfaction in her journal. An example from October 26, 1856, illustrates her opinion: "Remained talking with George, after breakfast, for some time, about military matters, and also when we walked out with him later. I must say I think he is much devoted to his office and very active and energetic, in getting things into good and proper order."[36]

---

34 RA VIC/E2/58, Letter from Colonel Grey to the Duke of Cambridge, dated February 7, 1853 and enclosed "Memorandum: Formation and Distribution of Proposed Provisional Battalions." Prince Albert and his military secretary, Colonel Grey, responded favorably to the Duke's memoranda and saw the need for additional standardization of the regiments throughout the army.

35 RA VIC/E8/64-114 passim. Between October 13, 1856 and December 24, 1856 the Duke bombarded Lord Panmure, Prince Albert and the Queen with his suggestions for army organization.

36 RA QVJ: 29 October 1856, journal entry of Queen Victoria, dated October 29, 1856.

Undaunted by the inertia of military bureaucracy, Cambridge continued writing letters and memoranda. Another long-sought goal was to hold large-scale organized maneuvers–it had happened once during the summer of 1853 for two months at Chobham. For the first time since the defeat of Napoleon, regiments conducted coordinated operations in the field simultaneously. Although not solely the result of his advocacy, Cambridge's numerous memoranda from 1852 had impressed Prince Albert and Lord Hardinge. For two months in the summer of 1853, tens of thousands of soldiers were encamped in the field. The maneuvers attracted great attention, being a completely new phenomenon within the United Kingdom, and the *Times* followed them in "the wilds of Surrey" with great interest.[37] Almost two decades would pass before they were again attempted, and they did not accomplish much of anything, certainly not the army's ability to fight, as the war in the Crimea would shortly demonstrate. In the words of an officer in the Royal Artillery, the maneuvers proved, "This Army is in shambles."[38]

By 1857, despite his desire to make the Surrey maneuvers of 1853 a recurring event, the Duke reversed his earlier position. Many regiments returning from the Crimea were garrisoned at Aldershot, a suitable site for large-scale maneuvers. Presented with a contemporary-sounding dilemma, Cambridge weighed troop welfare against readiness and in this case, the moniker, "the soldier's friend," proved accurate. Extended encampments in isolated locations lacking permanent infrastructure were horrible for troop morale, welfare, and recruiting. While officers had the means and permission to leave, regular soldiers were relegated to living in tents pitched in mud–the only leisure activity was drink. Recognizing that garrisoning large formations restricted available space for maneuvers, thus mitigating the reason for them in the first place, while the impact on morale and recruiting was disastrous, Cambridge postponed them indefinitely due to the poor conditions at Aldershot.[39] For almost two years, Aldershot

37 *Times* (London), August 16, 1853. Articles covering the maneuvers continued on to the breakup of camp on August 20, 1853.

38 Christopher Hibbert, *The Destruction of Lord Raglan* (London: Longmans, 1961), 8. From a technical and tactical standpoint, the maneuvers were less than impressive indeed. Commanders frequently lost control of their units and occasionally became lost themselves so that a common sight was the ridiculous spectacle of units maneuvering aimlessly while the commander was out of sight on a wild goose chase of his own. A lasting consequence which remains to the present day was the purchase of nine thousand acres in Hampshire for the purpose of future maneuvers. The site is today known as Aldershot and it remains as one of the major training areas of the British army.

39 In 1871 and 1872 under the auspices of the Secretary of State for War, Lord Cardwell, and the Duke

remained a large encampment for returning regiments from the Crimea and soldiers stationed there were subjected to conditions which Cambridge lamented. It was the first peacetime organization above regimental level, but only temporary, and it would not occur again until 1901.[40]

III

The Duke of Cambridge's greatest success at reform involved military education. Prior to his assumption of duties as Commander-in-Chief, there had been other prominent advocates of improving officer education, most notably Lord Panmure's predecessor, Sidney Herbert–Secretary of State for War from 1852-1855–the Prime Minister–Lord Palmerston–and Prince Albert.[41] Even before their interest, the matter had received inconsistent emphasis during the preceding half century.[42] Due to the poor performance of British officers, especially staff officers,[43] during the wars against France in the 1790s, the Duke of York[44] founded a Royal Military College in 1799 with a cadet department temporarily founded at Marlowe, but permanently at Sandhurst in 1812. A staff department was formed at High Wycombe, and it later joined the junior department at Sandhurst, quickly developing into a quality institution producing capable officers by the final years of the Napoleonic Wars. Decades later on June 5, 1856, Sidney Herbert would inform Parliament that "During the last five years of the Peninsular War I believe there was but one officer on the staff of the Quartermaster General who had not passed through our staff school at High Wycombe."[45]

The courses taught at the staff school were overwhelmingly practical and focused primarily on surveying and sketching and in no way attempted

---

of Cambridge, large scale maneuvers would once again take place, although it was to be the last time during the 19th century.

40 Verner, vol. 2, 445.

41 Verner, vol. 1, 132.

42 See "Chapter Two: The Decline of the Senior Department and the Foundation of the Staff College 1815-1858" in Brian Bond, *The Victorian Army and the Staff College* (London: Eyre Meuthen, 1972), 51-81.

43 There were three categories of staff officer: the personal staff to general officers, staff members of the civilian departments and officers belonging to the Department of the Adjutant General and the Department of the Quartermaster-General.

44 Although the Duke of York was the sponsor and founder of the Royal Military College, it was the capable and veteran cavalry officer, Colonel (later Major General) John Gaspard Le Marchant, who was the driving force behind creating the Royal Military College.

45 *Hansard's Parliamentary Debates 1066-1918*, 3rd Series, Vol. 142, 996.

to produce the type of staff officer to be found in the Prussian system.[46] The British goal was to create staff officers who were technically proficient, but not necessarily independent thinkers with much individual authority.[47] Despite its success by the end of the Napoleonic Wars, the staff school fell into disfavor between Waterloo and the Crimean War for a variety of reasons. The Duke of Wellington never supported the staff course or its graduates, preferring instead officers of "family, fortune, and influence."[48] Wellington's attitude and comments obviously did not help the school. The never-ending governmental drive for economy resulted in ever-smaller budgets until funding went away altogether in 1832.[49]

As noted, the Crimean War revealed great inefficiency and incompetence, generating demand for serious reform in virtually every area of army organization and training. Thinking officers quickly realized that the absence of a trained corps of senior staff officers was a serious deficiency. The aforementioned *Report of the Select Committee on the Royal Military College* released June 18, 1855, was testament to the gravity of the situation.[50] Shortly before Cambridge became Commander-in-Chief, Sidney Herbert, as a back bencher in Parliament, once again raised the issue of educational reform. Supported by General Sir De Lacy Evans and other influential back benchers, Herbert reminded the House of

---

46 An important work in English dedicated strictly to the Prussian General Staff is Walter Görlitz, *The History of the German General Staff, 1657-1945* (New York: Praeger, 1953). Although a journalist, Görlitz presents a useful but uneven account. For the larger relation of the Prussian General Staff and the army's relation to the state, see Gordon Craig, *Politics of the Prussian Army, 1640-1945* (Oxford: Oxford University Press, 1955). Trevor N. Dupuy, *A Genius for War: The German Army and the General Staff, 1807-1945* (Englewood Cliffs, NJ: 1977) is also helpful, but must be treated with caution as the author does not take a critical approach to his subject.

47 Bond, *The Victorian Army and the Staff College*, 52. Unlike the Prussian system where the chief of staff had a great deal of autonomy and authority in relation to the commander, under the British system, the chief of staff had little if any decision-making authority and instead served primarily as an advisor to the commander.

48 S.G.P. Ward, *Wellington's Headquarters* (London: Routlege, 1957), 159.

49 The Parliamentary grant for the college ceased this year and students in the senior college had to pay an annual fee of £15. It is not surprising that the size of the class had by then shrunk to fifteen students.

50 The results of the *Report* were so deplorable that the new Secretary for War, Lord Panmure, formed a three-man committee to investigate the best way to reorganize the training of the officers belonging to the scientific corps (the Royal Artillery and the Royal Engineers). The committee traveled throughout the Continent and found that whereas Britain spent approximately £1,300 annually on officer education, Prussia spent £26,000, France spent £48,000 and Austria spent over £1127,000 annually. From Great Britain. Parliamentary (sessional) Papers. *Report of the Commissioners Appointed to Consider the Best Mode of Reorganizing the System for Training Officers and for the Scientific Corps*, Parliamentary Paper C.57, 1857, Session 1., VI, xix-xl.

his earlier pre-war proposals, urging restitution of the senior department of the staff school and the requirement that senior officers hold staff school certificates or substitute qualification to receive staff appointments.[51]

Concurrent with the drive for educational reform in the Commons, Prince Albert and the Duke of Cambridge agreed that the military educational system needed great improvement. Albert's memorandum of January 1855 stressed the need for educated, competent general officers and a staff corps to train subordinate officers for field duty.[52] Cambridge soon took the lead in pressing for reform. The Rev. George Robert Gleig, Chaplain General for her Majesty's forces, expressed his hope that Cambridge might bring a new attitude for reform: "Hitherto there has been a fixed determination at the Horse Guards not to move in the matter at all. And this underground hostility to change drove the War Office to do the work–which ought to have been done by the Duke of Wellington and Lord Hardinge."[53] Gleig informed Cambridge, "times, as well as men, are now changed, and it is, I think, in the power of Your Royal Highness to reassume the authority which to a considerable extent had passed out of the hands of your predecessors. You will be able to manage the education of the Army for yourself…"[54]

This prompting influenced the Duke to act and he consulted with Prince Albert on reforming the education system well into 1857. Here was a case where Prince Albert's advocacy of modernizing the army was put into effect. Cambridge organized a small committee of officers to report on the subject, and on November 27 he forwarded his findings to Prince Albert.[55] For several weeks the two worked through the details. The most serious item of contention concerned the educational background of future officers. Whereas Prince Albert believed all candidates for commissions should undergo military schooling before commissioning, Cambridge believed it crucial to have some officers with a public school[56] background,

---

51 Sidney Herbert speaking before the House of Commons, June 5, 1856, *Hansard's Parliamentary Debates 1066-1918*, 3rd Series, Vol. 142, 980-1001.
52 RA VIC/E5/5, Prince Consort's Memorandum on the Army, dated January 14, 1855.
53 RA VIC/Add E1/538 (M), Letter from Mr. Gleig to the Duke of Cambridge, dated November 1, 1856.
54 *Ibid.*
55 RA VIC/E8/93-94, Letter with enclosed memorandum from the Duke of Cambridge to Prince Albert, dated November 27, 1856.
56 Unlike the American usage, for the past several centuries public school in Britain has always meant the elite and very expensive private boarding schools whose pupils normally came from the upper class. The most famous were Eton, Harrow and Rugby. The name derives from the fact that anyone

even though "the education may be in some respects defective, but it is the education of the best class of English gentlemen." [57] Although he supported reforming army education, to him it was nonnegotiable that the gentry be the source for officers. Cadets then entered Sandhurst between the ages of thirteen and fifteen so some may not have had the opportunity to attend public school. Cambridge recommended the minimum age for entrance to Sandhurst be raised to sixteen and that there be two distinct classes of cadets: those from the public schools and regular Sandhurst cadets. All cadets would have to pass the same professional examinations.

Prince Albert and the Duke of Cambridge ultimately came to a consensus in December and forwarded the amended plan with progressive recommendations to the Secretary of State for War, Lord Panmure. [58] The educational system would be uniform for all officers, the Commander-in-Chief would have a special, directly subordinate department responsible for the army educational system, and there would be four subordinate educational department members dedicated to the four primary arms of service, infantry, cavalry, artillery, and engineers. [59]

Simultaneous to but not coordinated with Cambridge's efforts, Lord Panmure directed the War Office to undertake a similar initiative. A bright young artillery officer, John Henry Lefroy, famous for his assistance to Florence Nightingale in the Crimea, made proposals similar to those of Albert and Cambridge. [60] Months of extended negotiations ultimately bore fruit in April 1857 with the creation of the Council of Military Education. After considerable correspondence involving Panmure, Cambridge,

from the paying public could attend and that the school was not tied directly to a religious institution. A clear definition of what constituted a public school did not exist at this time; from 1861-1864 the Clarendon Commission investigated charges of abuse at public schools and the resulting Public Schools Act of 1868 clarified that there were nine public schools in England: Charterhouse School; Eton College; Harrow School; Merchant Taylor's School; Rugby School; Shrewsbury School; St. Paul's School; Westminster School; and Winchester College.

57 In the words of Cambridge, to deny entry to those with a public school background would remove from the army those "men who have formed their minds and tastes at the great public schools, together with the great majority of those who in after life are distinguished in statesmanship, in law, in literature, in religion, moral and physical science, and who, moreover, imbibe a tone at those great institutions, which is seldom found elsewhere." From Verner, vol. 1, 138.

58 RA VIC/Add E1/558 (M), Letter from the Duke of Cambridge to Lord Panmure, dated December 12, 1856.

59 *Ibid.* The proposal included much more than these items, but these were the essential recommendations.

60 Spiers, *The Army and Society, 1815-1914*, 153. For Lefroy's influence, see Brian Bond, *The Victorian Army and the Staff College*, 66-70. Bond makes a convincing argument that Lefroy greatly influenced the plan put forth by Cambridge and Prince Albert.

Albert, and Victoria, Cambridge sent a final draft of the proposal to the Queen on April 3, 1857 that she approved happily.[61] Cambridge served as the president of the Council; the Vice President, who would do most of the work, was Major General Duncan Cameron, while Lieutenant Colonel Lefroy was relegated to the post of Inspector-General of Army Schools.[62] The rather ignominious posting of Lefroy–Lord Panmure wanted him to be Director-General of Military Education–was the wish of Queen Victoria. She objected to Lefroy's junior rank and insisted the Director-General of Military Education should be directly under the Horse Guards.[63] Naturally Cambridge agreed with the Queen, and Panmure failed to overcome their united opposition.

A General Order dated April 9, 1857, stipulated that the Council of Military Education would select examiners and prepare examinations for those seeking army commissions as well as admission to the staff school. The Council would also oversee subsequent promotions and recommendations for instructors and professors at the Staff School, the Royal Military College, Sandhurst, and the Royal Military Academy, Woolwich. The Order further defined the qualities required of all staff officers by January 1, 1858. The focus was primarily upon practical skills, such as the ability to ride well, write legibly (rather ironic considering the Duke himself lacked this characteristic), demonstrate proficiency in sketching, trigonometry, military history, geography, at least one foreign language, the principles of fortification, as well as the ability to read terrain and determine its suitability for all branches of service.[64] Although the term would not have then been in vogue, the requirements would later be seen as core attributes of a professional officer. They were quite progressive.

Although the essential qualifications for staff officers had been settled, there was still no requirement for a separate staff school to produce these qualified officers. Determined to implement their reforms and concerned they would be neglected indefinitely, Sidney Herbert and General Sir

---

61 Letter from Queen Victoria to the Duke of Cambridge, dated April 4, 1857, reproduced in Verner, vol. 1, 141.

62 Spiers, *The Army and Society, 1815-1914*, 153; Bond, *The Victorian Army and the Staff College*, 70-71; Verner, vol. 1, 140-142.

63 Letter from Lord Panmure to Queen Victoria dated February 15, 1857 and reply by Queen Victoria to Lord Panmure dated February 17, 1857 reproduced in Sir George Douglas Bart and Ramsay, Sir George Dalhousie, eds, *The Panmure Papers*, vol. 2 (London: Hodder and Stoughton, 1908), 352-254 and 355-356.

64 Verner, vol. 1, 141-142; Spiers, *The Army and Society, 1815-1914*, 153.

George De Lacy Evans once again raised the issue before the House of Commons, urging that the level of instruction for the commissioned ranks in the army and especially that for the staff be raised significantly.[65] For the next few months the Council of Military Education debated the contents of the entrance examination and what the course of study at the Staff College should be. Cambridge and Prince Albert were especially concerned at what they viewed as an overemphasis on abstract mathematics. Albert wrote to the Duke asking, "What is to be gained by making the officers of the Army, and the Staff in particular, abstract <u>mathematicians</u> instead of <u>scientific</u> <u>soldiers</u>?"[66] Concurring with the Prince Consort, Cambridge forwarded Albert's comments on to Lord Panmure on November 3 with the observation that there was "a great deal of truth in them," and that the Vice President of the Council, General Cameron, was "inclined to think the same."[67] The Queen refused to sign the memorandum until the issue had been solved to the satisfaction of all parties. The provision for "abstract mathematics" was reduced and Cambridge, Panmure, and the Prince Consort agreed to a plan that represented the formation of a professional Staff College. The Council of Military Education issued a revised General Order and Regulations on December 17, 1857 and replaced the old title of the Senior Department with the Staff College after "fifty-eight years of chequered existence."[68] After January 1, 1860, the only way to become a staff officer was graduation from the Staff College unless the officer already held the rank of lieutenant colonel or he had already proved his fitness for staff appointments in the field.[69]

Thus after years of attempts by dedicated reformers, an essential prerequisite for a professional officer corps—a higher-level education system for senior officers—was finally established. Whether the Staff College would fulfill the highest expectations of ardent reformers remained to be seen. A General Order dated June 3, 1858 stipulated the College would be open to overseas- and home-stationed officers of all branches.[70] Officers with a minimum of three years' service could apply, but admission was by

---

65 Sidney Herbert speaking before the House of Commons, July 28, 1857, *Hansard's Parliamentary Debates 1066-1918*, 3rd Series, Vol. 147, 569-608.

66 RA VIC/E10/13, Memorandum by Prince Albert, Remarks on the 'Report of the Committee for Education on the reorganization of the R.M.C. at Sandhurst, dated October 31, 1857.

67 Verner, vol. 1, 143.

68 Bond, *The Victorian Army and the Staff College*, 73.

69 *Ibid.*

70 Verner, vol. 1, 143.

competitive examination only. Total enrollment would be thirty officers with twenty-five from the infantry and cavalry and five from the artillery and engineers, if any wished to compete for the two-year course, divided into four semesters, beginning on February 1 each year.[71] Examinations focused on Mathematics, Military History, French, Chemistry, German, Geology, Fortifications, and Military Drawing.[72] Cambridge inserted a significant loophole in the graduation requirements by allowing some officers to take the examination at the end of the first year without having attended and to attend the second year only, and, in extreme cases, be allowed to take all examinations without attending the course.[73] As Lieutenant Colonel Lefroy aptly noted, such a provision undermined the position of the college if it was possible to graduate without ever even going to Sandhurst.[74]

The Duke of Cambridge's involvement with the formation of the Staff College at Sandhurst runs counter to his subsequent reputation as an opponent of reform. In fact, he lent his name to Camberley.[75] Although his official military biographer, Colonel Verner, exaggerates when he writes, "so far from the Duke objecting to the Staff College, he made it,"[76] it is definitely the case that without Cambridge's influence the Staff College would not have been created when it was. While Sidney Herbert and General Sir George De Lacy Evans were instrumental in keeping alive the idea of a real Staff College, great opposition existed within the Horse Guards and many officers in the infantry and cavalry especially were steadfastly against it.[77] Prince Albert also offered key support to the creation of a professional Staff College. Significantly, the two men overcame the opposition of Queen Victoria, whose views were similar

---

71 Bond, *The Victorian Army and the Staff College*, 74.
72 Verner, vol. 1, 143; Bond, *The Victorian Army and the Staff College*, 74.
73 Verner, vol. 1, 143. The Duke presented a memorandum with this modification on June 7, 1858, immediately after the constitution of the Staff College was released.
74 Bond, *The Victorian Army and the Staff College*, 74.
75 Originally it was to be Cambridge, but that was too confusing given the existence of town of Cambridge in Cambridgeshire.
76 Verner, vol. 1, 147.
77 See Bond, *The Victorian Army and the Staff College*. For an investigation of the initial success of the Staff College see, "The New School: Major General Sir Patrick MacDougal" in Jay Luvaas, *The Education of an Army: British Military Thought, 1815-1940* (Chicago: University of Chicago Press, 1964), 101-129. General MacDougal was the Staff College's first commandant and he proved to be a serious contributor to military thought in Britain and Canada. He had a profound impact on the future of military education in the British army.

to Wellington regarding the Staff College and staff officers. Since the Duke of Cambridge was crucial to its creation, it was quite appropriate that the *Times* gave lead coverage to his cornerstone-laying ceremony for the new building on December 14, 1859.[78] Approximately one mile from the Royal Military College, Sandhurst, it was completed in 1862 and served its purpose until 1997, perhaps the most significant, lasting, and unrecognized legacy of the Duke of Cambridge on the subsequent history of the British army.[79]

IV

Although the years 1856 and 1857 witnessed serious attempts–and some successes–at reform in the organization, administration, and education of the British army, major developments in foreign affairs greatly affected and ultimately arrested the movement for reform. In the final months of 1856, a dispute with China developed into open conflict. The dispute originated with the seizure of a British-flagged vessel, the *Arrow*, and its crew. Registered under questionable circumstances in Hong Kong, although unknown to the Chinese authorities, the British Plenipotentiary in Hong Kong, Sir John Bowring, took punitive measures against the Chinese for what he determined was a violation of the 1842 Treaty of Nanking that had ceded Hong Kong to the British. Bowring destroyed Chinese forts. The situation escalated as the Chinese Governor Yeh put a bounty on Bowring's life, and he was almost assassinated through poison. By the end of the year, the British government sent an ultimatum to Governor Yeh, and Canton was bombarded and occupied by a joint British and French force. The Chinese refused to back down and the war continued until 1858 when Bowring was replaced with the more diplomatic Lord Elgin. The Treaty of Tientsin that year ended the war and granted most of the privileges to the British that Bowring had originally demanded.

The incident had political consequences back in London. In the House of Lords, Lord Derby introduced a motion condemning British actions,

---

78 *The Times* (London), December 15, 1859. The laying of the cornerstone and the foundation of the college by the Duke was the lead article in the *Times* that day.

79 The Staff College building now houses army administrative offices. The current Staff College is located at Watchfield near Shrivenham where budget cuts have forced a Joint–army, navy and air force–Services Command and Staff College. The last class graduated from Camberley in 1997.

subsequently defeated 146 to 110.[80] In the House of Commons things went differently. Richard Cobden introduced a similar motion on March 2, 1857, which brought Palmerston's government a vote of no confidence after four days of debate. In a curious coalition of Conservatives, Peelites, and the "Peace Party," Benjamin Disraeli, W.E. Gladstone, Lord John Russell, John Roebuck, and Lord Robert Cecil (afterwards Lord Salisbury) played prominent roles in the success of the motion which passed by sixteen votes: 263 to 247. Cambridge himself attended the debates and found them "very interesting."[81] In response to Disraeli's challenge, Palmerston dissolved Parliament, and new elections were held later that month. The elections destroyed the Peace Party and restored Palmerston's government in a decisive political victory.[82]

A much greater shock to the army, the government, and the British public was the Sepoy Mutiny in India in the summer of 1857. A local military mutiny in Meerut on May 10, 1857 quickly spread throughout the subcontinent in what was essentially a backlash against social, racial, and political developments caused by British rule in India. The immediate cause was cartridges in the new Enfield rifle. They were greased with fat from cows and pigs. To load the weapon, soldiers had to tear cartridges with their mouths, meaning that Hindus were participating in the slaughter of sacred cows while Muslim soldiers were ingesting forbidden pork. The combination of decades of economic and social reform according to British tastes coupled with a strong evangelical movement carried out by British missionaries sparked rebellion. Continued British territorial expansion and the ongoing British annexation of formerly independent Indian kingdoms under the "doctrine of lapse" also contributed to the unrest.[83] At first viewed as a local and spontaneous occurrence, the underlying causes had been mounting for years. British and colonial troops quelled the unrest by early 1858, but sporadic fighting continued for another two years.

The rebellion represented a decisive break in British policy toward India as the self-confidence of British rule was permanently undermined.

---

80 Sheppard, vol. 1, 183.

81 *Ibid.*

82 Benson and Esher, eds., *The Letters of Queen Victoria*, 1ˢᵗ ser., vol. 3, 283; *London Illustrated News*, January –May 1857.

83 The British doctrine of lapse was the system whereby and princely state of territory under the direct influence of the British East India Company would be annexed if the ruler of that state was incompetent or died without a direct heir. Under this policy large amounts of territory passed directly to the British, creating understandable anger amongst the Indians.

Writing to Queen Victoria shortly after the recapture of Delhi from the rebels, Lord Canning, Governor-General of India, reported that, "The reputation of England's power, too, has had a rude shake; and nothing but a long-continued manifestation of her might before the eyes of the whole Indian Empire, evinced by the presence of such an English force…will re-establish confidence in her strength."[84] Although the British public soon lost interest in Indian affairs, it meant the end of the East India Company as the Crown took direct control of the Indian government and the Indian army. The aftermath of the Mutiny also affected the post-Crimean reform movement for the army and allowed for a greater dominance of the conservative elements within the army. The relationship between India and Britain would never be the same. Many Indians reverted to an orthodox Hinduism and resented British progress and permanence. In turn, British civil servants lost respect and generosity towards the Indian people and saw increased firmness as the only solution to maintaining order.[85]

The incident in China and the Mutiny were the first military campaigns with which the Duke had to contend as Commander-in-Chief.[86] He was involved with military decisions but not as directly as might be supposed. The Secretary for War, Lord Panmure, made most of the decisions regarding the dispatching of regiments and naming individuals for command.[87] Nonetheless, Cambridge exercised great influence regarding the placement of individuals into command of the various regiments, although the ultimate approval rested with the Secretary of State for War, Lord Panmure, and then of course with the Queen herself.

---

84 Letter from Viscount Canning to Queen Victoria, dated July 4, 1857, reproduces in Benson and Esher, eds., *Letters,* 1st ser., vol. 3, 301.

85 Among many others, see Christopher Hibbert, *The Great Mutiny: India 1857* (New York: Viking, 1978).

86 Shortly before the crisis in China, the ongoing war with Persia had been settled. Technically the first war Cambridge encountered while Commander-in-Chief, Persia annexed the province of Heart in mid-1856 and Britain declared war on November 1, 1856. A small detachment of British and Indian troops under the command of Sir James Outram achieved local victories and by March 1857 the peace was signed. The Duke himself had little involvement and complained to Lord Panmure that he was insufficiently informed of developments. Panmure agreed and responded on March 18, 1857 that "the Y.R.H. [Cambridge] should see all military dispatches…" Letter from Lord Panmure to the Duke of Cambridge, dated March 18, 1857, reproduced in Verner, vol. 1, 149-150.

87 The personal papers of the Duke of Cambridge from this period are filled with correspondence with senior officers throughout the Empire and within England either accepting or rejecting commands. For example, Sir Colin Campbell writing to the Duke on May 9, 1857 thanking him for the "verbal offer" of service in China, but rejecting it on the basis of his 21 years of service in tropical climates. *Ibid.*, 151.

Perhaps more significant than the Duke's military correspondence and his continued frustration over inadequate direction of military operations in India–he again complained to Panmure about insufficient information[88]– was his frequent correspondence with the Queen. Cambridge and Victoria reinforced each other's position that army reductions had done irreparable damage and that the survival of the Empire was at stake. Both proceeded to bombard Panmure and Palmerston with their opinions regarding the size and condition of the army.[89] Cambridge was Commander-in-Chief of the forces at *home*, and therefore he could do little more than monitor events overseas–he certainly could not direct military operations. The Queen also had only the power of persuasion to influence how the military campaign was run. Prosecution of military action overseas was up to Parliament and the Prime Minister with the Secretary of State for War responsible for directing the government's military policy. It was the same for the funding of the army. The Queen and her cousin were therefore frustrated by the absence of real power while they also lamented the inadequate funding they were powerless to prevent.

For her part, the Queen saw the situation in India as a direct consequence of the Peace Establishment established after the Crimean War. Victoria corresponded frequently with Palmerston and Panmure expressing both detailed opinions as to which units should be sent to reinforce India and her great dissatisfaction over the reductions which developments in China had already stretched the army too thin. As a result, the army was unable to defend the homeland and send the required forces to India. A strongly worded letter to Lord Palmerston on July 19, 1857 is typical of many. She believed that "Contrary to the Queen's hopes and expectations, immediately after the late war the Army was cut down to a state even <u>below</u> the Peace Establishment recognized by the Government and Parliament in their own estimates…"[90]

---

88 In mid-August 1857 Cambridge complained that he was not being notified of matters relating to his command and in reply Lord Panmure wrote that the Duke received all of the material that Panmure did ("You see everything that comes to me at present, and I know of no military information which ought to have been communicated and which has not been so."), and besides much of it was political in nature ("There are many political matters often mixed up with some military details which reach the Government, but these of course are for the action of the responsible Ministers of the Crown."). Letter from Lord Panmure to the Duke of Cambridge, dated August 23, 1857, reproduced in *Ibid.*, 158.
89 Verner's biography presents extensive coverage both of the Duke's military correspondence and reproduces *in toto* the Duke's "Journal of the Mutiny Campaigns." What is telling throughout is how much the Duke is a commentator and observer, rather than a decision-maker. See *Ibid.*, 159-197.
90 RA VIC/E9/81, (Copy) Letter from Queen Victoria to Lord Palmerston, dated July 19, 1857.

The Queen's influence on the actual conduct of foreign policy was less than she would have hoped. The same held true for Cambridge. Both were forced to stand on the sidelines as the government dispatched forces, and the theater commander-in-chief reported back directly to the Secretary of State for War. Certainly the Queen held the Royal Prerogative and Cambridge protected it for her, but in actual practice such things meant little during military operations abroad. Issues that would have great effect on military operations–units to be sent, amounts of supplies, primary and secondary objectives of a certain campaign–were beyond the control of the royal cousins. The treatment afforded the Duke of Cambridge in the press was respectful, but it hardly portrayed him as being decisively involved with command decisions, army policy, or anything more than ceremony. Despite his great involvement with army reform during the first few years of his tenure, little of his efforts were reported. The rebellion in China and especially the Indian Mutiny caused great alarm in Great Britain, and the events were reported with great excitement in the national press. The actions of Cambridge, however, were not central to the coverage of either event, regardless of what may have occurred at the Horse Guards or within the War Office. For the most part, routine coverage of his actions detailed his addresses to various regiments being dispatched to China or to India.[91]

The popular but exclusive London weekly, *The Illustrated London News*, reflected fairly accurately how the Duke was portrayed and hence viewed by the reading public. Although the journal reported regularly on the weapons and tactics employed as well as the actions of key participants–the edition of March 14, 1857, depicted Chinese rebels in the attack and described the actions of Admiral Seymour against them[92]–the Commander-in-Chief was strictly a member of the royal family giving a pep talk to departing soldiers.[93] The most attention given to him at any

---

91 *The Illustrated London News* reported every Saturday the latest developments in domestic and international affairs with accompanying etchings for further edification of the stories contained therein. Whether it was "The War in China" covered in great detail throughout March, April and May 1857 (*The Illustrated London News*, March 14,21,28,April 4, May 9 1857, etc.), "The Mutiny in India" similarly reported from July 4, 1857 to the end of the year, or the various political developments such as the vote of no confidence in the government of Lord Palmerston in March 1857 and the subsequent elections which returned his government to power were detailed in the April 4th edition, the scope of the weekly was broad. Cambridge was frequently mentioned, but primarily as a figurehead.

92 *The Illustrated London News*, March 14, 1857.

93 The March 28, 1857 *Illustrated London News* listed those army and naval units destined as reinforcements for China, while it was reported "The General Commanding-in-Chief visited Portsmouth on Monday last to inspect the troops about to embark from that garrison for China...

point during the China rebellion or the Indian Mutiny occurred in a three-page article in the June 13, 1857 edition of the journal.[94] One full page was filled with a portrait of the Duke of Cambridge in uniform and another with two half-page etchings of the Duke in action followed by a full column detailing the actions of the Duke of Cambridge–the article was entitled "Inauguration of Calthorpe Park, Birmingham" and among other actions and speeches, it portrayed and described how the Duke planted a tree in the park.[95] The most detailed and reliable newspaper of the era, *The Times*, was similar in that it reported extensively on the developments in both crises, but coverage of the Duke was relegated to the section reporting on members of the royal family.

V

Still new to his position, the Duke of Cambridge occupied his post not only in the midst of a period of reform for the army, of which he was a surprisingly integral force, but also during a period of changing international relationships. It is clear he began his tenure firmly dedicated to improving certain areas of army organization, administration, and most especially education. Within a short time, however, Cambridge lost any reputation of being progressive. On the contrary, contemporaries soon came to regard him as an enemy of reform, a view which has become his legacy ever since. And while Cambridge was viewed as being progressive for at least a short period of time, Victoria was rarely if ever regarded as a proponent of reform for "her army." On the other hand, Prince Albert mitigated the Queen's more reactionary tendencies until his death in 1861. Over the long span of his tenure and her reign, Cambridge and Victoria drew closer together in their efforts to prevent or limit civilian interference with the military and to resist as much as possible further civilian control.

At the conclusion of the movements the troops formed hollow square, from the center of which the Duke addressed them, expressing his high admiration of the eminently-efficient manner in which they had performed the various manœuvres, the precision of their movements, and their soldierly front, proving themselves capable of adding to the fame of their several regiments and the glory of the British arms wherever they might be engaged…" Similar accounts followed, for example the May 9th edition reported with accompanying illustrations on "The Destruction of Piratical Junks" while on the following page an article described how "On Wednesday last the Duke of Cambridge reviewed the troops at Chatham."

94 *The Illustrated London News*, June 13, 1857.
95 *Ibid.*

Yet, as the China Rebellion and the Sepoy Mutiny starkly illustrated, the Duke of Cambridge and Queen Victoria had little actual influence on the army once it engaged in action overseas.

The combination of the ever-present demands by the government—regardless of ministry and party—as well as an altered international situation, perhaps coupled with the sense of ineffectiveness, made the Duke more of a reactionary. Whereas the Indian Mutiny in 1857 came as a tremendous shock to the army and to the nation, the army's reputation did not suffer, largely due to the absence of reporting in the style of Russell, as well as deep hatred for the supposed disloyalty of the Indians. The Great Invasion Scare of 1859 and the subsequent revelation of the lack of preparedness regarding Great Britain's defenses further reinforced the importance of national defense and rekindled a pride in both the army and its competence that had been lacking since the Crimean War.[96] The combinations of these two events, the consequences of which will be dealt with in the following chapter, placed a serious brake on the movement to reform the army. It is indeed rare for an army to undergo significant change when its leadership and its nation perceive it as being successful. The post-Indian-Mutiny British army was no exception.

Concurrent with this, the attitude of the Duke began to change as well. Although he was successful in the implementation of some of his reforms, overall, he felt restricted. Additionally, the demand for ever greater reductions—except during the Mutiny—caused him to become reactive rather than proactive. The protracted mourning of Queen Victoria beginning with Prince Albert's death at the end of 1861, the government's continued demands for retrenchment, and the increasingly reactionary views of the Duke of Cambridge marked a turning point not only for reforms within the army, but also the Duke's leadership of it. And as his attitude may have turned, his widowed cousin would only encourage it. Most of all Victoria feared and detested civilian control of the army and would reinforce Cambridge's resistance to the same as the next decade unfolded. What the immediate and long term consequences of their cooperation would have on the army and the nation remained to be seen.

---

96 The rise of Napoleon III in France in the 1850s created an exaggerated fear of a French invasion of Britain that culminated in 1859 with a Royal Commission charged with investigating the true state of Britain's homeland defenses. The following chapter will address this largely-forgotten episode of British history and how it revealed much about the relationship between the military and the monarchy.

CHAPTER 6:
The Royal Prerogative and the End of Reform 1858-1861

The decade of the 1860s would bring about important changes for Britain internationally, politically, and militarily. It was not only the Indian Mutiny that affected the future direction of army reform, but also the growing perception that perhaps England was no longer safe from invasion. Coupled with a changing international situation, these factors ushered in a new strategic position for Britain and its army. While the Crimean War had brought needed attention to the neglected condition of the British army, the Indian Mutiny brought a shock of a different kind. For those seeking an answer, the Mutiny demonstrated the flaws of British administration of the subcontinent and called into question the heavy reliance upon native troops. The renewed threat of French invasion in 1859, though exaggerated, brought new life to the volunteer movement and a drastic increase in coastal defenses as the experts of the day–the Duke of Cambridge included–concluded Britain was not prepared to defend itself against invasion.[1]

Politically, the period immediately prior to and during the Mutiny witnessed a new ministry under Lord Derby that was short-lived. More significantly, the death of Albert in 1861 provided a distinct end for one part of Victoria's reign and the beginning of another. His absence removed a reforming influence on the Queen, at least regarding the army. Military developments abroad coupled with dramatic technological advances brought about a reevaluation of many aspects of military weapons and doctrine. Although the French campaign in Italy would be of little immediate significance, the American Civil War and especially the German Wars of Unification would raise again the question of British military efficiency. The decade of the sixties would find Great Britain's place in the world dramatically changed; the demand for greater efficiency in the public services affected not just the army, but Parliament and the entire civil service as well.

While political developments continued, military technology advanced significantly during this period and would have substantial consequences for international relations. The volunteer movement of

---

1 Napoleon III never had any intention of invading the United Kingdom, but his increasing authoritarianism and nationalistic utterances in the late 1850's worsened relations between France and Britain. Specifics will be addressed below, but a consequence of domestic developments in France was heightened awareness of Britain's poor state of home defense.

1859, the Militia Act of 1860, and the Reserve Force Act of 1867 were all intended to strengthen home defense in response to increasing worries of unpreparedness and vulnerability. At sea, steam power and armor protection coupled with long-range guns had a tremendous impact on naval warfare. The launch of the French battleship, *La Gloire*, in November 1859 represented a great challenge to British naval supremacy due to its steam power and armor protection. The launch of the Royal Navy's *HMS Warrior,* the most powerful ship in the world in December 1860, demonstrated Britain's resolve and preeminence in naval affairs, but it also signaled an ongoing naval race and the end of the British-French alliance of the Crimean War. On land, armies had better small arms and artillery– the Enfield rifle replaced the Minié in 1856 and a breech-loading rifle, the Snider, was adopted in 1866, resulting in dramatically increased firepower for infantry–while breech-loading cannon with greatly improved ranges made artillery more effective. On the continent, Prussia continued to make great strides in the professionalization of its military, while Britain had its first stirrings in this direction–after years of unsuccessful attempts, hints of a professional army appeared with the founding of the Staff College in 1858 and the professional journal of the services, the *Journal of the Royal United Service Institution*, the previous year.[2]

Against this backdrop of dramatic change, introspection, and uncertainty, the Duke of Cambridge and Queen Victoria were each placed in new roles. Although she might not have been previously strongly disposed toward reform, Albert's death removed permanently any incentive the Queen might have had in promoting it. As for Cambridge, the army he had known–in fact the world he had known–was dramatically altered. How he would react to such a changed situation remained to be seen; however, his earlier enthusiasm for reform would be severely dampened. Furthermore, an issue which had been dormant, but not settled, was revived and it

---

2 The first volume detailed the purpose, membership and laws of the Institution. Under the heading of Laws, Section 1, Design explained, "The United Service Institution is founded as a central Repository for objects of Professional Art, Science, and Natural History, and for Books and Documents relating to those studies, or of general information. The delivery of Lectures on appropriate subjects included in the design of the Institution." *Journal of the United Service Institution* 1, no. 1 (1858): 2. Membership was open to all Princes of the Blood Royal, officers of the army, navy and marines, regular and local militia, East India's Land and Sea Services, Lords Lieutenants and Deputy Lieutenants of counties, Yeomanry and retirees, among others. *Ibid.* It is interesting to note that two prominent reformers were represented in the first issue: The Rev. George A. Gleig contributed an article, "On the Armies of Ancient Greece," *Ibid.*, 30-50; and Lieutenant Colonel MacDougal, later the first Commandant of the Staff College wrote "On the Genius and Campaigns of Hannibal," *Ibid.*, 120-146.

concerned the relationship between the Secretary of State for War and the Commander-in-Chief: who was to be subordinate to whom.

In 1860 the Select Committee on Military Organization recommended the Commander-in-Chief be subordinate to the Secretary of State for War, a conclusion Cambridge strongly rejected, and one that he would continue to reject to the end. In his view, matters of army command and discipline were matters of Royal Prerogative, and were therefore solely between the Commander-in-Chief and the Queen. Naturally Victoria agreed and the two presented a united front against any intrusion into the area of responsibility which they both held so dear. Until the advent of Edward Cardwell as Secretary for War toward the end of the decade, Cambridge and Victoria were outwardly effective at preserving the status quo. Unfortunately, the period from the end of the Indian Mutiny to Edward Cardwell's arrival at the War Office has been overlooked by scholars investigating army reform. The considerable influence of the Duke of Cambridge, the impact of the death of Prince Albert in 1861 on the Queen, and of course the actual changes which occurred six years later under Cardwell have overshadowed very significant developments in between. In many ways, Cambridge was successful for almost a decade in preventing reforms of which he did not approve.

I

The defeat of Palmerston's government in February 1858 and the Derby Ministry that replaced it did not in itself end the movement for reform in the wake of the Crimean debacle, but the change did bring the issue of the position of the Commander-in-Chief vis-à-vis the Secretary of State to the fore in late May 1858.[3] On May 30, a progressive officer and MP, Captain Vivian, introduced a motion in the House arguing for a clear definition of the responsibilities and duties of the military departments.[4] Vivian argued that although the previous consolidation of the departments of Ordnance, Commissariat, and the Secretary at War had improved matters somewhat, responsibility was still fragmented. To bring about greater efficiency, the Horse Guards and the War Office needed to

---

3 For a discussion of the end of the Palmerston's Ministry, see section II below.
4 For a little-known account of this case and its relation to British army reform in light of developments in Prussia, see Waldemar B. Campbell, "The Franco-Prussian War and British Military Reform" *The Historian* 4, no.2 (March 1942): 149-261.

be under the authority of a single minister. The House was divided on the issue, but the motion barely carried in a vote during which many members were absent: 106 for and 104 against. The official wording of the motion was, "That although the recent consolidation of the different Departments of Ordnance, Commissariat, and Secretary at War has to a certain extent improved the general administration of Military Affairs, a divided responsibility still exists; and that, in order to promote greater efficiency, the Departments of the Horse Guards and War Office should be placed under the control of one responsible Minister."[5] A changed position for the Commander-in-Chief was now a very real possibility.

Benjamin Disraeli, Lord Derby's Chancellor of the Exchequer, wrote to inform the Queen of this unfortunate news the evening the motion passed, but he tried to lessen the blow by informing her, "The motion, fortunately, was only a resolution and not an address to the Crown, which…would have required an answer."[6] He pointed out that even though it could be rescinded, it would be best to leave the issue alone. In Disraeli's opinion, if the government made no reaction, the issue would fade away.[7]

Cambridge's response was predictable. On June 1 he expressed his concern to Victoria that although he did not believe the motion would amount to much, it would "bring with it much mischief."[8] The issue at stake was the very one both the Queen and Cambridge believed crucial: the Royal Prerogative. This was a matter that touched directly upon the Queen's control of the army, as exercised through the Commander-in-Chief. As it stood, the current ambiguities worked to the advantage of the Crown. The lack of clearly defined duties and responsibilities of the Secretary of State for War and the Commander-in-Chief allowed royal control of the army to continue unchallenged. Were Parliament to undertake a move to define the duties of the two positions, it would be a further erosion of the Royal Prerogative in two ways. First, Parliament, by defining the actual role of the Commander-in-Chief, would be interfering directly with an area previously under the purview of the sovereign. Second, any discussion by Parliament of the proper relationship between the civilian Secretary for War and the military Commander-in-Chief would be bound to assert the

---

5 RA VIC/E10/73, List of Votes on Capt. Vivian's Motion, dated June 1, 1858.
6 RA VIC/E10/70, Letter from Benjamin Disraeli to Queen Victoria, dated June 1, 1858.
7 *Ibid.*
8 RA VIC/E10/71, Letter from the Duke of Cambridge to Queen Victoria, marked "most confidential," dated June 1, 1858.

dominance of the former over the latter; for Parliament to do otherwise would be to call into question the entire principle of civilian control of the army, something most unlikely. From the Duke's position, the best thing was to prevent the concrete discussion of any of these things because in the end, it would only mean a further diminution of the Royal Prerogative. Cambridge's concerns were well founded.

Cambridge also observed that the Duke of Wellington had guarded "this prerogative of the Crown with the greatest jealousy," and predicted it would be only a matter of time before the army became dangerous to the state.[9] In Cambridge's mind, abolition of the office of the Commander-in-Chief–the logical development of parliamentary control of the army–would encourage the development of a "Parliamentary Army."[10] In other words, only through an apolitical Commander-in-Chief would the army be prevented from being drawn into politics, with the legacy of Cromwell serving as an extreme example of what could happen.[11] Cambridge saw himself as following a succession of Commanders-in-Chiefs–Wellington and Hardinge in particular–who protected the army and the state from Parliamentary usurpation of what was indeed a prerogative of the Crown. The Duke believed that was why he was selected for the position he now held, and that to subordinate openly the Commander-in-Chief to the Secretary of State for War would be to politicize the position. He would not compromise on this matter he viewed as being central to the core of his duties. It was a point of view he would hold until his death.

Not surprisingly, Lord Derby wrote to the Queen the following day to state that he agreed with both Disraeli and Cambridge that the issue was a serious one, but he agreed with Disraeli's position that "it would not be desirable to ask the House of Commons formally to rescind its vote; but it is hoped that some member may be induced to ask whether it is the intention of Your Majesty's Servants to take any steps towards giving effect to the vote…"[12] Derby gave the Queen his full assurance that he would do whatever she felt right in this important matter, but essentially he believed the best thing to do would be to let the matter die under its own inertia. He closed with a very strong statement attesting to the importance of protecting the Royal Prerogative: "Your Majesty may rest assured that

---

9 *Ibid.*
10 *Ibid.*
11 See "Crown and Parliament" in Hew Strachan, *Politics of the British Army*, 44-73.
12 RA VIC/E10/72, Letter from Lord Derby to Queen Victoria, dated June 2, 1858.

not only no step shall be taken without Your Majesty's previous Authority, but that no step shall be taken...to weaken your Majesty's Prerogative in respect of the Army, or to hand over its control and discipline, apart from the Civil department, to the virtual government of the House of Commons."[13]

As soon as Queen Victoria learned of the vote in the Commons, she wrote to Lord Derby to emphasize "the absolute necessity for maintaining the authority and position of the Commander-in-Chief," and to point out that she understood Lord Derby shared her opinion.[14] She believed the situation might make it possible to define more accurately the relative duties of the Commander-in-Chief and the Secretary of State for the War Department, but that the authority of the Commander-in-Chief should not be lessened. Alarmed by the motion, she did not view her position as a weak one and actually saw the potential for good to arise from it; clearly she did not view the situation as gravely as her cousin did. However, she was adamant that "the authority and position of the Commander-in-Chief must not be deteriorated."[15] In response to her questions, Disraeli reassured Victoria that the best course would be to let the matter rest, for he believed that Parliament and the nation would react most harshly against "any move which threatened to touch Your Majesty's prerogative, would excite...indignation & resistance."[16] Furthermore, the number of members of Parliament present for the vote on Vivian's motion was so small that it did not reflect the genuine position of Parliament as a whole.[17]

The issue of Captain Vivian's motion is important despite having long since faded into obscurity. It highlights the nature of the relationship between Queen Victoria and Cambridge, while it also presents an example where the Queen was adamant—and successful—in preserving the Royal Prerogative. More shrewdly than her cousin—and most likely consistent with the influence of Albert[18]—she saw the potential for genuine reform of

---

13 *Ibid.*

14 RA VIC/E10/74, Letter from Queen Victoria to Lord Derby (copy), dated June 2, 1858.

15 RA VIC/E10/75, Letter from Sir Charles Phipps to Prince Albert, dated June 2, 1858, reporting the Queen's position on Captain Vivian's Motion.

16 RA VIC/E10/77, Letter from Benjamin Disraeli to Queen Victoria, dated June 3, 1858.

17 *Ibid.*

18 RA VIC/E10/76, Letter from General Grey to Prince Albert, dated June 2, 1858. Reporting to the Prince Consort the result of the House vote, General Grey observed that he did not attach as much importance to the matter as he believed that Prince Albert did and that "a change in the sense of Captain Vivian's Motion would be much more nominal than real...."

army administration. Whereas Cambridge saw any intrusion by Parliament as disastrous, the Queen, with the counsel of her ministers and her husband, was willing to view it as an opportunity. Writing to the Duke after receiving "satisfactory" answers from Lord Derby and Disraeli, Victoria passed on the advice of all three to her cousin. The best course was to do nothing for the moment–the Royal Prerogative was not threatened, there was no support for abolishing the position of the Commander-in-Chief, and perhaps the vote could "lead to a clearer and more satisfactory definition of the relative positions of the Commander-in-Chief and Secretary of State…"[19]

Having made her decision, Queen Victoria wrote to Lord Derby on June 4 to let him know she was quite satisfied with the course he and his ministry was following. Even though Cambridge seemed "rather uneasy altogether," she saw no threat to the Royal Prerogative.[20] Although other issues might be troublesome–rumors in the House of Lords suggested Lord Canning, the Governor General of India, had overruled the Commander-in-Chief of the military forces in India on a purely military matter[21]–the Queen saw no great threat arising from Vivian's motion. The Queen met with Lord Derby the following day and both agreed the matter should be left alone; the memorandum clarifying the duties of the Secretary for War and the Commander-in-Chief was still being revised and nothing would be formal without the Queen's signature.[22] Victoria had stood firm on the matter of Royal Prerogative and convinced Cambridge to overcome his concerns. Ultimately he admitted to her that Derby's advice was "very satisfactory."[23]

Although the memorandum defining the duties of the Commander-in-Chief in relation to the Secretary of State for War would languish in relative obscurity, the issue was by no means a dead one. For his part, the Prince Consort recognized that a memorandum defining the duties

---

19 Letter from Queen Victoria to the Duke of Cambridge, dated June 3, 1858, reproduced in Verner, vol. 1,109.
20 RA VIC/E10/78, Letter from Queen Victoria to Lord Derby, dated June 4, 1858.
21 Lord Derby responded to the issue directly in the House of Lords on June 4 pointing out that it was only natural that there would be tension between the civilian and military authorities in India and that this was not necessarily a bad thing. Furthermore, in the end it was only right that the Governor General should have the final word. Letter from Lord Derby to Queen Victoria, dated June 6, 1858, reproduced in Verner, vol. 1, 110.
22 RA VIC/E10/79, Minutes of Conversation between Queen Victoria and Lord Derby regarding Captain Vivian's Motion, June 5, 1858.
23 RA VIC/E10/81, Letter from the Duke of Cambridge to Queen Victoria, dated June 5, 1858.

of the Commander-in-Chief posed a potential danger even if it led to greater efficiency because it would prove "dangerous to the Sovereign's free action, to admit a right in any Member of either House, to ask for the production of such a paper..."[24] Ultimately, Albert decided that even though a memorandum was desirable, to release such a document would be a grave mistake–the best course would be to acknowledge the memorandum, but to refuse its production.[25] In the short run, that is exactly what happened; in the long run, his worst fears were realized.

Lord Derby wrote to the Queen on June 9, 1858 that the Cabinet had moved on to other issues–primarily the situation India–and that Captain Vivian intended to present another motion before the House, although he was not specific as to the nature of the motion.[26] Vivian would indeed present another motion, but not until months later on March 10, 1859. He moved for a select committee to determine whether additional changes were required to produce greater efficiency and economy. He also declared that if the duties of the Commander-in-Chief were clearly defined, it would assist the Secretary for War in carrying out his duties, even if the duties of the Commander-in-Chief were expanded.[27]

Overall, the combination of avoiding an open struggle in the House of Commons coupled with the quiet but firm reaffirmation of the Royal Prerogative proved to be quite successful. Part of the reason for the success was the major event affecting the army, quite unrelated to Captain Vivian's motion. The Mutiny in India had occupied the army and the nation from its outbreak and, unlike the Crimean War, it reflected well on the army. The *Times* covered the military actions of the army suppressing the Mutiny from a very supportive position. Perhaps because there was not a war correspondent of the caliber or persuasion of W.H. Russell (who did not arrive in India until January 1858), articles in the *Times* glowingly reported how the army overcame great difficulties and performed magnificently.[28] Even though such reporting was inaccurate–for example, of the 11,021 British soldiers who perished in quelling the Mutiny, 8,978 died from "sunstroke" and illness[29]–it effectively shielded the army from criticism.

---

24 RA VIC/E10/80, Memorandum by Prince Albert on the Production of Memorandum Defining Duties of Military Departments asked for in Captain Vivian's Motion (copy), n.d. [ca. June 8, 1858].
25 *Ibid.*
26 RA VIC/E10/84, Letter from Lord Derby to Queen Victoria, dated June 9, 1858.
27 Verner, vol. 1, 110-111.
28 Spiers, 132.
29 *Ibid.*, 135.

George, Duke of Cambridge, 1855

George, Duke of Cambridge, 1880s

Queen Victoria and Prince Albert, 1854

Queen Victoria, 1897

Queen Victoria and Prince Albert with their nine children, 1857

George, Duke of Cambridge, 1880s

British rule in India brought the subject of the Royal Prerogative to the forefront. Rather ironically, however, it also revealed the rather insignificant role of the Commander-in-Chief in relation to the Royal Prerogative, at least as far as foreign operations were concerned. The Government of India Act of 1858 had the full support of Queen Victoria and was the logical succession to the Queen's proclamation of November 1858 that converted former East India troops into soldiers of the Crown. The Act officially transferred the responsibility for governing India from the East India Company to the Crown and prevented the existence of a separate, locally-raised army that had been in control there for a century ever since the British victory at Plassey in June 1757. The Act established there would be only one British army in service of the Queen and in accordance with her position there should not be "a British Army distinct (in its existence and constitutional position) from that of the Crown."[30] Despite some strong opposition from the so-called "Indian officers"–most notably the "white mutiny" during which the 5th European Regiment refused the order to stand down–the matter was settled permanently.[31] The Queen made her position clear: she would have only one army and there would be no challenge to the Royal Prerogative.[32] Significantly, Cambridge played only a passive role in the whole transition. Although he received updates from India on a regular basis, he had no control and virtually no influence over actions there. The Indian Mutiny had been the single greatest threat to the Empire since 1776 and Cambridge had served no appreciable function in subduing the uprising. His only real contribution to the campaign was a "Military Journal" which he wrote during the crisis and recorded the events of the campaign.[33] Apart from his personal use, this journal had no larger purpose.

Against the backdrop of the Indian Mutiny and its resolution, the Queen successfully defended the Royal Prerogative. She thwarted the

---

30 Letter from Queen Victoria to Lord Derby, dated February 7, 1859, reproduced in Benson and Esher, eds., *The Letters of Queen Victoria*, 1st ser., vol. 3, 408.

31 For a contemporary discussion of the event in the larger context of the British involvement in India, see Peter Stanley, *White Mutiny: British Military Culture in India, 1825-75* (London: C Hurst & Co Publishers Ltd, 1998).

32 For a brief synopsis, see Spiers, 135-138; for a detailed account of the correspondence between Queen Victoria and the Duke of Cambridge, see "Chapter XI: The 'White' Mutiny in India – 1858-1859" in Verner, vol. 1, 222-247.

33 The Military Journal is reproduced in its entirety in Verner, vol. 1, 173-197 and begins on October 18, 1857 and ends on April 29, 1859. It provides a detailed and interesting view of the conduct of operations, but it also highlights the completely passive role of the Duke of Cambridge.

ongoing struggle of Captain Vivian and ultimately turned his motions in the House to her advantage. Vivian and his supporters failed to overcome the united efforts of Queen Victoria and the Duke of Cambridge, and as the Queen's advisors predicted, the issue was not fought openly in the House. This resulted in obscurity for Vivian's motion. Shortly after the presentation of Captain Vivian's second motion in 1859, the Queen wrote to the Duke of Cambridge and expressed her satisfaction that "all the mischief" of the previous year had been eliminated.[34] Although serious mischief would arise a decade later when Edward Cardwell served as Secretary for War, this time the issue was resolved decidedly in favor of the Queen and the Duke of Cambridge.

II

The issue of the Commander-in-Chief's position had been put to rest, at least temporarily, and Victoria and Cambridge greeted the end of the 1850's with the Royal Prerogative solidly in place. Furthermore, the mid-decade demands for serious army reform that arose from the poor army administrative performance during the Crimean War faded with the crisis in India—the clamor for reform had dwindled while support for the status quo grew stronger. The new challenge, which would remain a constant one for the Duke and the Queen, was the constant demand by the government for ever greater economy. His behavior during the exaggerated fears over French aggression contrasted sharply with his earlier inaction during the Indian crisis. Whereas before Cambridge could do little in a matter of great importance, now he could do a great deal in a situation that was more hype than substance. Taken in this light, the genuine authority of the Commander-in-Chief as exercised by the Duke of Cambridge is open to question.

By the end of the decade, peace returned to India while the rumblings of war elsewhere were as distant as ever. In northern Italy, the combined forces of France and Sardinia defeated the Austrians in 1859, but the threat to Britain was virtually nonexistent. Political leaders sought what governments typically desire when the threat to national security is low: reductions in military expenditure. The arrival of Palmerston's Liberal

---

34 Letter from Queen Victoria to the Duke of Cambridge, dated March 11, 1859, reproduced in Verner, vol. 1, 111.

Ministry in June 1859 meant the demand for reduction would likely be even greater. Apart from the routine maintenance of the colonies, the great national defense issue other than the naval race regarding ironclad steamships was the so-called "invasion scare" of 1859. A failed assassination attempt against Emperor Napoleon III on January 14, 1858 strained relations between France and Great Britain.[35] The Carbonari Society, a group of Italian nationalists, threw bombs under Napoleon's carriage in protest against the emperor's failure to support Sardinian efforts to unite Italy under the Sardinian king. The bomb wounded the emperor, killed several bystanders, and created an international incident. Ultimately it ended the Palmerston Ministry and resurrected the so-called Volunteer movement.

Reactionary French officers believed England to be complicit because the lead assassin, Orsini, and some conspirators had lived in England when the bomb and the plot had been hatched in London.[36] Press coverage exacerbated tensions between Britain and France, while Palmerston attempted to mollify the French by putting forth a bill in the House of Commons making conspiracy a felony rather than a misdemeanor. French aggressiveness combined with the perception that Palmerston went too far in acceding to French demands brought a return of Lord Derby's government for little more than a year. Even though the French threat was mainly national hysteria, relations between Britain and France were the lowest of any time since well before the Crimean War. British suspicions of the French grew as Austria went to war over the issue of Italian unification and invaded Piedmont in April 1859. The quick defeat of Austria further reinforced fears.[37] Napoleon III continued aggressive development of the French navy and coastal fortifications, keeping the threat of a French invasion alive in the British consciousness.

The civilian and military leadership of the army took the situation very seriously since Britain's capacity for homeland defense was poor. One concrete response was the appointment of Cambridge as president of a Royal Commission charged with assessing Britain's defenses against an invasion. In session for two years, the conclusion was not surprising in finding that defense preparedness was inadequate. The Duke believed

---

35 Benson and Esher, eds., *The Letters of Queen Victoria*, , 1ˢᵗ ser., vol. 3, 331.
36 Spiers, 164.
37 Benson and Esher, eds., *The Letters of Queen Victoria*, 1ˢᵗ ser., vol. 3, 394.

67,500 men and 2,645 guns assigned to Britain's fortresses, dockyards, and arsenals were insufficient; 100,000 men would be the minimum number required to defend the home islands. Yet such a number would be impossible to meet because of existing shortages throughout the empire–Ireland alone was 10,000 men short for adequate garrisoning.[38] The Report of the Royal Commission found that "neither our fleet, our standing army, nor our volunteer forces, not even the three combined, can be relied on as sufficient in themselves for the security of the Kingdom against foreign invasion."[39] The unanimous conclusions of the committee did cause a limited increase in defense spending.

In analyzing Britain's defensive posture against invasion, the Duke demonstrated a realistic understanding of the situation. The limitations of budget constraints obviously frustrated him and Queen Victoria equally. During the period of increased tensions between France and Britain, Cambridge and Victoria corresponded frequently on the topic of Britain's inadequate state of readiness, while both in turn wrote regularly to the ministers in the various governments. A regular topic of correspondence from Cambridge to the Secretary of War–whether it was Peel, Herbert, or Lewis–was the "totally inadequate" nature of Britain's defenses. The frequent refrain maintained that Britain's deplorable condition of defense was wholly unacceptable, and although he recognized it was "a most difficult matter to find a remedy, as any additional force must require increased expenditure," Britain was taking too great a risk.[40]

Although it would take the example of the American Civil War and the German Wars of Unification–especially the Franco-Prussian War–to demonstrate the full impact of new technology on warfare, Cambridge understood successful defense of Britain would require a mobile reaction force to meet any invasion force. Such an idea was not new, as the Norman conquest of 1066 had demonstrated. More recently, Wellington had pointed out the inadequacy of Britain's defenses in 1846. Still, the long-standing tradition of extensive coastal fortifications and the world's strongest navy to protect against foreign invasion provided reasonable security. The

38 Letter from Lord Panmure to the Duke of Cambridge, dated January 16, 1858, with enclosed letter from Lord Cowley, reproduced in Verner, vol. 1, 269-271.
39 "Report of the Select Committee on Military Organisation, 1859-1860" quoted in Brian Bond, "The Late-Victorian Army." *History Today* 11 (1961): 618.
40 Letters from the Duke of Cambridge to the Secretary for War, General Peel, dated November 26, 1860, and Sir George Lewis, dated October 8, 1861, reproduced in *Ibid.*, 271-272.

major wars of the next decade would demonstrate the great advantage of forces maneuvering with mobile long-range firepower. Traditional defensive fortifications could be bypassed easily and subsequently cut-off.

Cambridge was not alone in grasping the extent of the problem facing him; Palmerston's second Secretary for War, Sir George Lewis, perhaps saw the situation even more clearly. Both understood it would be "absurd to defend the Coast of England" as there was simply too much coastline to defend, but it seems that only Lewis recognized not every area could be fortified.[41] Although he appreciated the wisdom of fortifying arsenals and naval stations, he saw little utility in "dotting little forts" along the coast and wryly observed, "We have been building a little fort on the coast of Aberdeenshire of which I am unable to discover the use, unless it is to prevent the Norwegians from kidnapping the Queen from Balmoral…"[42] On the other hand, both men recognized that the likelihood of an approved budget adding tens of thousands of men to the active ranks was nonexistent. Whether he liked it or not, Cambridge had to seek other solutions.

The nation's regular reserve force, the militia, had served its purpose fairly well in the Crimean War. With approximately 38,000 men in 1855, that number had grown to 66,000 by 1856.[43] Militia regiments replaced regular regiments stationed throughout the empire, especially those in the Mediterranean, allowing the regular regiments to leave their home stations and head to the Crimea. In addition, thousands of militiamen volunteered for the active force. A similar process in both regards occurred during the Indian Mutiny in 1857 when some 25,000 militiamen reinforced garrisons throughout the empire and approximately 8,000 volunteered for active service.[44] In both cases, the militia received positive coverage from the press and genuine popular support, but it was not a combat-ready organization, nor was it ever seriously expected to be. With an attitude that remains true to the present day, regular army officers opposed any expansion of the militia due to its weakness as a fighting force. Furthermore, recruiting declined considerably in the wake of the Crimean War and the Indian Mutiny made its expansion doubtful because its use for extended periods

---

41 Letter from the Duke of Cambridge to Sir George Lewis, dated October 8, 1861, reproduced in *Ibid.*, 271.
42 Letter from the Secretary for War, Sir George Lewis to the Duke of Cambridge, dated October 8, 1861, reproduced in St. Aubyn, *The Royal George*, 116.
43 Spiers, 162.
44 *Ibid,* 163.

disrupted local economies and individual livelihoods. Still, something needed to be done quickly to make up the shortfall of homeland defense revealed during the invasion scare. The "Volunteer movement" presented one possible solution.

Creating units filled with volunteers in response to a national emergency was not a new idea. Quite a few volunteer battalions were raised during the Napoleonic Wars, and a derivative body of the Volunteer Corps raised in 1794 had become the Royal Victoria Rifle Club by the late 1850s.[45] The Volunteer movement offered an alternative to the rural militia units, many of which were socially exclusive, and a patriotic member of the middle class could serve while avoiding the social disgrace associated with enlisting in the regular army. In addition to long-standing rational arguments put forth by the movement's most prominent supporters–Hans Busk, Alfred B. Richards, and Nathaniel Bousfield among them–increased tensions with France created a genuine national frenzy. Yet even before then a steady increase in support arose throughout the 1850's. The *Times* suggested a Volunteer Corps be raised to assist in the suppression of the Indian Mutiny.[46] More liberal and radical newspapers saw a Volunteer Corps as an effective counter against the regular army and the Crown.[47]

For these reasons, the Duke of Cambridge had felt nothing but contempt for the idea of creating a volunteer corps, believing it would create "unmanageable bodies" and "an armed and dangerous rabble" that would ruin the army.[48] Most officers in the Horse Guards agreed with their chief. The Adjutant-General at the time, Lieutenant General Sir George H. Wetherall summed up conventional wisdom when he appeared before the Royal Commission on the Militia and expressed that a Volunteer Corps as an alternative to the Militia would be a "very bad principle."[49]

Rising tensions between Britain and France brought about a change of attitude rather quickly, and even Cambridge eventually changed his position, at least outwardly, as popular sentiment recognized the

---

45 *Ibid.*

46 *Times* (London), 22 September 1857.

47 *The Daily News* and *Reynold's Newspaper* both published articles to this effect. See in particular, *The Daily News,* 15 December 1859 and *Reynold's Newspaper* 25 October 1857.

48 Letters from the Duke of Cambridge to Lord Panmure, dated September 25, 1857 and October 2, 1857, reproduced in Sir George Douglas Bart and Sir George Dalhousie Ramsay, eds., *The Panmure Papers*, vol. 2 (London: Hodder and Stoughton, 1908) 435, 439.

49 Testimony of Lieutenant General Sir George H. Wetherall before Militia Commission of 1859, reproduced in Spiers, 164.

shortcomings of British national defense. Despite his aversion to the reserve forces, Cambridge had spent a great deal of time and effort throughout his career investigating their condition.[50] The Volunteer movement soon attracted greater popular attention than any other military-related issues, including Florence Nightingale's efforts to reform military medicine and create better living conditions for ordinary soldiers. An article from the *Times* in April 1859 reflected popular sentiment when reporting on a gathering of supporters for the Volunteer movement at St. Martin's Hall, Longacre: "There can only be one true defence of a nation like ours–a large and permanent volunteer force…"[51]

The growth of the Volunteer movement is an interesting topic, although its social significance is beyond the scope of this book. However, it is closely related to the issue of army reform and the connection between the army, the Crown, and Parliament. The Commander-in-Chief thought poorly of the volunteers and their movement, but he was convinced throughout his tenure that Britain's army was wholly inadequate to conduct homeland defense. Believing the French threat to be urgent, especially with a growing navy, Cambridge was willing to enact an expedient solution with volunteers to make up shortages facing the army as the threat rose. If there was to be Volunteer Corps, however, it would be on his terms and in a manner that did not threaten the relative position of the army in society. Queen Victoria's obvious support and interest undoubtedly influenced Cambridge's changed attitude.[52]

In the spring of 1859 the Duke of Cambridge wrote a memorandum that expressed his views and provided guidance. Naturally, a key consideration was discipline–for the force to be effective it must be subject to military discipline or it would prove unreliable, the main shortcoming of such units during the Napoleonic Wars. Furthermore, if such units were to be raised, units would have to arrive at appropriate times and perform required duties. Cambridge fully recognized that members of Volunteer units would be from a social class different from the ranks of the regular army and the rural militia. Accordingly, he believed that "service should be made as little irksome to the men as possible."[53] The War Office issued a

---

50 Throughout the fall and winter of 1858 and on into 1859, the volume of Cambridge's correspondence was astonishing, see RA E10/85-120.
51 *Times* (London), 19 April 1859.
52 Longford, 283.
53 "Memorandum on Volunteer Organization, 1859" reproduced in Verner, vol. 1, 272-273.

circular on May 12, 1859, largely based upon Cambridge's "Memorandum on Volunteer Organization, 1859." The circular required the Lords-Lieutenant of counties to raise a Volunteer Force and used a long-dormant act from the Napoleonic Wars, the Yeomanry and Volunteers Consolidation Act of 1804, as its legal foundation.[54] Cambridge's influence was clear; the Volunteer Corps would not become a freewheeling organization that was not responsible to the Crown. The War Office issued a second circular, drafted by Prince Albert, several days later stating that Volunteer units were to remain small bodies of men who were good marksmen rather than experts at drill, and who would serve in company-sized formations subordinate to the regular army, valued primarily for their knowledge of the local land.[55] Working together, Cambridge and Prince Albert thus ensured that units formed under the Volunteer system would not compete with the army, while remaining fully under the Crown's control and in accordance with the Royal Prerogative.

Just as the Duke of Cambridge and army officers in general ultimately accepted but did not embrace the Volunteer movement, the governments of Derby and Palmerston were equally ambivalent about the whole idea. The second circular issued in May 1859 stipulated that Volunteers had to pay for their own ammunition and equipment–something sure to dampen the enthusiasm of volunteers.[56] Lord Palmerston's Secretary for War, Sidney Herbert, disliked the whole movement but delegated control of the program to his Under-Secretary, Earl de Grey, who saw to it that volunteers were given weapons and ammunition. In fact, as Secretary for War from 1863 to 1866, he ensured the movement was well funded.[57] Regardless of the attitudes of Cambridge, army officers, and government ministers, public support for and interest in the movement remained quite high for several years after the invasion scare. Queen Victoria clearly enjoyed receiving a review of 21,000 volunteers in Hyde Park during the summer of 1860.[58] Newspapers, especially the *Times*, continued to support the movement, and officers soon learned that any public disparagement of the Volunteers would receive negative coverage. As noted, Cambridge modified his earlier stance and the *Times* reported in detail a speech at

54 Spiers, 165.
55 *Ibid.*
56 *Ibid.*, 166.
57 *Ibid.*
58 Benson and Esher, eds., *The Letters of Queen Victoria*, vol. 3, 485.

an Easter dinner in which he praised the Volunteers and their movement. He recognized their "admirable spirit" and believed the Volunteers would serve as "a great auxiliary" force to the defense of the nation.[59] Even though Cambridge accepted that the Volunteer movement was going continue for the immediate future, he was not above criticizing the organization, even to the Volunteers themselves, especially regarding large-scale maneuvers which would prove a disaster and actually look ridiculous.

Cambridge understood that bringing together large bodies of men unused to working together and leading them with an equally inexperienced staff would not lead to effective military exercises. At a banquet hosted in his honor by the City of London Rifle Brigade Volunteers, he showed his true feelings when he praised the spirit of his hosts but did not restrain his criticism of them in suggesting the Volunteers should spend much more time practicing their drill.[60] More surprisingly, he openly addressed the issue of whether he, or in his words, "the Horse Guards," was opposed to the Volunteer movement and reassured his audience that in fact he was a great supporter. It was his long term objective to improve as much as possible the Volunteer Corps so that they would serve the defense of the nation as effectively as possible.[61]

Despite the large numbers of men who volunteered–161,239 by 1861and 200,000 by 1869–national enthusiasm for the Volunteer movement did fade within several years of the invasion scare.[62] By mid-1862 the majority of Volunteers tended to be working class rather than middle class, and any social status associated with the Volunteer Corps evaporated with the changed social composition. The Volunteer Corps and their successor organization survived in one form or another until the First World War. Its military significance is debatable; the units never amounted to anything more than a manpower pool. The Volunteer movement certainly never fulfilled the hopes of radicals and some liberals looking for a counterweight to the Crown and regular army, but it did reflect for a short time a genuine groundswell of nationalism among the middle class. Most importantly, however, the Volunteer Corps was a victory for the Duke of Cambridge and the Crown because the Royal Prerogative was not only preserved, but actually reinforced. The Duke strengthened his ties with

59 *Times* (London), 9 April 1860.
60 *Times* (London), 15 April 1861.
61 *Ibid.*
62 Spiers, 166.

the Queen while at the same time he understood a changing public mood and reacted well to it.

III

In the fall of 1861, for the first time a document outlined the responsibilities of the Commander-in-Chief. Though little noticed at the time, it would eventually have a great impact on Cambridge's career, and more importantly, his office. The struggle for control of the army between the Commander-in-Chief and the Secretary for War, an issue which had arisen from administrative reforms during the Crimean War, was resolved through the issuance of a Royal Warrant. As discussed earlier, while the Crimean War was still ongoing, Palmerston's Ministry had attempted to restructure the War Department from thirteen virtually independent departments into a more manageable and efficient number. By the end of the decade only two departments remained, often referenced by their location rather than their actual title. They were the office of the Commander-in-Chief whose headquarters were located at the Horse Guards and the office of the Secretary for War whose office was located in the old War Office at Pall Mall.

Despite the questionable effectiveness of administrative reforms made in the wake of the Crimean War (Sir James Graham described military administration in 1860 simply as "chaos"[63]), the issue as to whether the Commander-in-Chief was subordinate to the civilian Secretary for War acting on behalf of the Crown, or simply the Crown alone, remained unresolved. With the apparent sanction of the War Department, the Assistant Commissary-General, Edward Barrington de Fonblanque, published a book in 1858 defining the duties of the Commander-in-Chief, "nominated by, and responsible to, the Crown, for the discipline and efficiency of the service, the conduct and capacity of general and other commanding officers, and the interior economy and organization of the army."[64] Direct responsibility to the Crown is, at first glance, unambiguous, but a footnote modifying the description of duties of the Commander-in-Chief presents an unresolved relationship:

---

63 Bond, "The Late-Victorian Army," 617.
64 Edward Barrington de Fonblanque, *Treatise on the Administration and Organization of the British Army, with Especial Reference to Finance and Supply* (London: Longman, Brown, Green, Longmans, and Roberts, 1858), 82. The former Secretary of State for War, Lord Panmure, commissioned it.

> The relative positions of the Minister for War and the Commander-in-Chief are not, perhaps, as clearly defined as is desirable for the efficient working of these two important departments, and it is probable that some changes will require to be made in order to bring them into more complete harmony.[65]

For Cambridge there was no issue: his position was subject only to the Royal Prerogative. Perhaps the most convincing argument in support of his position was his selection. His predecessor, Lord Hardinge, had consistently defended his position as one subject to the Royal Prerogative alone; the fact that a prince of the royal blood was his successor strongly supported this.[66] The Royal Commission that met in 1860 to resolve the issue permanently found constant opposition in the person of the Duke of Cambridge. Despite numerous attempts to create a document providing the Secretary for War with overall authority for command and control of the army, the Duke would not accept subordination to the Secretary for War rather than directly to the Queen. The reforms implemented in 1855 failed to make a clear distinction between the duties of the Secretary for War and the Commander-in-Chief. In fact, the creation of a separate Secretary of State for War may have exacerbated differences between the Horse Guards and the War Department.[67] In an attempt to resolve the issue permanently, Sir George Lewis had presented a draft warrant to Queen Victoria in May of 1855 outlining the specific duties of the Secretary for War.[68] Ultimately, Victoria agreed in rather ambiguous terms that the Commander-in-Chief was subject to the sovereign's "general control over the Government of the Army and the responsibility of the Secretary of State for the exercise of our Royal Prerogative."[69] In other words, the office of the Commander-in-Chief was in fact subordinate to the Secretary for War, but it was a

---

65 *Ibid.*, 83.

66 Strachan, *Politics of the British Army*, 62-63.

67 Sweetman, 126-131.

68 RA VIC/E13/90, Letter from Secretary for War Sir George Lewis to Queen Victoria, dated October 7, 1861.

69 Sweetman, 131.

matter still open to interpretation. Further obfuscation occurred because the Queen agreed to the draft of the warrant, but she never approved a formal draft as a Royal Warrant. The draft of 1855 only resurfaced in 1860 because Sir George Lewis had written the original draft over five years previously. The second time around, Lewis was not about to let the matter continue without a firm answer from the Queen.

For his part, it was not as if the Duke of Cambridge was demanding subordination of the Secretary of State for War; on the contrary, he preferred the lack of clear delineation as helpful to his cause. What mattered most was protection of the Royal Prerogative–the government might control the budget and state policy, but the sovereign alone exercised control over the army. Only a military officer–ideally of royal blood–could carry out the wishes of the Crown. Cambridge found it anathema to have a civilian execute the Royal Prerogative and the basis of his objections to subordination of his office to the Secretary for War always centered on what the Duke perceived as abrogation of the Royal Prerogative.[70] Furthermore, having the matter undefined suited his interests far better. The exact powers of the monarchy were not specified, and since Cambridge served the Queen directly, there was no need to have his duties defined as well. In one of the important political works of the era, Walter Bagehot, in defining the powers of the monarchy, wrote that the Queen had a hundred "powers which waver between reality and desuetude, and which would cause a protracted and very interesting legal argument if she tried to exercise them."[71] He argued that this did not mean the sovereign was without power or influence–it was simply that what she did defined what she was able to do. A similar situation could have been used to describe the position of the Commander-in-Chief, as both Cambridge and Victoria viewed it this way.

After many submissions of drafts to the Duke of Cambridge and Queen Victoria, the matter was finally resolved in the form of a Royal Warrant on October 12, 1861.[72] The Duke had resisted such an event for many months and opposed the last draft of October 7 over the inclusion of a semi-colon in the last sentence of the document which discussed the

---

70 RA VIC/E13 contains dozens of letters throughout the year 1861 which reflect Cambridge's dissatisfaction regarding proposed drafts for the powers of the Secretary of State for War.

71 Walter Bagehot, *The English Constitution* (London: Longmans, 1915; reprint, Ithaca, NY: Cornell University Press, 1963), 99.

72 RA VIC/E13/95, Royal Warrant Relating to the Business of the Military Departments, dated October 12, 1861.

Royal Prerogative.[73] As it stood, the Royal Warrant of 1861 closed with virtually identical language to the document Lewis had submitted in 1855. It was not very lengthy, but what it said was indeed portentous for the future of the Duke of Cambridge. Due to its subsequent importance and vagueness, it is repeated here in its entirety:

> Whereas we deem it expedient in order to prevent any doubt as to the powers and duties of the Commander-in-Chief with respect to the Government of Our Army and the Administration of Military Affairs to express Our Will and Pleasure thereon–Now Our Will and Pleasure is that the Military Command and Discipline of our Army and Land Forces, as likewise the appointments to and promotions in the same, together with all powers relating to the Military Command and Discipline of Our Army which, under and by any Patent or Commission for Us, shall have been, or shall from time to time be committed to, vested in, or regulated by the Commander-in-Chief of Our Forces, or the General Commanding Our Forces in Chief for the time being, shall be excepted from the Department of the Secretary of State for War.
>
> And we are further pleased to declare Our Will and Pleasure to be, that all powers relating to the matters above enumerated shall be exercised, and all business relating thereto, shall be transacted by the Commander-in-Chief of Our Forces for the time being, and shall be deemed to belong to his Office;–subject always to our General Control over the Government

73 RA VIC/E13/91, draft of Royal Warrant Relating to the Business of the Military Departments, dated October 7, 1861.

> of the Army, and to the responsibility of
> the Secretary of State for the exercise of
> Our Royal Prerogative in that behalf and
> subject to any power formerly exercised
> by the Secretary at War.[74]

Even by Victorian-era writing standards, the Royal Warrant is quite vague. It deliberately attempts to state that the Commander-in-Chief is the supreme military authority, but ultimately that he is subordinate to Secretary of State for War. Although "all business" would be transacted by the Commander-in-Chief, the Secretary of State had the overall responsibility to exercise the Royal Prerogative. The language may have been purposely clouded to appease the Duke of Cambridge and Queen Victoria as much as possible, but it represented nonetheless a serious defeat for the interests of the Duke of Cambridge. On the other hand, the Queen made it explicitly clear to Sir George Lewis that the document was to be kept most confidential and never to be made public out of fear that the instructions contained within "might be moved for in Parliament, and, having been once treated as a public document, their production could not be refused."[75] It appears Lewis followed the Queen's instructions very well, for nothing became of the document for almost a decade–until Edward Cardwell found it while rummaging through papers at the War Office.[76]

Remarkably, investigations of the career of the Duke of Cambridge have neglected the significance of this Royal Warrant during the reign of Queen Victoria and the various reforms of the War Office. The "Royal Warrant Relating to the Business of the Military Departments" is important for a number of reasons. Above all, the Warrant reveals that despite the subsequent upheaval that occurred under the tenure of Lord Cardwell as Secretary of State for War at the end of the 1860s and early 1870s, the

74 RA VIC/E13/95, Royal Warrant Relating to the Business of the Military Departments, dated October 12, 1861. This was the final version of many previous drafts with which the Duke of Cambridge took great exception. As is made clear by the awkward language, the Duke did not wish to accept a subordinate role to the Secretary of State for War, and this final version almost hides that essential fact.
75 RA VIC/E13/90, Letter from Secretary for War Sir George Lewis to Queen Victoria, dated October 7, 1861. In the letter, Lewis is repeating the Queen's instructions back to her to demonstrate that he fully understood her concerns.
76 For a full account of the impact of Cardwell's term as Secretary of State for War, see Chapters 8 and 9.

issue of who was ultimately in command of the army was written down and approved by the Queen and Cambridge long *before* Edward Cardwell became Secretary for War in 1868. Second, the document raises the question of why there was not a more vigorous reaction by the Queen and her cousin since the document obviously infringed upon the Royal Prerogative. The final issue prompted is why nothing became of the Warrant after it was approved. The answers to each are interrelated.

Clearly, the authority of the Commander-in-Chief to be the sole executor of the Royal Prerogative is eliminated by the Royal Warrant. Despite Cambridge's strong attachment to the idea that *he* was solely responsible to the Crown for the army, the historical precedent was not so clear. As has been addressed before, the position of Commander-in-Chief had possessed an uneven history prior to the Duke's assumption of office. From the day he assumed office, the issue of his relationship to the Secretary for War remained an open one–it had never been proved one way or the other. Instead, Cambridge carried on as his predecessors did: relying upon a combination of force of personality and influence with the Queen.

Significantly, neither Cambridge nor Victoria mentions the matter after the fact in their correspondence or journals.[77] At first glance, this absence might indicate a lack of importance over the issue, but the repeated references to the Royal Prerogative by both parties make this explanation most unlikely. Since no concrete evidence survives, a more plausible explanation is that both believed the issue to be settled. At one level, they clearly understood that Parliament controlled the army and its funding. Any protracted and public fight over this issue could only do more harm than good. If the Warrant were kept secret–as Queen Victoria expressly commanded[78]–the matter might quietly fade away (as it did for almost a decade). Furthermore, since the matter was now settled and the Secretary for War was placated, the ordinary business of the War Office and the Horse Guards could continue. But the precedent had been set–

---

77 The published extracts from Queen Victoria's correspondence and journal as well as Queen Victoria's journal itself in the Royal Archives make no special mention of the document, and after the Royal Warrant was signed, the published and unpublished letters and journal entries of the Duke of Cambridge never mention the Warrant as a concern.

78 RA VIC/E13/90, Letter from Secretary for War Sir George Lewis to Queen Victoria, dated October 7, 1861. Lewis acknowledges the Queen's desire to keep the document confidential and he assures her that he will.

the Royal Prerogative as defined by the Queen and Cambridge had been substantially weakened.

As for why nothing became of the Warrant until Edward Cardwell arrived at the War Office, the explanation is fairly simple. The frequent turnover of personnel–Sir George Lewis lasted but two years, the Earl de Grey occupied the position for three, and Lord Hartington, General Peel, and Sir James Pakington each occupied the position of Secretary for less than one year prior–hindered continuity. More importantly, reduced army estimates coupled with growing international commitments and a less secure international position placed increased demands on Secretaries and their staffs. The major operations underway consisted of settling any remaining problems in India, the Chinese expedition, and a rebellion in New Zealand that lasted from March 1860 to the end of 1863. As the impetus for reform faded within the War Office and throughout the army, the demand to define the relationship of the Commander-in-Chief and the Secretary of State for War was no longer very pressing. For the most part, the decade of the 1860s witnessed a reaction against army reform. If the Secretary for War did not make the issue of the Commander-in-Chief's position a priority, it was unlikely that anyone else would.

Another aspect was the manner in which the Royal Warrant was developed. Sir George Lewis did not arrive at the War Office with the expectation of increasing his own authority at the expense of the Duke of Cambridge; he merely sought clarification of his duties, something he had attempted in the wave of reform that swept through the War Office the last time he was there. Part of the reforms of 1855 dictated that the Secretary of State for War receive, in addition to the seals and letters-patent constituting his office, a supplementary patent that prevented him from interfering directly with military affairs such as discipline, promotion and command. Lord Panmure had received such a patent in 1855 conferring on him all powers with respect to the army, except those of military command, discipline, appointments, and promotions.[79] Previously, Secretaries of State for other departments had not seen such an explicit limitation of power placed upon them; when the House Committee established to review the position of the Secretary for War considered the situation in 1860, its members determined that because the Secretary for War was responsible to the Crown and removable as well, there was no need for

79 Verner, vol. 1, 111-112.

a supplementary patent. Rather surprisingly, the Duke of Cambridge stated before the House Committee that he always sought the Secretary of State's consent before he made any important appointments. If the two men disagreed, ultimately the final say rested with the Secretary.[80]

Without any obvious reason for its continuance, the supplementary patent was eliminated. Even though the restriction was now gone, the respective positions of the Commander-in-Chief and the Secretary of State for War remained without a clear definition. In 1861 Sir George Lewis moved from the Home Office to the War Office. Since he was already a Secretary of State, he did not require a new patent, but he prepared a memorandum and obtained the Queen's signature to it. With a view toward more clearly defining the situation, it provided that the command and discipline of the army and the promotion and appointments in it should be carried out by the Commander-in-Chief, subject of course to the control of the Sovereign, "and to the responsibility of the Secretary of State for the exercise of Our Royal Prerogative, and subject to any powers formerly exercised by the Secretary at War."[81]

For several interrelated reasons, therefore, the Royal Warrant abolishing the independence of the Commander-in-Chief from the Secretary of State for War caused little commotion when it was signed. Despite the large amount of attention Edward Cardwell attracted as Secretary for War, a defining aspect of his struggle with the Duke of Cambridge over the relative position of the Commander-in-Chief had already been settled. Sir George Lewis and his successors never chose to challenge the Duke of Cambridge and the Royal Prerogative in such a public manner. More importantly, Cardwell was the first Secretary of State for War who actually tried to enforce the provisions of the Royal Warrant or matters that actually touched upon the heart of Royal Prerogative, such as the Purchase System.

IV

Perhaps more than anything else, the demise of the movement to abolish the purchase of commissions signaled that serious reform of the army was a dead issue for the decade of the 1860s. The disappointments

---

80 *Ibid.*, 112.
81 Biddulph, *Lord Cardwell at the War Office*, 238.

of the Crimean War had long since been forgotten while Cambridge and staunch supporters of tradition dominated the army with the backing of key members of Parliament. Although the effort to abolish the Purchase System could be traced to the statement of General Sir George De Lacy Evans' public criticism of the practice during a speech in the House of Commons in 1832 ("...the command of regiments ought not to be open to purchase by majors who happen to have plenty of money in their pockets..."),[82] by 1861 the steam behind the effort that grew out of the debacle in the Crimea had run out. The purchase system served as a lightning rod for those interested in army reform, and when the press and members of Parliament criticized the practice, other questionable practices of the army such as flogging or bureaucratic bungling came under attack as well. When the system went relatively unnoticed, it indicated a more widespread satisfaction with the status quo.

Prior to the Crimean War, small but vocal outbursts existed against the practice. De Lacy Evans was a respected and decorated army officer. It was only his military credentials that gave him any public voice at all, because conventional opinion of both serving and retired army officers regarded Purchase as one of the cornerstones of the strength of the officer corps. Undaunted, speaking before the House of Commons De Lacy Evans attacked the system again in 1846 and 1847.[83] Other members of Parliament also began to criticize the system, among them Sir William Molesworth, Joseph Hume, and Bernal Osborne. Overall, however, there was little support or even interest at the national level for abolishing Purchase. Wellington had remained a staunch supporter til the very end and, predictably, senior officers who had served under him on the Peninsula believed similarly. Not surprisingly, prior to the Crimean War both within the army and without, there was little interest in, and even less support for, abolishing the system. The Great War against Napoleon had apparently vindicated the system, and it was only natural for the officer corps that grew up under it to continue its support until there was a reason to reconsider.

Besides General De Lacy Evens, there were occasional concentrated efforts end the practice, but overall they were inconsequential. The only other prominent military officer who had challenged the merits of

---

82 *Parliamentary Debates* (Third Series) XI, 1039.
83 *Parliamentary Debates* (Third Series) LXXXVIII, 881-884; *Parliamentary Debates* (Third Series) XCI, 713-725.

the Purchase System prior to the Crimean War was Major General John Mitchell.[84] Mitchell and an accomplice, Colonel Maurice Firebrace, wrote several articles highlighting the need to abolish the system, but their efforts proved unsuccessful. Apart from the *United Service Magazine*, and occasionally the *Times*, few journals or newspapers addressed the topic.[85] Mitchell and Firebrace tried to bring about legislative reform but failed. It would take something dramatic to bring attention to the subject; the Crimean War did just that.

At first, reformers achieved great success in generating attention to the topic of Purchase, as they did regarding other areas of inefficiency in the army. The first issue of a journal representing the Army Reform Association, *The Army Reformer*, published on March 10, 1855, stated it was dedicated to "keep before the public the necessity for a thorough change of the system."[86] Overall, however, the Army Reform Association and groups like it had little effect. They provided a platform for members of Parliament who opposed Purchase, and therefore seemed to back up the efforts of reformers within Parliament. The most influential reformer within Parliament, Viscount Goderich (originally Frederick John Robinson and later Earl de Grey and Ripon), met frequently with other members and supporters–including General Sir William Mansfield, later an ally of Cardwell–to promote the interests of reforming education within the army and the abolition of Purchase. When Goderich put forth a motion before the House of Commons in early 1855 recommending the abolition of Purchase, it was soundly defeated 158 to 114.[87]

Although discontent was indeed widespread over the current state of affairs, Goderich had identified a problem but not offered a solution. Even Palmerston admitted the faults of the system, suggesting no one would purposely create such a system, but that its existence would be quite difficult and expensive to abolish it.[88] Goderich may have overplayed his

---

84 For Mitchell's attempts at instigating reform, see "Chapter 2, The Neglected Rebel: Major General John Mitchell," in Jay Luvaas, *The Education of an Army: British Military Thought, 1815-1940* (Chicago: University of Chicago Press, 1964), 39-64.

85 For a detailed account of the articles by Mitchell, see *ibid.* above. Major articles attacking purchase in the *Times* were as follows: *Times* (London), 28 October 1841; 18 November 1841; 24 November 1841; 30 November 1841; 4 December 1841; 18 December 1841; 24 December 1841.

86 From *The Army Reformer* 1 (10 March 1855), 1, reproduced in Anthony Bruce, *The Purchase System in the British Army, 1660-1871* (London: Royal Historical Society, 1980), 101.

87 Godersich's expressed his views in the form of an address to the Crown. *Parliamentary Debates* (Third Series) CXXVI, 2107.

88 Bruce, 103.

hand with his motion, but he led the way for other reformers challenging Purchase, most notably a radical Member of Parliament, Henry Rich, who introduced a motion advocating its end on July 4, 1855, and another by De Lacy Evans, seconded by Goderich, in March of 1856.[89] Not surprisingly, both motions were defeated. Although the motions failed, they prompted Lord Palmerston to create a commission to investigate the subject. As he subsequently explained to Queen Victoria, the true purpose of the commission was to preserve the status quo rather than actually end Purchase. Accordingly, Palmerston ensured that only one member of the Royal Commission would be a dedicated reformer, De Lacy Evans.[90]

The "Report of the Commissioners appointed to inquire into the system of purchase and sale of commissions" was published in August of 1857.[91] It found many of the same problems that had existed prior to the Crimean War. The Duke of Cambridge appeared before the Royal Commission and defended Purchase on the basis that it prevented army involvement in politics; if purchase were abolished, the Crown would be subject to charges of favoritism and prejudice. In his opinion, the system was vital to maintaining the integrity of the entire defense establishment and allowed him to veto appointments with which he did not agree, something that would not continue if the practice were abolished. Even though every other aspect of the system made it quite disagreeable, Cambridge found that for protection of the Crown from politics, the system had to be maintained.[92]

The Royal Commission, however, found great problems with the system. Purchase was hurting efficiency and professionalism in the officer ranks, while it allowed the commissioning of "idle young men, who, having money at their disposal, regard the army as a fashionable past-time for a few years of leisure, and bring with them habits of expense and dissipation."[93] In spite of these strong words, the report did not recommend dramatic change. Above all, it did not advocate the abolition of the purchase system. The most radical suggestion was the selection of

---

89 *Parliamentary Debates* (Third Series) CXXXIX, 429-430; *Parliamentary Debates* (Third Series) CXL, 1791-1850.

90 Bruce, 104.

91 House of Commons, "Report of Royal Commission on Purchase," *Sessional Papers*, 1857, XVIII, 1-316.

92 *Ibid.*, 256-268.

93 From "Arguments For and Against the Purchase System," by Lord Granville, 1871 reproduced in Arvel B. Erickson, "Abolition of Purchase in the British Army," *Military Affairs.* 23 (1959): 67.

regimental commanders by merit.[94] The Royal Commission met the goals which Palmerston had envisioned–preservation of the status quo. Rather than provide a platform to end Purchase, the committee instead provided a written defense and explanation for its continuation. Compounding this was the Indian Mutiny, which dampened earlier public clamor for increased military effectiveness. The inefficiencies of the Crimean War clearly were forgotten.

By the early 1860s the demand for reform was all but gone. The Volunteer Movement, though a potential threat to the army's traditional position in society, had been co-opted by the Duke of Cambridge and ended up reinforcing his position rather than weakening it. The Duke of Cambridge and Queen Victoria had quietly acceded to a challenge to the Royal Prerogative, but outwardly their positions were reinforced. The preservation of Purchase was an additional reinforcement of their position. The two royal cousins had every reason to suppose that for the time being the Royal Prerogative would not be threatened any further, although the army itself could not be guaranteed to maintain its present state. Cambridge was in perhaps his most secure position yet, but a curious byproduct of that security was the lack of real power and authority that came with it. The Indian crisis had revealed just how (un)important the current iteration of the position of Commander-in-Chief was for serious military operations, while the "Royal Warrant Relating to the Business of the Military Departments" proved conclusively that the Commander-in-Chief was indeed subordinate to the Secretary for War. Cambridge had enhanced the *appearance* of his authority during the Invasion Scare, but the substance of his position was arguably as low as it had ever been. It is doubtful, however, whether he or Victoria recognized that fact since outwardly the Royal Prerogative of the Crown and the Commander-in-Chief was secure.

---

94 House of Commons, "Report of Royal Commission on Purchase," 32-34.

CHAPTER 7:
Consequences of the Death of Albert 1862-1868

Having experienced serious challenges to the Royal Prerogative and a changed world position, the recurring governmental theme which the Duke of Cambridge faced throughout the mid-1860s was governmental parsimony. Whereas some inroads toward change may have been made at the end of the previous decade and the beginning of the new one, the middle years of the 1860s witnessed a full retreat from any reformist tendencies by both the Duke of Cambridge and Queen Victoria. Although a dated history of the War Office exaggerates that, "Probably there has been no short period more fruitful in army reforms than the two years from 1859-1861, during which Sidney Herbert…and the Duke of Cambridge… laboured shoulder to shoulder for the good of the Service,"[1] the first half-decade of the Duke's tenure as Commander-in-Chief was the time during which he was most open to reform. Between 1859 and 1861 Cambridge and Herbert *did* work well together in a spirit of cooperation to improve the soldier's lot.[2] Although Cambridge naturally fought additional cuts in the strength of the army, as he always would, the tone of the previous decade was not as adversarial as it became a decade later.

From the beginning of the 1860s until the end of his tour as Commander-in-Chief, Cambridge resisted any changes he viewed as detrimental to the interests of the army and the Crown. Naturally, he and his cousin viewed the interests of each as being inextricably linked. It was during this period that his earlier, more progressive attitude hardened fully into the reactionary feelings for which he would become known as the government's desire for economy pushed the Duke of Cambridge ever deeper into a feeling of great distrust of parliamentary interference and control of the army. It was during this decade, even before the advent of Edward Cardwell, that he came to be regarded as a man "to whom a new idea was perdition."[3]

As a whole, the period of the 1860s was not completely without improvement regarding the army. Most notably, the efforts of Florence Nightingale and her supporters to improve the medical and living conditions of the British soldier met with a good deal of success. But overall, the decade witnessed the death of major initiatives to reform the army. The

---

1 Owen Wheeler, *The War Office Past and Present* (London: Methuen, 1914), 169.
2 Gordon, 55.
3 *Ibid.*

public issue of the abolition of Purchase, and the more private one of the position of the Commander-in-Chief in relation to the Secretary of State for War, however, did not undergo any significant alteration. The Duke of Cambridge and Queen Victoria successfully resisted any attempts toward change that threatened or even affected the Royal Prerogative. Despite Britain's changed international position, great political developments and profound changes in the prosecution of warfare, the two cousins successfully withstood repeated and concerted attempts to challenge their united position. Without support from the War Office, the press, or Parliament, reformers were largely unsuccessful. A new Secretary of State for War at the end of the decade would provide a completely new challenge, but for the majority of the decade it appeared the issues of abolition of Purchase and royal control of the army were settled issues.

The period immediately following the Crimean War and, of course, the actions of Edward Cardwell as Secretary of State for War from 1868 to 1874 are clearly important areas of investigation regarding the administration and reform of the British army, but the years between these two dramatic periods–1862 to 1868–are frequently neglected although they are also crucial.[4] This is unfortunate because the intermediate years are crucial to understanding the changing attitudes of the Duke of Cambridge and Queen Victoria and the changed relationship between the military and the monarchy following the death of Prince Albert. It was precisely during this period that the relationship between the two cousins improved to a level previously not seen. When Albert died, it meant the passing of Victoria's most persistent and influential advocate for improving the army. With his death, the Queen lost her most important advisor and the army lost its only progressive voice near the monarchy: reform came to an end, reactionary forces within the army and without it were dominant, and the Duke of Cambridge stepped in to exercise the role of military advisor previously filled by Albert.

I

The death of the Prince Consort on December 14, 1861, represents a significant break in the reign of Queen Victoria and serves as more than

---

4 The principle biographies on Cambridge–Sheppard, Verner, St. Aubyn–and even the minor one by Duff, all neglect this period and instead transition from 1861 to 1868. The major works investigating reform of the army–Bond, Strachan, and Spiers–suffer from the same defect as well.

a convenient period of transition. The nature of her reign would be quite different without her husband. The years immediately following the death of Albert witnessed the Queen's retreat from an active role in government affairs. In the years following his passing, she lessened her involvement and interest even in the army, arguably her favorite institution. With Albert's passing, Disraeli commented, "…we have buried our sovereign. This German Prince has governed England for twenty-one years with a wisdom and energy such as none of our kings have ever shown…"[5] Whether Albert deserved such high praise is most unlikely, but anyone close to Queen Victoria could not have helped noticing how central a role he played as a counselor to her. Despite the fact that she was admittedly "miserably weak and utterly shattered," the Queen was determined to make it her "*firm* resolve, my *irrevocable decision*, viz. That *his* [Prince Albert's] wishes–*his* plans–about everything, *his* views about *every* thing are to be *my law!*"[6]

Whether this would be the case remained to be determined, for privately even more so than publicly, Albert had been a significant influence on the Queen. Since they had been married all of her letters had in fact first been written by her husband–Victoria would not even choose a bonnet without soliciting Albert's opinion.[7] To suppose that her reign would not undergo any change and that she could remain true to her late husband's ideas was an unlikely proposition. At forty-two years of age, like it or not, she entered a new phase and was forced to take on a new role. Her early political mentors and friends–most notably, Lord Melbourne, Sir Robert Peel, the Duke of Wellington, and Lord Aberdeen–were all dead. Only three elder statesmen remained who were prominent at the time of her accession: Lord Palmerston, the serving Prime Minister; Lord Russell, Foreign Minister; and Lord Derby, Leader of the Conservative Opposition.[8] And of these men, none had been a trusted advisor to the degree that Melbourne, and subsequently, Peel, had been.[9] The most

---

5 Strachey, 300.

6 Letter from Queen Victoria to the King of the Belgians, dated December 24, 1861, reproduced in Benson and Esher, eds., *The Letters of Queen Victoria*, 1st ser., vol. 3, 605-606. Victoria went on in the same letter to express her determination that "*no human power* will make me swerve from *what* he decided and wished."

7 Longford, 307.

8 Palmerston would be dead within three years, Derby would die in 1869 and Russell in 1878.

9 George E. Buckle, ed., *The Letters of Queen Victoria*, 2nd ser., *A Selection From Her Majesty's Correspondence Between the Years 1862 and 1878*, vol. 1 (New York: Longmans, Green and Co., 1926), viii-ix.

important private confidant and correspondent in the wake of Albert's death was Victoria's uncle, King Leopold I of the Belgians, who himself would die in four years. In the 1860s Victoria was on her own to a degree she had never experienced as a monarch.

Yet the demands of state on the grief-stricken Queen were great while the prospect of greater delays in getting her to sign actions or make decisions was irksome to her advisors. On June 7, 1862, she agreed at last to a change that distanced her somewhat from the process by which officers in the army were promoted. Previously, all commissions and subsequent promotions required her signature. Sir George Lewis, her Secretary of State for War, recommended that instead the Queen need only sign the initial commission of each army officer rather than each subsequent promotion. This was a change Albert had long recommended, and the Queen's military counselors thought it wise as well, so without much hesitation she agreed with the recommendation of her Council.[10]

Whereas prior to Albert's passing Victoria had steadfastly resisted all attempts to limit her involvement with army matters–the protection of the Royal Prerogative remained paramount–in her reduced state, she proved less able to resist such changes. In fact, several days after she consented to the change regarding commissions, she agreed to additional administrative changes concerning pay and retirement. Although he did not mention the Queen's condition directly in the wake of Albert's death, the consequences of her reduced condition were clearly an underlying theme of Lewis's letter to Her Majesty dated June 17, 1862. Acknowledging the large number of documents the Queen had to sign throughout the year, Lewis expressed his desire to reduce her burden regarding army administrative matters.[11] Pointing out that in the previous year the Queen had signed at least 838 documents addressed to the Paymaster General, Lewis argued that it would accomplish the same purpose if the Queen directed and empowered the Paymaster General through the person of the Secretary of State for War to act on her behalf in such matters. Had this measure been enacted the previous year, according to Lewis, Victoria would have only had to sign approximately fifty "submission papers."[12]

---

10 RA QVJ: 7 June 1862, journal entry of Queen Victoria dated June 7, 1862.
11 RA VIC/E14/47, letter from Sir George Lewis to Queen Victoria, dated June 17, 1862.
12 RA VIC/E14/48, "Memorandum for the consideration and approval of Her Majesty, undated, enclosure to RA VIC/E14/47.

The Queen agreed with her Secretary for War that it would be prudent for her to delegate to him "cases of half pay, pension and retirement."[13] Reassuringly, the memorandum detailing the changes in procedure pointed out that instead of her having to sign hundreds of purely administrative documents in the course of the year, the Queen "with the least trouble, would be enabled to give directions, to the Secretary of State."[14] Victoria would still be informed of "every case and the particulars of it" so that she could render her judgment, but cases of similar subject matter could be grouped together for much greater efficiency. Further, this same principle could be equally applied to other administrative army matters, such as the "names of Officers, in the Store, Commissariat, Militia and Volunteer forces."[15] Without reservation–and apparently with little consideration– the Queen approved the memorandum.[16] Quite clearly, Albert's death had influenced her resolve to maintain her detailed interest in army issues, at least for the time being.

Although Victoria's interest in all things military would eventually return, for the time being her correspondence with the Secretary of State for War and the Commander-in-Chief declined considerably.[17] She continued to receive a large amount of detailed information on all matters military, but it was years before she regained her former interest in her favorite area. As for the larger issues of the state, the Schleswig-Holstein dispute forced Victoria from her isolation somewhat, but again it was a gradual return to the affairs of state. Perhaps the arrival of the subsequently famous– and controversial–Highlander, John Brown, helped return the Queen to a more active role.[18] Something had to be done, however, as the *Times*

13 *Ibid.*

14 *Ibid.* The memorandum mentions convenience or burden a number of times: "practical difference would be that Her Majesty's time and trouble would be economized"; "Convenience would suggest"; etc.

15 *Ibid.*

16 Writing only several years after this change was enacted, Walter Bagehot found Victoria's decision a welcome one, as he pointed out that commissions had been in arrears in the thousands (undoubtedly an exaggeration), and now that the Queen was not so bogged down by unnecessary duties on the Queen who had so many formal duties to society. Walter Bagehot, *The English Constitution* (Ithaca, New York: Cornell university Press, 1976), 101.

17 More accurately, the amount of military correspondence which was sent to Queen Victoria in 1862 and 1863 was indeed large, it was the Queen's capacity to respond to it appropriately that was diminished.

18 St. Aubyn, *Queen Victoria*, 356-364; Longford, 324-345. Two of the Queen's advisors, Sir William Jenner and Colonel Sir Charles Phipps, dispatched Brown to assist the Queen in October 1864 in the hopes of convincing her to ride once more and thus bring the Queen to a more normal condition. To a degree, the effort was a success despite the problems it created in its own right. One consequence

observed on the third anniversary of Albert's death: "The living have their claims as well as the dead; and what claims can be more important than those of a great nation."[19] Overall, however, it could be argued Victoria continued her mourning to the last of her days maintaining a number of morbid routines.[20] Far more important than her peculiar personal behavior was the opportunity Albert's death created for the Duke of Cambridge–he was now able to assume a much larger role in influencing the military attitudes of the Queen.

II

Just as the death of Albert would serve as a decisive turning point in the life and reign of Queen Victoria, it would also mark a crucial juncture in the career of the Duke of Cambridge. While Victoria had scrupulously followed Albert's advice that she not "*sign anything* until he had read and made notes,"[21] information presented to the Queen would now be a different matter for her and her advisors. No longer would the sure presence of Albert guide her; she would be on her own. This is not to say that she did not have military secretaries–Phipps, Ponsonby, and Biddulph–but they were *servants*. In such a situation, the position and influence of her royal cousin could only improve, assuming of course that Cambridge played his part correctly.

In the months following Albert's death, correspondence between the two was rather limited. Quite literally, however, the Duke of Cambridge assumed the role of Prince Albert when he took over what had been a primary occupation of the late Prince: the Great International Exhibition to be opened in London on May 1, 1862. The Queen remained in seclusion, the Prince of Wales was away in the Mediterranean, and the Queen's other children were still too young to officiate. Despite poor weather, the crowds were enthusiastic, and the Duke thought that, "The success was complete and everybody appeared pleased."[22] Taking part in ceremonies on behalf

of John Brown's success at bringing the Queen out of her borderline dysfunctional state was that the favoritism she afforded him created controversy and additional problems of its own.

19 *Times* (London), 14 December 1864.

20 St. Aubyn, *Queen Victoria*, 348-349. In addition to her predilection for black attire, she ensured that twice daily a change of ironed clothes, soap and hot water be delivered in Albert's room.

21 *Ibid.*, 340.

22 Diary entry of the Duke of Cambridge, May 1, 1862, reproduced in Sheppard, vol. 1, 230. Cambridge

of the Queen was by no means a new phenomenon for a member of the royal family, but the direct substitution of the Duke of Cambridge for the Prince Consort is suggestive nonetheless. Whereas previously Albert had been the primary military advisor to the Queen–and arguably no one could completely fill that role–it was only natural that Victoria's first cousin would take a correspondingly important position, not only as Commander-in-Chief but also as a counselor to the Queen.

While the veil of depression covered Victoria and those around her, Cambridge continued his normal duties without interruption. Although his detailed oversight of the army and the massive volume of correspondence that came with those duties continued, he had a very active social calendar as well. In the months prior to Albert's death, he had left London for a family reunion at Rumpenheim from August 18 to September 13, 1861, followed by a four day trip to Prussia to witness army maneuvers.[23] In the months following Albert's passing, he fulfilled the role of Albert in a number of ceremonies, attended weddings, made social calls, and attended formal functions.[24] Newly promoted to the rank of Field Marshal by the end of 1862,[25] Cambridge was again agitated over proposed further reductions to the army, and reductions in the Estimates would be a recurring challenge facing him throughout his remaining thirty-three years as the Commander-in-Chief. Resistance, though largely unsuccessful, would be a major joint endeavor of Cambridge and Victoria. Their shared effort and frustration gave them a mutual sense of purpose, no matter how futile. The Army Estimates for 1863-1864 were a crucial event in this process that continued for the remainder of their lives. It was the first time Victoria would examine them without any assistance from Albert.

---

returned to the Exhibition again on July 11th to distribute prizes on behalf of Queen Victoria. In this case, Cambridge was not representing Albert but rather Victoria herself as she was still in a deep state of mourning and was quite incapable of venturing out in public.

23 Diary entries of the Duke of Cambridge, August 18, 1861, August 28, 1861, September 17, 1861, reproduced in *ibid.,* 218.

24 For example, on May 1, 1862, Cambridge visited Fritz William, Prince of Prussia and Prince Oscar of Sweden. He attended the marriage of Princess Alice later that day. The next three days were spent at the great exhibition. The following month he visited the Pasha of Egypt where he was staying in London. Although not particularly exciting, such activities comprise the majority of his diary entries reproduced in *ibid.,* 229-232.

25 The Duke of Cambridge was promoted to the rank of Field Marshal on November 9, 1862, an honor which he believed to be due to the efforts of Sir George Lewis, to whom the Duke wrote on November 11th expressing that he felt "very much obliged." Letter from the Duke of Cambridge to Sir George Lewis, dated November 9, 1862, reproduced in Verner, vol. 1, 358.

In early December 1862, Cambridge received a copy of the proposed Estimates for the upcoming year and was concerned that Palmerston's government anticipated a significant reduction in the army. Cambridge wrote to Sir George Lewis that he would let the Prime Minister and the Cabinet members[26] see his lengthy memorandum detailing the consequences of the proposed reductions.[27] Analyzing the current composition, disposition, and strength of the various branches of service, he made a compelling case. For example, the practice of deploying one-third of artillery batteries at home and two-thirds abroad as opposed to the previous practice of half and half was not working–it was his "duty to state that...[n]either horse [n]or field batteries can be maintained on an efficient footing, if they are to be but five years at home to 10 abroad."[28] Further reductions of the force would only worsen an already dangerous situation. A similar condition existed with the Royal Engineers–twenty-two companies were stationed at home against nineteen abroad. Again, to cut the number or strength of the engineer companies any more would be an invitation to disaster.

As dire as the situation with the support branches was, however, the status of the combat arms of maneuver–cavalry and infantry–was even worse. The continuing need to pacify India demanded a greater demand for such troops. He stated emphatically that he could "...not recommend any reduction of Rank and File for the Regiments."[29] Besides, Cambridge had already proposed a "savings of about £10,000" by temporarily dismounting one regiment of cavalry and keeping another permanently dismounted, saving the need for some 400 horses. This could be accomplished by rotating one regiment back and forth to India. Again, to further reduce this force would be unwise. As for the Footguard, they were composed of seven of the most serviceable battalions "Kept at all times in the highest state of efficiency and always available for immediate Service though ordinarily kept for Home Service." Because of the nature of requirements throughout the Empire, there were two battalions of Footguards stationed in Canada. Categorically, the Duke argued that "No Reduction in this valuable Force can be contemplated."[30]

---

26 Letter from the Duke of Cambridge to Sir George Lewis, dated December 6, 1862, reproduced in *ibid.*, 277.
27 RA VIC/E14/56, Memorandum by the Duke of Cambridge for Sir George Lewis: "Estimates for 1863-4" dated December 5, 1862, copy.
28 *Ibid.*
29 *Ibid.*
30 *Ibid.*

As for the status of infantry regiments of the line, they were already over-stretched beyond the "normal" state and were unable to meet the standard of battalions spending one-third of their time stationed at home and two-thirds abroad. Cambridge then added rather plaintively that "I hope therefore I have clearly demonstrated that any reduction of Battalions of Infantry is wholly out of the question," although as a small concession he could offer a reduction of perhaps fifty men per battalion.[31] Confident that he had adequately demonstrated the army's thin ranks, Cambridge rounded out his argument with the admonition that the military train, commissariat, and staff corps were already very low and were "really a mere nucleus to form upon in the event of War."[32]

Despite his detailed and logical argument, Cambridge clearly recognized that his analysis mattered little in the world of politics. Civilian control of the budget meant he could do little to affect it other than present his position, and he acknowledged this with his closing statement to the Secretary of State for War: "With the political portion of the question I have no right to interfere, but…I hardly think the state of any portion of the world…would justify the belief that the moment was an opportune one for diminishing the available power of the Empire."[33] As strongly as Cambridge saw his role as protector of the army and preserver of the Royal Prerogative, he understood the appropriations for the army were beyond his control. This is important because as conservative as he was and still became, he did not question the underpinnings of civilian government, despite believing the current government pursued disastrous policy.

Although the likelihood of resisting the reductions was small– and Cambridge knew it–he continued to object vehemently to further reductions. Unfortunately for his efforts, his memorandum of December 5 merely prompted Sir George Lewis to ask Cambridge to consider an additional reduction of ten percent to the Army Estimates for 1863-64.[34] Undaunted, he replied on December 19 that the army had already been cut too much as it was, closing with an emphatic postscript: "I cannot help thinking must have originated in the brain of some gentleman totally unacquainted with military matters."[35]

31 *Ibid.*
32 *Ibid.*
33 *Ibid.*
34 Letter from Sir George Lewis to the Duke of Cambridge, dated December 17, 1862, reproduced in Verner, vol. 1, 277.
35 Letter from the Duke of Cambridge to Sir George Lewis, dated December 17, 1862, reproduced

Shortly after Christmas of 1862, Cambridge learned that despite his frequent protests to the Secretary for War, it seemed the Palmerston Ministry was seeking additional savings from the army budget. In addition to the reductions already proposed, the government was considering eliminating another fifty men–perhaps even 100–per battalion for a total reduction of some 3,500 to 7,000 men.[36] Although the entire strength of the army in 1861 was 217,922 men,[37] individual infantry battalions had an authorized strength of 900 men. Therefore a reduction of fifty men per battalion was significant, and the reduction of an additional fifty would profoundly affect the capabilities of an infantry battalion. Writing to Lewis on January 20, 1863, Cambridge conceded that they had already discussed the possibility of reducing infantry battalions by fifty men, but the reduction by another fifty "would make a very large one indeed in men, and I think it would really be *too large*."[38] He went on to remind the Secretary again how precarious Britain's position was in the world, and that if only he would show his previous memorandum to Lord Palmerston–which Lewis had not yet done and likely never did–it would all be made very clear to the Prime Minister and catastrophe would be avoided.

Frustrated by the lack of responsiveness from the Secretary of State for War, Cambridge turned to the person he knew would serve as a natural ally in his struggle to protect the army as it stood. Writing to Queen Victoria on January 15, January 20, and February 13, 1863, he expressed his dismay over the reductions contained in the Army Estimates.[39] To emphasize his position, the Duke included a copy of the memorandum he had prepared for Sir George Lewis the previous December with the second letter of the three.[40] Despite her weakened condition, he hoped the Queen could still assist in preventing the reductions even though it had already "been decided upon" by the Cabinet.[41] His efforts came to naught, but it

---

in *Ibid.*, 277.

36 *Ibid.*, 280.

37 Peter Burroughs, "An Unreformed Army? 1815-1868" in David Chandler, ed., *The Oxford Illustrated History of the British Army* (Oxford: Oxford University Press, 1994), 164.

38 Letter from the Duke of Cambridge to Sir George Lewis, dated January 20, 1863, reproduced in Verner, vol. 1, 280-81.

39 RA VIC/E14/54, Letter from the Duke of Cambridge to Queen Victoria, dated January 15, 1863, RA E14/61, Letter from the Duke of Cambridge to Queen Victoria, dated January 20, 1863, RA E14/61, Letter from the Duke of Cambridge to Queen Victoria, dated February 13, 1863.

40 RA VIC/E14/56, Memorandum for Sir George Lewis: "Estimates for 1863-4," dated December 5, 1862.

41 RA VIC/E14/61, Letter from the Duke of Cambridge to Queen Victoria, dated February 13, 1863.

would by no means be the last time the Duke fought reductions nor sought his cousin's intervention in the process. Rather, it was the first episode in a repetitive process that continued for the next three decades.

The following December, the process regarding the Army Estimates played itself similarly. The government sought economy and the army was an easy–and large–target. Cambridge resisted and did his best to demonstrate that the force as it stood was inadequate. Domestic and international considerations both complicated and reinforced the Duke's position. First and most obviously from an administrative standpoint, he had a new civilian counterpart at the War Office. Palmerston appointed a new Secretary of State for War, Lord de Grey (subsequently Lord Ripon), who had succeeded the late Sir George Lewis. Whereas he had worked well with Lewis in the past, Lord de Grey presented a new challenge. Internationally, additional developments affected Britain's world position. The Civil War in the United States continued unabated; Lincoln's Emancipation Proclamation had taken effect January 1, and the northern forces seemed likely to win, which made it impossible to support the southern states. Although this lessened the likelihood of armed intervention in North America–never a great possibility–the most important development was the changed strategic position of Prussia. As the Prussian Prime Minister, Otto von Bismarck demanded settlement of the Schleswig-Holstein issue; despite the Queen's sympathy for Germany's cause, the potential for an aggressive and growing Prussia posed a real threat to European stability and Britain's part in it.[42]

In the course of getting to know the new Secretary of State for War and developing a working relationship, Cambridge kept him well informed of the true state of Britain's defenses and the alarming degree to which the British army was stretched. Writing to Lord de Grey on October 20, 1863, Cambridge explained in a lengthy memorandum of twenty pages of legal-pad sized paper the inadequate state of recruiting for the army and its impact on readiness.[43] His main complaint was that the Ten Year's Enlistment Act had not done the army any good.[44] Although Cambridge incorrectly argued

---

42 Despite Palmerston's avowed support for Denmark and keeping the principalities of Schleswig and Holstein in Danish hands, the Cabinet was divided, the Queen was sympathetic to Prussia and the French under Napoleon III were unwilling to commit. The final result was never in question.

43 RA VIC/E14/77, "Memorandum for the Secretary of State on recruiting for the Army and the Ten Year's Enlistment Act," presented from the Duke of Cambridge to Lord de Grey, dated October 20, 1863.

44 More accurately, it was known as the Reserve Warrant Act of 1859. Although known by its major

the Ten Year's Enlistment would drain men from the regular force–only 3,000 opted[45]–he also pointed out the dangerous situation posed by an inadequate force. Recruiting woes worsened an already poor condition,[46] but not until March of 1866 would a Royal Commission be established to investigate the recruiting crisis. Despite failure after failure, however, Cambridge persevered tirelessly to protect his institution.

The Army Estimates for 1864-65 once again presented the opportunity for the Commander-in-Chief to make the case for increased spending and against reductions. By this stage it was standard procedure: a lengthy and detailed letter to the Secretary of State for War laid out the Duke's position. Citing his itemized memorandum of the previous December, Cambridge explained, "the Establishment proposed for last year must be looked upon as barely sufficient to meet the ordinary requirements of our Service, and that any unusual demands upon them would therefore require additional means in order to meet them efficiently."[47] The army's total force of 206,969 had 71,763 men serving in India, 58,739 in the Colonies and an additional 76,467 stationed at home–there were too few to meet homeland defense.[48]

Essentially, Cambridge argued forcefully that at the very least the forces should be maintained to the level they were the previous year. He detailed where and how the members of each branch of service were deployed–for instance, there were now only 44,685 infantrymen in England whereas there had been 50,000, and of this reduced number, 14,636 belonged to the Depôt Battalions for home defense and could not rotate with infantry battalions stationed abroad.[49] To make matters worse, the reduction of battalions to 800 men from the previous authorized strength of 900, rather than 850 which Cambridge had recommended as a compromise, made them significantly less capable since they still had administrative and logistics functions as before, making it "next to impossible" to dispatch infantry

result, the Act allowed regular soldiers of the line–infantrymen–to accept a discharge after ten year's service rather than the normal 21 if they transferred to the reserve. Cambridge objected, fearing it would drain men from the regular army, although it did not. Spiers, 169.

45 *Ibid.*

46 RA VIC/E14/77, "Memorandum for the Secretary of State on recruiting for the Army and the Ten Year's Enlistment Act," presented from the Duke of Cambridge to Lord de Grey, dated October 20, 1863.

47 RA VIC/E14/83, "Memorandum for Lord de Grey – Estimates 1864-65," dated December 5, 1863 and from the Duke of Cambridge (copy).

48 *Ibid.*

49 *Ibid.*

battalions abroad. Finally, he recommended the Estimates be increased by 1,000 men as that number was required to be sent to New Zealand.[50] Cambridge's closing words reiterated his position that the forces were too low and "the only question is whether we do not run considerable risk in leaving our Establishments at so low a figure."[51]

In what had by now become an annual and predictable pattern, the Duke of Cambridge wrote to Queen Victoria for the express purpose of keeping her informed, but also to gain her support for their common cause. Almost two years after the death of Albert, the Queen was more willing to take an active role in preventing further reductions of the army. In response to his letter of December 10, 1863,[52] in which Cambridge notified Victoria that he had sent a confidential memorandum to Lord de Grey[53] protesting further reductions, the Queen replied through her personal secretary, "that Your Royal Highness [Cambridge] may depend on HM's support in opposing any reduction in the present strength of the Army."[54] In a tacit acknowledgement of her lengthy absence of active participation in army affairs and her future intention to remain involved, the Queen's letter closed with the information that she would "be glad to hear more frequently from Your Royal Highness and to be kept acquainted, in the same manner, as you were in the habit of acquainting the Prince Consort, with anything of interest that may occur in the administration of the army."[55] Although the effectiveness of the united efforts of the Duke of Cambridge and Queen Victoria were yet to be determined concerning army reductions, the Queen's relationship with her cousin and their mutual concern for the army would help bring her out of her dysfunctional mourning while also bringing her closer to her cousin.

---

50 The dispatch of troops to New Zealand was the result of the ongoing effort to fight the Wars, begun in 1845 and not finally extinguished until 1872. See below.

51 RA VIC/E14/83, "Memorandum for Lord de Grey – Estimates 1864-65," dated December 5, 1863 and signed by the Duke of Cambridge.

52 RA VIC/E14/80, Letter from the Duke of Cambridge to Queen Victoria, dated December 10, 1863.

53 RA VIC/E14/83, "Memorandum for Lord de Grey–Estimates 1864-65," dated December 5, 1863 and signed by the Duke of Cambridge.

54 RA VIC/E14/81, Letter from General Grey to the Duke of Cambridge, dated December 12, 1863.

55 *Ibid.*

III

In the short run, the efforts of the Duke of Cambridge and a partially reinvigorated Queen Victoria were unsuccessful in preventing additional army reductions. Although future cuts would be rather small, they would be enacted despite repeated and articulate arguments of Cambridge backed by the open support of Victoria. Somewhat ironically, the day following the Prussian invasion of Schleswig-Holstein supported by a minor Austrian naval force on February 1, 1863, Lord de Grey wrote to the Queen and informed her the Cabinet proposed further reductions amounting to 1,449 fewer men to offset the increased cost of the "hostilities in New Zealand."[56] To provide the proper funding and transport of the troops, cuts had to be made to other units throughout the Empire. Believing the proposed cuts would not "interfere with the practical efficiency of the Army," de Grey explained the reductions were to be effected by diminishing battalions in the branches of service which had not been reduced in the previous year's reductions.[57] He did not even mention the war which had just broken out between Prussia and Denmark. Cambridge, however, was well aware what the war entailed for Britain's strategic position.

Once Cambridge understood the magnitude of the Prussian invasion, he wrote to the Secretary of State for War and requested that, at the very least, infantry regiments be returned to their previously authorized strength of 900 men per infantry battalion.[58] Noting the combined Prussian-Austrian force mobilized and deployed a very large force–"at least 50,000 men"–within the space of a fortnight, with justified alarm, Cambridge observed that in light of "what the Continental Armies have just accomplished," Britain "literally can do nothing but call our Militia and recruit up as fast as the labour market will permit us to obtain men."[59] The Militia could not be called out without war. Arguing that Britain was in a poor strategic position and that regiments be increased up to 1,000 men, he closed his letter with the request that de Grey present it to Lord

---

56 RA VIC/E14/86, Letter from Lord de Grey to Queen Victoria, dated February 2, 1864. New Zealand officially became a colony of Great Britain in 1840, but the indigenous Maori tribes resented the land distribution to European settlers. Tribal resistance and unrest lasted from 1845 to 1872, generally known as the New Zealand Land Wars or the Maori Wars.

57 *Ibid.*

58 Letter from the Duke of Cambridge to Lord de Grey, dated February 2, 1864, reproduced in Verner, vol. 1, 286-288.

59 *Ibid.,* 287.

Palmerston immediately or meet with Lord Palmerston in person.[60] The not-too-surprising result was no change.

Cambridge had attempted to prevent further reductions and the changed situation in Europe bolstered his position, but the reductions went through anyway. Belatedly, the Queen accepted the reality that government economy would win out over her wishes and those of her cousin, and on her behalf her private secretary, General Grey, wrote to Lord de Grey on February 4, that if there were no other way to make up the required troops for New Zealand, then it would be acceptable to reduce the other branches of service, except the Royal Engineers, "already too weak should be the last to be reduced."[61] She recognized that neither the government nor the country was prepared to get involved in the war on the continent and that there was no support for increased defense expenditures. The invasion scare was by now a distant memory and the Prussian-Austrian alliance did not present as clear an enemy to Great Britain as France historically had. In response to the Queen's wishes, Lord de Grey informed her the reductions of the support branches would be carried out, but the Royal Engineers would be the last to be reduced and that further reductions would not be undertaken.[62] Two days later, de Grey's letter was amended, "Reduction approved under the circumstances. By Command of the Queen. Feb 7/64."[63]

With time the Queen's interest in army affairs increased markedly and Cambridge continued managing postings and promotions of senior officers throughout the Empire. Despite Denmark's defeat, the consolidation of Schleswig-Holstein into Prussia, and the promotion of the Duke of Cambridge to the rank of Field Marshal, most of his correspondence was routine–routine for an Empire that continued to cover an ever-larger portion of the globe. Throughout 1864, most of the letters written by the Duke of Cambridge affected the recommendation of officers for commands throughout the world, recommendations of awards or promotions.[64] As Cambridge continued his correspondence with the Queen and his senior officers, she did not hesitate to express the suitability

---

60 *Ibid.*, 288.
61 RA VIC/E14/87, Letter from General Grey to Lord de Grey, dated February 4, 1864.
62 RA VIC/E14/88, Letter from Lord de Grey to Queen Victoria, dated February 5, 1864.
63 *Ibid.*
64 RA E14/92, RA E14/93, and RA E14/94, dated April, letters from the Duke of Cambridge to Queen Victoria, recommending the approval of awards or promotions of senior officers stationed in Canada, Gibraltar, India and England.

of one officer over another. The interchange highlights the evolving relationship between the two cousins. As had always been the case, the Queen approved the promotion and command assignments of all senior officers in the British army. Such approvals, however, came after the Commander-in-Chief, in consultation with the Secretary of State for War, put those recommendations forward to the Queen. Technically, the chain of responsibility ran from officers in the field to the Duke of Cambridge, to the Secretary for War, and then to the Queen. For her part, however, the Queen did not always acquiesce if she felt strongly enough, or especially against, a certain officer.

As has been well documented, Queen Victoria was not always amiable. Even though Cambridge and Victoria grew closer together in the wake of Albert's death, it by no means meant the Queen always agreed with her cousin. Later, her influence with Cambridge figured quite prominently in forcing him to accept the reforms and changes put forth by Lord de Grey's successor, Edward Cardwell.[65] A case in point concerns an area where the power of the Queen and especially the Duke of Cambridge was indeed large: the posting and promotion of senior army officers. Specifically, the Queen sometimes challenged the appointment of certain officers whom she found objectionable. The selection of General Sir Hugh Rose (later Lord Strathnairn) for command in Ireland is useful to examine the relationship between the two when they disagreed.[66]

Although as a Cabinet member the Secretary of State for War ultimately presented the names of officers for promotion to senior rank and command of key billets, the Commander-in-Chief really held sway in this area and reported directly to the sovereign. Although the issue of *command* of the army would come to a head when Cardwell became Secretary of State for War, governments of both parties up to 1868–and generally thereafter–did not question that "The Military command and discipline of the Army, and also the appointments and promotions therein, are declared...to be vested in the Commander-in-Chief."[67] The Royal Warrant of October 11, 1861,

---

65 The interaction between the Duke of Cambridge, Queen Victoria and Edward Cardwell will be discussed in depth in the following chapter.

66 Rose was a prominent and successful officer who had spent much of his military career in India, to include playing a major role in suppression of the Mutiny and most recently, command in Bombay.

67 Charles M. Clode, *The Military Forces of the Crown; Their Administration and Government*, vol. 2 (London: John Murray, 1869), 351. Although the significance of Clode's work will be addressed more fully in the following chapter, it is important to note that he wrote it while he was serving as an official at the War Office with the full support of the Secretary for War, Edward Cardwell. Clode's work was

drafted under Sir George Lewis had codified this relationship, although in principle the rights of the Commander-in-Chief in areas of "command and discipline" of the army had never been openly challenged.

As the Queen became more involved in army matters, Cambridge corresponded with her more frequently and the two regularly exchanged thoughts as to the suitability of various officers for various command billets throughout the Empire. In November 1864 Cambridge informed her of his choice for selections to command in India and Canada, against which the Queen had no objection. In agreeing to the selections, she asked the Duke to have the army barracks at Windsor modernized.[68] Further selections occurred in the New Year–General Airey to command the fortress at Gibraltar and General Scarlett to command at Aldershot–without any disapproval from the Queen.[69]

Although Victoria normally concurred with her cousin's selections, she fiercely objected to the Duke's decision to post the aforementioned General Sir Hugh Rose to command in Dublin because "his moral character is so <u>very</u> bad."[70] Perhaps as a consequence of his service in India–Rose was serving as the Commander-in-Chief of the forces in India, most recently having overseen the campaign in the North-West Frontier in 1863 and the little-remembered Umbeyla Campaign in 1863[71]–but more likely due to Rose's numerous affairs, the Queen viewed him as bad choice. Based upon information she had heard "from all quarters," she believed that "Dublin, where society is notoriously lax, will, I fear, have a bad effect, & do harm."[72] Not swayed by the Queen's adamant objection,

---

intended to be a Whig interpretation of the history of civilian control of the army and it began its analysis with the year 1688.

68 RA VIC/E14/103, Letter from the Duke of Cambridge to Queen Victoria, dated November 25, 1864 reference selection of General Napier to command in Bombay, approved by Queen Victoria November 28, 1864; RA VIC/E14/104, Letter from the Duke of Cambridge to Queen Victoria, dated November 29, 1864 reference selection of General Michel to command in Canada; RA VIC/E14/105 Letter from Sir C. Phipps [on behalf of Queen Victoria] to the Duke of Cambridge, dated December 9, 1864, reference modernization of army barracks at Windsor.

69 RA VIC/E14/111, Letter from the Duke of Cambridge to Queen Victoria, dated January 22, 1865 reference selection of General Airey to command Gibraltar and Scarlett at Aldershot.

70 RA VIC/E14/114, Letter from Queen Victoria to the Duke of Cambridge, dated January 24, 1865, reference selection of various officers, including Rose, to command in various assignments. In the same letter she approved the assignment of Scarlet for Aldershot and Airey for Gibraltar.

71 For a brief but lively account of these campaigns, see "Chapter 13, The North-West Frontier 1855-63" and "Chapter 14, The Umbeyla Campaign 1863" in Byron Farwell, *Queen Victoria's Little Wars* (New York: W.W. Norton & Co., 1972), 144-162.

72 RAVIC/ E14/114, Letter from Queen Victoria to the Duke of Cambridge, dated January 24, 1865.

Cambridge refused to yield, replying instead that he would "do all that is right to prevent General Sir Hugh Rose from doing anything objectionable in Ireland."[73] Furthermore, argued the Duke, Rose had done great things for the army in India, was a "first rate soldier" and although he was not loved by the civilian authorities, he was loved by the troops. In effect, Cambridge was thanking Victoria for her advice, but he was definitely going to assign Rose to command in Ireland, which he did. In the same letter he discussed other officers for commands elsewhere. So it continued for the remainder of his time as Commander-in-Chief.

The disagreement over the assignment of General Sir Hugh Rose is instructive for what it reveals about the relationship between Queen Victoria and the Duke of Cambridge. Although the two disagreed completely over an issue important to both, the Queen actually deferred to her cousin, while Cambridge for his part felt quite comfortable in standing up to her. Ultimately she accepted his authority and expertise when it came to officer placement. Equally significant is that Cambridge, owing his position to the Queen, was quite willing to oppose her. Overall, such disagreements would occur with a fair degree of regularity throughout the coming years, but the two never differed on the matter they both held to be especially important–preservation of the Royal Prerogative.

IV

With mind-numbing regularity, the Duke of Cambridge, supported by Queen Victoria, continued to wage his Sisyphean struggle against further reductions of the army. The annual Estimates battle once again raged in December 1864 over the shape of the force for 1865-66, only to be followed by a similar struggle the following December regarding the force for 1866-67. Except for the death of Lord Palmerston on October 18, 1865, and his replacement by Earl Russell as Prime Minister, there was virtually no substantive difference between the battle over the Army Estimates for 1865-66 and 1866-67.[74] The political changes caused Victoria to "*feel* ALL these changes sadly, painfully!" Although they made her "feel more and more alone!," she promised to "strive to *do* my *duty* courageously and

---

73 RA VIC/E14/115, Letter from the Duke of Cambridge to Queen Victoria, dated January 26, 1865.
74 Obviously, the death of Lord Palmerston meant the passing of another elder statesman who had been prominent from the start of Victoria's reign. Earl Russell would lead the Whig government until Derby once again became the Prime Minister the following June.

conscientiously."[75] In subsequent years, the Army Estimates debate played out in the normal fashion–Cambridge and the Queen were steadfastly against additional reductions, while Palmerston's (and subsequently Russell's) Secretary of State for War, Lord de Grey, implemented the fiscal limitations imposed by the government.

In December 11, 1864, Cambridge made it clear once again that he was "opposed to <u>all</u> reductions of <u>men</u>."[76] The arguments had been heard before–uncertainty in Canada, potential unrest in Ireland, the changed nature of politics on the Continent–and Cambridge reaffirmed that his duty was to advise while political matters were beyond his responsibility. As expected, the Queen dutifully protested additional "diminution of force" although she did "not withhold her consent" because she could not challenge budgetary matters.[77] Ultimately, Lord Grey informed that the Estimates would be implemented. In December 1865, Lord de Grey, the Duke of Cambridge, and the Queen went through the same process for the upcoming year, this time "for the reduction of Infantry."[78] The Queen was opposed, fearing "that the reduction of the officers must necessarily cause much hardship."[79] Cambridge registered his objections for familiar reasons directly to the Prime Minister, Lord Russell, on January 25th to protest further reductions.[80] Predictably, the Prime Minister did not agree with the Duke's position, and he saw "no cause, either in regard to Ireland or in regard to Canada, against the contemplated reductions of the Army."[81]

---

75 Letter from Queen Victoria to the King of the Belgians, dated October 25, 1865, reproduced in Buckle, ed., *The Letters of Queen Victoria*, vol. 1, 280. Several days earlier Victoria had written to her uncle that she had "*never liked*" or even respected Palmerston, because "He was very vindictive, and *personal* feelings influenced his political acts very much." And yet despite her strong feelings, she felt completely on her own as she observed, "Still, he is such a loss! I shall have troubles and worries, and to face them *alone* without my Angel [Albert] is dreadful!" Letter from Queen Victoria to the King of the Belgians, dated October 20, 1865, reproduced in *Ibid.*, 279. The death of King Leopold of Belgium several weeks later on December 10, 1865 would complete the Queen's feeling of isolation, removing the old guard of close advisors.

76 RA VIC/E14/107, Letter from the Duke of Cambridge to Queen Victoria, dated December 11, 1864.

77 RA VIC/E14/109, Letter from General Grey to Lord de Grey, dated December 12, 1864.

78 Letter from Lord de Grey to the Duke of Cambridge, dated December 20, 1865, reproduced in Verner, vol. 1, 291; RA VIC/E14/144, letter from Lord de Grey to Queen Victoria, dated December 20, 1865, reference Army Estimates for 1866-67.

79 RA VIC/E14/145, Letter from Sir Charles Phipps [Keeper of the Privy Purse] to Lord de Grey, dated December 22, 1865.

80 Letter from the Duke of Cambridge to Lord Russell, dated January 25, 1866, reproduced in Verner, vol. 1, 294. The basis for Cambridge's objection was the "anxiety felt in Canada on the subject of the Fenian raids."

81 Letter from Lord Russell to the Duke of Cambridge, dated January 26, 1866, reproduced in *Ibid.*

The advent of a new Secretary of State for War, whether it was Lord Hartington in February 1866 or Sir John Pakington (along with a Conservative Ministry under Lord Derby) in July 1866, and another Prussian War–the Austro-Prussian War of 1866[82]–did little to affect the Army Establishments. Although Cambridge did not advocate any direct involvement with the fighting on the continent, he recognized that Prussia clearly possessed a land warfare capability surpassing Britain's. Although he did not grasp the genuine strengths of the Prussian army based upon the few written thoughts he left on the subject–he apparently attributed the Prussian victory to the Prussian breech-loading needle rifle over the Austrian muzzle-loading rifle[83]–Cambridge did indeed realize that Britain's strategic position was now even more precarious. What should have troubled him more than Prussian rifles was the strategic mobility provided by the Prussian rail system and the consequences of a professional officer corps and general staff. He also should have recognized the impressive ability to mobilize such a large force so quickly and capably by the Prussian General Staff of Helmuth von Moltke. Since the likelihood of continental engagement was quite limited, however, the government– under Lord Derby as well as Russell before him–continued a policy of economy toward the army and assumed the risk that war on the Continent was unlikely.

While government policy toward the army underwent little significant change in the mid-1860s,[84] the Queen and the Duke of Cambridge focused their attention on army matters generally within their purview and beyond the scope of the government's interest. For her part, in addition to the larger issues of the defense establishment or the numbers of troops by branch and location, the Queen also revived and intensified her previous interest in

---

82 One consequence of the Prussian victory was the annexation of Hanover to Prussia, depriving the royal family of the throne of that kingdom.

83 Diary entry of the Duke of Cambridge, dated July 4, 1866, "The Needle Musket [*sic*] of the Prussians, it appears is so offensive, that all the gallantry of the Austrians cannot stand up against it." Reproduced in Sheppard, vol. 1, 262.

84 Cambridge and Victoria were unsuccessful in stemming reductions to the army, but they were not more than one or two thousand per year–the army was much larger than it had been prior to the Crimean War in the wake of the post-Napoleonic draw-down. However, it was true that Britain's worldwide commitments were far greater than they had been prior to the 1850's. For a colorful but scholarly analysis of the relationship between expanding Empire and the British Army, see P.J Marshall, ed., *The Cambridge Illustrated History of the British Empire* (Cambridge: Cambridge University Press, 1996).

other aspects of "her army."[85] In addition to commands and promotions, she also followed uniform and drill policy very closely. Sometimes her degree of interest was astonishing, and overall it demonstrated a lack of proportionality. Since she was interested in virtually all aspects of her army, matters of minor detail and no importance received an amount of attention equal to ones that really did, such as the army Estimates. A salient example involved lace and drums.

A proposal to change the pattern of lace used by drummers throughout the army in 1865 brought about a united action of the Queen and the Duke of Cambridge as the two worked together to prevent change they viewed as detrimental. The episode is interesting not only for its absurdity, but more importantly because it highlights once again the unity of effort of the two royal cousins while revealing the degree to which Victoria remained interested in army matters. On March 1, 1865, the Queen's private secretary, General Grey, informed Victoria that a change in the pattern of lace for drummers had been put forth by General Scarlett at Aldershot with the intention of standardizing drummers' lace.[86] Subsequent updates from Scarlett through General Grey kept Victoria abreast of the situation, as well as the Duke of Cambridge, until at last Scarlett realized the futility of his struggle: the change was not going to happen. Scarlett wrote to the Queen through General Grey on March 7, 1865 that since the appropriate paperwork had not been "signed by the Queen...nothing more will be done in the matter" and he realized the error of his ways while thinking "it only just to His Royal Highness [Cambridge]" to say that he also was very "unwilling to make any alterations."[87] Accordingly, the revision to the patterns of lace on drums was not carried out and tradition was preserved.

As ridiculous as this and many of the other issues with which the Queen involved herself–and many were quite ridiculous, at least to the modern reader; e.g., bearskin caps for the Fusiliers regiments[88]–they

---

85 It is telling that when Lord de Grey wrote to the Queen on December 10, 1864 with the proposed army estimates he apologized–"Lord de Grey trusts that Your Majesty will pardon him for the length"– for going into such detail, but in reality he knew very well that she expected such a lengthy letter. RA VIC/E14/106, Letter from Lord de Grey to Queen Victoria, dated December 10, 1864, reference Army Estimates 1865-66 and further reductions.

86 RA VIC/E14/119, Letter from General Grey to Queen Victoria, dated March 1, 1865.

87 RA VIC/E14/122, Letter from Sir J.Y. Scarlett to General Grey, dated March 7, 1865.

88 A uniform change in the Fusiliers regiments had recently altered soldiers' headgear so that bearskin caps were no longer worn. This caused understandable consternation within the regiments as the bearskin caps were a distinctive and prized symbol of regimental service. With Cambridge's sanction, General Scarlett at Aldershot sent potential replacement bearskin caps to the Queen for her approval

also represent an area where the authority of the Queen and the Duke of Cambridge was not either implied or the result of persuasion, but instead a real power which no other government body could counter. In this way she achieved tangible results in the institution which mattered more to her than any other than perhaps her own family. Whereas the responsibilities of the Crown weighed heavily upon her head, Victoria looked upon her duties as head of the kingdom's armed forces with unreserved pride. Unlike many duties she had to endure–and she made it clear to those around her that she worked very hard [89]–army matters were not a burden but a pleasure.

These same things could be said of the Duke of Cambridge, although his powers in the army were more direct and tangible. Even though he was Commander-in-Chief, his authority was often less direct than the title implies, for he never was the commander of overseas operations. As for matters of command and discipline of the army, the cornerstone of the position, civilian control of the budget and various reform initiatives by Parliament had limited much of the independence of the Commander-in-Chief. It is in no way surprising that Cambridge sought to control as much of his organization as he still could, while the budget constraints forced upon him made him more inclined to limit not just reform, but change of almost any kind.

V

Compared to what came after it as well as the period before it, the history of the office of the Commander-in-Chief Duke at the Horse Guards and its relationship to the Crown during the mid-1860s appears calm, if not outright dull. Often overlooked, this was a period that witnessed an important, but gradual change in Cambridge's outlook while it was also a very important period for further cementing the cooperation of the Queen and Cambridge. Albert had taken great interest in military affairs and

---

beginning in mid-May 1865. In addition to their other responsibilities, Cambridge, and through him, Victoria, were regularly apprised of new cap design and modifications until a satisfactory model was finally developed in the course of the next several weeks. RA VIC/E14/125-127, correspondence between Sir J. Scarlett, General Grey, the Duke of Cambridge and Queen Victoria, dated 18-19 May 1865.

89 One thing that is certain about Queen Victoria is that she worked very hard indeed. Refusing to delegate anything–two of her private secretaries, Sir Henry Ponsonby and General Grey, died of strokes–she toiled every day of the year through mountains of correspondence. For a discussion of the workload of Victoria, see St. Aubyn, *Queen Victoria*, 340-342.

was genuinely committed to serious reform. With his absence, the role of Cambridge as a trusted advisor was undoubtedly enhanced. Furthermore, Victoria and Cambridge regarded their roles–or more accurately, their callings–to preserve what they viewed as the traditional duty their respective positions encompassed. Thrust into a changing society and an altered international framework, Cambridge became increasingly conservative. Victoria reinforced and reflected this conservatism and the two supported one another in their moral convictions. The two were indeed representative of the attitudes prevalent throughout the army as the impetus for reform had virtually disappeared.[90]

The period cannot be seen as one of great triumph for Cambridge because he was singularly unsuccessful in limiting the reduction of the army. On the other hand, the issue of the Royal Prerogative was not threatened and the thorny issue of the relationship between the Commander-in-Chief and the Secretary of State for War was not resurrected. Furthermore, despite his frustration over the Army Estimates, the Duke fully accepted the notion that financial matters were for the politicians to decide, and therefore was a matter which he hoped perhaps to influence but ultimately not one he could control. Cambridge had not fully accepted the Royal Warrant of 1861. Although he did not fight it openly, he hoped the issue would fade away and the physical and functional separation of the Horse Guards and the War Office would let the issue die a quiet death. In this he was successful–for the time being.

The advent of Edward Cardwell, Gladstone's Secretary of War from 1868 to 1874, would mark the turning point of Cambridge's tenure as Commander-in-Chief. Against the fierce opposition of the Duke, Cardwell would attempt complete reform of the War Office, ending the system of dual control of the army and bringing the administration of the army under closer control of the Secretary of State. Cardwell would introduce a number of reforms that struck at the heart of Cambridge's vision of the Royal Prerogative; whether they would be effective or meaningful reforms was another matter entirely. The entire Cardwellian issue will be dealt with fully in the following chapters, but the impact of Cardwell and his

90 As an authority on the British army and its administration has said, "After the enthusiasm for army reform generated by the Crimean War and reinforced by the shock of the Indian Mutiny and the fear of French invasion, the 1860's constituted a lull or trough during which Britain's military authorities were slow to grasp the significance of developments in the American Civil War and the Austro-Prussian War." Bond, *The Victorian and the Staff College*, 111.

struggle with Cambridge, backed frequently by the Queen, is meaningful only when examined from the perspective of the events and relationships that preceded Cardwell's tenure as Secretary for War and, of course, the events that followed it.

Historically, Cambridge has been considered important only as the foil against whom Cardwell had to implement his intended reforms. To examine the few years in which the two men occupied their respective offices is to miss the larger question of the relation of Cambridge to the Queen and the common objectives the two shared. Above all, the royal cousins wished to preserve the army as an institution subject to the Royal Prerogative and one which would be protected from undue parliamentary influence and political association. Cardwell may have burst onto the scene as a relative newcomer with a flurry of reforms, and Cambridge may have had a much lengthier tenure in office, but the lasting legacy of the two men is important to consider. In the end, Cambridge outlasted his civilian counterpart, but while he may have retained his position–barely–the nature of that office, not to mention the army as a whole, was irrevocably altered. Whether such changes accomplished Cardwell's long term goals is another issue that will be addressed later, but the larger consideration is the degree to which the united front of Cambridge and Victoria could prevent unwanted changes to the army and their relationship to it. Thus far they had been outwardly successful when confronted with ministries not dedicated to a fundamental transformation of the army. It remained to be seen whether the same could be said when faced with the determined and reform-minded government of Gladstone.

CHAPTER 8:
Opening Skirmishes 1868-1870

When the Gladstone Ministry came into power with a decisive Liberal victory near the end of 1868, it brought with it a new Secretary of State for War. If the death of Prince Albert marks a decisive point in the reign of Queen Victoria, the return of Gladstone to power from December 1868 to February 1874 represents not only an important period for the history of Great Britain, but also a decisive phase for the office of the Commander-in-Chief and the career of the Duke of Cambridge. While there had been a number of struggles over civilian control of the army and preservation of the Royal Prerogative, the next five years would be the ones that determined not only the legacy of the Duke of Cambridge, but more importantly they clarified and changed fundamentally the relationship between the military, the monarchy, and Parliament.

While the bond between Cambridge and the Queen had evolved and strengthened considerably up to this point, the arrival of Edward Cardwell (1813-1886) at the War Office tested the powers and influence of the Duke and the Queen to a degree not seen before or after during their long tenures. Cardwell's legacy and his rivalry with Cambridge are crucial and thoroughly investigated aspects of the Gladstone Ministry. Until now, accounts of the period have left Cambridge strictly as a backdrop for the more gifted Cardwell. When he is addressed, if he is addressed at all in either political or military studies, the Duke is cast as the main obstacle to serious reform.[1] No less an authority than Brian Bond has referred to him as a "Bow-and-Arrow General."[2] Perhaps the most lasting example is found in the masterful account of British history between the Franco-Prussian War and the First World War by R.C.K. Ensor portraying the

---

1 A telling example is Sir John W. Fortescue's thirteen-volume history of the British Army which mentions the Duke of Cambridge as Commander-in-Chief *only three times*. Sir John W. Fortescue, *A History of the British Army,* 13 vols. (London: MacMillan and Co., 1910-1930); vol. 13, pp. 55, 557 and 559. Studies of the British army of the Victorian period that mention Cambridge focus his role in preventing or delaying effective British army reform. See Brian Bond, *The Victorian Army and the Staff College, 1854-1914* (London: Eyre Methuen, 1972); Gwyn Harries-Jenkins, *The Army in Victorian Society* (London: Routledge & Keegan Paul, 1977; Edward M. Spiers, *The Army and Society, 1815-1914* (London: Longman, 1980); Jay Luvaas, *The Education of an Army: British Military Thought, 1815-1940* (Chicago: Chicago University Press, 1964) and *The Military Legacy of the Civil War: The European Inheritance* (Chicago: University of Chicago Press, 1988); and Hew Strachan, *European Armies and the Conduct of War* (London: Routledge, 1983).
2 Bond, *The Victorian Army and the Staff College,* comment beneath illustration of the Duke of Cambridge placed between pages 126-127.

"very able man of affairs, Edward Cardwell" as bringing much needed reform to the army while the Duke "opposed all change."[3]

It is only natural that Cambridge serves as the foil against reform, which in many ways he certainly was. However, for Ensor, and others, to put "Cardwell's place among statesmen…[as] the greatest British army reformer during the nineteenth century" may be a bit of an exaggeration.[4] Under his term as Secretary for War, a number of well-publicized and tangible changes were enacted–most prominently the enactment of short-service enlistment and the abolition of Purchase–but the long term consequences of his proposals may not have been what he envisioned. More importantly, the behavior of Cambridge and how his actions related to those of the Queen, and what it all meant for the powers of the Crown have not been sufficiently explored or explained.

Despite the progressive image of Cardwell that has persisted, it now seems clear that the reforms he implemented did little to transform the army, and what is incontrovertible is that Cambridge continued as Commander-in-Chief for over two decades *after* Cardwell left office.[5] Furthermore, the Franco-Prussian War of 1870-1871 changed forever the strategic position of Britain as the newly created German Empire displaced France as the preeminent military and economic power in Europe. The struggle between the Horse Guards and the War Office took place while Britain's international position both militarily and economically was fundamentally changing. It is certainly debatable whether Cardwell did any better than Cambridge in preparing the army to deal with the new realities that Britain faced. What is without question, however, is that despite Cardwell's numerous "victories" over Cambridge–the most visible and the most resented by the Duke being that of physically relocating his office from the Horse Guards to the War Office at Pall Mall–the Duke nonetheless survived in his position as Commander-in-Chief. Although Cambridge maintained his

3 R.C.K. Ensor, *England 1870-1914,* Vol. 14 of *The Oxford History of England*, edited by G. N. Clark (London: Oxford, 1936), 9.

4 Ensor, 9. For an important and traditional portrayal of Cambridge as the obstructionist to the enlightened Cardwell, see William Robertson, *From private to Field-Marshal* (London: Constable, 1921).

5 Despite the controversy generated by Cardwell, the British army was not really transformed and the composition of the officer corps was not changed in the least. For the most convincing arguments revealing the limitations of the Cardwell Reforms see Gallagher, "British Military Thinking and the Coming of the Franco-Prussian War," 20-21; Spiers, "The Cardwell Reforms" in *The Army and Society1815-1914*, 198-200; Bond, "Edward Cardwell's Army Reforms," 116-117; and Gallagher, "Cardwellian Mysteries," 347-348.

post, the nature of his authority, and influence over the army as a whole had been diminished, and by extension, the Crown's as well.

I

Even though Benjamin Disraeli had successfully extended the franchise in 1867 as a result of the Second Reform Bill, the General Election in the fall of 1868 did not bring Conservative victory. Instead, William E. Gladstone and the Liberals won a commanding share of the seats in Parliament by a margin of 112. Although Cambridge noted the progress of the General Election with considerable alarm–"The elections are going most horribly for the government and I fear the next Parliament will be a most mischievious and radical one. God knows what they will not do! [*sic*]"[6]–the ultimate outcome did not overly concern him. He generally did his best to remain above politics, although as a staunch supporter of the maintenance of tradition he was understandably more inclined to support the positions of the Conservative Party. So when Gladstone announced his ministers on December 7, 1868, Cambridge described his new civilian counterpart in the following terms: "Mr. Cardwell is the new Secretary for War, a most gentlemen like man, with whom it will be pleasant to act."[7] Although Cambridge was fully aware that the new ministry was likely to impose considerable reductions and once again force Cambridge to face a difficult struggle, it is unlikely he understood the overall challenge that Cardwell would pose to Cambridge and his principles. For his part, Cardwell had had an admirable record as a progressive attorney. Before addressing in depth the ensuing struggle that would shape the future of the War Office and the Horse Guards while attempting to subject the latter to the former directly, it will be helpful first to discuss the struggle that preceded it, but on a larger scale. This larger battle was by no means settled permanently when Gladstone assumed office.

When Viscount Palmerston died in October of 1865, he was succeeded by Lord John Russell, a Liberal. Since he had been created an earl in 1861, he sat in the House of Lords, and it was Gladstone who led the Liberal members of the House of Parliament. The two men led an effort in 1866 to

---

6 Letter from the Duke of Cambridge to Sir William Mansfield, dated November 21, 1868, reproduced in St. Aubyn, *The Royal George*, 135.
7 Letter from the Duke of Cambridge to Sir William Mansfield, dated December 10, 1868, reproduced in Verner, vol. 1, 387.

reform Parliament, but a curious alliance between right wing Liberals and Conservatives defeated it for being too radical. As a consequence, both Russell and Gladstone resigned over their failure to pass the bill. Lord Derby's Conservative ministry then took over, similar to the government that had preceded it. Derby sat in the Lords while Benjamin Disraeli led in the Commons. This new Conservative alliance in turn passed a reform bill that was in fact more radical than the one which Gladstone and Russell had been unable to get through Parliament. Thus it was a Conservative Ministry that brought about a genuine broadening of the franchise, but the larger electorate also served as Disraeli's undoing in the General Elections of 1868 which brought Gladstone back to power, where he remained as Prime Minister until 1874.

The struggle between the Duke of Cambridge and Edward Cardwell represented a smaller version of the one between Disraeli and Gladstone, although to compare the two sets of men would be overstating their similarities, for Cambridge and Disraeli could not have been more dissimilar in background or demeanor. Nonetheless, the intensity of the contest makes the connection a useful one. All four individuals were extremely capable and effective at achieving their desired goals, but in very different ways. Just as Disraeli mastered the art of how to manage Queen Victoria, Gladstone never figured it out. Cambridge *understood* the army and was in it "for the duration," while Cardwell forced through a great deal but it is arguable that he never really understood the army. In a curious reverse symmetry, Disraeli as the ultimate outsider to politics and Cambridge the ultimate insider worked toward conservative ends. It is easy to stretch the comparison too far, for Cambridge never really understood expediency and considered himself instead a man of hard and fast principles, a description that could never be applied to Disraeli.

Whereas the demand for reform in all sectors of British society had abated somewhat in the first half of the 1860s–Cambridge had done his best to limit army reform–Gladstone's return to power in 1868 both reflected and propelled the growing movement for renewed progressive action. Palmerston's death in 1865 ended the mid-Victorian era and opened a new period of support for reform. The appearance of Gladstone and Disraeli as the primary politicians of the new era coincided with dramatic domestic and international developments. The year 1865 witnessed popular alienation within Britain due to an economic downturn, a cotton shortage, and a serious outbreak of cholera. The defeat of the Confederacy and the end of slavery in the United States,[8] as well as the unification of Italy under Garibaldi, brought about a renewed optimism in democratic principles and desire for reform.[9] Although many factors were involved and demand for reform in 1865 was strong, the demand was not as strong as it had been prior to the Reform Act of 1832. It was against this backdrop that Gladstone's fairly mild Reform Bill of 1865 was generated and subsequently defeated by an alliance of skeptical radical Liberals and the Conservatives. It was then that Disraeli did what only he could do: he introduced a bill more radical than Gladstone's that became the Reform Act of 1867, doubling the size of the electorate.[10] Disraeli's achievement, however, was his undoing and the General Election of December 1868 returned the Liberals to power with a commanding majority that kept Gladstone in power until 1874.[11]

As Prime Minister, Gladstone would push for reforms throughout Britain affecting education, Parliament, Ireland, and most importantly for the present purpose, the army. In pursuit of his progressive agenda, he filled his Cabinet with like-minded individuals. Edward Cardwell was not particularly interested in army matters, but since he was a zealot, his selection for Secretary of State for War was an ideal choice.[12] Possessing an impressive education from Winchester and Balliol College, Oxford, Cardwell was every bit the high-minded Liberal for whom the liberal ideal was more than a good idea; it was a calling bordering on obsession.[13] Cardwell had received a first in mathematics and the Classics while at Oxford and had also been President of the Union, and then admitted

8 Even Queen Victoria was not immune from the developments surrounding the end of the American Civil War. She wrote to Mary Lincoln on April 29, 1865 to express her heartfelt condolences after the assassination of President Lincoln. See Buckle, ed., The *Letters of Queen Victoria*, vol. 1, 265-7.

9 The end of the Civil War in itself did not immediately reduce the tensions between Great Britain and the United States, but rather intensified them in the short run over naval disputes and the defense of Canada.

10 The intricacies of the debates and skillful maneuvering of Disraeli leading up to it, as well as the genuine consequences of the Reform Act of 1867 are beyond the scope of this book. Among many others, see F.B Smith, *The Making Of The Second Reform Bill* (Cambridge: Cambridge University Press, 1966) and Maurice Cowling, *1867 Disraeli, Gladstone and Revolution The Passing of The Second Reform Bill* (Cambridge: Cambridge University Press, 1967).

11 In the long run, however, it was Disraeli's achievement of the Second Reform Act that would return the Conservatives to power in 1874 and maintain them as the "natural party of government" until after the turn of the century.

12 Cardwell had thus far in his career demonstrated virtually no interest in army affairs. He had not participated in the Purchase debates earlier in the decade. Spiers, 177-179.

13 St. Aubyn, *The Royal George*, 135-7. For a glowing, but unbalanced account of Cardwell and his accomplishments, see Ralph Biddulph, *Lord Cardwell at the War Office* (London: John Murray, 1904).

to the Bar in 1838 and became a Member of Parliament in 1842.[14] Six years older than his counterpart at the Horse Guards, he was every bit as serious in disposition as Cambridge and had previously demonstrated administrative competence throughout his time in government service.[15] Appointed Secretary to the Treasury by Peel, Cardwell later served as Chief Secretary for Ireland and Secretary of State for the Colonies. In addition to his demonstrated administrative efficiency and liberal credentials, he possessed the added benefit of not having attracted the unwanted notice of the Duke of Cambridge or Queen Victoria by promoting radical change of the army.[16]

Upon learning that Cardwell would be the new Secretary for War, Cambridge's first reaction was one of relief, for he had been expecting it to be a known "troublemaker," the radical and extremely eloquent John Bright.[17] As for his opinion of Cardwell, he admitted to Lord Granville that he "thought Cardwell would be weak" and feared Bright far more as a choice.[18] Regardless of who filled the Cabinet position, Cambridge knew he would again face the ever-recurring battle over the Army Estimates.[19] With Gladstone leading a new government, he braced himself for the worst and did his best to prepare. He was quite right to suppose that a Gladstone Ministry would demand greater economy. Whether in the long run the changes enacted during this period brought about savings of any kind is extremely doubtful.

It was not only Cambridge whose fears of the new Gladstone administration were initially assuaged. Victoria's initial agitation over a reinvigorated Liberal government's design on the country and her army softened after her customary conference with Gladstone. After meeting with the new Prime Minister, she reflected he "was most cordial and kind in his manner, and nothing could be more satisfactory than the whole

---

14 St. Aubyn, *The Royal George*, 136.

15 For a detailed account of the earlier accomplishments of Edward Cardwell, see A.B. Erickson, *Transactions of the American Philosophical Society*, New Series, vol. 49, II, 1959.

16 Sir George de Lacy Evans' motions to abolish Purchase did not prompt Cardwell to speak or vote on the proposals. Bruce, 119.

17 Spiers, 178; Memorandum by General Grey, dated December 4, 1868, reproduced in Buckle, ed., The *Letters of Queen Victoria*, vol. 1, 559-564.

18 British Library, Gladstone Papers, Add. Mss., 44165, 170. The Duke of Cambridge's opinion was repeated in a letter from Earl Granville to Gladstone, dated August 2, 1868. Granville was the leader of the Liberals in the House of Lords.

19 St. Aubyn, *The Royal George*, 135-6.

interview."[20] Furthermore, she found little to worry her over the choice of Edward Cardwell to be Secretary of State for War and readily accepted Gladstone's assessment that Mr. Cardwell was "a cautious, conciliatory and experienced man."[21] Initial impressions by the two cousins would soon change.

II

The Duke of Cambridge and Queen Victoria quickly grew concerned over developments coming from the War Office once the new government was in place. Cardwell started with an aggressive policy and literally within days of his arrival it became clear he was committed to instituting dramatic change at the War Office and the army as a whole. Certainly there was nothing new in demanding greater economy and efficiency from the army–every Secretary of State for War with whom Cambridge had worked had this primary mission. It was only natural that Cardwell continue as his predecessors had done. Where he differed was in the scope of what he regarded as his domain. A memorandum he wrote for Gladstone before assuming office made his guiding principle quite clear:

> I contend for the principle of plenary responsibility to Parliament on the part of the parliamentary head of the Department; and consequently, for the absence of all reservations, express or implied, from authority of that office.[22]

The Secretary for War would be responsible for more than budgetary and political matters. In Cardwell, Cambridge would face a civilian counterpart not content to bypass the awkward issue of dual control of the military. Rather, Cardwell would face the issue head on and make the authority of the Secretary of State for War supreme in all aspects of army administration and control.

---

20 Memorandum by Queen Victoria, dated December 3, 1868, reproduced in Buckle, ed., The *Letters of Queen Victoria*, vol. 1, 564.
21 *Ibid.*, 565.
22 Memorandum from Edward Cardwell to W.E. Gladstone, dated December 3, 1868, reproduced in Verner, vol. 1, 388.

Before his first month was out, Cardwell made it painfully clear to the Duke of Cambridge and Queen Victoria that he fully expected to take charge with the complete backing of Gladstone's Liberal Ministry behind him. The desire to reduce the Army Estimates came as no surprise, but the extent for the year 1869-1870 certainly did. Writing to General Grey for the benefit of Queen Victoria on December 29, 1868, Cardwell proposed the most ambitious reductions of the decade–almost 9,000 men–citing as the rationale the situation in "B.N. America, where the circumstances have ceased to exist, which led to our maintaining there a great force."[23] Although Cardwell's assessment regarding North America was entirely accurate, it was not the best possible beginning with Cambridge and Victoria. Aware of her sentiments, Cardwell attempted to compensate with the net result of a greater number of troops at home and an increase in the militia.[24] Even though Cardwell would successfully withdraw thousands of troops from the colonies, especially Canada, in turn allowing reductions to take place at home, Victoria was not pleased. A letter to Cardwell in March 1869 expressed her "misgivings as to the extent to which it is proposed to withdraw troops from the Colonies, & to carry reductions in the staff at home," but she trusted that the matter had been "well considered in the Cabinet" and let it pass.[25]

Cambridge, on the other hand, never adjusted to the overseas withdrawals. In the years to come with the process well underway, he continued to express his misgivings to Cardwell. He cited reasons as varied as better climate than in India,[26] the need to garrison the fortress in Quebec by the "Mother Country,"[27] and the overall concern that the reduction was too much, too soon throughout the Empire.[28] Even though the withdrawals

23 RA VIC/E15/190, Letter from Cardwell to General Grey, dated December 29, 1868. Cardwell proposed an Establishment of 130,000 rather than 138,691. His decision was astute since the likelihood of conflict between the US and Britain was nonexistent and the Fenian threat was not sufficient to maintain so large a troop presence in Canada.

24 For example, writing to the Queen's Private Secretary on January 26, 1869, about the ongoing discussion over the Army Estimates in the Cabinet, Cardwell observed that the Estimates would provide "3,100 more than by the distribution of last year. In addition to this,-the Estimates provide for 81,000 militia, or 13,400 more than last year:-making a total of 16,500, regulars & militia together." RA VIC/E16/10, Letter from Cardwell to General Grey, dated January 26, 1869.

25 RA VIC/E58/37, Letter from Queen Victoria to Edward Cardwell, dated March 2, 1869.

26 Letter from the Duke of Cambridge to Mr. Cardwell, dated August 3, 1869, reproduced in Verner, vol. 1, 394-396.

27 Letter from the Duke of Cambridge to Mr. Cardwell, dated December 14, 1869, reproduced in *Ibid.*, vol. 1, 396-399.

28 Letter from the Duke of Cambridge to Mr. Cardwell, dated January 11, 1870, Reproduced in *Ibid.*,

were primarily from settler colonies where the threat was negligible and a greater number of troops in England resulted, Cambridge was unable to adapt. Maintaining a large presence where the national interest was not threatened did not make sense when deeper cuts were coming. More importantly, the growing power of North German Confederation– subsequently an even more powerful German Empire–changed national strategic considerations that Cambridge did not fully grasp. His attention was soon focused much more on domestic considerations than drastic changes in the stationing of the forces abroad.

In addition to the immediate struggle over the Annual Estimates, a relatively minor incident foreshadowed what was to come. Several days into the New Year of 1869, a speech from an outspoken member of Gladstone's Ministry highlighted the rift that would soon develop between the War Office, backed fully by the government, and the Horse Guards, supported by the Queen. The incident incited the wrath of the Queen and the Duke of Cambridge and quickly reinforced the growing hostility between the friends of the army on the one hand and those who wished to transform it on the other. The episode is revealing for what it demonstrates about the limit of Gladstone's reforming ministry and the political influence of both the Duke of Cambridge and Queen Victoria.

George Otto Trevelyan, the newly appointed Civil Lord of the Admiralty, presented a public speech criticizing the close connection between the Crown and the army, suggesting it was royal influence that blocked army reform.[29] Unfortunately for Trevelyan, the speech was subsequently printed in the *Pall Mall Gazette*.[30] When the Queen read a summary of the speech she was shocked and demanded a full explanation. Accordingly, General Grey passed on the Queen's concerns about the "most outrageous speech" to Gladstone on January 6 along with the article from the *Pall Mall Gazette*.[31] What disturbed her most was the "untrue" nature of Trevelyan's statements, including the "'tremendous influence of the Court' as one of the obstacles to be overcome by anyone who desires

---

399-400.

29 Sir George Otto Trevelyan served as a Liberal member of the House of Commons from 1865 to 1897. In addition to being a dedicated Whig politician, he was also a respected historian, whose first biography was about his uncle, Lord Macaulay. He was the father of George Macaulay Trevelyan.

30 Trevelyan made his exuberant speech in celebration of his reelection to Parliament on Monday, January 4, 1869.

31 RA VIC/E16/1, Letter from General Grey to W.E. Gladstone, dated January 6, 1869.

to reform the War Office."[32] Additionally, she found the jab at her cousin ("Royal Duke in permanent command of the Army") quite upsetting (Cambridge himself would be equally outraged), despite the veracity of Trevelyan's speech.

Gladstone immediately expressed his hope to the Queen that the article was an exaggeration, but he warned against punishment so severe that its consequences might be more injurious in the long run as "a nucleus of mischief."[33] Predictably, Cambridge quickly registered his unhappiness with Victoria. At her insistence, General Grey had sent the Duke a copy of the article, and Cambridge explained how he felt the "attack made upon me to be a most unjustifiable one."[34] Furthermore, he made it clear he had served with several governments and Secretaries of State, always maintaining "the most friendly and cordial relations." Trevelyan's speech attacked both Cambridge and his position directly. He was therefore aware that great danger loomed with the new administration. Cambridge expressed his fears openly and asked the Queen for her support in a most forthright manner.[35]

As has been established, it had become common for Cambridge to rely upon Victoria for support and to attempt to combine her influence with his to accomplish objectives they both deemed beneficial. The advent of Gladstone and Cardwell marks the beginning of a new stage in the connection between the military and the monarchy, however, because very early into Gladstone Ministry, Cambridge foresaw that not only his beloved institution was to be "attacked" but also that his individual position as Commander-in-Chief was to be challenged. It was therefore convenient–and vital–that criticism of Cambridge be linked with that of the Crown. And it was here that the strategy of the Duke of Cambridge began to take shape. Not only did the Commander-in-Chief serve at the pleasure of the sovereign, but the position was tied directly to the Crown as part of the institution. It followed logically then, that any attempt to alter or remove the position of the Commander-in-Chief was by extension an attempt to weaken the prestige of the Queen. Therefore, an important and neglected consideration in assessing Cardwell's tenure is how the Duke and the Queen perceived the threat and how well they resisted it.

32 *Ibid.*
33 RA VIC/E16/2, Letter from W.E. Gladstone to Queen Victoria, dated January 7, 1869.
34 RA VIC/E16/3, Letter from the Duke of Cambridge to Queen Victoria, dated January 7, 1869.
35 *Ibid.*

The criticism of the Queen and Cambridge from the newly appointed Civil Lord of the Admiralty, G.O. Trevelyan, and the response from the government and the Crown demonstrate that in this case the Duke of Cambridge was quite successful in harnessing the support of Queen Victoria. More accurately, she took the lead, and Cambridge, in turn, used his influence to gain her assistance. The same day he wrote to her expressing his concerns, Cambridge wrote a second letter that pointed out the dangers of such negative commentary against the Crown coming from "a Member of the Government, even in a subordinate position." [36] He would bring the matter to the attention of Edward Cardwell to avoid similar mishaps in the future.

The response was swift. The combined efforts of the Queen and Cambridge brought an immediate apology from Gladstone and Trevelyan. Gladstone wrote to Victoria on January 10 and included with his letter one from Trevelyan to him. Gladstone's letter was earnest and devoid of emotion, as was his style, explaining his minister's behavior as being "in part due to...inexperience, but undoubtedly in part also to a slip of the tongue, the employment of words he did not mean to use, and then a momentary confusion resulting from a painful sense of his lapse."[37] Although Gladstone regretted the offending words, he did not intend to remove Trevelyan, a genuine gentleman, who had "received a lesson for life."

As for the harm done to Cambridge, Mr. Cardwell would address that. Trevelyan's apology was more heartfelt than Gladstone's, expressing "feelings of real mortification" over the fact that his words did not express his "real meaning."[38] Accepting full responsibility for the mishap, Trevelyan offered his resignation, but Gladstone did not accept it. Cardwell was also critical of Trevelyan's behavior, not for the ideas expressed, but for the manner in which he did so. He believed in the long run injurious language would hurt the cause of reform.[39] Although none of the parties involved expressed it, the reaction of Victoria and Cambridge and subsequent speedy apologies proved Trevelyan's point. It is likely the irony was not lost on him.

36 RA VIC/E16/4, Letter from the Duke of Cambridge to General Grey, dated January 7, 1869.
37 RA VIC/E16/5, Letter from W.E. Gladstone to Queen Victoria, dated January 10, 1869.
38 RA VIC/E16/6, Letter from G.O Trevelyan to W.E. Gladstone, dated January 9, 1868 [*sic*]. In his haste, Trevelyan made the all-too-common mistake of failing to remember the correct year so quickly after the New Year.
39 Verner, vol. 1, 401.

Victoria and Cambridge were satisfied by the government's response, and they used it to their advantage. The Queen found the apologies satisfactory but made it very clear that since Trevelyan, as a member of the government, had advocated the removal of Cambridge as Commander-in-Chief, the government must distance itself from that position.[40] Ultimately, however, she accepted Gladstone's advice not to press the issue too hard for fear of drawing unwanted attention–it could do more harm than good.[41] As long as Cardwell and Gladstone understood that the official government position was that Cambridge should remain as Commander-in-Chief, she would let the matter drop. Cambridge also accepted the letters of apology, although he found Trevelyan's, which was given to him by Cardwell, to be less satisfactory than the one from Gladstone.[42] Nonetheless, as long as he had the assurance from the government that this was not the official attitude, he had no desire to prolong "this disagreeable matter."

Still, the battle lines had been drawn. The new administration was going to be aggressively reformist and most likely challenge the Royal Prerogative. The relationship between the Crown and the army exercised through the office of the Commander-in-Chief would be stressed as it had not been at any time, not simply during Cambridge's tenure, but in the history of the position. Initially it seemed the combined efforts of the Queen and her cousin had been successful, but in the succeeding months the stakes would be far greater.

III

The tone set during the initial weeks remained relatively constant throughout the Gladstone Ministry. The Army Estimates proposed for 1870-71 ended up being even more severe than originally proposed in December; rather than a reduction of almost 9,000, the actual number decided by the Cabinet was in excess of 15,000.[43] The following year's Annual Estimate for 1871-72 left only 23,941 British troops abroad–not

---

40 RA VIC/E16/7, Letter from Queen Victoria to W.E. Gladstone, dated January 12, 1869.

41 RA VIC/E16/9, Letter from General Grey to the Duke of Cambridge, dated January 20, 1869.

42 RA VIC/E16/8, Letter from the Duke of Cambridge to Queen Victoria, dated January 18, 1869.

43 RA VIC/E16/10, Letter from Cardwell to General Grey, dated January 26, 1869. The total reduction was to be 11,166 men. This was accomplished by withdrawing troops primarily from Canada. Finally, Cardwell announced reductions of 15,173 on March 11, 1869 which also mainly came from Canada. 34,852 troops remained abroad outside of India. From Bond, "Edward Cardwell's Army Reforms, 1868-74," 109.

including those in India–concentrated mainly in Gibraltar, Malta, Bermuda, and Halifax.[44] But Cardwell had far greater goals than merely reducing the army and its budget; he intended "wide and extensive changes."[45] Shortly after his appointment on December 3, 1868, Cardwell laid out his plans regarding the War Office and the army for Gladstone.[46] Although the origins of this memorandum are a matter of debate–Cardwell and Cambridge's biographers, among others unconvincingly cite it as proof that Cardwell had had designs on overhauling the War Office for many years[47]–the document does indeed foreshadow much of Cardwell's subsequent program. In conservative language that acknowledged Cardwell's predecessors, the short memorandum focused on reforming the administration of the War Office, including subordination of the Horse Guards to the War Office, but also recommended reducing colonial stationing from 50,000 to 26,000, reorganizing and expanding the militia, and most significantly, abolition of Purchase, significant changes in promotion and retirement, and the introduction of short service.[48] Not one of these topics was new to reformers and Cambridge had personally considered some of them.[49] What *was* new was that for the first time there was a military secretary who arrived in office equipped with a comprehensive plan.

Although the reductions for 1870-71 were the most drastic ones seen since the end of the Crimean War, they were really the culmination of work begun by Cardwell's predecessor, Sir James Pakington. The Gladstone Ministry merely intensified planned withdrawals, but the germinal idea was not theirs. The first initiative Cardwell undertook–consolidation of the Horse Guards into the War Office–would be the most dangerous challenge Cambridge had yet faced. The name Edward Cardwell is most often

---

44 *Ibid.,* 109-110.

45 Undated letter from Cardwell, reproduced in Bond, "Edward Cardwell's Army Reforms, 1868-74," 108-109.

46 The memorandum, "The Army," is reproduced in its entirety in Biddulph, "Appendix I" in *Lord Cardwell at the War Office,* 249-254.

47 Cardwell's biographer, Sir Robert Biddulph suggests the detailed nature of the memorandum proves it was the work of many years, see *Ibid.,* v; Cambridge's military biographer argues similarly, see Verner, vol. 1, 386-390; an insightful journal article does likewise, see Gallagher, "Cardwellian Mysteries," 329. On balance, however, Cardwell had given little thought to the matter prior to his selection and wrote the memorandum to plan his Secretariat. The previous lack of interest in army affairs argues against a longstanding plan for army reform. See Bond, "Edward Cardwell's Army Reforms, 1868-74," 108-109; Spiers, *The Army and Society 1815-1914,* 177-178.

48 Biddulph, 249-254.

49 Verner, vol. 1, 389.

associated with the abolition of the system of purchase, but this was not the most significant reform he implemented. It was merely the most fiercely resisted, and therefore the most publicized. As Cardwell himself viewed it, the move to end Purchase was only one step in a larger process of creating a unified and rational army organization.[50] The actions of Cambridge, Victoria, and others to preserve Purchase are well documented, but the more relevant topic of subordination of the office of the Commander-in-Chief to the Secretary of State for War is crucial to understanding the relationship of the Duke, the Queen, and civil government. Fiercely resisted by Cambridge, it was a crucial personal battle he did not win.

When Cardwell assumed his duties, he found an organization that offended his lawyer's sense of order and logic. Having devoted his adult life to increased efficiency, he found the War Office anything but. Despite previous efforts at reform in the wake of the Crimean War, the structure of the War Department and the administration of the army as a whole remained muddled. The War Office building–more accurately building complex–was located on the south side of Pall Mall between the Oxford and Cambridge and Carlton Clubs. It had once belonged to the Culloden Duke of Cumberland, but army administration quickly outgrew the confines of the Duke's former town house. Nineteen neighboring houses were incorporated into a War Office occupied by over 800 officials and clerks and over 100 messengers by the 1870s.[51]

More troubling still was the concept of dual government, or at least the lingering doubt that it still existed. While the Secretary for War resided at Pall Mall, the Commander-in-Chief maintained his office at the Horse Guards. In the eyes of Cardwell, the physical separation was more than symbolism; however, for appearance reasons alone he found it objectionable. Both physically and literally, the most important step in uniting the War Office under Cardwell's authority would be moving the Commander-in-Chief into his headquarters building. This would remove permanently any ambiguity regarding the command relationship between the two positions. For these same reasons Cambridge found the move unacceptable. Previous attention on Cardwell's reforms has overlooked this important fact. Yet, ironically, it was the settlement–or

---

50 Bond, "Edward Cardwell's Army Reforms, 1868-74," 113.
51 W.S. Hamer, *The British Army: Civil-Military Relations 1885-1905* (Oxford: Clarendon Press, 1970), 8.

partial settlement–of the issue upon which all other changes implemented by Cardwell depended.

Cardwell did not attempt to disguise his intention to end dual control and force Cambridge's compliance; the memorandum of December 3, 1868 made this point clearly. Cardwell consistently argued that constitutionally, the matter had been settled for quite some time. Cambridge hoped he could continue as he did under Sir George Lewis and the issue would fade to the background, but such a tactic would not work with Edward Cardwell. On March 11, 1869, still barely into the new ministry, a Radical Member of Parliament, James White, raised the issue of dual control. Despite White's contentious statements in the House condemning "dual government" and his introduction of a resolution to end the practice of the Secretary of State for War having to share his power with the Commander-in-Chief, Cardwell replied simply that such a situation did not exist. According to Cardwell, there was only one military administrative authority in the country, and he was it.[52]

Although the dispute between the Horse Guards and the War Office would grow in intensity in the succeeding months and years, Cambridge had indeed agreed to the subordination of his office to the War Office at the start of the decade under Sir George Lewis.[53] The Cardwell administration discovered the Royal Warrant of 1861 codifying the relationship between the Secretary of State and the Commander-in-Chief– it had not faded into oblivion as Cambridge had hoped. The warrant was a serendipitous discovery which merely reinforced Cardwell's conviction that constitutionally there was no dispute. The same month he spoke in Parliament on the matter of dual control, a more weighty account of his views was published.

A long-time member of the staff at the War Office, Charles M. Clode, approached Cardwell about producing an official history of the War Office to which Cardwell readily agreed. The resulting *Military Forces of the Crown* was produced in an astonishingly short amount of time–less than six months–considering its length of over 1,400 pages and breadth of material covered.[54] Written with the express approval of Cardwell, the

---

52 *Hansard's Parliamentary Debates 1066-1918*, 3rd Series, Vol. 194, 1094-1109.
53 See above, Chapter 7.
54 Charles M. Clode, *The Military Forces of the Crown; Their Administration and Government*. 2 vols. (London: John Murray, 1869). Clode dates his preface as March, 1869 and states that he approached the Secretary with the idea of the book in September of 1868.

two-volume history provides excellent insight into Cardwell's "Whig" interpretation of civilian control of the army from 1688 to that time. Most pertinent are those sections defining the duties of and relationship between the Secretary of State for War and the Commander-in-Chief: "Extracts from the Records of the War Office and Ordnance Department" and "Public Documents."[55] Unfortunately for Cambridge, and apparently not recognized by contemporary historians, it was only because Clode was conducting research for this book–a fact previously neglected–that the Royal Warrant of 1861 was even discovered.[56] The author published the warrant in full, as well as a significant number of other documents relating to the history of the office of the Commander-in-Chief.[57]

In unambiguous language, Clode recounts the constitutional history of civilian control of the armed forces of the Crown and uses the concluding chapters of his lengthy work to state the official position of the War Office: dual control of the military does not exist, and the Secretary of State for War is supreme over all departments of the army, to include the office of the Commander-in-Chief.[58] Clode's *Military Forces of the Crown* serves as an excellent guide to the Cardwellian view of how it should all work, and it explicitly resolves a number of issues which, though he may not have directly challenged, the Duke of Cambridge certainly resisted. Although it is stated in a number of ways and pains are taken to point out that the Commander-in-Chief is still responsible for command and discipline and possesses important powers, it is clear that his is a subordinate position: "24. The Office of the Commander-in-Chief is *strictly* Executive, and for the discharge of his duties he is directly responsible to the Constitutional Ministers of the *Crown*."[59] It can be seen that despite attempts to finesse the language to avoid offending the Crown or the Duke, there was no escaping the reality that the Commander-in-Chief was subordinate to the Secretary for War.[60] Publishing the opinion of the Secretary of State for

---

55 *Ibid.*, vol. 1, iii-vi.

56 In a footnote, Clode explains that "I am not aware that it [Royal Warrant of 1861] came under the cognisance of any official (save the author), until it had been submitted to a section of the Cabinet." *Ibid.*, vol. 2, 351.

57 "Appendix CXLI" in *Ibid.*, vol. 2, 738-739.

58 "Chapter XXV, The Office of the Secretary of State," "Chapter XXVI, The Office of the Commander-in-Chief," and ""Chapter XXIX, The Consolidated War Office" in *Ibid.*, vol. 2, 316-334, 334-358, 390-427.

59 *Ibid.*, vol. 2, 344.

60 To prevent repetition, the context of the positions stated in the concluding chapters of Clode's work will be omitted. The vast majority of the last 100 pages of the second volume, as well as a substantial

War was one thing, but getting Queen Victoria and the Duke of Cambridge to accept that position was another matter entirely.

On March 1, the Queen wrote to Cardwell regarding what she believed to be excessive colonial troop withdrawals.[61] Realizing her objections would have little practical effect, she was "anxious…to the fact that a disposition exists in some quarters to run down the C.-in-C. and generally to disparage the military authorities as obstacles to all improvements in our Army administration."[62] Victoria observed that Cambridge had always acted "most cordially" with the previous secretaries. She had learned about the plan to move the Commander-in-Chief's office to the War Office and could not support it because "Such a step could not fail to damage the position of the C.-in-C."[63] In other words, financial matters were beyond her control, but she was prepared to resist to her utmost any damage to her cousin's prestige.

Cardwell tried not to contradict the Queen, but he did not deny he wanted to do exactly that. Waiting two days, he sidestepped the issue stating he was unaware of any plan to move the offices at the Horse Guards; there was insufficient space at Pall Mall to house them anyway.[64] Additionally, he affirmed he would never implement any plan before receiving the Queen's approval. Several months after their correspondence, it was apparent Cardwell had every intention of implementing the very thing of which the Queen had accused him. For the time being, however, the matter was deferred, and instead Cardwell allowed his capable and far more affable subordinate, Lord Northbrook, to work the details of the planned move. In the end, Cardwell knew he was operating from a position of strength–he had the backing of Gladstone as well as Parliament. There was no point in deliberately provoking the Queen, but he did not need to take her wishes into account.

---

number of the appendices, are dedicated to stipulating that the Secretary for War is responsible for the army as a whole and that the Constitution is quite clear on the matter.
61 Letter from Queen Victoria to Edward Cardwell, dated March 1, 1869, reproduced in Buckle, ed., The *Letters of Queen Victoria*, vol. 1, 584-585.
62 *Ibid.*, vol. 1, 585.
63 *Ibid.*
64 Letter from Edward Cardwell to Queen Victoria, dated March 3, 1869, reproduced in *Ibid.*, vol. 1, 585-586.

IV

In December of 1868 the new Gladstone Ministry appointed a War Office Committee to investigate army organization and recommend improvements. The chairman was the Under-Secretary of State for War, Lord Northbrook, whom Cardwell had asked Gladstone to appoint as his under-secretary when Cardwell accepted his position as Secretary for War.[65] Northbrook had previously served as the under-secretary and understood how the War Office operated, as well as ways to improve the bureaucratically awkward situation there. Not surprisingly, Cardwell and Northbrook held similar attitudes about what needed to be changed at the War Office. Fortunately for Cardwell, his subordinate was a gifted administrator who had great diplomatic abilities and liberal ideas. As chairman of the committee charged with investigating army organization, Lord Northbrook could propose ideas which Cardwell shared while also benefiting from the appearance of neutrality offered by a committee.

The Committee on Army Organization began its work without generating much attention, not even from the Duke of Cambridge. Several interim reports were issued: on March 11, 1869, the committee recommended the creation of the position of a Financial Secretary and Surveyor-General of Ordnance and on May 7, 1869 it recommended modifications to the army system of supply.[66] Unlike these two, the next area the committee investigated directly challenged Cambridge: the establishments at the Horse Guards. In taking on the organization of the Horse Guards and the relationship of it to the War Office, the committee was entering an area where consensus was unlikely. Thus began an investigation that ultimately would threaten not only the physical location of the office of the Commander-in-Chief, but the nature of the position, and indeed its continued existence.

Presented in November of 1869, the report of the War Office Committee on the Conduct of Business in the Army Departments recommended the reassignment of the Commander-in-Chief's staff to other departments within the War Office, changing (and reducing) the status of the Commander-in-Chief's military secretary to a private secretary, and the movement of the Commander-in-Chief's office to the War Office

---

65 Verner, vol. 1, 389-390; St. Aubyn, *The Royal George*, 135-137.
66 Verner, vol. 1, 403.

building where his position would be equal to the chiefs of other military departments and subordinate to the Secretary of State for War.[67] This was the opening shot in a conflict that would drag on for several years. Clearly, the Duke of Cambridge would not easily accept such obvious degradations of his authority and neither would the Queen. Gladstone, however, did not believe the committee had clearly recommended and stated directly a decrease in authority for the Commander-in-Chief.[68] As for Cardwell, he was committed to a complete reorganization of the army and saw modification of the Commander-in-Chief's position merely as a vital first step in that process.

Before the year was over, tension between Cambridge and Cardwell had risen to the gravest condition yet. Initially, Cambridge avoided cooperating in any way with Lord Northbrook's committee until he realized this helped Cardwell's cause. Erroneously, Cambridge had thought the Northbrook committee would build upon the ideas generated from the last such investigation headed by Sir James Graham in 1860.[69] Previously, there had not been consideration of subordinating the Commander-in-Chief to the Secretary for War, and Cambridge was not pleased with the creation of a chief of staff position, implying replacement or redefinition of the Commander-in-Chief's position.[70] Although Cambridge had earlier recognized this actual relationship—his consent to the Royal Warrant of 1861 demonstrates this conclusively—he did not expect it to be stated openly. What perturbed the Duke was the public demonstration of the subordination of the ranking military officer to a civilian minister.

On December 5, 1869, Cambridge expressed his sentiments to Cardwell in a typical lengthy and detailed letter. An article had appeared in the *Army and Navy Gazette* in which the opinions of the Secretary for War were presented as official opinion. Astonished, Cambridge wrote to Cardwell to remind him of the importance of presenting any major changes regarding the army to the Queen beforehand. Noting he felt he was not being consulted on the most important army matters despite his many years of experience, he could scarcely contain his anger. The Queen

---

67 House of Commons, "Report of the War Office Committee on the Conduct of Business in the Army Departments," *Sessional Papers*, 1870, XII, 1-17.

68 British Library, Add. MSS 44537, f. 146, Letter from W.E. Gladstone to Edward Cardwell, dated November 21, 1869.

69 House of Commons, "Report of the Select Committee on Military Organization," *Sessional Papers*, 1860, VIII.

70 Verner, vol. 1, 402-408.

agreed. The distinct duties of the Secretary of State and the Commander-in-Chief demanded their separation. Consolidation of the latter into the former would not improve efficiency. Cambridge believed the core of the matter was exemplified by the physical relocation of the office of the Commander-in-Chief.[71]

For months following the report of Lord Northbrook's committee, Cambridge and the Queen challenged Cardwell and Gladstone on a regular basis, arguing against the subordination of the Commander-in-Chief to the Secretary of State for War, and subsequently virtually all of the changes attempted by the Cardwell administration at the War Office.[72] Cambridge and Queen Victoria were united against Gladstone and Cardwell as to where and what the office of the Commander-in-Chief would be.

In mid-January 1870, the Queen raised the issue of the "subordination" of the Commander-in-Chief to the War Office with Cardwell. In reply, the Secretary of State for War explained that although he had no desire to interfere with the command and discipline of the troops: "if they were not well commanded & disciplined I should be bound to recommend to H.M. to change the Com. In Chief & should be pretty subject to Parliamentary censure if I failed to do so."[73] Naturally this did not please her Majesty, and she reasserted her position to Cardwell in early February that the Commander-in-Chief executed those duties of a "purely military & executive character." In her opinion, the "constitutional control of the Sovereign over the Army" meant that the Secretary for War had responsibility for financial and administrative control of the army, but the Secretary had no "right of interfering at the Horse Guards in all the details affecting the command and discipline of the Army, & to this the Queen will not consent."[74] She was not going to allow civilian interference in an area she held dear, and the positions of Cambridge and Victoria were one in the same. In response with more passion than was customary, Gladstone stated he had no desire to see "a practical invasion or curtailment" of the functions of the Commander-in-Chief. Nonetheless, it had been settled by

---

71 Letter from the Duke of Cambridge to Edward Cardwell, reproduced in *Ibid.*, 408-411.
72 Indeed, if the folios dealing with the issue of the relationship of the Commander-in-Chief to the Secretary of State for War were simply reproduced as written, the result would be several hundred pages. The documents within files RA VIC/E17 and RA VIC/E/18, especially, are filled with such correspondence.
73 Letter from Cardwell to Gladstone, dated January 16, 1870, reproduced in Gallagher, "Cardwellian Mysteries," 340.
74 RA VIC/E17/8, Letter from Queen Victoria to Cardwell, dated February 7, 1870.

the Royal Warrant of 1861, and for the sake of clarification, he would like to have a "new document...trace...the duties of the Field Marshal commanding."[75] The Prime Minister hoped such a document would bring about greater harmony and unity of purpose at the War Office as a whole.

General Grey tried to convince the Queen that Cardwell and Northbrook were "making a fuss about nothing at the War Office" because the Royal Warrant of 1861 was quite clear; it might even prove to be an opportunity to clarify the present correct relationship between the two positions.[76] The Queen was partially convinced by Grey's suggestion and replied fairly quickly to Gladstone. Although she thought Gladstone had misinterpreted the "clear and intelligible" language of the warrant, she would have no objection to a new warrant, "provided care is taken to say nothing that shall seem to weaken the authority of the Commander in Chief in all Military questions." Furthermore, she added that "The superior control of the Queen, exercised through her Minister & the responsibilities of that Minister, have never been denied, & no man admitted this more cordially than the Duke of Wellington."[77] Regardless of the current state of affairs, the Queen closed her letter by stating that the confusion was due to the War Office and the "constant succession of changes–old offices abandoned & again restored–amalgamated & again separated."[78] This was in direct contrast to the Horse Guards where duties were "well defined & efficiently executed." The Queen had come down firmly in defense of her cousin, and it remained to be seen how easily any change could be implemented given the hostility of the Queen and the determination of Cambridge. In the end, however, she consented to a new document articulating the exact relationship between the Secretary for War and the Commander-in-Chief. Perhaps, as Grey had suggested, it would provide an opportunity to preserve the Royal Prerogative after all.

The subsequent wrangling lasted for months, even though the formal statement delineating the duties of the two positions came quickly. Cardwell presented Northbrook's findings as the War Office Bill to Parliament in February of 1870 where it encountered little opposition. Ultimately, the statement articulated that legally there was no dual control of the army, and sole responsibility for the army rested with the Secretary

---

75 RA VIC/E17/9, Letter from W.E. Gladstone to Queen Victoria, dated February 8, 1870.
76 RA VIC/E17/11, Letter from General Grey to Queen Victoria, dated February 9, 1870.
77 RA VIC/E17/12, Letter from Queen Victoria to W.E. Gladstone, dated February 9, 1870.
78 *Ibid.*

for War. In practice, dual control existed in terms of executing government commands–the War Office executed financial and administrative matters while the Horse Guards discharged matters of command and discipline. The War Office Act of 1870, passed in February, placed the supreme authority of the office of the Secretary of State for War on a statutory basis. Subsequently supplemented by an Order in Council, the end result was the military authority of the Horse Guards and the Civil Administration carried out at the War Office under the sole and immediate control of the political chief.[79] Such a finding was hardly new, and even the *Times* recognized that the ideality of dual government had never existed. Instead, there was a separation of responsibilities, but clearly "The military element is distinctly subordinate; the civil element distinctly supreme."[80]

The War Office Act of 1870 divided the administration of the War Office under three officials. The Commander-in-Chief's authority was not really diminished, and actually grew in responsibility as he was now responsible officially for the personnel of both the regular and auxiliary forces, something Cambridge had wanted all along. The Surveyor-General of Ordnance was responsible for the purchase, construction, and charge of *materiel*, while the Financial Secretary was made responsible for the preparation of the Estimates and the accounting and audit of all sums voted. Thus the War Office was now divided into three major areas of responsibility, all of which came under the immediate and direct control of the Secretary of State.[81]

In practice, at least pertaining to the War Office Act, the position of the Duke of Cambridge was not diminished as he had feared. The actions undertaken by the Queen and Cambridge ensured that the language of the War Office Act continued the Royal Prerogative, but significantly it admitted the ultimate subordination of the Horse Guards to the civilian minister. This was not revolutionary; the Queen and Cambridge had never questioned this fact. Although they did not want the issue publicly addressed, as it was the language which ensured the Commander-in-Chief continued to execute the Crown's authority over the army. More importantly, the Duke of Cambridge now held responsibility not only for the regular army, but the combined reserve forces and education departments. The

79 Spiers, *The Army and Society, 1815-1914*, 186-187.
80 *Times* (London), 2 March 1869.
81 Verner, vol. 1, 113-114.

consolidation that took place under Cardwell had the unforeseen effect of placing a greater proportion of the army under the control of the Duke. The combined efforts of Victoria and Cambridge had prevented a diminution of both the Royal Prerogative while actually increasing the power and influence of the Commander-in-Chief. Yet this triumph of increased–and unintended–authority for the Duke of Cambridge settled permanently and publicly the issue of the subordination of the Commander-in-Chief to the Secretary of State for War. In exchange for the preservation of the language of the Royal Prerogative, an ambiguous term, they sacrificed permanently the ability to question the relationship between the Horse Guards and the War Office. With this relationship clearly defined, there would be little way of preventing the Secretary for War from implementing other changes on his military subordinate.

V

Although the authority of the Commander-in-Chief vis-à-vis the Secretary of State for War had been settled early, Cardwell wanted other important changes–most significantly, the introduction of the so-called Short Service and the abolition of the purchase system. Although the end of Purchase in 1871 represented a major defeat for the Duke and the Queen, another important setback occurred that same year when he was forced at last to move his office from the Horse Guards into the War Office. The Short Service Act will be addressed later, while the end of Purchase will be covered in detail in the following chapter. Against the backdrop of these dramatic changes implemented by Cardwell, Prussia's decisive victory over France in the Franco-Prussian War further altered the continental balance of power. Surprisingly, the Prussian's effective, large, and quickly-mobilized reserve had little impact on the Cardwell's reforms.[82] He generated his ideas from the domestic situation alone and pushed innovation with the help of loyal, like-minded subordinates. Edward Cardwell represented the greatest threat to the interests of the Duke and the Queen, and by the second year of his tenure the extent of that challenge was even greater. It was not the result of external developments, but instead the product of a genuinely reformist ministry.

---

82 Gallagher, "British Military Thinking and the Coming of the Franco-Prussian War," 19-22.

Cardwell sought short-service enlistments out of economy rather than improved readiness.[83] Colonial withdrawals were crucial to the subsequent implementation of short-service, and Cardwell built upon the work of his predecessor, General Jonathan Peel, who had served as Disraeli's Secretary for War from 1866 to 1867. Whereas economy motivated Cardwell, Peel had recognized that modern warfare made a large, trained reserve essential as demonstrated by the Prussians in the Austro-Prussian War. Cardwell sought to reduce the number of pensioners burdening the Army Estimates. Short-service enlistments would reduce the number of pensions to be paid. Although Peel was successful in getting the Enlistment Act of 1867 passed–the act enabled the creation of a reserve of 20,000 men who had served a minimum of twelve years active service–in a few years it was obvious the reserve concept was not working since fewer than 1,000 joined the reserves as a result.[84] Enlistment into line infantry regiments had traditionally entailed a commitment of twenty-one years, which obviously limited the appeal, further diminished by the low regard for army life in general. Peel had hoped the reduced term of service would increase the appeal of enlistment, which it did not. Furthermore, the commitment to serve in the reserves proved undesirable because reservists suffered great economic hardship when activated. Modest bonuses were ineffective while other ideas, such as offering shorter terms of enlistment for those serving at home and a longer term for Indian troops, were not acceptable either. Long term service in India was seen as deleterious to the health of European troops–as well as discipline–while short term Indian service was considered beneficial for troops stationed at home.[85]

Shortly after becoming Secretary for War, Cardwell quickly realized the Enlistment Act of 1867 had failed. His solution, The Army Enlistment Act of 1870, passed without difficulty and allowed the shortening of enlistments to a greater degree than Peel's act had done, in some cases to as little as three years, although in general the standard was to be for six years active service to be followed by six in the reserve.[86] Cardwell's

---

83 Spiers, "The Late Victorian Army 1868-1914," in *Th e Oxford Illustrated History of the British Army*, 190.

84 Gallagher, 19.

85 *Ibid.*; Speech by Edward Cardwell, June 10, 1869, *Hansard's Parliamentary Debates 1066-1918*, 3rd Series, Vol. 196, 1544-1545.

86 For troops other than infantry, the term of enlistment was to be eight years active followed by four in the reserve.

system remained in effect long after he had left office, although long term enlistments continued to make up a sizeable percentage of the force.

Cambridge recognized the shortcomings of the new system because its major impetus was economy and not the creation of a trained, expandable reserve on the Prussian model, but instead a method to reduce further the active force. He expressed his concerns to Cardwell in January of 1870 that, "though we hope to have…a Reserve…[it] does not really belong to Regiments, & can only be incorporated with them in the breaking out of a war. Consequently, in times of emergency or anxiety short of war, we can do nothing but recruit up, & we may have difficulty in obtaining them."[87] Despite his concerns, Cambridge did not see the creation of a capable reserve as a great danger and the system functioned fairly well in the long run.[88] The timing of the bill was another hindrance since Cardwell introduced it in Committee on July 18, 1870, shortly after the start of the Franco-Prussian War. It remained unclear whether Britain would become involved to guarantee Belgian neutrality and military members of the House fought it, but it passed with little difficulty. On July 26, 1870, the Duke of Cambridge spoke in favor of the measure in the House of Lords, and it passed without a division. The following day, Cardwell's deputy, Lord Northbrook, wrote him a letter in which he expressed "thanks for the cordial and effective support which your excellent speech in the House of Lords last night gave to the Army Enlistment Bill. It made my task a very easy one."[89] The example of the Short Service Act is surprising because Cambridge worked well with Cardwell. It is largely an exception, however, because Cambridge had indeed been concerned for some time over Britain's lack of an adequate reserve. It just so happened that this was an area where Cambridge and Cardwell agreed.

For the Duke of Cambridge, there were two great developments to occur in 1871 that represented the lowest ebb of his tenure as Commander-in-Chief, the consequences of which shall be addressed in the following chapter. The first defeat, one which has been addressed in depth by historians and the issue for which Cardwell is most remembered, was

---

87 P.R.O. 30/48/3/13, fo. 17, Letter from the Duke of Cambridge to Edward Cardwell, dated January 11, 1870.

88 For a long term assessment of the Enlistment Act's effectiveness, see Spiers, "The Cardwell Reforms" in *The Army and Society, 1815-1914,* 190-193.

89 Letter from Lord Northbrook to the Duke of Cambridge, dated July 27, 1870, reproduced in Verner, vol. 2, 31.

the end of the system of purchase. The second, which has passed largely unnoticed, was a more personal defeat for Cambridge: his physical relocation from the Horse Guards to the War Office at Pall Mall. Both events clearly demonstrated the limits of royal influence against a reform-minded government. On the other hand, the continued survival of the Duke of Cambridge as Commander-in-Chief with an unlimited term of office is itself an indicator of the limitations of a reform-minded ministry against united royal opposition. Queen Victoria and the Duke of Cambridge may have been powerless to affect the larger issues of reform, but they did preserve and protect the relationship between the military and the monarchy. Although the monarchy was never threatened, the language of the Royal Prerogative was preserved at the cost of the diminution of the position of the Commander-in-Chief. The office, if not its holder, existed not at the pleasure of the Crown, but at the mercy of the ministry.

CHAPTER 9:
Closing Engagements 1870-1874

Without question, the year 1871 proved to be the most eventful one in the long tenure of the Duke of Cambridge as Commander-in-Chief. With some prescience he noted in his diary on New Year's Day, "The year begins sadly and anxiously. I am myself far from well and begin the year alone, and moreover in bed. Political matters are in a most serious and precarious state, and the future is most dreary."[1] Although Cambridge was most affected at the time by the military reversals the French had suffered at the hands of the Prussians,[2] Cambridge was well aware that the Gladstone Ministry represented the greatest threat to his and the Queen's interests regarding the army either had encountered thus far. The Duke had survived the previous year with his office, but he had precious little success otherwise, except perhaps for the Short Service Act. Against his strong objections, Parliament had passed the War Office Act in February 1870 based upon the recommendations of Lord Northbrook and his committee. Though its implementation actually increased the forces over which the Duke exercised authority, he viewed it as a personal defeat since it publicly subordinated the Commander-in-Chief to Secretary of State for War.

Although Cambridge and Cardwell had differed over many issues affecting army reform, none received the national attention attached to the issue of the abolition of Purchase. More than any other, Cardwell's triumph over the conservative and royal interest in Purchase marks his most public and permanent accomplishment. Though less remembered, but perhaps the most troubling of all indignities Cambridge believed Cardwell had inflicted upon him, was the relocation of his office. He and the Queen resisted the changed location of the office of the Commander-in-Chief with all of their will, but together they proved powerless to prevent the move. And again, this represented a serious defeat for Cambridge and the Crown. The significance of that forced move was overshadowed at the time and ever since by the debate over the abolition of Purchase. Furthermore, Cambridge continued to resist fiercely the War Office Act of 1870, an event which further added to his lasting reputation as an opponent of change and reform.

---

1 Diary entry of the Duke of Cambridge, dated January 1, 1871, reproduced in Sheppard, vol. 1, 291.
2 The definitive work is still, Michael Howard, *The Franco-Prussian War* (New York: Methuen, 1961).

Whereas the beginning years of the relationship between Cambridge and Cardwell were not very successful for the interests of the Duke and the Queen, the remaining years were not a complete disaster only because Cambridge remained in position long after Cardwell's departure. Otherwise, however, they represented the lowest ebb of his tenure and his New Year's sentiments were prophetic. The role of the Commander-in-Chief had been defined and therefore weakened permanently in the eyes of Cambridge and Queen Victoria through Cardwell's efforts. In fact, the outcome could have been worse because several weeks into 1871, it was not certain Cambridge would even remain in office.

While the first two years of the Gladstone ministry established the relationship between the Secretary of State for War and the Commander-in-Chief, the remainder of Cardwell's tenure colored permanently the last two decades of Cambridge's active service. More importantly they marked the final step in ending the debate as to whether the army would be a parliamentary institution. Its most visible sign was the public subordination of the highest ranking uniformed officer to a civilian minister rather than to the monarch. Cardwell's success was the conclusion of two conflicting visions of how to prevent a recurrence of the Cromwellian experience.

From the Crown's perspective, only royal control of the army and the preservation of the Royal Prerogative could prevent the politicization of the army and the subordination of the army to the influence of party politics. In the extreme case, so went the argument of those in favor of the preservation of the Royal Prerogative, loss of royal control over the army could subject it to parliamentary extremism of the type as occurred under the Lord Protector. The conflicting and ultimately triumphant liberal view was that a parliamentary army was the only way to protect the constitution and ensure that the army remained an efficient institution, subject to legal legislation and enlightened reform. Although the relationship between Cardwell and Cambridge may have been settled by the beginning of 1871, such larger issues remained as yet unresolved.

I

Before the larger debate over the abolition of Purchase dominated the attention of those interested in army reform, the Duke of Cambridge was most concerned with the physical location of his office and the status that he believed was linked directly with its whereabouts. Of all of the struggles he waged over the years against *nineteen* Secretaries of State for War with whom he served, arguably none mattered more than keeping his position at the Horse Guards. Since this was a battle of no national importance and little publicity, it reveals much about the relative balance of power between the forces of the army and the Crown represented by Cambridge and Parliament represented by Cardwell. More than any other, this defeat revealed the true state of affairs. Obscured by the much more public debate over Purchase, this smaller contest was largely ignored by contemporaries and has since been neglected by historians as well.

The issue of the Commander-in-Chief's location was indeed more important symbolically than for any matter of army efficiency. It was also a one-sided battle. With the passage of the War Office Act of 1870, the movement of the office was a forgone conclusion–to leave the Duke in his own separate location once the office of the Secretary of State for War had been consolidated would violate the spirit and the letter of the act. The guiding principle of the Northbrook Committee stated it bluntly: "Indeed as a practical question, no scheme which is not based upon the accomplished fact that all the departments of military administration are housed under one roof can be otherwise than abortive."[3]

When Cardwell took over the War Office, it was in administrative confusion, but Cambridge's forced move to Pall Mall had as much to do with the exercise of authority as bureaucratic efficiency. This is precisely why Cambridge and the Queen resisted. Even though he lost, the Duke never fully accepted his defeat and posted "Horse Guards" on his correspondence until well into the 1880s.[4] Aware of the inevitability of the consolidation once the War Office Act had been passed, he realized afterward that he had not been presented with the full plan. Cambridge had been led to believe that a new building was going to be constructed for the War Office. Since both Cardwell and Cambridge would have had to relocate to new offices, the ambiguity of their relationship would continue, at least publicly. The Duke of Cambridge had been duped and so had the Queen. That it came from Gladstone only made it worse.

This was the main reason why Cambridge's reaction against the War Office Act became far more strident after its passage. Gladstone

3 Verner, vol. 1, 418.
4 St. Aubyn, *The Royal George*, 193.

had repeatedly reassured Queen Victoria, and therefore the Duke of
Cambridge, that the government would never do anything "adverse to the
Horse Guards."[5] Cardwell also furthered the impression that relocating
the Commander-in-Chief would only occur under circumstances favorable
to the Duke. Reassuring the Queen on February 19, 1870, Gladstone
reported that, "the Cabinet today heard a statement from Mr. Cardwell
with reference…[to] military administration. Mr. Cardwell read a letter…
carrying Your Majesty's desire that the…Horse Guards should be
preserved."[6] The Cabinet agreed with the recommendation, according to
Gladstone, and an estimate for the construction of a new building on the
Thames Embankment would be prepared shortly.

With evident satisfaction, General Grey informed Cambridge
several days later about the above-mentioned letter from Gladstone
reassuring Her Majesty that there would be "<u>no</u> interference with the
Horse Guards" and that plans for a new building to house the combined
War Office were being created.[7] He also expressed his personal views
and dissatisfaction with the War Office that caused "all the mischief."
General Grey's reassurances notwithstanding, the Duke of Cambridge
sensed (correctly) that events were not going his way at all. The language
and tactics employed by Cardwell, with the full backing of Gladstone,
were an effort to minimize or even nullify the resistance of Cambridge
and the Queen to the reorganization and consolidation of the War Office
with the subordination of the Commander-in-Chief to the Secretary of
State for War. Most of all, Cambridge fervently wished to avoid a public
demonstration of his subordination to the civilian Secretary of State by
having to leave the building he regarded not only as his headquarters, but
also the very symbol of his command. To relocate to a building already
occupied by Cardwell meant more than a move to a different facility that
happened to house the War Office–the existing complex was the physical
symbol of the Secretary of State for War. In response to General Grey's

---

5 RA VIC/E17/13, Letter from W.E. Gladstone to Queen Victoria, dated February 10, 1870. Gladstone
wrote many letters during deliberation of the War Office Act assuring her that he would do no harm to
the reputation or position of her cousin.
6 RA VIC/E17/16, Letter from W.E. Gladstone to Queen Victoria, dated February 19, 1870. Regarding
the building of the Horse Guards, Gladstone was true to his word as the building stands to the present
day.
7 RA VIC/E17/18, Letter from General Sir Charles Grey to the Duke of Cambridge, dated February
23, 1870.

letter, Cambridge admonished the Queen's secretary that "they are quite determined to combine the War Office and Horse Guards."[8]

The Duke of Cambridge was suspicious of Cardwell's plans, but rather than simply fight them outright, he offered a modification of the existing plan. In an adept move, he presented a solution that appeared to accept Cardwell's plan but also would not diminish Cambridge's prestige as Commander-in-Chief: construct the new War Office building on the site of the current Horse Guards.[9] The existing building could be left standing, thus preserving a venerable structure, and extensions could be built to the right and left as far as the Home Office and the Admiralty building, respectively. He suggested the Queen either present the suggestion to Cardwell or authorize Cambridge to do it for her. Convinced that the army was now in good shape–other than its "<u>alarmingly</u> <u>reduced</u>" size–the main hindrance to greater efficiency was interference from the War Office, or as the Duke put it more bluntly, "If they would only leave us alone."[10] Intent on avoiding an open conflict, he sought to preserve his position through a redirection of Cardwell's efforts rather than risk a direct challenge from Gladstone's Ministry.

General Grey did as Cambridge requested, and with the Queen's permission Grey presented the Duke's plan to Cardwell the following day.[11] Grey pointed out that Gladstone had already promised the Queen that the Horse Guards building would not be disturbed while plans were being crafted for the new War Office building on the Thames Embankment. Perhaps, argued Grey, the expansion of the building at the Horse Guards might make more sense. Most of all, General Grey–in reality, the Queen and Cambridge–wanted to know exactly what was planned. Gray closed his report with a telltale impression that despite the "fancied" reforms of the previous decades, military administration remained more confused than ever.[12] Against the combined efforts of the Duke of Cambridge, the Queen, and General Grey, Cardwell's reaction was predictable.

---

8 RA VIC/E17/20, Letter from the Duke of Cambridge to General Sir Charles Grey, dated February 24, 1870.

9 *Ibid.*

10 *Ibid.*

11 RA VIC/E17/21, Letter from General Sir Charles Grey to Edward Cardwell, dated February 25, 1870.

12 RA VIC/E17/22, Letter from General Sir Charles Grey to the Duke of Cambridge, dated February 26, 1870.

On February 26 Cardwell informed Queen Victoria that the Cabinet had considered the Duke of Cambridge's proposal, but expansion of the existing Horse Guards building would prove inadequate for a consolidated War Office and would also violate the Queen's desire that the building be left unchanged. A new structure on the Embankment would allow a fresh start, housing the War Office and the Admiralty in a facility accessible by road, rail, and boat.[13] Land would not prove difficult and construction could begin quickly, making temporary arrangements unnecessary. It was in this back-and-forth manner that Cambridge and Cardwell struggled over the War Office location.

Although neither Cardwell nor the Gladstone Ministry were to be deterred from moving the Commander-in-Chief's office into the same building as the Secretary of State for War, Cambridge continued to fight the change even after it was clear he could not win. While the Queen accepted Cardwell's position, Cambridge never did. In a letter on February 27, 1870, Grey observed "there is a great deal to be said for the proposed scheme" of Mr. Cardwell.[14] Queen Victoria's private secretary's commentary and Cardwell's reminder about the preservation of the Horse Guards–at the urging of Cambridge–swayed her. Since obviously any expansion would violate her previous dictum regarding the Horse Guards, Cardwell's plan made sense. Furthermore, she believed there was no loss of prestige because both her cousin and the Secretary of State for War would have to move. Against such logic Cambridge had no chance.

The final proof that Cambridge had lost the Queen's support on the proposed expansion of the Horse Guards in place of the relocation of his office was Victoria's often-repeated sentiment, "that by giving in on these questions, she will be better able to take an effectual stand on the more important point of the Changes proposed in the Organizations of the two Departments."[15] Giving in on a minor issue in exchange for greater influence on a major issue was a common refrain throughout Victoria's long reign, despite little evidence of success. More importantly, regarding the military and the monarchy, Cardwell had skillfully convinced the Queen to back his position rather than her cousin's and in the process he divided

---

13 RA VIC/E17/23, Letter from Edward Cardwell to General Sir Charles Grey, dated February 26, 1870.
14 RA VIC/E17/26, Letter from General Sir Charles Grey to Queen Victoria, dated February 27, 1870.
15 RA VIC/E17/27, Letter from General Sir Charles Grey to the Duke of Cambridge, dated February 28, 1870.

these normally united forces. Furthermore, since the reorganization of the War Office had the full backing of the Cabinet while the War Office Act of February 1870 made it governmental policy, there was no real chance of preventing it.

The Duke of Cambridge obviously had good reason to question Edward Cardwell's long-range goals. Although genuinely committed to army efficiency, he rightly saw Cambridge as the major obstacle to army reform. Although essentially correct, the disagreement was more than professional differences. Cambridge's reputation and identity was so closely associated with the Horse Guards that Cardwell's unyielding efforts to pry the Duke from his beloved building could only be interpreted as a personal affront. For his part, Cardwell saw the issue of civilian control of the War Department as a *sine qua non* and believed that his responsibilities encompassed the entire army. Cardwell had no doubt that the Commander-in-Chief was his subordinate, and therefore efficiency demanded the consolidation of his key department heads–including Cambridge–into a single building. With the full backing of the Prime Minister and the Cabinet on the more public and complicated issue of army reorganization, the new War Office building was simply a component of the reorganization. Once the Queen agreed to the general plan, Cardwell proceeded without informing her in advance. Perturbed, as she always was when not informed in advance of changes affecting the army, she expressed her displeasure at being left in the dark.[16] In reply, Cardwell wrote a perfunctory apology explaining he had thought she was aware of the plan, and he continued with his plans.[17] The matter was settled: Cambridge would leave the Horse Guards and move to the location Cardwell wanted. In the meantime, much more public and important changes affecting the army would overshadow the issue of an office location, namely the War Office reorganization and the abolition of Purchase.

Despite the importance of two significant areas of reform–War Office reorganization, discussed in the previous chapter, and abolition of Purchase, to be discussed later–Cambridge never relented in his futile attempt to remain at the Horse Guards. Typical of his efforts was a very lengthy memorandum in March 1870 arguing why the reorganization

16 RA VIC/E17/29, Letter from General Sir Charles Grey to Edward Cardwell, dated February 28, 1870 (draft).
17 RA VIC/E17/30, Letter from Edward Cardwell to General Sir Charles Grey, dated March 1, 1870.

would not lead to greater efficiency.[18] His criticisms came too late and had no impact, although Cardwell dutifully sent a copy to the Queen and the Northbrook committee.[19] For weeks after passage of the War Office Act, Cambridge, Cardwell, General Grey, and Queen Victoria corresponded extensively regarding the reorganization, but in the end the Duke and the Queen were powerless to prevent it. However, these changes were quickly overshadowed by the Purchase debate, first surfacing in a letter from Cardwell dated March 13, 1870.[20] Before delving into the important issue of the abolition of Purchase, the fate of the Duke's office and his failure to resist the reorganization of the War Office demonstrate a significant and ironic change in position.

Cambridge fought the consolidation of the army into three main departments: the office of the Commander-in-Chief with responsibility for personnel of the Regular and Auxiliary forces, the office of the Surveyor-General of Ordnance, responsible for the purchase, construction, and charge of *materiel*, and the office of the Financial Secretary, responsible for preparation of all army financial matters. In a strongly-worded letter to Cardwell dated March 17, 1870, he stated why: "My firm belief is that you cannot separate the responsibility for moving, feeding, and quartering the army, from the direct command of it."[21] His objection was that other military advisors besides Cambridge would be responsible to the Secretary for War.

Ironically, in objecting to the reorganization, the Duke now admitted openly he was directly subordinate to the Secretary for War; he just wanted to be the highest-ranking military advisor. As he observed, "The Secretary for War, being a civilian, <u>cannot</u> go right, with a multiplicity of military advisers: the C^{mdr} in Chief should be his <u>sole</u> adviser and subject to the control of the Secty. of State…[*sic*]"[22] This was a remarkable admission by Cambridge. He was now willing to accept direct subordination to prevent a further reduction of his prestige. Despite the Duke's remarkable *volte face*, Cardwell created an advisory body known as the War Office Council, which proved to be *exactly* what Cambridge did not want. The council was

---

18 RA VIC/E17/33, "Confidential Memorandum for the Secretary of State," by the Duke of Cambridge, dated March 4, 1870.
19 RA VIC/E17/32, Letter from Edward Cardwell to Queen Victoria, dated March 7, 1870.
20 RA VIC/E17/40, Letter from Edward Cardwell to Queen Victoria, dated March 13, 1870.
21 RA VIC/E17/44, Letter from the Duke of Cambridge to Edward Cardwell, dated March 17, 1870.
22 *Ibid.*

a consultative group to the Secretary of State for War consisting of the Commander-in-Chief, the Adjutant-General, the Quartermaster-General, the Inspector-General of Fortifications, the Director-General of Ordnance, and the Director-General of Mobilisation and Intelligence.[23] The Duke had lost to Cardwell once again.

The proposed new War Office building on the Thames Embankment never materialized, and Cambridge's worst suspicions were justified. In the end, Cambridge was forced to move to Pall Mall. He apparently first learned of the decision to relocate him to Pall Mall on January 18, 1871 and scarcely concealed his feeling of betrayal when he informed Cardwell, "I certainly had no idea from our conversation of yesterday morning that you intended at once to carry out the proposed removal of the Horse Guards to the present War Office." [24] Invoking the Queen's name did not help: "At all events I presumed that the Queen's pleasure would first be taken." After two years with Cardwell, realizing he really had no leverage against a united Liberal government, he revealed his powerlessness by pleading that he be spared: "in the eyes of the Army and the country it would be a serious lowering of the status of the Commander-in-Chief to remove his department from the present Horse Guards to Pall Mall."[25] For good measure, he then stated that if he could avoid "this annoyance" he would be deeply grateful to both Cardwell and Gladstone. The Duke closed this remarkable letter by stating that if there were no way to avoid it, he could move to Pall Mall because his "personal convenience must not for a moment stand in the way of the public service," but Cardwell must inform the Queen that Cambridge did so against his will and that the Queen should actually approve any such decision in advance.[26] This correspondence is striking in that it starkly reveals how little power and influence the Duke now had over his own fate. The Queen could not prevent Cambridge's removal, and there was no one else to turn to other than Gladstone and Cardwell, as Cambridge himself realized. Cardwell's brief and perfunctory response made it quite clear that Cambridge's opinion counted very little: "But I most strongly advise Your Royal Highness to assent to it [the move

---

23 Verner, vol. 1, 429-430.
24 Letter from the Duke of Cambridge to Edward Cardwell, dated January 18, 1871, reproduced in *Ibid.*, 430-431.
25 *Ibid.*, 430.
26 *Ibid.*

to Pall Mall] freely. No other course is, in my opinion, open to us or to yourself."[27]

Despite his concerted efforts over the course of an entire year, in the end he had no choice. He had written dozens of letters to the Queen, the Queen's secretaries, Cardwell, and Gladstone.[28] Even the death of the Queen's private secretary–General Sir Charles Grey had died of stroke the previous April–did not dissuade him. In a letter to the Queen on the occasion of Grey's death, Cambridge dedicated the majority of its content to the importance of building "a new War Office & Horse Guards combined in the Thames Embankment."[29] The Queen's new private secretary, Colonel Sir Henry Ponsonby, provided Cambridge with the answer he had fought against for so long: "The Queen expresses herself willing to allow a temporary arrangement to be made with the transference of the offices to the War Office provided it is temporary & that Your Royal Highness' accommodation is separate and is still called the Horse Guards."[30] With a sense of sadness, and perhaps a final realization over his actual position politically and militarily, Cambridge noted in his diary the day he relocated, "Went to War Office, where alas! the dear old Horse Guards are now established. It is a sad change, and the state of discomfort from all being unfinished is something really quite dreadful, and makes me feel very unhappy."[31]

As Cambridge feared, the move was not temporary–from 1871 until his retirement in 1895, the office of the Commander-in-Chief was modest and rather Spartan.[32] Budget constraints prevented the creation of the

---

27 Letter from Edward Cardwell to the Duke of Cambridge, dated January 18, 1871, reproduced in *Ibid.*, 431.

28 A sampling of the correspondence dating from several weeks in just one month–in this case, April 1870–reveals the extent to which the Duke attempted to get his way: RA VIC/E17/48, Letter from Sir Thomas Biddulph to Queen Victoria, dated April 12, 1870; RA VIC/E17/51 Letter from the Duke of Cambridge to Sir Thomas Biddulph, dated April 17, 1870; RA VIC/E17/53, Letter from Sir Thomas Biddulph to Queen Victoria, dated April 22, 1870; RAVIC/E17/54, Letter from Sir Thomas Biddulph to Queen Victoria, dated April 22, 1870; RAVIC/E17/55, Letter from Sir Thomas Biddulph to Queen Victoria, dated April 22, 1870; RAVIC/E17/56, "Memorandum" from Sir Thomas Biddulph relative to the future building for the Horse Guards, dated April 23, 1870.

29 RA VIC/E17/26, Letter from the Duke of Cambridge to Sir Thomas Biddulph, dated April 12, 1870.

30 RA VIC/E18/26, Letter from Sir Thomas Biddulph to the Duke of Cambridge, dated January 29, 1871.

31 Diary entry of the Duke of Cambridge, dated September 23, 1871, reproduced in Sheppard, vol. 1, 299.

32 A photograph picturing the office is to be found in Verner's biography entitled, "The Duke's Room at the War Office 1871-1895," Verner, vol. 2, between pp. 96 and 97. In this case a picture is worth a thousand words for it shows a rather typical Victorian-era room with a high ceiling, two desks,

proposed new War Office building, although Cambridge continued to post his letters "Horse Guards" almost to the very end. At the time of his forced relocation, the continuation of Purchase and his very position served as his main preoccupation. He had lost a most important and personal matter of self-esteem–the next struggle would involve the very survival of his position.

II

The army reform for which Edward Cardwell is most well remembered was not one of his primary reformist goals when he came into office. It was instead the unintended consequence of what Cardwell's predecessor, Sir John Pakington, had believed to be an uncontroversial decision to abolish the lowest commissioned rank of ensign or cornet.[33] Although it is now quite clear that the consequences of the end of Purchase were not nearly as significant in the long run as the supporters had hoped–the composition and competence of the officer class was hardly affected by the end of purchase[34]–the issue was the most public and most hotly debated aspect of army reform during Cambridge's tenure as Commander-in-Chief.

The Duke was quite literally at the center of the storm surrounding the debate over the end of Purchase, and he was placed in the unenviable position of being staunchly opposed to its abolition yet faced with a ministry that eventually came to be committed to its end, almost regardless of the consequences–even if it meant the abolition of Cambridge's position. The abolition of Purchase is important as it relates both to the case and career of the Duke of Cambridge and his relationship with the Queen in that it reveals how the powers and influence of the Duke of Cambridge had been greatly–and permanently–diminished. The Duke proved to be completely powerless to prevent the abolition of Purchase, despite near

---

several book shelves, a fireplace and three chairs. The photograph conveys no sense of majesty or awe expected from the office of the Commander-in-Chief of the British army and when placed next to a photograph entitled, "View of the old Horse Guards: H.R.H.'s offices 1856-1879 [sic],"*Ibid.,* vol. 1,between 114 and 115. The comparison is striking for the former photograph shows a large, three-story building complete with sentries, canon, multiple archways and even a clock tower depicted. It is obvious why Cambridge wished to remain at his beloved Horse Guards.

33 Anthony Bruce, *The Purchase System in the British Army, 1660-1871* (London: Royal Historical Society, 1980), 121. Ensign was the lowest commissioned rank in the infantry and cornet was the same for the cavalry.

34 See especially, Tucker, "Army and Society in England 1870-1900: A Reassessment of the Cardwell Reforms," 122-129.

universal support by the officer corps for the system's continuance. Not surprisingly, the Queen greatly favored preservation of Purchase as well and saw the issue tied to the Royal Prerogative. When the issue was settled permanently, however, the Duke of Cambridge was fortunate to have escaped with his title and position, and the larger matters of principle no longer seemed as important to him as merely keeping his position indefinitely.

The injustices of the system of Purchase were well known prior to Cardwell's arrival at the War Office. Key figures in the early days to end the practice were General Sir George De Lacy Evans before and after the Crimean War, while George Trevelyan became an outspoken critic during the late 1860s.[35] Although the practice's shortcomings generally received little publicity because the officer corps was overwhelmingly supportive, the *Times* occasionally published articles condemning such a seemingly unfair system. Typical was an article written shortly after the Crimean War from an officer serving in the office of the Commander-in-Chief at the Horse Guards that highlighted the contradictions inherent in the commissioning system. [36] Clearly such a system could make little claim of selection based upon merit, but this was not then considered a negative assessment. Purchase had functioned without significant change since the beginning of the 19th century, and many army officers regarded it not as a weakness but rather a strength of the army.[37] Above all, the practice ensured the overwhelming majority of army officers came from the upper-middle and upper class and therefore had a great stake in the status quo. Men of property would have little reason to challenge the existing order. Additionally, the government saved a great deal of money as commissions were an investment that a serving officer could be confident he could one day sell again. For this reason, the thought of ending the system of purchase was an expensive prospect since the government would have to compensate all serving officers for the original cost of their commissions.

---

35 See Chapter 6, above, for De Lacy Evans' efforts to abolish purchase.

36 *Times* (London), 21 April 1856. For additional coverage of criticisms of the purchase system occasioned by the Crimean War, see: Fortescue, *A History of the British Army*, vol. 13, 169-171; W.J. Reader, *Professional Men: the Rise of the Professional Classes in Nineteenth-Century England* (London: Weidenfeld and Nicholson, 1966), 74-84; Asa Briggs, *Victorian People: A Reassessment of Persons and Themes 1851-1867* (Chicago: University of Chicago Press, 1983), 60-61; and Harries-Jenkins, 78-86.

37 A Royal Statute of 1809 had fixed the legal status of purchase from that point forward, although by that point the system had already been functioning for over a century.

This fact alone made it a difficult proposition even for the most reform-minded ministers due to the prohibitive cost of compensating thousands of officers for a total of perhaps millions of pounds. Furthermore, it was the only system every serving officer had known and therefore great inertia weighed against any change to the time-honored practice.[38]

The purchase of commissions had been a regular occurrence at least as far back as the Restoration of 1660, and the practice may have had its origins prior to the Commonwealth period.[39] It is difficult to pinpoint the exact beginning of purchase. Direct evidence from 1672 reveals there were differing rates for the sale of commissions for those within and outside of various regiments.[40] A Royal Warrant of Charles II sanctioned the practice March 7, 1683.[41] The practice then became the cornerstone of army officer accession and promotion throughout the entire 18th century and most of the 19th until Cardwell and Gladstone succeeded in having it abolished.

The history of Purchase, especially in the latter part of the 17th century and early 18th century, was an uneven one. William III attempted to end the practice, but Queen Anne allowed it to thrive and issued a Royal Warrant of May 11, 1711 that attempted to prevent the sale of commissions by officers who had either served twenty years or more or been permanently disabled during their service.[42] After George I acceded to the throne, purchase became a regular practice in which the Crown regulated prices. Although there were infrequent attempts to limit the "over-regulation payments" for commissions, such as a Royal Warrant issued by George III in 1766 that set limits on prices, the actual method of purchasing commissions and subsequent promotions underwent little significant change until it was abolished in 1871.[43] Even with a limit on cost for commissions, over-regulation payments were an accepted aspect of the purchase system and usually prices paid were approximately twice that of the official prices. Official recognition of the legality of Purchase was reaffirmed in 1809

---

38 See Anthony Bruce, *The Purchase System in the British Army, 1660-1871* (London: Royal Historical Society, 1980) for a complete but concise history of the purchase system.

39 Erickson, 65-66; Verner, vol. 2, 1-9; Bruce, 9-11. Bruce argues unsuccessfully the sale of commissions can be traced as far back as the Norman Conquest and the feudal system. Such a linkage is strained. *Scutage*, payment in lieu of military service by a knight to his lord, was a different matter entirely.

40 Erickson, 65-66.

41 Verner, vol. 2, 2.

42 *Ibid.*, 3.

43 Biddulph, 3. The prices established were as follows: ensigns, £400; lieutenants, £550; captain-lieutenants, £800; captain, £1500; major, £2600; lieutenant-colonel, £3500.

via the Statute of 1809 issued under the name of George III. This made it a crime to buy or sell any office except for commissions in the army.[44] Command of regiments and ranks above that of lieutenant colonel could not be purchased. As for the technical branches of artillery and engineers, promotion occurred through what was incongruously termed selection, although it was actually advancement through merit. Since these branches were not generally officered by those of gentle birth and technical skills were required, the practice did not occur.[45]

Although the system appeared unfair and inefficient, it had developed out of expediency. Whereas Purchase may not have been the most just method of selecting and grooming army officers, it had proved to be effective at providing Britain with army officers capable of leading the nation's generally small army for over two centuries. From shortly after the Restoration and the creation of a permanent standing army, the money raised by Parliament was given to the Treasury, which was then disbursed to gentlemen through the Minister of War for the purpose of raising regiments. In exchange for the money and the responsibility of the regiment, these gentlemen with whom the government had entered into an agreement in turn had the right to appoint their own officers. Since the money provided by Parliament was normally quite inadequate to provide for the cost of raising a regiment, the regimental commander sought captains as company commanders and lieutenants in charge of subdivisions who would volunteer to cover the cost of raising their respective units. Although the regimental commander might be willing to divide some of his funding, his subordinates were compensated by the ownership of their commissions, which they in turn could sell to offset the cost of purchasing a higher position or to provide monetary benefit when leaving the army. Such a system ensured that only men with high social position and means could serve as officers; it also meant the only path for promotion during peacetime was through purchase.

It was possible to receive a commission without purchasing it in branches other than the Royal Artillery or Royal Engineers, although this point was usually overlooked by reformers then and many historians ever since. Part of the reason for this neglect is that the awarding of non-purchase commissions was not designed to acquire officers of ability into

---

44 Erickson, 66.
45 *Ibid.,* 66-67.

the infantry or cavalry. The apt words of a contemporary commentator put it succinctly: "in no case, are the personal merits of the applicant considered for one single moment."[46] All so-called "free commissions" were instead an extension of the powers of patronage of the Commander-in-Chief, as it was he who had to approve all commissions without Purchase. The majority of these free commissions were granted to the sons of army officers so that they could join regiments directly or receive an appointment to Sandhurst.[47] Ironically, one of the most famous British officers, and an arch enemy of the Duke of Cambridge, was commissioned without Purchase as an ensign on March 12, 1852 by the Duke's predecessor, Lord Hardinge: Garnet Wolseley.

Whatever the system's merits–or the excuses employed to preserve it–Purchase was objectionable to those interested in serious army reform because of the type of officer corps it perpetuated. While the other European nations were devoting ever more resources to the creation of professional army officers through improved education and training, Purchase ensured that ability had negligible impact on promotion. Furthermore, it actually discouraged expertise and instead undermined discipline as the least industrious often rose to high rank, while inconvenient or dangerous foreign assignments–most notably India–could be avoided through a combination of adept purchases and skillful politicking at Whitehall. It would be no exaggeration to state that Purchase allowed incompetents to advance while it thwarted the careers of those with great ability who lacked adequate resources. Such findings were made clear in a committee commissioned by Cardwell in 1870 to look into the subject, and yet many of the findings were no different from those of the previous commission of 1857.[48]

A central problem to those who wished to reform or abolish Purchase was the economy that the system allowed and the great cost to the government of ending it. Since the officer class was overwhelmingly composed of men with suitable resources, there was little need to pay officers the full amount they would otherwise have to be paid. To end the

---

46 Letter from M.J. Higgins dated 1855, "Letter on Army Reforms," reproduced in Gwyn Harries-Jenkins, *The Army in Victorian Society* (London: Routledge & Kegan Paul, 1977), 65.
47 *Ibid.*
48 House of Commons, "Report of the War Office Committee on the Conduct of Business in the Army Departments," *Sessional Papers*, 1870, XII; House of Commons, "Report of the Royal Commission on Purchase, House of Commons, Sessional Papers," 1857, XVIII.

practice the War Office estimated it would cost the government between £8,000,000 and £12,000,000–a vast sum in the 1870s for either political party.[49] Another argument offered repeatedly was that Purchase enabled the great commanders of English history–particularly Marlborough and Wellington–to attain high rank while still very young and ensuring that only the best elements of British society would command the various units of the army. Wellington himself testified before the Finance Committee in 1828 that the system recruited officers whose "education, manners, and habits, [made] the best officers in the world, and that to compose the officers of a lower class would cause the army to deteriorate."[50]

Defenders of the system also argued it prevented stagnation yet did not foster unhealthy competition. Leadership by independent gentlemen also served as a counterweight to the traditional fear of a standing army that developed during the Interregnum with Cromwell's New Model Army. As Wellington testified in 1830:

> [Purchase] brings into the service men of fortune and education–men who have some connection with the interests and fortune of the country besides the commissions which they hold from His Majesty. It is this circumstance which exempts the British Army from the character of being a 'mercenary' army, and has rendered its employment for nearly a century and a half, not only inconsistent with the constitutional privileges of the country, but safe and beneficial [*sic*].[51]

---

49 Erickson, 68.

50 Testimony quoted in Verner, vol. 2, 5. Verner and conservatives like him lamented the passing of British army traditions at the end of the 19th Century. They neglected to observe that it was oftentimes a combination of coincidence and chance that allowed those with financial means, social connection *and* ability to advance. It would be impossible to determine exact numbers, but is indisputable that a system not based upon promotion by merit thwarted the careers of a large number of more capable officers who failed to advance through lack of resources rather than ability.

51 "Memorandum of the Duke of Wellington," 1830, reproduced in Harries-Jenkins, 84.

The influence of the Duke of Wellington's support for Purchase was substantial while his legacy and views influenced the character of the British army for the majority of the nineteenth century. By the latter third of the century, the shadow of Wellington still loomed, but continental military developments and the changing nature of society and politics weakened his influence. In the end, however, the debate centered on whether the British army officer corps would be composed of amateurs of gentle birth or it would transition to the creation of a body of skilled professionals similar to continental armies, most spectacularly, Prussia.[52]

The event which started the process to abolish purchase was on the surface unremarkable. Cardwell's predecessor, Sir John Pakington, had suggested the elimination of the ranks of ensign and coronet as a way to help reduce the army estimates with minimal disruption. Before he could submit the plan, however, Disraeli's government was defeated in the national elections, and the Liberals came to power.[53] In the flurry of new proposals and initiatives brought about by Cardwell's arrival at the War Office, his subordinates advised him to resurrect Pakington's plan to eliminate the most junior officer ranks. Gladstone's Ministry decided to abolish the positions of cornet and ensign to save the government money—the move had nothing to do with reforming or ending Purchase when it was first introduced.[54]

The decision aroused little controversy and General Grey presented the matter to the Queen for her signature along with three other items on February 20, 1870. The manner in which her private secretary presented it demonstrates its lack of importance, listing it on his cover letter with the attached documents after the final iteration of the army establishment for 1870-1871 as, "2. Abolition of the titles of Cornet & Ensign. This seems quite right on every consideration—& the conditions for regulating the future purchase in those ranks are simple."[55] Obviously it was thought

---

52 Success of the Prussians in 1864 and 1866 was not a direct influence on the debate, but it was obvious even to the most casual of observers that officer training on the continent followed a distinctly different pattern. Michael Gallagher, "British Military Thinking and the Coming of the Franco-Prussian War," 19-20, argues convincingly that the Prussian successes of the 1860's had limited influence, except that conscription greatly impressed British observers.

53 Bruce, 121.

54 *Ibid.* By raising the price of a first commission from £450 to £600, the government reduced the amount it would have to pay to retiring officers.

55 RA VIC/E17/17, Memorandum from General Sir Charles Grey to Queen Victoria, "Four submissions for Your Majesty's approval & signature," dated February 20, 1870. The last two items in the memorandum were, "3. Abolition of the African Artillery. 4. General Napier to be director of

to be not a significant matter; when Cardwell put forth a bill crafted by Pakington to the House of Commons to compensate army officers who had in the past purchased the ranks of ensign and cornet, he called upon the "generosity" of the members of the House to do the correct thing.[56] The cost of reimbursing the officers of their past purchases Cardwell estimated to be £509,500, which he argued was not an excessive amount, but then fatefully remarked that the system of purchase was indefensible.[57]

Caught completely off guard, Cardwell had not anticipated the vehemence of reaction from both sides over the issue of Purchase. Radical members of Parliament attacked the Secretary of State for War for failing to address the heart of the problem and eliminate the entire system of purchase.[58] The following week, Cardwell was again criticized in the House by Colonel C.W. White who motioned for the postponement of the issue until officers had the opportunity to "consult their interests" in the matter.[59] Cardwell's failure on this army bill was the first serious setback he encountered, but rather than encourage him to become more conservative, the defeat inspired a more radical approach. Cardwell withdrew his bill on March 14 concerning the abolition of the ranks of ensign and cornet and instead requested and received the creation of a royal commission to investigate the problem of over-regulation of payments. The commission met from March to June of 1870 and addressed the subject of excessive prices for commissions.[60] During the summer of 1870, the royal commission produced its report, and it was this very detailed and damning document which convinced Cardwell to abolish Purchase in its entirety.[61] Many motives have been assigned to this document, but its intention was not to make the officer corps more middle class in character. The main purpose was to document the abuses of the system and determine whether regulations were being violated–they had no motive to cause a transformation of the social background of the officer corps.[62]

Military Education, instead of President of Council of Ditto, the council being abolished."

56 Edward Cardwell's speech before the House of Commons, March 3, 1870, reproduced in *Hansard's Parliamentary Debates 1066-1918*, 3rd Series, Vol. 199, 1172-1174.

57 *Ibid.*

58 *Ibid.*, 1204-1206.

59 Speech of Colonel C.W. White before the House of Commons, March 10, 1870, reproduced in *ibid.*, 1629.

60 Gallagher, "Cardwellian Mysteries," 330-331.

61 House of Commons, "Report of the Royal Commission on Over-Regulation," House of Commons, *Sessional Papers*, 1870, XII.

62 Gallagher makes this point conclusively. See Gallagher, "Cardwellian Mysteries," 330-335.

There remains little concrete evidence as to why Cardwell decided to end the system of purchase when he did, other than the logic that once he faced opposition over any sort of tampering he figured he might as well end the entire practice since it was an affront to his efforts at making the army more efficient and modern. On the other hand, the attitude of the Duke of Cambridge toward Purchase was consistent with his overall view of the army. His views on the subject were well known and a large body of correspondence has preserved his fixed opinion on Purchase. Sometime before Cardwell considered ending Purchase, Cambridge had written to him in November of 1869 with his own views on the subject.[63] Cardwell had requested Cambridge's opinion as to whether the purchase of commissions should begin with the rank of captain or major, and Cardwell was attempting to determine how best to resurrect Pakington's earlier proposal to eliminate the ranks of ensign and cornet. In response Cambridge argued the system had to be continued as it then existed because "it has worked favourably to the interests of the service. It has enabled us to officer our Army with gentlemen, and it has kept our officers comparatively young in years compared to the other armies of Europe."[64]

Rather than modify the system, Cambridge thought it best to leave the entire practice undisturbed. It preserved the officer corps and maintained the army in a manner he thought vital: an institution in which gentlemen commanded, unhealthy competition was prevented, and the officer corps was vigorous and youthful. His views mirrored those of his most famous predecessor, the Duke of Wellington, and Cambridge believed the preservation of the Royal Prerogative was tied intimately with the system of purchase. He put forth a final argument for leaving the system in tact: to eliminate any ranks would result in "additional public expense...at a time when rigid economy is enforced on every department of the State. Are you prepared for this additional expense?"[65] Cambridge closed his letter prophetically, suggesting that rather than tamper with the system, it would be best to eliminate the system in its entirety rather "than to adopt the alternative one of selection commencing from the rank of Major."[66] Although it is difficult to ascertain whether the views of Cambridge had

---

63 Cardwell Mss., P.R.O. 30/483/12, folio 150, Letter from the Duke of Cambridge to Edward Cardwell, dated November 24, 1869.
64 *Ibid.*
65 *Ibid.*
66 *Ibid.*

any influence on Cardwell, it is no small irony that at first he disregarded Cambridge's advice and then followed the Duke's take-it-or-leave-it recommendation.

Whereas Cardwell may not have arrived at the War Office with strong feelings about Purchase, some of his key subordinates were staunchly opposed to the system. Outside of the prominent reformers in Parliament such as Trevelyan, a young and progressive artillery officer, Lieutenant Evelyn Baring (later Lord Cromer), Chief of the Topographical and Statistical Department of the War Office, led the charge against Purchase from within. With the backing of the senior staff at the War Office, Baring wrote a confidential memorandum, "Arguments For and Against the Purchase System," which argued intelligently and forcefully that the system had to be abolished above all because it lowered the quality of the officer corps.[67] Since purchase determined promotions rather than "selection" as in the navy and many of the European armies, the officer corps was populated with men who sought a life of leisure rather than those who were earnest about their profession. In Baring's damning but accurate assessment, "The British Officer, as a rule, prefers a shooting jacket to a tunic, and the amusements of civil life to the practical exercises or theoretical studies incident to his profession."[68] In Baring's view, selection would eliminate those seeking an idle existence and a comfortable escape from school life while it would retain a body of men dedicated to the profession of arms. Baring's memorandum was widely distributed within the War Office and the argument it espoused was in turn used by cabinet ministers during the subsequent debates within the House of Commons.[69]

The debate over the abolition of Purchase occupied Parliament and the press throughout the second half of 1870 and well into the following

---

67 Granville Mss., P.R.O., 30/29/68, folios 232-51, Memorandum by Evelyn Baring, "Arguments For and Against the Purchase System," dated February 14, 1871.

68 *Ibid.*, 241. In the course of research trips for this book, I had the pleasure to stay at the Royal Military College, Sandhurst, where my hosts were most gracious. Additionally I have had the great privilege of serving with and sometimes under British officers in the Balkans, Afghanistan and Iraq. Although Baring's comments generally would not apply to the modern officer corps, it might be slightly relevant with certain officers belonging to the Household Regiments. For an essay on the function of class and social affectations in the modern British army, see Christopher Jary, "Class In the Army: An Observer's Perspective," *British Army Review*, 117 (December 1997): 50-55.

69 Gallagher's article, "Cardwellian Mysteries," illustrates the importance of the document and its subsequent influence within the War Office. Speeches by Cardwell, among others, in the House of Commons mirrored the arguments put forth in "Arguments For and Against the Purchase System." See speeches on March 3, 1871, in *Hansard's Parliamentary Debates 1066-1918*, 3rd Series, Vol. 204, 1416-1469, March 9, 1871 in *ibid.*, 1705-1741, and March 13, 1871 in *ibid.*, 1902-1951.

year.[70] Despite the best efforts of determined reformers such as Cardwell, Trevelyan, and Northbrook, great opposition to ending the practice remained. Lord Northbrook aptly identified part of the reason for the opposition. Even some of the more reform-minded individuals within the Liberal party would have difficulty in the House of Commons promoting the idea of ending Purchase because, as he explained, there was "hardly a member of Parliament who has not some relative personally interested in the Purchase system."[71]

Supporters of the status quo did not further their interests in the best manner possible. A group of officers in the House of Commons who became known collectively and pejoratively as "the Colonels" also strongly opposed the end of purchase. In fact, they were so opposed that even the conservative military press criticized them for their narrow interest in the protection of wealthy officers.[72] Even though they received fairly wide support from within the army, their efforts achieved little. Sir George Trevelyan recognized the negative but powerful influence they exerted in a letter to Gladstone on March 15, 1871: "the Colonels have showed themselves…to be a fourth power in the state, and are a terrible obstacle to economy. The abolition of purchase will, by an obvious process, weaken or destroy their hold on legislation…"[73]

The debate over Purchase occurred against the backdrop of the stunning Prussian successes against France in the Franco-Prussian War. Even though the two matters were not related, it was obvious the military situation on the continent was forever altered. The pressure on Cardwell was immense. He found himself caught between trying to implement further reforms to make the army more efficient, while he was also accused of letting the army deteriorate so it could not meet the defense needs of the home islands. The Prussian army's speedy and efficient mobilization of a large pool of trained reserves proved decisive, and the British army had nowhere near the same number of reservists or detailed planning required to carry out a comparable mobilization. Northbrook and even Trevelyan

---

70 Fortunately, this is a subject where scholarship has revealed a great deal and need not be repeated here in detail. One of the best accounts of the subject can be found in Spiers, *The Army and Society*, 177-200.

71 Letter from Lord Northbrook to Edward Cardwell, dated September 30, 1870, cited in Gallagher, "Cardwellian Mysteries," 336.

72 Bruce, 170.

73 Gladstone Papers at the British Museum, Add. MS. 44225,27, letter from Sir George Trevelyan to W.E. Gladstone, dated March 15, 1871.

became muted in the face of harsh criticism from the press and political opposition. On January 3, 1871, Cardwell even offered his resignation to Gladstone because of the "altered state of the public mind on military questions."[74] He believed that the public expected an even greater army for home defense while at the same time demanding reduced spending on military defense. To bring about effective reform in such a charged political environment might prove beyond Cardwell's ability.

True to form, Gladstone remained undeterred by the obstacles facing him and his ministry. He therefore sought additional support for Cardwell. Obtaining a seat in Parliament for General Sir Harry Storks, the chief of the Control Department of the War Office, Gladstone ensured that Cabinet completely backed Cardwell and his intended reform. Accordingly, Cardwell introduced the Army Regulation Bill in the House of Commons on February 16, 1871, confident that he had the complete confidence of the entire Gladstone Ministry.[75] The bill proposed to abolish the purchase system, provide full compensation of officers' investments, and unify the regular, auxiliary, and reserve forces under one command.[76] Not surprisingly, almost from the start the bill encountered opposition in the House of Commons. Although the bill eventually passed the House of Commons on July 3, 1871, the several months of debate proved a setback for Gladstone's ministry.

In the first half of February 1871, when the Cabinet discussed the exact nature of the bill to be introduced regarding the abolition of Purchase, one of the main topics was the future of the position of the Commander-in-Chief. At first they considered limiting his tenure to a period of five years, although Cardwell wrote to reassure Queen Victoria that he had "no other wish than to uphold the just authority of the Commander-in-Chief."[77] Even so, Cardwell did not rule out "change in the tenure of the Commander-in-Chief's office" because the Duke's powers would substantially increase as a result of his holding the single command for regular, reserve, and auxiliary forces. As expected, the Duke of Cambridge strenuously fought such a limitation and wrote repeatedly to the Queen for her assistance in

---

74 Letter from Cardwell to Gladstone, dated January 3, 1871, reproduced in Spiers, *The Army and Society,* 191.

75 Speech by Edward Cardwell, February 16, 1871, *Hansard's Parliamentary Debates 1066-1918,* 3rd Series, Vol. 204, 338-349.

76 The estimated cost to reimburse the affected officers was £7,500,000 to £8,500,00–not an insubstantial sum. From *ibid.*

77 RA VIC/E18/40, Letter from Edward Cardwell to Queen Victoria, dated February 2, 1871.

the matter. The Queen agreed with her cousin that such a change would be quite damaging to the Royal Prerogative, and she in turn wrote to Gladstone expressing "her earnest wish and hope" that the position of the Commander-in-Chief would be preserved as it stood.[78] The Queen went on to complain of her cousin's unfair treatment by a large portion of the public, and that it was imperative that the government treat the matter properly.

Perhaps the strenuous disagreement by the Queen and the Duke of Cambridge influenced Cardwell to shy away from tampering with the position of the Commander-in-Chief. More likely, the Secretary of State for War probably believed the issue of Purchase would generate more than enough controversy on its own–there was no need to make matters more difficult by taking on another issue that struck at the heart of the Royal Prerogative. Furthermore, Cardwell had every reason to be satisfied because the Army Bill of the previous year had demonstrated conclusively that the Commander-in-Chief was subordinate to the Secretary of State for War. Whatever his reasoning, Cardwell wrote to the Queen the day before he introduced his bill to inform her the Cabinet had considered "The following words…'The position of the officer Commanding-in-Chief must be looked upon as an exceptional one, as compared with that of any other staff officer, and therefore cannot be regulated by a mere reference to time.'"[79]

Once again, Cambridge had survived with his position intact, but again it was a matter largely out of his control, and an implicit threat lingered with his continued tenancy. In his letter to the Queen, Cardwell ominously added that the Cabinet said of the Commander-in-Chief, "It will of course be necessary for him to be in harmony with the Government of the day,–and his continuance or removal must depend upon considerations of public policy."[80] Gladstone wrote to the Queen that same day to reassure her that the office of Commander-in-Chief would be "treated in a manner suited to its dignity and importance."[81] Thus, the situation and position of the Commander-in-Chief now had the potential to become that which both the Duke and Queen had feared the most–a post subject to political fortune. As long as the occupant of the office met with the approval of the party

78 RA VIC/E18/42, Letter from Queen Victoria to W.E. Gladstone, dated February 14, 1871.
79 RA VIC/E18/49, Letter from Edward Cardwell to Queen Victoria, dated February 15, 1871.
80 *Ibid.*
81 RA VIC/E18/50, Letter from W.E. Gladstone to Queen Victoria, dated February 15, 1871.

in power, his position was assured, but it was, according to the opinion of Cardwell and Gladstone, subject to recall. This aspect of the relationship between the office of the Commander-in-Chief and the government would figure prominently in the debate over the abolition of purchase as it moved to the House of Lords.

Despite having passed in the House of Commons, the Army Regulation Bill still had to survive the House of Lords to become law. Since the Duke of Cambridge had a seat in the House of Lords, he held the awkward position of being expected to speak on behalf of the government in favor of a bill to which he was steadfastly opposed. Although he opposed the bill, he also fully understood that he had barely escaped having the terms of his office attached to the present bill. Cardwell made it quite clear that he expected Cambridge–ostensibly his subordinate–to speak publicly and forcefully in support of the bill. The Duke resented this duty and resorted once again to asking for help from the only person who could intervene on his behalf: the Queen. On May 31, 1871, he "was annoyed at Mr. Cardwell's expression of hope that he would support the Army Bill in the House of Lords."[82] Cambridge realized there would be much opposition to the bill in the Lords and that his vote might end up being the deciding one–he was loathe to tie the prestige of the Crown and the Royal Prerogative with a political issue. Several days later Cambridge wrote directly to Cardwell that "it has ever been understood by myself, and certainly admitted by all previous Governments, that the officer holding the position of Commander-in-Chief could have and ought to have no politics."[83]

Over the next few weeks, Cambridge wrote a number of similar letters to the Queen and to Cardwell; the Queen in turn generally supported her cousin's position. Cambridge believed the system to be flawed since it prevented the advance of socially and militarily qualified officers because of inadequate financial resources, but overall it had worked well for the nation and the army. Although imperfect, there could be no way to modify Purchase without ending the entire system, but to run the army without it would invite radical and perilous change. Cambridge's attitude toward the matter had not changed since he first expressed his opinion to Cardwell

---

82 RA VIC/E18/92, Letter from Colonel Ponsonby to Queen Victoria, dated May 31, 1871.
83 Letter from the Duke of Cambridge to Edward Cardwell, dated June 3, 1871, reproduced in Verner, vol. 2, 10-11.

almost two years earlier. When Cardwell asked Cambridge directly to speak publicly for the abolition of purchase on June 18, Cambridge responded that he could not and again asked for the Queen's assistance.[84] All of this prompted Gladstone to intervene and present his opinion that Purchase was not a political matter, but instead one that rose above party. For good measure he pointed out that the Duke of Wellington had spoken on behalf of the Short Service Bill in 1847 even though Wellington had not been in political sympathy with the government at the time.[85]

Despite additional letters and further resistance from the Duke of Cambridge, Gladstone made a blatant threat. In a lengthy letter, the Prime Minister stipulated seven distinct reasons why the Commander-in-Chief had to support the government's position. The first point, however, was the point that mattered most: "Mr. Cardwell has acquainted the House of Commons that, in the view of the Cabinet, it is requisite that the Commander-in-Chief should, on military subjects, be in harmony with the Executive; and this is the understanding which the five-years rule has been declared inapplicable [*sic*]."[86] Gladstone explained that he respected the position of the Commander-in-Chief and wished no hard feelings, but that the debate over the continued existence of Purchase was over—it only remained to be seen how the system would finally be ended. Although at the last minute, the Prime Minister sent Cambridge a telegram in which he informed him he did not have to vote on the abolition, only speak for it. The true state of affairs was clear.

Cambridge survived the ordeal, but only through the generosity of the ruling party. In the end, he made the desired speech—lengthy, bland, and without emotion—before the House of Lords, vaguely supporting a change which he despised. The vote afterwards was actually a non-vote as the decision reached was a postponement of the issue. A rather surprising irony was that the Queen herself abolished Purchase through a Royal Warrant of July 20, 1871. With the advice of her ministers and following the logic that the Royal Warrant of 1809 had first regulated purchase, it followed that the Crown could in turn abolish the ancient practice just as it had first regulated

---

84 Letters from Edward Cardwell to the Duke of Cambridge, dated June 18, 1871, Letter from the Duke of Cambridge to Edward Cardwell, dated June 19, 1871 and Letter from the Duke of Cambridge to Queen Victoria, dated July 6, 1871, reproduced in *ibid.*, 13-14.

85 Letter from W.E. Gladstone to the Duke of Cambridge, dated July 9, 1871, reproduced in *ibid.*, 14-15.

86 Letter from W.E. Gladstone to the Duke of Cambridge, dated July 14, 1871, reproduced in *ibid.*, 17-18.

it. Rather paradoxically, a practice both the Queen and Cambridge viewed as being intimately tied with the prestige of the Crown was ended through the exercise of the Royal Prerogative. Sensing accurately the low morale of her cousin, the Queen wrote to Cambridge several days after the issue was settled to show her support but also explaining, "that the interest of the Crown is so intimately connected with that of the Commander-in-Chief, that any diminution of the authority of the latter is highly injurious to the Crown."[87]

The Regulation of the Forces Act came into effect on November 1, 1871, and the purchase of commissions passed into history. Along with the purchase system, a new era had arrived with respect to the position of the Commander-in-Chief. Although by no means the end of his tenure, or even the end of his relationship with Cardwell, a watershed had been passed. The remaining years in which Cardwell served as Secretary of State for War were far less contentious than those preceding them. No doubt Cambridge and Cardwell were exhausted by the struggle. In 1872 Cardwell successfully engineered the Localization Bill of 1872 by which the country was divided into sixty-six territorial districts in an effort to shore up home defense by fostering local connections and improve the efficiency of the auxiliary forces. The bulk of reform was over, however, and along with its end came the permanent resolution of the position of the Commander-in-Chief. Despite the supportive words of Queen Victoria above, nothing could hide the fact that the Duke served at the mercy of his civilian counterpart. The nature and consequences of the Cardwell reforms may be debated, but there can be little doubt that the position of the Commander-in-Chief was now clearly shown to be held at the pleasure of the governing party and the Queen's connection to the army was reduced.

III

A bizarre but revealing incident involving the Duke of Cambridge occurred shortly after the New Year of 1874 and serves as a convenient allegory to describe the warrior spirit of the Commander-in-Chief. While walking in Park Lane, London, the Duke was physically attacked by a "well dressed man." Cambridge did not resist in any way and instead fled

---

87 Letter from Queen Victoria to the Duke of Cambridge, dated July 24, 1871, reproduced in Buckle, ed., *The Letters of Queen Victoria*, vol. 2, 150-151.

across the street, only to learn that the assailant had followed him, and hit him "again in the same place." The Duke did not hit the stranger in return, because he "thought it would not be a very dignified proceeding."[88] Although the incident in no way relates to the larger issue of the role of the Commander-in-Chief, it is perhaps representative of the attitude of the Duke of Cambridge during his final years working with Edward Cardwell, and maybe even the remainder of his tenure. Rather than stand and fight a battle which by now he knew he could not win, Cambridge instead withdrew to a position of safety from which he criticized from afar and after the fact events he was now powerless to affect. The Duke would survive, but his honor and prestige would not be enhanced in the process.

For the dozen years prior Edward Cardwell's arrival, Cambridge's role had been one of great apparent importance. He was the Commander-in-Chief of the British army, the highest-ranking officer in the service responsible only to the Queen. Although his duties were not clearly defined when he began, such a condition was perfectly acceptable–indeed preferable–since the duties of the Queen were similarly unspecified but still very real. With the passage of years in the office, the Duke of Cambridge failed to expand his real powers, even when he worked with a ministry favorable to his interests. Wars abroad and reforms at home proved the true extent of his influence and power. Unfortunately for Cambridge, he was not a Wellington or even a Cumberland–his own wartime example, though it miraculously did not prevent his occupation of the office, certainly did not add anything to his powers when he was at the Horse Guards. The continued support of the Queen was of general assistance, but as the Crown had been forced to recognize long ago, ultimately the power of the monarchy could not withstand the determined opposition of the Parliament. The experience of Edward Cardwell in the War Office starkly demonstrated the limits of power a royal duke had against a united and liberal ministry committed to implementing a progressive program of reform.

Fortunately for Cambridge, Gladstone's was the most effective and determined agenda-driven government he would face in his long career and one of the strongest and most reform-minded ministries of the 19th century. The Liberal ministry of 1868-1874 defined as no other government had or would Cambridge's genuine position–and also, by extension, the

---

88 RA VIC/E21/1, Letter from the Duke of Cambridge to Queen Victoria, dated January 6, 1874.

Queen's relationship–in the realm of the army and politics. Cambridge kept his title as Commander-in-Chief of the British army, but the job was now clearly defined as one subordinate to the Secretary of State for War. By no means did the military-monarchical connection disappear, but it was now apparent that the Commander-in-Chief, whether or not he was a member of the royal family, worked primarily for the civilian government. The changes carried out during the period that Edward Cardwell served as Secretary of State for War fundamentally and permanently altered the role of the Commander-in-Chief of the British army and its relation to the Crown. The Duke of Cambridge and Queen Victoria had failed to prevent what both feared: significant diminution of the Royal Prerogative.

CONCLUSION:
The Legacy of a Royal Duke

The Marquis of Lansdowne opened the debate in the House of Lords on the afternoon of March 17, 1904, shortly after learning about the death of the Duke of Cambridge earlier that day. In praising the accomplishments of the Duke, Lansdowne said of Cambridge, "He chose the profession of a soldier, and for fifty-eight years he followed that profession."[1] Further explaining that Cambridge had held many prominent appointments and seen service in the field, Lansdowne suggested that, "the most remarkable feature in his [Cambridge's] military career is that for almost forty years he filled the high and distinguished office of Commander-in-Chief of the Army." With unintended irony, he then added, "That office has now ceased to exist, but I venture to say that when we refer to it and look back to it, we shall invariably connect it with the long and honourable career of his late Royal Highness."[2] Undoubtedly the end of the office of the Commander-in-Chief had something to do with the Duke's "long and honourable" association with it.

Shortly before Cardwell left the War Office, he was created Viscount Edward Cardwell, but with the defeat of the Liberals in the General Election of February 1874, his association with the army was soon ended permanently. The political turn of events had no immediate impact on the office of the Commander-in-Chief, and the Duke of Cambridge remained "in command" for another two decades. After the election of 1874, Gladstone explained his defeat at the hands of the Conservatives over a tax on spirits saying, "We have been bourne down in a torrent of Gin and Beer."[3] Regardless of how it happened, the return of the Conservatives assured the continued survival of the Duke of Cambridge as Commander-in-Chief.

In fact, Cambridge remained in office almost a decade after the death of Cardwell in 1886. It would be some time before the Duke again faced a threat to his position similar to Edward Cardwell, and though his position was now formally and permanently diminished as had been made clear above, he kept his job. Cambridge perhaps also drew some satisfaction from outlasting Cardwell politically and physically. In the course of the years following Cardwell's departure, Cambridge witnessed another

---

1 *The Times* (London), March 18, 1904.
2 *Ibid.*
3 St. Aubyn, *The Royal George*, 169.

seven changes of government and worked with another ten Secretaries of State for War. Although he had established his reputation as a strong conservative regarding army reform while Cardwell was Secretary of State, it was in the years after Cardwell's departure that the Duke's name was linked permanently with tradition and conservatism, to the point that by 1890 even Queen Victoria would refer to her cousin as "retrograde and old-fashioned."[4] The issue of subordination of the Commander-in-Chief to the Secretary for War had been settled permanently by the War Office Act of 1870, but the passage of the act only increased Cambridge's resistance to innovation in almost any form.

For the next decade and a half, Cambridge lamented the inadequacy of the army estimates to the Queen, but he remained as powerless as ever to alter them. In the realm of military operations overseas, there was plenty of action for the British army. Between 1879 and 1882, Cambridge wrote about the Afghan, Zulu, and South African Wars, while in 1882 and 1883, and again from 1883 to 1886, the skirmishes in Egypt and the Sudan occupied the attentions of the Queen, the army, and the nation. As had been the case before, Cambridge's role was little more than that of a chronicler.[5] These were the years when the army was engaged continuously in a series of often small but always tenacious fights on the periphery of the Empire.[6] Apart from the occasional visit to the continent, Cambridge spent these years safely ensconced in the fashionable parts of London. However, before he retired there would be one more concerted effort to remove him from office in the hopes of bringing the British military into the modern world. As before, it revealed much about the relationship between the Crown and the army.

---

4 Letter from Queen Victoria to Sir Henry Ponsonby, dated August 12, 1890, reproduced in George E. Buckle, ed., *The Letters of Queen Victoria*, 3rd ser., *Selection from Her Majesty's Correspondence and Journal Between the Years 1886 and 1901*, vol. 1 (New York: Longmans, Green and Co., 1930), 630. Victoria was comparing Cambridge to her son, the Duke of Connaught, whom she was hoping succeed Cambridge as Commander-in-Chief, to be discussed below.

5 Diary entries from these years present a detailed account of the combat activities of the British army abroad. Sheppard, vol. 2, 65-123.

6 For a concise and readable account, see Byron Farwell, *Queen Victoria's Little Wars* (New York: W.W. Norton & Co., 1972).

I

In the late 1880s, another movement to modernize both the army and the navy gained momentum as the result of overseas developments and reactions to them at home. The heroic death of the popular and eccentric General Charles "Chinese" Gordon at the fall of Khartoum in January 1885, the fear of Russian expansion toward India, and the increase of the German army in 1886 and 1887 all served to make government ministers aware that Britain's foreign policy and defense needs appeared to be inadequate. More dramatically, however, the resignation of two high ranking officers within the armed services signaled another wave of reform; Lord Charles Beresford resigned from the Board of Admiralty; shortly after, Viscount Wolseley quit his position as Adjutant-General. Both acted out of frustration with their respective service's lack of preparation for war, fostering a renewed demand for serious reform of the services. Beresford believed the navy was making insufficient preparations for war, while Wolseley suggested the army was seriously disorganized. In a rare visit before the House of Lords, Wolseley suggested the army could not even protect London.[7]

In response to mounting evidence that military readiness needed to be examined, Lord Salisbury's Cabinet instituted a Commission in 1886 to be chaired by Lord Hartington to investigate the efficiency of both the army and the navy.[8] Hartington was a former Secretary of State for War, as were two of his assistants, W.H. Smith and Henry Campbell-Bannerman.[9] By far this was the most competent group of individuals representing the most determined effort to investigate the state of the army since the days of Edward Cardwell. The Commission's most important observation for the Duke of Cambridge was its advocacy of the need for a general staff. The Hartington Commission issued its final report on May 11, 1890, and the chief recommendation was the creation of a Chief of Staff whose duties would be:

---

7 Brian Bond, "The Retirement of the Duke of Cambridge" in *Journal of the Royal United Services Institution* 106 (1961): 545.

8 For a detailed discussion of the Hartington Commission, see "Chapter IV. The Hartington Commission 1886-1892," in W. S. Hamer, *The British Army Civil-Military Relations 1885-1905* (London: Oxford University Press, 1970), 93-147.

9 The other members of the Commission were Major General Henry Brackenbury from the War Office, Lord Randolph Churchill and Sir G. S. Clarke (later Lord Sydenham). *Ibid.*

1. To advise the Secretary of State generally on military policy, and to strength.

2. To collect and co-ordinate all military information.

3. To propose and devise schemes for the defence of the Empire; and to prepare plans of action.

4. To communicate direct to the First Naval Lord on inter-departmental policy, and conduct correspondence with other Departments of State, and with General Officers commanding, on military policy.[*sic*][10]

The apparent overlap of recommended responsibilities for the Chief of Staff with those of the Commander-in-Chief was not coincidental. Although the members of Commission scrupulously avoided any direct criticism of the Duke of Cambridge, they argued "that no possible successor could enjoy a position and influence which years of service to the State are alone capable of establishing."[11] What really concerned Hartington and his assistants was the amount of administrative influence Cambridge wielded. Salisbury's ministry had previously issued two Orders in Council on December 29, 1887 and February 21, 1888 that reorganized the War Office. The resulting readjustment concentrated sole military responsibility into the office of the Commander-in-Chief and eliminated Cardwell's earlier subdivision of the War Office into three departments: the office of the Commander-in-Chief, the Financial Secretary, and the Surveyor-General of Ordnance.[12]

Cambridge obviously never liked Cardwell's reorganization since it limited the powers of the Commander-in-Chief. As a result of the Salisbury alterations, Cambridge was now the sole military officer responsible directly to the Secretary of War, a compromise he had earlier argued for in vain with Cardwell.[13] Anyone in favor of improved army efficiency could not be pleased since Cambridge arguably had more power over the army now than at any time since the arrival of Cardwell at the War Office. The Hartington Commission found Cambridge responsible for too many things, and although the report did not say it directly, the description of duties for the proposed Chief of Staff position would be a way to get around the

10 Report of the Hartington Commission, dated May 11, 1890, reproduced in Verner, vol. 2, 355.
11 *Ibid.*
12 *Ibid.*, 350.
13 Verner, vol. 2, 350.

obstinate presence of Cambridge. The proposed Chief of Staff would have responsibility for many of them. Britain's army needed to be modernized, as the better-staffed continental forces–especially Germany's–had already made clear, and the growing military and economic power of Germany seemed to demand.[14] It was also clear that Cambridge would do all in his power to prevent any such development and his conservative outlook had become legendary. He wore his resistance to change like a badge of honor during his final years in office and delighted in thwarting the efforts of more progressive officers, such as Wolseley, immortalized by Gilbert and Sullivan in the *Pirates of Penzance* as "the very model of a modern Major-General." Several years later at a dinner in honor of his retirement, Cambridge revealed his genuine outlook, remarking, "Gentlemen, there have been great changes in my time–great changes. But I can say this. Every change has been made at the right time, and the right time is when you cannot help it."[15] As long as Cambridge remained in office, he would act as an effective brake on any efforts towards improvement.

Even though Cardwell had established the subordination of the Commander-in-Chief to the Secretary of State for War, it is doubtful any member of the Hartington Commission relished the thought of a revisiting a major struggle with the Duke of Cambridge. The sheer longevity of the Duke of Cambridge as Commander-in-Chief, coupled with the constant support of Queen Victoria, made him a force of great inertia within the War Office. Fully conscious of the important relationship between the Queen and Cambridge, the Hartington Report addressed the touchy subject of the Royal Prerogative directly. Acknowledging the relationship between the monarch and the Commander-in-Chief, it questioned its importance: "It has been contended that the existence of the office of the Commander-in-Chief in its present form is essential to the maintenance of the Royal Prerogative of the Sovereign as head of the Army. We are unable to accept this view."[16] Curiously, however, it offered no proof why the Royal Prerogative would

---

14 The volume of literature on this topic is large. For the impact of the accession of William II on the German army, see Gordon Craig, *Politics of the Prussian Army 1640-1945*. For foreign policy issues related to the growing German navy, see Paul Kennedy, *The Rise of Anglo-German Antagonism, 1860-1914* (London: Prometheus, 1980).

15 St. Aubyn, *The Royal George*, 329. The date is not cited, but the event would have occurred in late October 1895 as Cambridge retired on October 31, 1895.

16 Report of the Hartington Commission, dated May 11, 1890, reproduced in Bond, "The Retirement of the Duke of Cambridge," 546.

not be diminished by placing a military officer in a position superior to the Commander-in-Chief.

The closing words of the document revealed perhaps the ultimate desire of its authors. The members of the Commission challenged the continued tenure of the Duke by recommending a change "at the occurrence of a vacancy in the office of the Commander-in-Chief, or at any favourable opportunity."[17] Perhaps the Duke of Cambridge would retire voluntarily or be forced to do so. With the Duke gone at last, a professional advisor to the civilian secretaries for the army and the navy could create the equivalent of a modern joint general staff and provide to the Secretary for War a rational defense strategy. The Hartington Report was bold and progressive. It was a worthy and long-overdue effort. It was never carried out.

II

The Duke of Cambridge reacted to the recommendations of the Hartington Commission predictably. Already upset over an article by Wolseley, the Adjutant-General, and theoretically Cambridge's subordinate, in *Harper's Magazine* some weeks previously, Cambridge believed Wolseley indirectly accused him of using "his rank and favoured position to stifle well-informed military criticism."[18] Perhaps because Wolseley was quite accurate, Cambridge was angry and therefore tried to convince the Queen "that she might write me [Cambridge] a private note to show Wolseley...saying for instance, that she thought it would be so much better for him as Adjutant-General not to publish anything or even to speak as seldom as possible on Army matters."[19] The Queen decided not to respond to Wolseley's article as Cambridge wished, because she thought it "unnecessary to prolong the discussion."[20]

It was in the wake of this article in *Harper's* that the Hartington Commission produced its report. Cambridge recognized immediately a renewed threat to his position. He noted, "the Report of the Royal Commission, which recommended the prospective abolition of the Com.-

---

17 *Ibid.*
18 Bond, "The Retirement of the Duke of Cambridge," 546.
19 Letter from the Duke of Cambridge to Sir Henry Ponsonby, dated February 17, 1890, reproduced in Buckle, ed., *The Letters of Queen Victoria*, 3rd ser., vol. 1, 570-571.
20 Letter from Sir Henry Ponsonby to the Duke of Cambridge, dated February 26, 1890, reproduced in *ibid.*, 574-575.

in-Chief—a most deplorable recommendation!"[21] The members of the Commission were plotting either to force him from office or to make his position irrelevant if he remained.[22] The Queen was upset as well. Even before Cambridge had seen the Hartington Report, he sent a letter to Victoria notifying her of his concerns, which she endorsed by writing on the margin, "This cannot be allowed for one moment, and Sir Henry [Ponsonby] should take steps to prevent this being even discussed."[23] On the March 20 she wrote to Ponsonby, "over the subject of this really abominable report, which beyond measure she is shocked should have come from a Conservative Government."[24]

Victoria had discussed the matter with Cambridge and the two agreed something must be done to prevent its implementation; she listed six reasons why this must be so. The first point was a typical refrain of hers that nothing should be done during the Queen's absence, but the second point was revealing, for she argued what she had during the time of Edward Cardwell. Namely, she believed, "That the Army *must* remain as heretofore in direct communication with the Sovereign through the C.-in-C., who is unpolitical, and who, with the assent of the S. of W[ar], must have the dispensation of patronage." For the Queen, this was "the greatest safeguard against the Army becoming political and parliamentary."[25] She went on to point out that she was not against the idea of a Chief of Staff, something Wellington and Prince Albert had also recommended, *as long as the position was subordinate to the Commander-in-Chief.* This was indeed a remarkable letter.

The Queen still wanted to preserve the Royal Prerogative through the office of the Commander-in-Chief and prevent the army from becoming a parliamentary army. She was too late. Cardwell had proven almost two decades previously that Parliament was indeed the army's master, and although the appearance of the Royal Prerogative had been preserved, the victory of Cardwell had allowed the continuance of the semblance of command without much of the substance. Cambridge occupied his

---

21 Diary entry of the Duke of Cambridge, dated March 18, 1890, reproduced in Sheppard, vol. 2, 214.
22 Bond, "The Retirement of the Duke of Cambridge," 546.
23 Letter from Sir Henry Ponsonby to Queen Victoria, endorsed by Queen Victoria, dated March 4, 1890, reproduced in Buckle, ed., *The Letters of Queen Victoria*, 3rd ser., vol. 1, 577.
24 Letter from Queen Victoria to Sir Henry Ponsonby, dated March 20, 1890, reproduced in *ibid.*, 582.
25 *Ibid.*

position not out of any inherent strength of his own, but ultimately at the mercy of civilian ministers. Although the Queen wanted to preserve the Royal Prerogative, she was really attempting to protect the appearance of its continuance. And her original command to Ponsonby to "take steps to prevent this being even discussed" was adroitly carried out.

Acting very much as a go-between for Cambridge and the Queen, Ponsonby, with great delicacy, convinced the Duke it would be wise to offer to relinquish some of his duties, "which at present are only placed under your responsibility without corresponding power, such as the manufacture of Ordnance."[26] The most important consideration was for Cambridge to "remain at the Head of the Army, whether with the present or any other title."[27] Furthermore, if Cambridge formed a council subordinate to the Commander-in-Chief it might forestall the drive to create a Chief of Staff. Queen Victoria, meanwhile, met with Lord Salisbury and W.H. Smith, the Conservative leader in the House of Commons, to discuss the future of the office of the Commander-in-Chief. When Salisbury hinted it might be prudent to have Cambridge's successor not be a royal prince, Victoria was dismissive and said the issue would not be a factor any time soon.[28]

Fortunately for Cambridge and Victoria, Wolseley was in almost complete agreement over the importance of maintaining the position of the Commander-in-Chief as the highest position in the army and to leave it as it essentially stood.[29] Wolseley might have hoped to preserve the position for himself. He also could have been motivated by his politically conservative outlook that the best way to effect reform was by having the right military man at the top. Regardless, his support carried great weight with the government.[30] By the end of April, the threat to Cambridge's position was over. The Secretary of State for War, Edward Stanhope, wrote to the Duke of Cambridge on April 28, 1890 and explained that the Cabinet had met and considered the proposals of the Hartington Report, and decided the post of Adjutant-General, which would be "vacant in the autumn, should be filled up, without the intervention of a Chief of Staff in

---

26 Letter from Sir Henry Ponsonby to the Duke of Cambridge, dated April 5, 1890, reproduced in Verner, vol. 2, 356.

27 *Ibid.*

28 Bond, "The Retirement of the Duke of Cambridge," 547.

29 Letter from Sir Henry Ponsonby to the Duke of Cambridge, dated March 25, 1890, reproduced in Buckle, ed., *The Letters of Queen Victoria*, 3rd ser., vol. 1, 589.

30 Bond, "The Retirement of the Duke of Cambridge," 547. Bond portrays Wolseley's motives as being one factor or the other – more likely it was a combination of the two.

any form."[31] Apart from the vague recommendation that the "meetings" of the War Office become more "systematised" there would be little actual change as a result of the Hartington Report. The combined efforts of Victoria, Cambridge, and Wolseley, along with the skillful maneuvering of Ponsonby, had preserved the office of the Commander-in-Chief with Cambridge still firmly in it. For the Queen, the next concern was to ensure that her cousin's successor would be as devoted to the preservation of the Royal Prerogative as Cambridge had been. For Victoria that meant another royal duke.

The Queen's third son and seventh child, Arthur, Duke of Connaught, was a successful career army officer who had attended the Royal Military Academy, Woolwich, from 1865-1868 and had risen rapidly through the ranks ever since. Unlike virtually all of his high-ranking military contemporaries, however, he had never seen combat and was unlikely to be given command in war.[32] Significantly, the Queen hoped to have her son, the Duke of Connaught, take over Cambridge's position to protect the Royal Prerogative. Cambridge clearly was not successful in resisting reform as has been demonstrated above. However, by remaining in office for so long, inertia developed, and he acted as a significant bulwark against further change throughout the 1880s. Had he retired sooner and let a more reform-minded individual take his place, change could have occurred more readily. The sequence of events that then followed, though complicated and hinging upon the vacancies of a number of key commands throughout the army, revealed the extent to which Salisbury's ministry wished to avoid having another royal duke succeed the Duke of Cambridge. No matter how fervent the desire of the Queen to place another royal prince in the office of the Commander-in-Chief, it had to be prevented.

The position of Adjutant-General, which Wolseley was scheduled to leave in the autumn, was considered the most prestigious post after that of Commander-in-Chief. Had Cambridge resigned in 1890 as he threatened to do when he first learned of the Hartington Report, Wolseley would have taken over as Commander-in-Chief without opposition.[33] Although the

---

31 Letter from Edward Stanhope to the Duke of Cambridge, dated April 28, 1890, reproduced in Verner, vol. 2, 357.

32 Bond, "The Retirement of the Duke of Cambridge," 547.

33 Letter from the Duke of Cambridge to Sir Henry Ponsonby, dated April 9, 1890, reproduced in Buckle, ed., *The Letters of Queen Victoria*, 3rd ser., vol. 1, 594. In his letter, Cambridge stated that he could not accept any altered title, "and could not for one moment accept that of Chief of Staff. If that is insisted I MUST resign." See also, H.M. Kochanski, "Field Marshal Viscount Wolseley as

Queen would have wanted Connaught even then, he would have been too junior and inexperienced to rise to the top so quickly. Since Cambridge had survived the latest challenge with his command intact, the Queen hoped that Sir Frederick Roberts, Commander-in-Chief in India, arguably the third most prestigious command in the army, would succeed Wolseley as Adjutant-General. Connaught would then take over from Roberts and be well placed to take over as Commander-in-Chief once the position came open.[34] It would all work out to preserve the Royal Prerogative.

The Duke of Cambridge, however, did not want Roberts and thus ruined the designs of the Queen. Cambridge did not want another officer in the style of Wolseley under him, as he explained to Ponsonby in February of 1890 when he first learned Roberts was being considered. The problem with Roberts was, "Having been Commander-in-Chief in India, he would not submit himself to a higher military authority with comfort to himself, and he ought to hold an independent post, Malta, Gibraltar, or the Irish command."[35] In other words, Roberts was too independent.

Furthermore, although Cambridge did not say it explicitly, the fact that he was an "Indian officer" did not act in his favor. Unfortunately for Stanhope, he had already offered the post to Roberts and had to withdraw it, while in April Salisbury informed the Queen he could not countenance having Connaught take over in India. The problem then was how to fill the vacant slot in India. Salisbury asked Wolseley to fill it on the basis of an emergency, but Wolseley declined on account of "Indian fever." Wolseley, in a letter to Ponsonby, after giving the excuse of the fever as to why he could not go to India, spoke truthfully: "I see through the little game, which is to pretend that there is some serious emergency in India as an excuse for having refused the Duke of Connaught to go there."[36] He then offered to go to Dublin or Aldershot, whichever the Duke of Connaught did not want, but to go to India, "in a state of profound peace," would be "professional suicide."[37] The final solution worked out by Salisbury and Stanhope satisfied everyone but the Queen. Wolseley would go to Aldershot, Roberts would remain in India for another two years, Sir

Commander-in-Chief: A Reassessment." *The Journal of Strategic Studies*, 20 (June 1997): 120.

34 Bond, "The Retirement of the Duke of Cambridge," 547.

35 Letter from the Duke of Cambridge to Sir Henry Ponsonby, dated April 9, 1890, reproduced in Buckle, ed., *The Letters of Queen Victoria*, 3rd ser., vol. 1, 571.

36 Letter from Viscount Wolseley to Sir Henry Ponsonby, dated May 9, 1890, reproduced in *ibid.*

37 *Ibid.*

Redvers Buller–whom Cambridge had found "so rough"[38]–would become Adjutant-General, while Connaught was shuttled off to the relatively peaceful Southern Command at Portsmouth.[39] Clearly, even before Cambridge's retirement, a *Conservative* ministry was making sure that a royal duke would not succeed the current one as occupant of the office of the Commander-in-Chief.

Victoria recognized what was happening and expressed her indignation to Ponsonby in a letter of July 30, in which she accused the "so-called Conservatives" of wishing "to pander to the Radicals!"[40] The Queen believed her son was eminently qualified for the position, with great exaggeration stating he had "gone through *every grade* from the lowest with honour and distinction…"[41] In her mind, the only reason he was being excluded was because he was a royal duke. Rather surprisingly, Wolseley was also disappointed at the turn of events, and he actually supported Connaught, finding it sad "that a man should be held to be disqualified for high military command because he is the Queen's son."[42] The source of his concern likely originated from his desire to one day be the Commander-in-Chief himself, so he believed it to mean "they [Salisbury's ministry] have made up their minds to do away with the office of Commander-in-Chief, and are afraid that, if they allowed the Duke of Connaught in here, they could not refuse to make him Commander-in-Chief by and by."[43]

Thus it was settled before Cambridge retired. No longer would a royal duke serve as Commander-in-Chief. The recommendations of the Hartington Commission urged the abolition of the position in its entirety–the neglect of Britain's strategic situation had gone on for too long. The changed international situation required greater coordination than could be accomplished simply by the head of the army. When the Liberals returned to power in 1892, Sir Henry Campbell-Bannerman took over as Secretary of State for War. Although favorably disposed to reform, his

---

38 Letter from the Duke of Cambridge to Sir Henry Ponsonby, dated April 9, 1890, reproduced in *ibid.*, 571.
39 Bond, "The Retirement of the Duke of Cambridge," 547.
40 Letter from Queen Victoria to Sir Henry Ponsonby, dated July 30, 1890, reproduced in Buckle, ed., *The Letters of Queen Victoria*, 3rd ser., vol. 1, 624.
41 *Ibid.*
42 Letter from the Viscount Wolseley to Sir Henry Ponsonby, dated August 2, 1890, reproduced in *ibid.*, 624-625.
43 *Ibid.*

greater concern was a familiar one: keeping the army estimates down.[44] More importantly for our present purpose, however, it was Campbell-Bannerman who secured the retirement of the Duke of Cambridge. By May of 1895, the Duke of Cambridge was seventy-six years of age. Parliament renewed its demand for the implementation of the Hartington Report. Aware of the changing situation, Cambridge wrote in desperation to the Queen to try and hold onto his position, forgetting his earlier, youthful admonitions against allowing aged senior officers to continue on active service.[45] He wrote, worrying, "It is especially felt that my age is much against me...I should therefore feel grateful to you if you would let me know Your views on the subject."[46]

This letter stands in marked contrast to the countless others written from Cambridge to Victoria throughout their decades of mutual support. There is no invective, there are no demands, just a simple realization that this time it is serious and there seems to be little that can be done. At this point, all Cambridge needed to know is how the Queen really felt. The Queen delayed two weeks before giving her answer. A meeting with the Secretary for War, Campbell-Bannerman, was clearly instrumental in helping her make up her mind, and as she noted in her journal the evening after having had luncheon with him on May 18, she found him to be "most kind about George C. and the great trouble his retirement was causing me. He read me a draft of a letter he thought I might write to George, urging him to retire sooner."[47] The following day she sent her answer that, based upon the need to bring about "considerable changes," the Queen thought, despite the great pain it caused her to say it, for the Duke's "*own* sake as well as in the public interest, it is inexpedient that you should much longer retain that position, from which I think you should be relieved at the close of your autumn duties."[48] At long last, Cambridge's career was ending.

---

44 During this period the Queen continued, without success, to secure India for her son, but there was strong opposition in Parliament to such a move. Roberts retired in 1893 and Connaught took command at Aldershot.

45 See Chapter 2 for a discussion of Cambridge's memorandum, "The Age of General Officers."

46 Letter from the Duke of Cambridge to Queen Victoria, dated May 4, 1895, reproduced in Verner, vol. 2, 395.

47 Journal entry of Queen Victoria, dated May 18, 1895, reproduced in Buckle, ed., *The Letters of Queen Victoria*, 3rd ser., vol. 2, 512. The previous day, Campbell-Bannerman had met with Cambridge and discussed at length the possibility of the Duke's retirement.

48 Letter from Queen Victoria to the Duke of Cambridge (copy), dated May 19, 1895, reproduced in *ibid.* 512-513.

For Cambridge, the suddenness of the Queen's decision came as quite a blow, and it caused him "great pain and deep sorrow," especially because he was not at all prepared for "an immediate decision."[49] He really did not take it well and noted in his diary the evening he received the news that he was filled "with the deepest sorrow, as I still feel quite equal to the performance of my duties, and never anticipated such a decision being made without my consent, but I must submit…to the inevitable, but I… am disgusted, with this…most unjustifiable proceeding."[50] Cambridge continued to resist his forced retirement, going so far as to question the legality of it since his appointment was by patent at the Queen's pleasure.[51] Nonetheless, in the end there was nothing he could do, and the Duke relented and agreed with the Queen, the Prime Minister, Rosebery, and Campbell-Bannerman, that Buller would be the best replacement for Cambridge.

On June 21, 1895, the Liberal government was brought down by a surprise vote of censure against the Secretary for War over the issue of keeping "an insufficient reserve of cordite ammunition."[52] Shortly before this occurred, Campbell-Bannerman had made the announcement of the retirement of the Duke of Cambridge. Now the Conservatives were back in power. After a short suspense for Wolseley, Lord Lansdowne offered him the job without first notifying the Queen, which in turn angered her greatly. Wolseley accepted Lansdowne's offer on the condition that there be no material change in the office of the Commander-in-Chief.[53] Unfortunately for Wolseley, the terms of the position offered presented a significantly altered role—an Order in Council would make the Commander-in-Chief one of *five* advisors to the Secretary of State for War.

Overall, Wolseley's five-year tenure would be regarded as unsatisfactory and he had the misfortune of serving as the head of the army during the disastrous experience of the Boer War.[54] But it was indeed

---

49 Letter from the Duke of Cambridge to Queen Victoria, dated May 20, 1895, reproduced in *Ibid.*, 513.
50 Diary entry of the Duke of Cambridge, dated May 19, 1895, reproduced in Sheppard, vol. 2, 241.
51 Bond, "The Retirement of the Duke of Cambridge," 551.
52 Buckle, ed., *The Letters of Queen Victoria*, 3rd ser., vol. 2, 460.
53 Kochanski, 121.
54 *Ibid.*, 120. Kochanski's article is an excellent account of Wolseley's performance as Commander-in-Chief, but it tries to hard to rehabilitate his legacy. It is true that Wolseley was old and in ill health by the time he took, over, that he inherited the problems he found in the War Office and the Order in Council severely weakened his position. Nonetheless, there is no escaping the truth that Wolseley did not fulfill the high expectations of his supporters and the Boer War was a great embarrassment for the

a remarkable irony of fate that the Cardwellian policy of reform to limit the power of the Commander-in-Chief should at last have been carried to a triumphant conclusion at the expense of Lord Wolseley, who had always been one of its most enthusiastic advocates. Furthermore, for it to have been carried out by Cardwell's former parliamentary under-secretary, Lord Lansdowne, made it especially so.

III

"The dukedom of Cambridge is now extinct" was the last sentence in the obituary of the Duke of Cambridge printed in the *Times* on March 18, 1904.[55] Although the article was referring specifically to the absence of an heir due to Cambridge's morganatic marriage, it serves as a fitting epitaph for his office. Several weeks previously, the office of the Commander-in-Chief had been abolished. The judgment of history on the experience would not be a good one. In the short term, the second Boer War, which began in earnest in 1899, revealed the British army was woefully unprepared to face a determined opponent equipped with modern weapons. The absence of suitable training, equipment, logistics, and a capable staff seemed to be a revisitation of the inadequacies of the Crimean War some forty years earlier. Even though the Boer army was outnumbered and largely composed of irregulars, it would take two years and eight months for the British army to subdue it. As Wolseley himself said, the Boer War demonstrated that "the British Army was under-manned, ill-equipped, poorly trained and commanded."[56] Although Cambridge cannot be blamed for all of these shortcomings, especially the poor funding about which he complained incessantly throughout his four decades as Commander-in-Chief, there can be no avoiding the fact that he promoted an air of stagnation and resistance to change which proved deadly in Britain's first war of the 20th century. The British army that deployed to South Africa in October 1899 was in many ways his most immediate legacy.

Politically, the Duke of Cambridge made it impossible to give command of the army to a royal duke. Throughout his many years of service to the Horse Guards, Cambridge earnestly thought he was protecting the Royal Prerogative. Because of his obstinate resistance to virtually all

army. See Thomas Pakenham, *The Boer War* (New York: Random House, 1979).
55 *The Times* (London), March 18, 1904.
56 Kochanski, 137.

types of reform, especially in the later years of his tenure–for example, he opposed the use of Khaki uniforms in the desert–there is little evidence he actually enhanced or even affected the Royal Prerogative. In her own right, Queen Victoria had a great interest in the army and was fiercely determined to hold on to as much control over it as she could. On the other hand, she sometimes seemed to have a better sense than her cousin when to give up a fight that could not be won and to save the effort for one that could. Whereas Victoria often understood the limitations of the power of the monarchy, it is not clear that Cambridge comprehended the confines of his. By the end of his tenure, Cambridge had become a laughing stock in some quarters of the army and society–the great German Bumble Bee with his penchant for pork chops. Such a view could hardly have improved the popular view of the monarchy, at least in its connection to the Commander-in-Chief. The monarchy, especially in the final decades of Victoria's reign, was not made more glorious by its association with the Duke of Cambridge. If anything it was becoming more glorious in spite of, or without him, as Victoria's assumption of the title of Empress of India in 1876 and the celebration of the Diamond Jubilee in 1897 made so clear.

Parliamentary control of the army was never in question at any point during Queen Victoria's reign. Although Cambridge and Victoria may have contested the manner in which that command would be portrayed and what the exact relationship between the royal duke in command of the army and the civilian minister responsible to Parliament for its efficient operation should have been, even that question was settled relatively early. Edward Cardwell's public demonstration of the exact nature of the relationship altered the appearance, perhaps, but not the substance. In striving to keep the army above politics, Cambridge and Victoria thought the presence of an "unpolitical" Commander-in-Chief essential. Over a century later, the British army has proved their fears to be wholly unfounded. The most significant difference peacetime ministries have displayed toward the military has been in the realm of budgets. Although all political parties see the military as a prime target for reduction in the absence of a major conflict, the difference is usually how much to spend as opposed to which weapons to select or how to train a staff. Yet this was the one area Cambridge never questioned; it was always Parliament's right to determine the budget.

After Cambridge left office, the relationship between the military and the monarchy would never again be the same. This is not to suggest that the sovereign was not regarded as the symbol for command of the armed forces; quite the contrary, George V and George VI most decidedly were during the First and Second World Wars, respectively, while Queen Elizabeth II remains so today for the ongoing wars in Iraq and Afghanistan. It also did not mean the end of the close familial association between the armed services and the Crown. Earl Mountbatten, the great-grandson of Queen Victoria, was a significant example of a member of the royal family who went on to great accomplishment in the naval service, but it was due to as much to his own accomplishments as it was any factor of his royal birth. Furthermore, he did not command an entire service. Although he reached the rank of admiral and later served as the last Viceroy to India, he was not continuing the tradition of his great-great uncle. Even the current monarch, Queen Elizabeth II, was commissioned in the Auxiliary Territorial Service while she was still Princess Elizabeth. She learned to drive and maintain military vehicles during the Second World War.

In the present, the issue remains current with Prince Andrew, son of Queen Elizabeth II, and Prince Harry, grandson of Queen Elizabeth II and son of the Prince of Wales, Prince Charles. As a helicopter pilot flying combat missions during the Falklands War, Prince Andrew proudly continued the legacy of his royal ancestors, though in a far more modern conveyance. The issue of whether Prince Harry, third in line to the British throne, would serve in Iraq with his regiment dominated international media in the spring of 2007, drawing renewed attention to the connection between the military and the monarchy. Thus the Duke of Cambridge clearly did not end the Crown's association with the military nor did he dampen the enthusiasm with which royals have undertaken and continue to seek careers in the armed services. He did, however, make it quite impossible for a royal duke to command.

It now seems clear that the career of the Duke of Cambridge and his lifelong and intimate association with the monarchy marked an important period of transition both for the army and the Crown. Though it would clearly be an exaggeration to suggest that Parliamentary control of the army was ever in question at any point during Cambridge's tenure as Commander-in-Chief, it is nonetheless true that his career witnessed the final clarification of the relationship between the military, the monarchy, and Parliament. It was during Cambridge's command that the army witnessed not merely the final assertion of civilian control–something which had not been contested for some time–but more accurately the ultimate definition of duties and responsibilities regarding the army, the Crown, and Parliament. As it turned out, it was a relationship neither the Duke of Cambridge nor Queen Victoria would have chosen.

Cambridge viewed his primary mission to be one of preserving the Royal Prerogative and preventing undue civilian interference in the command, discipline, and efficiency of the army. The Queen supported her cousin fully and overall agreed with his interpretation of his role, but in the end it was to no avail. Even when it came to specific reforms of the army rather than the larger question of the constitutional relationship between the two positions of the military and the monarchy, Cambridge, in his capacity as Commander-in-Chief and again with the full support of the Crown, was unable to prevent major changes in the organization and administration of the army. The first government of William Ewart Gladstone, one of the most powerful and reform-minded ministries of the 19th century and certainly the most determined one Cambridge ever faced, was able to champion its will over the strongest possible objections of the Duke of Cambridge. Even though the career of the Duke of Cambridge spanned almost four decades, before the end of his second decade in office he had failed to accomplish those objectives which mattered most to him. Cambridge continued in office for some two decades after the definition of his duties had been resolved at his expense, but for the most part, his importance as a military, political, and even as a royal figure was substantially and permanently diminished. The Duke of Cambridge left the office of the Commander-in-Chief in a far different condition than he had found it; indeed, his impact on the office was such that soon after he left, few within the government or the army saw any benefit to preserving the position. Such was Cambridge's legacy of four decades of service as Commander-in-Chief of the British army.

Author's Note

Since the death of Prince George, 2nd Duke of Cambridge, in 1904 the title of Duke of Cambridge has lain dormant, but just prior to the publication of this book the title of Duke of Cambridge was restored. As is customary on the occasion of a royal wedding, Queen Elizabeth II bestowed the title of Duke of Cambridge on her grandson, Prince William, following his marriage to commoner Catherine Elizabeth Middleton on April 29, 2011.[1] Unlike the previous Cambridge, Prince William's wife shares the title and formally the couple is known as His Royal Highness the Duke of Cambridge and Her Royal Highness the Duchess of Cambridge. Additionally Princess William and Princess Catherine also have Scottish and Northern Irish titles: Earl and Countess of Strathearn and Baron and Baroness Carrickfergus.[2]

---

1 Martin Beckford, "Prince William and Kate Middleton's new titles revealed," *The Telegraph*, 29 April 2011.
2 *Ibid.*

BIBLIOGRAPHY

I. MANUSCRIPT SOURCES

British Library, London

    Army Papers Relating to the Abolition of Purchase
    Campbell-Bannerman Papers
    Cardwell Papers
    Gladstone Papers
    Ripon Papers
    Napier Papers
    Peel Papers

National Army Museum, London

    Private Papers of General Sir William Codrington

Public Record Office, London

    Cabinet Papers
    Cardwell Papers
    Granville Papers
    War Office Papers

Royal Archives, Windsor Castle, Berkshire

    Queen Victoria's Journal
    Victorian Archive

II. PRINTED PRIMARY SOURCES

Bart, Sir George Douglas and Ramsay, Sir George Dalhousie, eds.
    The Panmure Papers. 2 vols. London: Hodder and
    Stoughton, 1908.

Benson, Arthur C. and Viscount Esher, eds. *The Letters of Queen Victoria*, 1st ser., *A Selection From Her Majesty's Correspondence Between the Years 1837-1861*, 3 vols. New York: Longmans, Green and Co., 1907.

Biddulph, Ralph. *Lord Cardwell at the War Office*. London: John Murray, 1904.

Buckle, George E., ed. *The Letters of Queen Victoria*, 2nd ser., *A Selection From Her Majesty's Correspondence Between the Years 1862 and 1878*, 2 vols. New York: Longmans, Green and Co., 1926.

Chesney, Kellow. *Crimean War Reader*. London: Frederick Muller, Ltd., 1960.

Clode, Charles M. *The Military Forces of the Crown; Their Administration and Government*. 2 vols. London: John Murray, 1869.

De Fonblanque, Edward B. *Treatise on the Administration and Organization of the British Army, with Especial Reference to Finance and Supply*. London: Longman, Brown, Green, Longmans, and Roberts, 1858.

Fulford, Roger, ed. *Your Dear Letter: Private Correspondence of Queen Victoria and the Crown Princess of Prussia 1865 -1871*. New York: Charles Scribner's Sons, 1971.

Hibbert, Christopher, ed. *Queen Victoria in her Letters and Journals*. London: John Murray, 1984.

Higginson, Sir George. *Seventy-one Years of a Guardsman's Life*. London: Smith, Elder and Co., 1916.

Illustrated London News. London.

Journal of the United Service Institution. London.

Punch. London.

Reynold's Newspaper. London.

Sheppard, Edgar, ed. *H.R.H. George Duke of Cambridge: A Memoir of His Private Life Based on the Journals and Correspondence of His Royal Highness.* 2 vols. London: Longmans, Green & Co., 1906.

The Daily News. London.

The London Gazette. London.

Times. London.

United Kingdom. *Hansard Parliamentary Debates*, 3rd Series (1830-91).

_____. *Hansard Parliamentary Debates*, 4th Series (1892-1908).

United Services Journal. London.

Verner, William W., and Erasmus D. Parker, eds. *The Military Life of H.R.H. George, Duke of Cambridge.* 2 vols. London: John Murray, 1905.

III. SECONDARY SOURCES

Allen, Louis. *Singapore 1941-1942.* London: Frank Cass, 1977.

Anderson, Olive. *A Liberal State at War: English Politics and
    Economics during the Crimean War.* London: MacMillan,
    1967.

Arnstein, Walter L. *Britain Yesterday and Today: 1830 to the
    Present.* 4th ed Lexington, MA: D.C. Heath & Company,
    1983.

Auchinloss, Louis. *Persons of Consequence: Queen Victoria and
    her Circle.* London: Weidenfield & Nicolson, 1979.

Beier, A.L., David Cannadine and James Rosenheim, eds. *The First
    Modern Society: Essays in Honour of Lawrence Stone.*
    Cambridge: Cambridge University Press, 1989.

Bagehot, Walter. *The English Constitution.* Ithaca, NY: Cornell
    University Press, 1963.

Barnett, Correlli. *Britain and Her Army 1509-1970.* New York:
    William Morrow & Co., 1970.

Bayly, C.A. *Imperial Meridian: The British Empire and the World
    1780-1830.* London: Longman, 1989.

Black, Jeremy. *European Warfare 1660-1815.* New Haven: Yale
    University Press, 1994.

Blake, Robert. *Disraeli.* London: Eyre and Spottiswoode, 1966.

Bond, Brian. "Edward Cardwell's Army Reforms 1868-1874." *The
    Army Quarterly and Defence Journal* 84 (1962): 108-117.

_____. "The Effect of the Cardwell Reforms on Army Organization,
    1874-1904." *Journal of the Royal United Services Institution*
    105 (1960).

_____. "The Late-Victorian Army." *History Today* 11 (1961): 616-624.

_____. "Prelude to the Cardwell Reforms 1856-1868." *Journal of the Royal United Services Institution* 106 (1961): 229-236.

_____. "The Retirement of the Duke of Cambridge." *Journal of the Royal United Services Institution* 106 (1961): 544-553.

_____. "The Territorial Army in Peace and War." *History Today* 16 (1966): 157-166.

_____. *The Victorian Army and the Staff College, 1854-1914.* London: Eyre Methuen, 1972.

Brewer, John. *Party Ideology and Popular Politics at the Accession of George III.* Cambridge: Cambridge University Press, 1976.

Briggs, Asa. *Victorian People, A Reassessment of Persons & Themes 1851-1867.* Chicago: University of Chicago Press, 1983.
Brown, R. Allen. *The Origins of Modern Europe.* London: Boydell, 1972.

Bruce, Anthony. *The Purchase System in the British Army, 1660-1871.* London: Royal Historical Society, 1980.

Burne, A.H. *The Noble Duke of York: The Military Life of Frederick, Duke of York and Albany.* London: Oxford, 1949.

Butterfield, Herbert. *George III and the Historians.* London: Cassell, 1957.

Cain, P.J. and A.G. Hopkins, *British Imperialism*, 2 vols. London: Longman, 1993.

Campbell, Waldemar B. "The Franco-Prussian War and British Military Reform" *The Historian* 4, no.2 (March 1942): 149-261.

Cannadine, David. *Aspects of Aristocracy: Grandeur and Decline in Modern Britain.* London: Yale University Press, 1994.

_____. *G M Trevelyan A Life in History.* New York: W.W. Norton, 1993.

_____. "The Brass Tacks Queen." *New York Review of Books*, 34 (23 April 1987): 30-31.

_____. *The Decline and Fall of the British Aristocracy.* New York: Anchor Books, 1990.

_____. "The Ideal Husband." *New York Review of Books*, 31 (8 November 1984): 22-24.

_____. "The Merry Wives of Windsor." *New York Review of Books*, 33 (12 June 1986): 15-17.

Cannadine, David and Simon Price, eds. *Rituals of Royalty: Power and Ceremonial in Traditional Societies.* Cambridge: Cambridge University Press, 1987.

Carver, Michael. *The Seven Ages of the British Army.* London: Weidenfeld and Nicholson, 1984.

Chandler, David and Ian Beckett, eds. *The Oxford History of the British Army.* Oxford: Oxford University Press, 1994.

Chandler, David G. *The Campaigns of Napoleon: The Mind and Method of History's Greatest Soldier.* New York: Scribner, 1966.

Churchill, Winston S. *The Hinge of Fate.* Vol. 4 of *The Second World War.* London: Cassell & Co., 1951.

Clark, J.C.D. *English Society 1688-1832.* Cambridge: Cambridge University Press, 1985.

Coleridge, Thomas. *This for Remembrance.* London: Fisher Unwin, 1925.

Colley, Linda. *"The Apotheosis of George III: Loyalty, Royalty and the British* Nation 1760-1820." *Past and Present,* 102 (February 1984): 94-129.

_____. *Britons: Forging the Nation 1707-1837.* New Haven: Yale University Press, 1992.

Cook, Edward T. *The Life of Florence Nightingale.* 2 vols. London: Macmillan and Co., Ltd., 1914.

Coward, Barry. *The Stuart Age.* New York: Longman, 1980.

Cowling, Maurice. *1867 Disraeli, Gladstone and Revolution The Passing of The Second Reform Bill.* Cambridge: Cambridge University Press, 1967.

Craig, Gordon A. *The Politics of the Prussian Army 1640-1945.* New York: Oxford University Press, 1955.

Denholm, A. "Lord De Gray and Army Reform, 1859-1866." *The Army Quarterly and Defence Journal.* 102 (1971).

Duff, David. *Albert and Victoria.* London: Muller, 1972.

Duff, Ethel M. *The Life Story of H.R.H. the Duke of Cambridge.* London: Stanley Paul & Co., 1938.

Dupuy, R. Ernest and Trevor N. Dupuy. *The Harper Encyclopedia of Military History: From 3500 B.C. to the Present.* 4th ed. New York: HarperCollins, 1993.

Dupuy, Trevor N., Curt Johnson and David L. Bongard. *The Harper Encyclopedia of Military Biography.* Edison, NJ: Castle Books, 1992.

Dupuy, Trevor N. *A Genius for War: The German Army and the General Staff, 1807-1945.* Englewood Cliffs, NJ: Prentice-Hall, 1977.

Emden, Paul. *Behind the Throne.* London: Hodder and Stoughton, 1934.

Ensor, R.C.K. *England 1870-1914.* Vol. 14 of *The Oxford History of England,* edited by G. N. Clark. London: Oxford, 1936.

Erickson, Arvel B. "Abolition of Purchase in the British Army." *Military Affairs* 23 (1959): 65-76.

Farwell, Byron. *Eminent Victorian Soldiers: Seekers of Glory.* London: W.W. Norton & Co., 1985.

_____. *Mr. Kipling's Army.* New York: W.W. Norton & Co., 1987.

_____. *Queen Victoria's Little Wars.* New York: W.W. Norton & Co., 1972.

Fichtenau, Heinrich. *The Carolingian Empire.* Toronto: University of Toronto Press, 1978.

Fieldhouse, David. "Can Humpty-Dumpty be put together again? Imperial History in the 1980's," *The Journal of Imperial and Commonwealth History,* XII (JAN 1984).

Figes, Orlando. *The Crimean War: A History*. New York: Metropolitan books, 2010.

Fortescue, John William. *A History of the British Army.* 13 vols. London: MacMillan &Co., 1899-1930.

Fulford, Roger.
George the Fourth. New York: Capricorn, 1963.

_____. *Hanover to Windsor.* Glasgow: Fontana/Collins, 1960.

_____. *Royal Dukes: The Father and Uncles of Queen Victoria.* London: Gerald Duckworth & Co., Ltd., 1949.

Fuller, J.F.C. *War and Western Civilization 1832-1932.* London: Duckworth, 1932.

Gallagher, John. *The Decline, Revival and Fall of the British Empire: The Ford Lectures and Other Essays.* Cambridge: Cambridge University Press, 1982.

Gallagher, Thomas F. "British Military Thinking and the Coming of the Franco-Prussian War." *Military Affairs* 39 (1975): 19-22.

_____. "'Cardwellian Mysteries': The Fate of the British army Regulation Bill, 1871." *Historical Journal* 18 (1975): 327 348.

Görlitz, Walter. *The History of the German General Staff, 1657-1945.* New York: Praeger, 1953.

Gordon, Hampden. *The War Office*. London: Putnam, 1935.

Halévy, Elie. *A History of the English People in the Nineteenth Century*. Vol. 4. *Victorian Year 1841-1895*. London: Ernest Benn Limited, 1961.

Hallows, Ian S. *Regiments and Corps of the British Army*. London: New Orchard, 1994.

Hamer, W.S. *The British Army: Civil – Military Relations 1885-1905*. Oxford: Clarendon Press, 1970.

Hamley, Edward. *The War in the Crimea*. New York: Charles Scribner's Sons, 1891; reprinted, Westport, CT: Greenwood Press, 1971.

Hardie, Frank. *The Political Influence of Queen Victoria 1861-1901*. London: Oxford University Press, 1935.

Harling, Philip. *The Waning of "Old Corruption:" The Politics of Economical Reform in Britain, 1779-1846*. Oxford: Clarendon Press, 1996.

Harpin, Paul H. "The British War Office: From the Crimean War to Cardwell, 1855-1868." Unpublished Master's Thesis, University of Massachusetts, 1976.

Harries-Jenkins, Gwyn. *The Army in Victorian Society*. London: Routledge & Keegan Paul, 1977.

Harrison, J.F.C. *The Early Victorians, 1832-1851*. New York: Praeger, 1971.

Haswell, Jock. *The British Army: A Concise History*. London: Thames and Hudson, 1975.

Hibbert, Christopher. *George IV*. Harmondsworth: Harmondsworth, 1976.

_____. *The Destruction of Lord Raglan.* London: Longmans, 1961.

_____. *The Great Mutiny: India 1857.* New York: Viking, 1978.

Hill, Christopher. *The Century of Revolution 1603-1714.* New York: W.W. Norton, 1961.

Hobhouse, Hermonie. *Prince Albert: His Life and Work.* London: Hamish Hamilton, 1983.

Hobsbawm, Eric and Ranger, Terence, eds. *The Invention of Tradition.* Cambridge: Cambridge University Press, 1983.

Holborn, Hajo. *A History of Modern Germany 1648-1840.* New York: Knopf, 1971.

Howard, Michael. *The Franco-Prussian War.* New York: Methuen, 1961.

_____. *War in European History.* Oxford: Oxford University Press, 1976.

Howard, Michael, ed. *The Theory and Practice of War.* Bloomington, IN: Indiana University Press, 1965.

Hurt, John. *Education in Evolution: Church, State, Society, and popular Education, 1800-1870.* London: Hart-Davis, 1971.

Hyam, Ronald and Martin, Ged. *Reappraisals in British Imperial History.* London: MacMillan, 1975.

Hyam, Ronald. *Britain's Imperial Century, 1815-1914: A Study of Empire and Expansion* London: MacMillan, 1993.

Jary, Christopher. "Class In the Army: An Observer's Perspective." *British Army Review,* 117 (December 1997): 50-55.

James, Robert Rhodes. *Prince Albert: A Biography.* London: Hamish Hamilton, 1983.

Judd, Denis. *The Crimean War.* London: Hart-Davis, MacGibbon, 1975.

Keegan, John. *A History of Warfare.* New York: Alfred A. Knopf, 1993.

Kennedy, Paul. *The Rise and Fall of the Great Powers: Economic Change and Military Conflict from 1500-2000.* New York: Random House, 1987.

_____. *The Rise of Anglo-German Antagonism, 1860-1914.* London: Prometheus, 1980.

Kishlansky, Mark. *A Monarchy Transformed: Britain 1603-1714.* The Penguin History of Britain, ed. David Cannadine. London: Penguin Books, 1996.

Kochanski, H.M. "Field Marshal Viscount Wolseley as Commander-in-Chief: A Reassessment." *The Journal of Strategic Studies* 20 (June 1997): 119-139.

Lee, Sidney, ed. *The Dictionary of National Biography: Supplement January 1901-December 1911.* Oxford: Oxford University Press, 1958.

Le May, G.H.L. *The Victorian Constitution: Conventions, Usages and Contingencies.* London: Duckworth, 1979.

Longford, Elizabeth. *Queen Victoria: Born to Succeed.* New York: Harper & Row, 1964.

_____. *Wellington.* 2 vols. London: Weidenfield & Nicolson, 1972.

Luvaas, Jay. *The Education of an Army: British Military Thought, 1815-1940*. Chicago: University of Chicago Press, 1964.

_____. *The Military Legacy of the Civil War: The European Inheritance*. Chicago: University of Chicago Press, 1988.

Lyttelton, Neville. *Eighty Years: Soldiering, Politics, Games*. London: Hodder and Stoughton, 1927.

Marshall, P.J., ed. *The Cambridge Illustrated History of the British Empire*. Cambridge: Cambridge University Press, 1996.

Martin Beckford, "Prince William and Kate Middleton's new titles revealed," *The Telegraph*, 29 April 2011.

McElwee, William. *The Art of War: Waterloo to Mons*. Bloomington, IN: Indiana University Press, 1974.

Myatt, Frederick. *The Soldier's Trade: British Military Developments, 1660-1914*. London: MacDonald and Jane's, 1974.

Norton, Philip. *The British Polity*. 2d ed. New York: Longman, 1991.

Omond, J.S. *Parliament and the Army 1642-1904*. Cambridge: Cambridge University Press, 1933.

Otley, C.B. "The Social Origins of British Army Officers." *Sociological Review* 18 (July 1970).

_____. "The educational Background of British Army Officers." *Sociology* 7 (May 1973).

Pakenham, Thomas. *The Boer War*. New York: Random House, 1979.

Pares, Richard. *King George III and the Politicians.* Oxford: Clarendon Press, 1953.

Paret, Peter. *Yorck and the Era of Prussian Reform 1807-1815.* Princeton: Princeton University Press, 1966.

Parker, Harold T. *Three Napoleonic Battles.* Durham, NC: Duke University Press, 1983.

Phipps, Ramsay W. *The Armies of the First French Republic and the Rise of the Marshals of Napoleon I.* 5 vols. London: Oxford University Press, 1926-1939.

Plumb, J.H. *et al., The English Heritage.* Arlington Heights, IL.: Forum Press, 1978.

Plumb, J.H. *The First Four Georges.* New York: Macmillan, 1957.

_____. *The Growth of Political Stability in England 1675-1725.* London: Penguin, 1969.

Pockock, J.G.A. *The Ancient Constitution and the Feudal Law: A Study of English Historical Thought in the Seventeenth Century.* New York: Cambridge University Press, 1987.

Pool, Daniel. *What Jane Austin Ate and Charles Dickens Knew: From Fox Hunting to Whist – the Facts of Daily Life in 19th Century England.* New York: Simon and Schuster, 1993.

Porter, Roy. *English Society in the Eighteenth Century.* London: Allen Lane, 1982.

Preston, A.W. "British Military Thought, 1856-1890,"*Army Quarterly*, vol. 89, no. 1 (1964), 57-74.

Razzell, P.E. "Social Origins of Officers in the Indian and British Home Army." *British Journal of Sociology.* 14 (September 1963).

Reader, W.J. *Professional Men: the Rise of the Professional Classes in Nineteenth-Century England.* London: Weidenfeld and Nicholson, 1966.

Robertson, William. *From Private to Field-Marshal.* London: Constable, 1921.

Robinson, Ronald *et al. Africa and the Victorians: The Climax of Imperialism in the Dark Continent.* New York: St. Martin's Press, 1961.

Ropp, Theodore. *War in the Modern World.* London: Collier MacMillan Publishers, 1959.

Rose, B. "The Volunteers of 1859." *Journal of the Society of Army Historical Research,* 37 (1959).

Ross, Steven T. *Quest for Victory: French Military Strategy 1792-1799.* New York: A.S. Barnes & Co., 1973.

Rothenberg, Gunther E. *The Art of Warfare in the Age of Napoleon.* Bloomington, IN: Indiana University Press, 1978.

St. Aubyn, Giles. *Queen Victoria: A Personal Portrait.* New York: Athenaeum, 1992.

_____. *The Royal George: The Life of H.R..H. Prince George, Duke of Cambridge, 1819-1904.* London: Constable, 1963.

Scott, Samuel F. *The Responses of the Royal Army to the French Revolution.* Oxford: Oxford University Press, 1978.

Skelley, Alan Ramsay. *The Victorian Army at Home: The Recruitment and Terms and Conditions of the British Regular, 1859-1899.* London: Croom Helm, 1977.

Smith, F.B. *The Making Of The Second Reform Bill.* Cambridge: Cambridge University Press, 1966.

Smyth, John George. *Sandhurst: The History of the Royal Military Academy, Woolwich, the Royal Military College, Sandhurst, and the Royal Military Academy Sandhurst, 1741-1961.* London: Weidenfeld & Nicolson, 1961.

Sommerville, J.P. *Politics & Ideology in England 1603-1640.* New York: Longman, 1986.

Spiers, Edward M. *The Army and Society, 1815-1914.* New York: Longman, 1980.

Stanley, Peter. *White Mutiny: British Military Culture in India, 1825-75.* London: C Hurst & Co Publishers Ltd, 1998.

Stephen, Leslie and Sidney Lee, eds. *The Dictionary of National Biography: From the Earliest Times to 1900..* Oxford: Oxford University Press, 1922.

Strachan, Hew. *European Armies and the Conduct of War.* London: Routledge, 1983.

_____. *From Waterloo to Balaclava: Tactics, Technology, and the British Army, 1815-54.* Cambridge: Cambridge University Press, 1985.

_____. *The Politics of the British Army.* New York: Oxford University Press, 1997.

_____. *Wellington's Legacy: The Reform of the British Army 1830-54.* Manchester: Manchester University Press, 1984.

Strachey, Lytton. *Queen Victoria.* New York: Harcourt, Brace & Co., 1921.

Sweetman, John. *War and Administration: The Significance of the Crimean War for the British Army.* Edinburgh: Scottish Academic Press, 1984.

Tennyson, Alfred, Lord. *Selected Poems.* Toronto: Dover Publications, 1992.

Tomalin, Claire. *Mrs. Jordan's Profession: The Actress and the Prince.* New York: Alfred Knopf, 1995.

Trevelyan, G.M. *British History in the 19th Century and After, 1782-1919.* New York: Harper & Row, 1966.

Tucker, Albert V. "Army and Society in England, 1870-1900: a Reassessment of the Cardwell Reforms." *Journal of British Studies* 2 (1963): 110-141.

University of Chicago Press. *The Chicago Manual of Style.* 14th ed. Chicago: University of Chicago Press, 1993.

Ward, S.G.P. *Wellington's Headquarters.* London: Routlege, 1957.

Webb, R.K. *Modern England.* 2d ed. New York: HarperCollins, 1980.

Weintraub, Stanley. *Victoria: Biography of a Queen.* London: Unwin Hyman, 1987.

Wheeler, Owen. *The War Office Past and Present.* London: Methuen, 1914.

Willcox, William B. and Walter L. Arnstein. *The Age of Aristocracy 1688-1830.* 6th ed. Lexington, MA: D.C. Heath & Company, 1992.

Williams, Richard. *The Contentious Crown: Public Discussion of the British Monarchy in the Reign of Queen Victoria.* Aldershot, UK: Ashgate Publishing Co., 1997.

Woodham-Smith, Cecil. *Queen Victoria 1819-1861.* London: Hamish Hamilton, 1972.

_____. *The Reason Why.* New York: E.P. Dutton, 1960. Reprint, New York: Barnes and Noble Books, 1998.

Woodward, E.L. *The Age of Reform 1815-1870.* Vol. 13 of *The Oxford History of England,* edited by G. N. Clark. London: Oxford, 1938.

Wright, Gordon. *France in Modern Times: From the Enlightenment to the Present.* 4th ed. New York: W.W. Norton and Co., 1987.

Young, Peter & Lawford, J.P., eds. *History of the British Army.* New York: G.P. Putnam's Sons, 1970.

ACKNOWLEGEMENTS

A work such as this could not be undertaken without the assistance of many people who facilitated my efforts and allowed the transition of a general idea into concrete reality. I wrote this book while serving as a faculty member in the Department of History at the United States Military Academy, and I have benefitted immeasurably from the assistance, advice, and support offered by its faculty. Brigadier General Robert A. Doughty, US Army, Retired, Colonel Cole Kingseed, US Army, Retired, Colonel Lee T. Wyatt, III, US Army, Retired, Colonel J.S. Wheeler, US Army, Retired, Colonel Matthew Moten, and Colonel Lance Betros provided vital support and assistance in the completion of this book. In addition, several visiting scholars to the Department of History, United States Military Academy, offered tremendous insight and friendship, and in particular I must thank Professor Robert Citino, Professor Joe Guilmartin, Professor Dennis Showalter, and Professor Linda Frey. Furthermore, the support, valuable insight, and camaraderie of my friends and colleagues made this a much better book, and I especially would like to thank Brigadier General H.R. McMaster, Colonel Christopher Kolenda, Colonel Gian Gentile, Colonel Ty Seidule, Colonel Gregory A. Daddis, Lieutenant Colonel Paul Krajeski, Lieutenant Colonel Gail Yoshitani, Major Brian Schoellhorn, Major Edwin Werkheiser, and Professor Jonathan Gumz. Each individual is a distinguished professional who helped me maintain my focus and sense of balance throughout.

This book could never have been written had I not been able to access the materials needed to undertake it. I gratefully and humbly acknowledge the gracious permission of Her Majesty Queen Elizabeth II for admitting me to the Royal Archives at Windsor Castle, Berkshire, England. Without access to the Royal Archives this book and its novel approach would have been impossible. Once inside Windsor Castle, I would have been lost had it not been for the patient and kind assistance of Mr. Oliver Everett, Assistant Keeper to the Royal Archives, Lady de Bellaigue, former Registrar, Miss Pamela Clark, Registrar, and the entire staff of the Royal Archives. Simply being within the Round Tower and getting to know the wonderful people who work there will forever provide me some of my happiest memories. I would also like to thank Brigadier General Fletcher M. Lamkin, US Army, Retired, and Brigadier General Patrick Finnegan, US Army, Retired, former Deans of the Academic Board, United States Military Academy, for approving several grants to help defray the costs of my research trips to England. Similarly, I would like to acknowledge the generous assistance of the Omar N. Bradley Historical Research Fellowship and the George C. Marshal European Center for Security Studies for providing essential funding for research trips to England. Were it not for the patient, professional, and dedicated assistance of the hardworking team at the University Press of North Georgia this manuscript would never have made it into print. In particular, I would like to acknowledge the assistance of Professor Timothy May, Professor Bonnie Robinson, and Ms. April Loebick.

I have benefited immeasurably from the world class scholars associated with Columbia University's Department of History. I am deeply indebted to Professor Fritz Stern who has been a source of unending inspiration and guidance. Professor Sir David Cannadine has been a friend, advisor, and mentor from the day I met him. He, more than anyone, has inspired me toward excellence as an historian and without him this book would have not been possible. Professor Walter Arnstein, Professor Emeritus, University of Illinois, also provided invaluable assistance in this book's completion. I am truly humbled to have benefited from the tutelage of such fine historians and first class gentlemen.

I would be remiss if I did not mention finally the support of my family throughout this enterprise. First of all, my mother, Carol Farrell, a professional educator, taught me from an early age the importance of learning and gave me the rare gift of always wanting to do better. It is to her that original credit must belong. Secondly, I must thank my father, William E. Farrell, who taught me the essential ingredient of success: never give up. And finally, to my wife and children I offer my heartfelt gratitude. My darling children, Elizabeth, William, and Caroline, have grown accustomed to thinking their father a cellar dweller – soon we may see the light of day together. As for my beautiful and charming wife, Sheila, who was with me every step of the way, I am deeply indebted. At times she must have believed she was married more to the Duke of Cambridge than to me – and maybe believed it to be a more agreeable arrangement – but her editing and revisions made it a much better book.

To those named above, and to all others whom I may have unintentionally omitted, I express my thanks and gratitude. Any mistakes in this book are mine and mine alone.

West Point, New York
August 5, 2011

The Descendants of George III
(Simplified)

King George III = Charlotte of Mecklenburg-Strelitz
(1738-1820)   (1744-1818)

George IV
(1762-1830)
=
Caroline of
Brunswick
(1768-1821)

William IV
(1765-1837)
=
Adelaide of
Saxe-Meiningen
(1792-1849)

Charlotte
(1796-1817)
=
Leopold of
Saxe-Coburg
(1790-1865)

Edward
Duke of Kent
(1767-1820)
=
Victoire of
Saxe-Coburg
(1786-1861)

QUEEN
VICTORIA
(1819-1901)
=
Albert Prince
Saxe-Coburg
(1819-1861)

Ernest
Duke of Cumberland
King of Hanover
(1771-1851)
=
Frederica of
Mecklenburg-Strelitz
(1778-1841)

George V
King of Hanover
(1819-1878)
=
Mary of
Saxe-Altenburg
(1818-1907)

Adolphus
Duke of
Cambridge
(1774-1850)
=
Augusta of
Hesse-Cassel
(1797-1889)

GEORGE
2nd DUKE of
CAMBRIDGE
(1819-1904)

Mary
(1776-1857)
=
William
Duke of Gloucester
(1776-1834)

Sophia
(1777-1848)

Index

About the Author

Kevin W. Farrell is an associate professor of history at the United States Military Academy at West Point, New York, where he oversees the military history program. A 1986 graduate of West Point, he earned his Ph.D. from Columbia University in New York City. Also a colonel in the U.S. Army, he has commanded at the platoon, company and battalion level with extensive combat and leadership experience in the Balkans, Afghanistan and as a battalion commander in Iraq. He is married to the former Sheila Newman of Lugoff, South Carolina, and together they have three children.